The following map key is to be used with the Belváro ⟨...⟩
Please disregard the map key on pp86-7.

P9-ELX-237

LONELY PLANET PUBLICATIONS

STEVE FALLON

BUDAPEST
CITY GUIDE

INTRODUCING BUDAPEST

Revel in Budapest's architectural and cultural gems, such as the Great Synagogue (p96)

Straddling the romantic Danube River, with the Buda Hills to the west and the start of the Great Plain to the east, Budapest is the most beautiful city in central Europe.

And the human legacy is just as remarkable as Mother Nature's. Architecturally, Budapest is a gem, with enough baroque, neoclassical, Eclectic and art nouveau (or Secessionist) buildings to satisfy anyone's appetite. With parks brimming with attractions, museums filled with treasures, pleasure boats sailing up and down the scenic Danube and Turkish-era thermal baths belching steam, the Hungarian capital is a delight both by day and by night. The food and wine are excellent, cheap and in abundance and the nightlife is hot. Indeed, in recent years, Budapest has taken on the role of the region's party town, especially in the warmer months when outdoor entertainment areas called *kertek* (literally 'gardens') heave with party makers.

Budapest does have its scars, of course, with organised crime, pollution, international fast-food eateries at every corner and mindless graffiti covering much of that gorgeous architecture. But come a fine spring (or summer or brisk autumn) day and all that will go by the by. Stroll along the Duna korzó, the riverside embankment on the Pest side, or across any of the Danube bridges past young couples embracing passionately. It's then that you'll feel the romance that, despite all attempts from both within and without to destroy it, has never died.

BUDAPEST LIFE

…though sometimes it feels like they haven't stopped trying. After years of serious training in the fine art of whinging, Budapesters now find they really *do* have something to complain about. The Hungarian economy is shot to hell, the city is torn apart by metro 4 construction and (sometimes violent) protests during each and every public holiday, and everyone but everyone holds a mortgage in Swiss francs, which now cost a wheelbarrow full of weak forint to repay. It all makes life just a few short years ago – when unemployment and inflation were down, real income and tourism figures were up and *fapados* (wooden bench – ie budget) airlines like easyJet and Wizz Air were winging Mr and Mrs Kovács and their 1.3 kids to Corsica for a 10-day holiday – look like paradise. But even then people here weren't happy. In 2006 only 36% of the population – the lowest in the EU and less than half the EU average of 73% – said they were satisfied with their quality of life.

Still, it's not all bad. While Hungarians may 'take their pleasure sadly', a bizarre arrangement for which there's even a phrase *(sírva vigadni)*, they continue to take them and with gusto. The clubs heave at the weekend, there's often a queue at the Gellért Baths and you won't get a table at the Ruszwurm on Castle Hill in a month of Sundays. Once upon a time in the east the man they call 'the greatest Hungarian' (and my namesake), István Széchenyi, wrote: 'Many people think that Hungary was. I like to believe that she will be!' We're still counting on you, Steve. Maybe this is just a bad patch.

'István Széchenyi wrote: "Many people think that Hungary was. I like to believe that she will be!"'

Sample traditional Hungarian fare at Nagycsarnok (Great Market; p120)

3

HIGHLIGHTS

THERMAL BATHS & SPAS

Budapest sits on a crazy quilt of more than 100 thermal springs, and 'taking the waters' is very much a part of everyday life. Some baths date from Turkish times, others are art nouveau wonders, and still others are spick-and-span modern establishments.

① Lukács Baths
Housed in a sprawling 19th-century complex and offering a very serious spa experience (p165)

② Széchenyi Baths
Popular indoor and outdoor bathing venues in City Park (p165)

③ Rudas Baths
Recently renovated, the most Turkish of all the baths in Budapest by day hosts Cinetrip monthly on Saturday nights (p165)

④ Gellért Baths
Taking the waters here has been likened to bathing in a cathedral (p164)

THE DANUBE & ITS BRIDGES

Budapest's 'dustless highway' is ever present, serving – still – as an important means of communication and neatly dividing the city into Buda and Pest. The Danube bridges are not just pretty faces but the lifelines that keep those two parts whole.

1 Liberty Bridge
Opened for the millenary exhibition in 1896 (p68)

2 The Danube
Beautiful at any time and from any perspective; enjoy the view across to the Parliament building from Batthyány tér (p66)

3 Széchenyi Chain Bridge
The city's oldest span was built by a Scotsman (p68)

BUDAPEST TODAY

Cultural centre… The place for nightlife in the region… Culinary bright spot of eastern Europe… The place for romance… Budapest has always been and will always be a lot of different things to a lot of different people.

❶ Nightlife
No other city in the region offers as pulsating a nightlife; see cutting-edge DJs at the underground bar Vittula (p151)

❷ Cafe Life
The cafe scene is alive and well and oh so sweet in Budapest (p144)

❸ Hungarian State Opera House
A night at the opera is a must (p161)

MONUMENTS & ICONS

Budapest's iconic buildings may not be immediately familiar to you but they certainly will be by the time you leave. The city's street art immortalises not just its larger-than-life heroes, but mythical creatures and unknown characters too.

1 Parliament Building
Designed in the Eclectic style by Imre Steindl and completed in 1902 (p86)

2 Anonymous statue
This 13th-century chronicler is a magnet for writers (p110)

3 Memento Park
Nothing beats this well-manicured socialist 'zoo' (p80)

4 Basilica of St Stephen
See the king's Holy Right (hand) (p84)

5 Liberty Monument
The lovely lady with the palm frond atop Gellért Hill is a much-loved monument (p69)

FOOD & DRINK

Hungary's larder offers a cornucopia of surprises, but why ignore the drinks cupboard? The country's wine – from the big-bodied reds of Villány to honey-sweet Tokaj – is world-renowned, and the fruit-flavoured pálinka (brandy) kicks like a mule.

❶ Eating Out
Budapesters tend to entertain outside of their homes, at cafes and restaurants (p124)

❷ Sausages and Salamis
Almost icons, especially the Pick brand (p134)

❸ Tokaj
Sweet Tokaj really is the 'king of wines and the wine of kings' (p145)

❹ Goulash and Gulyás
Goulash here is a rich 'stew' called *pörkölt* while *gulyás* is actually a meat soup (p123)

❺ Pálinka
Fruit-flavoured brandy punches much higher in the alcohol stakes (p144)

EXCURSIONS

In a country the size of Hungary (think Florida, or two Switzerlands) finding a worthwhile destination within easy striking distance is a snap. The only difficult part is deciding which one to choose.

1 **Pécs' Mosque Church**
The main church in the centre of Pécs was once a mosque (p196)

2 **Valley of the Beautiful Women**
Near Eger, this is the place to sample Bull's Blood wine (p196)

3 **Gödöllő's Royal Mansion**
Hungary's largest baroque manor house (p191)

CONTENTS

THE AUTHOR

Steve Fallon

Steve, who has written every edition of *Budapest,* first visited the Hungarian capital in the early 1980s and immediately fell in love with thermal baths, Tokaj wine and the voice of Marta Sebestyén. Not able to survive on the occasional fleeting fix, he moved to Budapest in 1992, where he could enjoy all three in abundance *magyarul* (in Hungarian). Now based in London, Steve returns to Hungary regularly for all these things and more: *pálinka* (fruit brandy), art nouveau and the best nightlife in the region.

STEVE'S TOP BUDAPEST DAY

Let's just say for the sake of argument that I wake up late on my last day in Budapest, work accomplished and conscience (if not head) clear. This is my day and I'm going to do what I want to do, damn it! I skip breakfast and head for the Rudas Baths (p165); some things are best done on an empty stomach and what a cure for a hangover! After a therapeutic soak and a 15-minute tussle with a mountainous masseur, I hobble across Liberty Bridge (p69), glancing up behind me at my best girlfriend,

Lady Liberty (p68), holding a palm frond above her head atop Gellért Hill. Across the bridge, I jump on tram 2, which runs along the river to Újlipótváros, Budapest's leafy Upper East Side (sort of). There's no better place in town than the Móri Vendéglő (p136) for some Hungarian soul food. From here it's just a hop, skip and a jump to Margaret Island (p76). I may stroll, I may cycle, I may kip in the sun. But I'm sticking to the beaten track, thank you very much. In this city of passion and a dearth of affordable apartments, lovers seize every opportunity and, frankly, any bush will do. Walking past parliament (p86), the crown, orb and upended sword tempt and it seems a shame to pass up the chance for another look at the Ethnography Museum (p87) across the way – who can ever get enough of those butter churns, mangles and hammers and sickles? But I need a fix of Secessionist architecture and the M1 metro (the 'little underground') just never fails me. Sinuous curves, asymmetrical forms and other bizarre shapes firmly under my belt, I can now concentrate on the really serious things. A slice of something sweet at the Lukács coffee house (p150) or a sundowner at one of the terrace cafe-bars on Liszt Ferenc tér (p150) while eavesdropping on some diva climbing and then falling down her scales at the adjoining Ferenc Liszt Music Academy (p156). Dinner will be a stone's throw away at Klassz (p136), my favourite new wine restaurant, and I'll sturch and lumble (pardon, lurch and stumble) into Giero (p137) for some honest-to-goodness Gypsy music to get my *tuchus* in motion. The rest of the evening will hopefully be spent debauched at various of the city's finest *kertek* (literally 'gardens', but in Budapest any outdoor spot that has been converted into an entertainment zone; p158) that open at night in the warmer months. In the morning I'll be thanking (and seeing) my lucky stars for the simple fact that last night was my last night in old Bp.

GETTING STARTED

To be honest, a trip to Budapest can be done with very little advance planning. Free tourist literature abounds, maps are excellent and readily available and staff at tourist offices, travel agencies, hotels, train stations and so on are usually knowledgable (if not always so welcoming). In fact, almost everything can be taken care of after you've arrived. And as most experienced travellers know, the difficulties or problems that occurred to you at home usually turn out to be irrelevant or sort themselves out once you are on the road.

But all this applies only if you have an unlimited budget, you don't have an interest in a particular activity, type of architecture or kind of music and you'll eat or drink anything set in front of you. Those who do have to put a cap on the amount they can spend while travelling, or want better value for money, will benefit immensely from prior knowledge and planning. And if you have specific interests – be it art nouveau architecture, city cycling or fine dining – you'll certainly want to make sure that the things you came to see and do will be possible at that time of year.

WHEN TO GO

Every season has its attractions – and its limitations – in Budapest. Though it can be pretty wet in May and early June, spring is just glorious. The summer is warm, sunny and unusually long but, as elsewhere in continental Europe, Budapest comes to a grinding halt in August, which Hungarians traditionally call 'the cucumber-growing season' – because that's about the only thing happening (although lots more festivals are now scheduled in that month than there were in years past).

Autumn is also beautiful, particularly in the Buda Hills. Winter can be wonderful, with bright blue skies; a light, ornamental-looking dusting of snow on church spires; occasional ice floes floating majestically down the Danube and ice skating in City Park. But it can also be cold and bleak, with museums and other tourist sights closed or their hours sharply curtailed. For more climate information, see p206.

FESTIVALS & EVENTS

Countless festivals and events are held in and around the capital each year. The following abbreviated list gives you a taste of what to expect, but get hold of the Hungarian National Tourist Office's annual *Events Calendar* brochure for a complete listing. To ensure that your trip does not coincide with a public holiday, when almost everything will be closed, see p208.

January

NEW YEAR'S DAY CONCERT
www.hungariakoncert.hu
This annual event, usually held in the Duna Palota (p156), ushers in the new year.

INTERNATIONAL CIRCUS FESTIVAL
www.maciva.hu
This biennial (2010, 2012, 2014 etc) event has been held under the big top of the Municipal Great Circus (p109) in late January every other year since 1996.

DON'T LEAVE HOME WITHOUT...

- a swimsuit for use in the mixed-sex thermal spas and pools, and plastic sandals or thongs (flip-flops)
- a towel and soap if you're staying in hostels
- an adapter plug for electrical appliances
- an immersion water heater or small kettle for an impromptu cup of tea or coffee
- premoistened towelettes or a large cotton handkerchief to soak in fountains and use to cool off in the hot weather
- sunglasses and sunblock, even in the cooler months
- binoculars for viewing detail on churches and other buildings
- a Swiss Army knife, with such essentials as a bottle opener and strong corkscrew
- a few words of Hungarian, and a phrase book – a little goes a long way (for a start, see p218)

February

OPERA BALL
www.operabal.com
This very prestigious annual event is held, usually in the third week of February, at the Hungarian State Opera House (p94).

March

BUDAPEST SPRING FESTIVAL
www.festivalcity.hu
The capital's largest and most important cultural festival (with 200 events) takes place for two weeks in late March/early April at five dozen venues across the city.

BUDAPEST FRINGE FESTIVAL
www.budapestfringe.com
This three-day festival of non-mainstream theatre, music and dance in Millennium Park (p66) and other venues around town is a kind of sideshow to the Budapest Spring Festival.

April

NATIONAL DANCE HOUSE FESTIVAL
www.tanchaztalalkozo.hu/eng
Hungary's biggest *táncház* (folk music and dance workshop; p42) is held over two days in early April at the Buda Concert Hall (Map p62) and other venues.

June

DANUBE FOLKLORE CARNIVAL
www.dunaart.hu
A pan-Hungarian international 10-day carnival of folk and world music and modern dance held from mid-June in Vörösmarty tér (p90) and on Margaret Island (p76).

FERENCVÁROS FESTIVAL
http://kultucca.hu
Local groups perform music and dance in the streets of Budapest's district IX from mid-June to early July.

BUDAPEST FAREWELL FESTIVAL
www.festivalcity.hu
Citywide 'Budapesti Búcsú' of concerts, folklore performances, street theatre and a carnival to mark the departure of Soviet troops from Hungarian soil on 19 June 1991.

top picks

UNUSUAL EVENTS

- Budapest Farewell Festival June (below left)
- International Circus Festival every other January (opposite)
- Jewish Summer Festival August (below)
- Museum Night June (below)
- National Dance House Festival April (left)

BRIDGE FESTIVAL
www.festivalcity.hu
One-day festival of music, dance and street theatre held on the city's bridges and by the river on or around 21 June to mark the start of summer.

MUSEUM NIGHT
www.museum.hu/events
Two dozen museums across town mark the summer solstice by re-opening their doors at 6pm and not closing them till the wee hours (usually 2am).

August

FORMULA ONE HUNGARIAN GRAND PRIX
www.hungaroring.hu
Hungary's premier sporting event is held in early August at Magyoród (Map p189), 24km northeast of the capital.

SZIGET MUSIC FESTIVAL
www.sziget.hu
Now one of the biggest and most popular music festivals in Europe, the 'Island' festival is held in mid-August on Budapest's Hajógyár (or Óbuda) Island (Map p74).

CRAFTS DAYS
www.nesz.hu
Prominent craftspeople from around Hungary set up kiosks and hold workshops in the Castle District (p61) over three days in mid-August. Folk dancers and musicians perform.

JEWISH SUMMER FESTIVAL
www.jewishfestival.hu
This weeklong festival starting at the end of August showcases Jewish culture through music and theatre performances, exhibitions, gastronomy and films, with many

events taking place at the Pest's Great Synagogue (p96).

September

BUDAPEST INTERNATIONAL WINE FESTIVAL
Hungary's foremost winemakers introduce their vintages to festivalgoers in mid-September in the Castle District (p61).

BUDAPEST MUSIC WEEKS
www.filharmonikusok.hu
Sacred and profane classical music is performed at venues across Budapest for a month from late September.

October

BUDAPEST INTERNATIONAL MARATHON
www.budapestmarathon.com
Eastern Europe's most celebrated foot race goes along the Danube and across its bridges in early October.

BUDAPEST AUTUMN FESTIVAL
www.bof.hu
Cultural events are held at venues throughout the city from late October until early November.

BUDAPEST ART FAIR
www.budapestartfair.hu
Hungary's only forum for representing classical and contemporary fine art and sculpture takes place in late November in the Palace of Art (Műcsarnok; p107) in Heroes' Sq.

December

NEW YEAR GALA & BALL
www.viparts.hu
The annual calendar's most coveted ticket is this gala concert and ball held at the Hungarian State Opera House (p94) on 31 December.

COSTS & MONEY
Budapest is no longer the bargain-basement destination that it was even half-a-dozen years ago, but it is still much cheaper than most Western European countries. If you stay in private rooms, eat at medium-priced res-

HOW MUCH?
Litre of petrol 288Ft to 296Ft

Litre of bottled water 55Ft to 149Ft

Korsó (0.5L) of Dreher beer in pub/cafe 350Ft to 600Ft

Souvenir T-shirt 2500Ft

Street snack (lángos) 200Ft to 400Ft

Cheap/good bottle of wine (75cL) in supermarket 700/2500Ft

Bed in private room from 6000Ft

Cup of coffee in a cafe 250Ft to 450Ft

Local English-language newspaper 399Ft to 580Ft

Dinner for two (with wine) at a good restaurant 15,000Ft

taurants and travel on public transport, you should get by on €50 a day.

Travelling in more style and comfort – restaurant splurges with bottles of wine, a fairly active nightlife, small hotels/guesthouses with 'character' – will cost about twice as much. Those putting up at hostels or college dormitories, eating *lángos* (deep-fried dough with various toppings, usually cheese and sour cream) street food for lunch and at self-service restaurants for dinner could squeak by for as little as €35 a day.

For price ranges of accommodation in Budapest, see p173, and for the average cost of restaurant meals, see p125.

INTERNET RESOURCES
Budapest Sun Online (www.budapestsun.com) Popular English weekly online, with local news, interviews and features.

Budapest Tourism Office (www.budapestinfo.hu) Budapest's best overall website.

Caboodle (www.caboodle.hu) Hungary's best English-language portal with daily news, features and events and links to, among other sites, Politics.hu ('All Politics. All Hungary') and the incomparable Pestiside.hu (p44) – 'The Daily Dish of Cosmopolitan Budapest'.

Hub (www.thehub.hu) Excellent all-inclusive site on nightlife and culture, including performances and exhibitions.

Museums in Hungary (www.museum.hu) Detailed site on museums and exhibitions around Hungary and Budapest.

ADVANCE PLANNING

A month or two before you go Check the visa situation (p216) and your passport expiry date and organise a good health-insurance policy. Try to book your accommodation at this point if you will be travelling in the high season and you want to stay in a boutique hotel like Lánchíd 19 (p174), a 'find' such as the KM Saga Guest Residence (p185) or some place offering exceptional value for money like the Hotel Margitsziget (p177). Take a look at some of the 'what's on' websites (p154) or some of the local English-language media sites (opposite).

A couple of weeks before you go If you're interested in serious fine dining at a place like, say, Csalogány 26 (p127) and there's more than one of you, book a table now. Now is also the time to visit the Ticket Express or Ticket Pro (p154) to get seats for a big-ticket concert, musical or play.

A day or two before you go Make sure your bookings are in order and you've followed all the instructions outlined in this chapter.

SUSTAINABLE BUDAPEST

Budapest already has enough cars clogging its avenues and side streets. Not only does the ensuing air pollution damage the environment and people's health, it also ruins historic buildings and monuments – sometimes irrevocably. Do us all a favour: leave your car behind and resist the temptation to rent one unless you're touring farther afield into the countryside (see p188) – and even then you can reach the destinations described by public transport. Instead, bring or rent a bike (see p167), enjoy the city on foot (Budapest is an eminently walkable city) and/or use the public transport system – it's safe, extremely efficient and very, very cheap.

HISTORY

Strictly speaking, the story of Budapest begins only in 1873 when hilly, residential Buda and historic Óbuda on the western bank of the Danube (Duna) River merged with flat, industrial Pest on the eastern side to form what at first was called Pest-Buda. But like everything here, it's not that simple; a lot more had taken place before that time, and the Queen of the Danube is not as young as she may look at first glance.

EARLY INHABITANTS

The Carpathian Basin, in which Hungary lies, has been populated for at least half a million years. Bone fragments found and exhibited at Vértesszőlős near Tata, some 70km northwest of Budapest, in the 1960s are thought to be that old. These findings suggest that Palaeolithic humans were attracted to the area by its thermal springs and the abundance of mammoth, buffalo, woolly rhinoceros and reindeer. The capital may have been something of a slow starter, however; the earliest evidence of human settlement in the greater Budapest area is the remains of a Neanderthal hunting camp in a gorge on the Érd plateau to the southwest. Complete with stone tools, cutters and scrapers, the site dates back 'only' 50,000 years.

During the ice age, temperatures in the area rarely exceeded 16°C even in July. During the Neolithic period (around 5500 BC), a warming of the climate forced much of the indigenous wildlife to migrate north. The domestication of animals and the first forms of agriculture appeared, as they did in much of central Europe. The first permanent settlement in this area – on the Buda side near the Danube – dates from between 4600 and 3900 BC. Remains from this culture, including bone utensils, fishing nets and even a primitive loom, have been unearthed as far north as Békásmegyer and south at Nagytétény.

In about 2000 BC fierce Indo-European tribes from the Balkan Peninsula reached as far as the Carpathian Basin in horse-drawn wheeled carts, bringing with them bows and arrows and copper tools. After the introduction of more durable bronze, forts were built and a military elite developed. The remains of several settlements of these so-called Bell Beaker people, named after their distinctively shaped pottery, have been uncovered on Csepel Island in the Danube.

Over the next millennium, invaders from the west (Illyrians and Thracians) and the east (Scythians) brought iron, but the metal was not in common use until the Celts arrived in the area in the early 3rd century BC. The vanguard of the so-called La Tène culture, noted for its sinuous geometric ornamentation, they settled at Békásmegyer and Óbuda, and erected an *oppidum,* or hilltop settlement, on Gellért Hill. The Celts also introduced glass and crafted some of the fine gold jewellery that can be seen in Room 5 on the 1st floor of the Hungarian National Museum (p101). It was not until the advent of the late Iron Age La Tène culture (450–390 BC) of the European Celts that the distinctive S-shapes, spirals and round patterns developed.

TIMELINE

4600–3900 BC	AD 106	Late 430s
The first permanent settlement in today's Budapest is established on the Buda side of the Danube; remains uncovered in the area include bone utensils, fishing nets and even a primitive loom.	Roman Aquincum in today's Óbuda becomes the administrative seat of the province of Pannonia Inferior and a fully fledged colony less than a century later in 194.	Aquincum offers little protection to the civilian population when Huns burn the colony to the ground, forcing the Romans and other settlers to flee.

THE ROMAN CONQUEST

In about 35 BC the Romans conquered the area west and south of the Danube River. By 10 AD they had established the province of Pannonia, which was later divided into Upper (Superior) and Lower (Inferior) Pannonia. The Romans brought writing, viticulture and stone architecture to the area, as well as the new religions of Christianity and Mithraism, which competed with one another for converts for some three centuries. At the end of the 1st century AD the Romans established Aquincum, a key military garrison and trading settlement along the Danube in today's Óbuda.

Aquincum (see p73) became the administrative seat of Pannonia Inferior in AD 106. A fortress was built at Contra Aquincum in what is now V Március 15 tér (Map p85) in Pest and the proconsul's palace in Transaquincum on a secure island in the Danube (now Óbuda, or Hajógyári, Island; Map p85). Villages nearby, such as Vindonianus (Békásmegyer) and Vicus Basoretensis (Kiscell), were populated by Celts, who were not granted Roman citizenship.

THE GREAT MIGRATIONS

The first of the so-called Great Migrations of nomadic peoples from Asia reached the eastern outposts of the Roman Empire in Dacia (now Romania) early in the 3rd century AD. Within two centuries, the Romans were forced by the Huns, whose short-lived empire was established by Attila, to flee Aquincum and abandon the rest of Pannonia.

After the death of Attila in 453, Germanic tribes such as the Goths, Gepids and Langobards (or Lombards) occupied the region for the next century and a half until the Avars, a powerful Turkic people, gained control of the Carpathian Basin in the late 6th century. At first they settled on the Pest plains, but their chieftains soon established their main base at the northern end of Csepel Island.

The Avars were subdued by Charlemagne in the early 8th century and the area around Budapest and the Danube Bend was incorporated into the Frankish empire. By that time, the Carpathian Basin was virtually unpopulated except for scattered groups of Turkic and Germanic tribes on the plains and Slavs in the northern hills.

top picks

HISTORY BOOKS

- **Budapest: A Cultural & Literary History** (Bob Debt, 2007) Part of the Cities of the Imagination series, this somewhat dense 'textbook' by a long-term foreign resident is nonetheless filled with esoteric facts and overlooked history.
- **Budapest 1900: A Historical Portrait of a City and Its Culture** (John Lukacs, 1994) Still a classic, this illustrated social history presents the Hungarian capital at the height of its *fin-de-siècle* glory.
- **A Good Comrade: János Kádár, Communism & Hungary** (Roger Gough, 2006) Arguably the most definitive biography of a Communist official to date, this tome does much to explain the tour de force that transformed Kádár from traitor and most hated man in the land to respected reformer.
- **An Illustrated History of Budapest** (Géza Buzinkay, 1998) This large, illustrated and now dated book remains one of the easiest entries into the complicated history of the Hungarian capital.
- **One Day that Shook the Communist World** (Paul Lendvai, 2008) This gripping eyewitness account of the uprising by a Hungarian journalist is among the best accounts of the heady days of autumn 1956.
- **The Siege of Budapest: 100 Days in WWII** (Kriztián Ungváry, 2005) Ungváry examines the battle to capture a major European capital often overlooked in favour of Warsaw or Berlin.

BACKGROUND HISTORY

Early 8th century	896–98	955
The Avars, a powerful Turkic people who had occupied the Carpathian Basin since the late 6th century, are subdued by Charlemagne, and the area around Budapest and the Danube Bend is incorporated into the Frankish empire.	Nomadic Magyar tribes set up camp in the Carpathian Basin, with five of the seven original tribes settling in the area that is now Budapest.	Hungarian raids outside the Carpathian Basin as far as Germany, Italy and Spain are stopped for good by German King Otto I at the battle of Augsburg.

THE MAGYARS

The origin of the Magyars, as the Hungarians call themselves, is a complicated subject, not helped by the similarity (in English and some other languages) of the words 'Hun' and 'Hungary', which are *not* related. One indisputable fact is that the Magyars belong to the Finno-Ugric group of peoples, who inhabited the forests somewhere between the middle Volga River and the Ural Mountains in western Siberia as early as 4000 BC.

By about 2000 BC, population growth had forced the Finnish-Estonian branch to move west, ultimately reaching the Baltic Sea. The Ugrians moved from the southeastern slopes of the Urals into the valleys of the region, and switched from hunting and fishing to farming and raising livestock, especially horses. Their equestrian skills proved useful half a millennium later when more climatic changes brought drought, forcing them to move north onto the steppes.

On the grasslands, the Ugrians turned to nomadic herding. After 500 BC, by which time the use of iron had become commonplace among the tribes, a group moved west to the area of Bashkiria in Central Asia. Here they lived among Persians and Bulgars, and began referring to themselves as Magyars (from the Finno-Ugric words *mon* – to speak – and *er* – man).

After several centuries, another group split away and moved south to the Don River under the control of the Turkic Khazars. Here they lived among different groups under a tribal alliance called *onogur*, or '10 peoples'. This is thought to be the origin of the word 'Hungary' in English and 'Ungarn' in German. The Magyars' last migration before the so-called conquest (*honfoglalás*) of the Carpathian Basin brought them to what modern Hungarians call the Etelköz, the region between the Dnieper and lower Danube rivers and north of the Black Sea.

THE CONQUEST OF THE CARPATHIAN BASIN

Nomadic groups of Magyars, acting as mercenaries for various armies, probably reached the Carpathian Basin as early as the mid-9th century AD. It is believed that while the men were away during one such campaign in about 889, a fierce people from the Asiatic steppe called the Pechenegs allied themselves with the Bulgars and attacked the Etelköz settlements. When they were attacked again in about 895, seven tribes under the leadership of Árpád – the chief military commander *(gyula)* – struck out for the Carpathian Basin. They crossed the Verecke Pass in today's Ukraine sometime between 896 and 898.

The two principal leaders of the tribes made their bases in Budapest. Árpád established his seat on Csepel; according to the 12th-century chronicler Anonymous, it was Árpád's overseer, a Turkic Cuman called Csepel, who gave his name to the island. Árpád's brother, Kurszán, the chief shaman (*táltos*; see the boxed text, p24), based himself in Óbuda. On Kurszán's death, Árpád took all power for himself and moved his seat to Óbuda; at this time Buda and Pest were no more than small villages.

The Magyars had met almost no resistance in the Carpathian Basin. Being highly skilled at riding and shooting (a common Christian prayer during the Dark Ages was 'Save us, O Lord, from the arrows of the Hungarians'), they began plundering and pillaging in all directions, taking slaves and amassing booty. Their raids took them as far as Germany, Italy and Spain, but in the early 10th century the Magyars began to suffer a string of defeats. In 955 they were stopped in their tracks by the German king Otto I at the battle of Augsburg.

This and subsequent defeats – raids on Byzantium were ended in 970 – left the Magyar tribes in disarray, and they had to choose between their more powerful neighbours to form an alliance:

1000	1083	1220
Stephen (István) is crowned 'Christian King' of Hungary on Christmas Day with a crown sent from Rome by Pope Sylvester II.	King Stephen is canonised as St Stephen by Pope Victor III in Rome, and 20 August is declared his feast day.	The Gothic style of architecture extends into Hungary from northern France, superseding the heavier Romanesque style.

BACKGROUND HISTORY

THEY CAME FROM OUTER SPACE

It was the biggest 'missing link' story of the new millennium, almost as big as the discovery of Piltdown Man in England's East Sussex nearly a century earlier. In May 2007 an outfit called the Africa Research Institute (ARI) in Geneva announced that a team of anthropologists led by one Gábor Varga had found a 'lost' tribe in the northwestern region of the Democratic Republic of Congo, cut off by a protracted civil war. The tribe, it said, called themselves the Madjari.

Could it be? Were they? *Hihetetlen!* (Unbelievable!) All of Budapest was abuzz, and the news was splashed across the front pages and covers of such august publications as *Magyar Nemzet* and *Heti Világgazdaság* (see p44). The ARI researchers had scrutinised the tribe's language, customs and culture for months, and found that many Madjari words sounded Hungarian and the tribe's folk songs resembled traditional Magyar music. The team theorised that the tribe's 600-odd members were descendants of Hungarian soldiers stationed in Africa during Ottoman rule in the 16th and 17th centuries.

Fascinating story… Trouble was, like the infamous Piltdown Man claim, it was all a hoax – this time dreamt up by a Budapest-based filmmaker called David Kresalek. 'We wanted to show how the media works, including a media hoax,' he told reporters. 'We got the idea about a year ago. It has turned out much better than we expected.'

Indeed. But we wonder what all the fuss was about anyway. As fas as we're concerned, Italian-American Nobel Prize–winning physicist Enrico Fermi (1901–54) solved the riddle of the origin of the (Magyar) species more than half a century ago. When asked whether extraterrestrial beings existed, Dr Fermi replied: 'Of course they do…(and) they are already here among us. They are called Hungarians.'

Byzantium to the south and east or the Holy Roman Empire to the west. Individual Magyar chieftains began acting independently, but in 973 Prince Géza, Árpád's great-grandson, asked the Holy Roman emperor Otto II to send Catholic missionaries to Hungary. Géza was baptised in his capital city, Esztergom, 46km upriver from Budapest, as was his son Vajk, who took the Christian name Stephen (István). When Géza died, Stephen ruled as prince, but on Christmas Day in the year 1000 he was crowned 'Christian King' Stephen I. Hungary the kingdom and Hungary the nation had been born.

KING STEPHEN I

Stephen ruthlessly set about consolidating royal authority by expropriating the land of the clan chieftains and establishing a system of counties *(megyék)* protected by castles *(várak)*. Shrewdly, he transferred much land to loyal (mostly German) knights, and the crown began minting coins. Stephen did not find the area of Budapest suitable as a base; he made his seat at Székesfehérvár, 66km to the southwest, while Esztergom remained the kingdom's religious centre.

The king sought the support of the Church and, to hasten the conversion of the populace, ordered one in every 10 villages to build a church. He also established 10 episcopates throughout the land. Monasteries staffed by foreign scholars were set up around the country; in Óbuda it was the religious Chapter of St Peter. By the time of Stephen's death in 1038, Hungary was a nascent Christian nation, increasingly westward-looking and multiethnic. But pockets of rebellion remained; in 1046 a Venetian-born bishop named Gerard (Gellért), who had been brought to Hungary by Stephen himself, was hurled to his death from a Buda hilltop in a spiked barrel by pagan Magyars resisting conversion. Gellért Hill now bears the bishop's name.

1222	1241–42	1301
King Andrew II signs the Golden Bull, according the nobility more rights and powers; it is renewed nine years later in 1231.	Mongols sweep across the country, killing some 100,000 people in Pest and Óbuda alone and reducing the national population by up to a half.	The line of the House of Árpád ends with the death of Andrew III, who leaves no male heir; a period of great turmoil follows.

LIONS & EAGLES & BEARS, OH MY!

The ancient Magyars were strong believers in magic and celestial intervention, and the shaman (*táltos*) enjoyed an elevated position in their society. Certain animals – for example, bears, stags and wolves – were totemic, and it was taboo to mention them directly by name. Thus the wolf was 'the long-tailed one' and the stag the 'large-antlered one'. In other cases the original Magyar for an animal deemed sacred was replaced with a foreign loan word. Medve for 'bear', for example, comes from the Slavic *medved*.

No other ancient totemic animal was more sacred than the *turul*, a hawklike bird that supposedly impregnated Emese, the grandmother of the chieftain Árpád. That legend can be viewed in many ways: as an attempt to foster a sense of common origin and group identity in the ethnically heterogeneous population of the time; as an effort to bestow a sacred origin on the House of Árpád and its rule; or just as a good story – not dissimilar from the one about the Virgin Mary begotten with child by the Holy Spirit anthropomorphised as a dove. Today Hungarians view the turul as their heraldic 'eagle' or 'lion'.

THE HOUSE OF ÁRPÁD

The next two and a half centuries – the lifespan of the Árpád dynasty – would test the new kingdom to the limit. The period was marked by dynastic intrigues and relentless struggles among pretenders to the throne, which weakened the young nation's defences against its more powerful neighbours. There was a brief hiatus under King Ladislas I (László; r 1077–95), who fended off attacks from Byzantium, and under his successor Koloman the Booklover (Könyves Kálmán), who encouraged literature and art until his death in 1116.

Tension flared again when the Byzantine emperor made a grab for Hungary's provinces in Dalmatia and Croatia, which it had acquired by the early 12th century and, together with Slovakia and Transylvania, were deemed the 'crown lands of St Stephen'. He was stopped by Béla III (r 1172–96), who had a permanent residence built at Esztergom (by then an alternative royal capital to Székesfehérvár), but was headquartered at Óbuda. Béla's son Andrew II (András; r 1205–35), however, weakened the crown when he gave in to local barons' demands for more land in order to fund his crusades. This led to the Golden Bull, a kind of Magna Carta signed at Székesfehérvár in 1222, which limited some of the king's powers in favour of the nobility, recognised the 'Hungarian nation' and allowed for a diet, or assembly, of nobles to meet regularly in Pest.

When Béla IV (r 1235–70) tried to regain the estates forfeited by Andrew, the barons were able to oppose him on equal terms. Fearing Mongol expansion and realising he could not count on local help, Béla looked to the west and brought in German and Slovak settlers. In March 1241 Béla gathered his troops at Óbuda and crossed over into Pest. But his efforts were in vain. The Mongols, who had raced through the country, attacked from every direction. By the end of the final attack in January 1242, Pest and Óbuda had been burned to the ground and some 100,000 people killed.

To rebuild the royal capital as quickly as possible, Béla, known as the 'second founding father', again encouraged Germans and Turkic Cuman (Hungarian: Kun) tribes displaced by the Mongols in the east to settle here. He also ordered those still living in Pest and Óbuda to relocate to Castle Hill and build a fortified town. Béla proclaimed Buda a municipality by royal charter in 1244 and bestowed civic rights on the citizens of Pest in 1255; another century would

1458–90	1514	1526
Medieval Hungary enjoys a golden age under the enlightened reign of King Matthias Corvinus and Queen Beatrix, daughter of the king of Naples.	Peasant uprising is crushed and 70,000 people are executed, including leader György Dózsa, who dies on a red-hot iron throne wearing a scalding crown.	Hungary is soundly defeated by the Ottomans at the Battle of Mohács and young King Louis is killed; the Turkish occupation lasting more than a century and a half begins.

go by before Óbuda's citizens won the same rights. By the start of the 14th century, all three areas had begun to develop into major towns.

But Béla did not always play his cards right. In a bid to appease the lesser nobility, he handed them large tracts of land. This enhanced their position and bids for more independence even further. At the time of Béla's death in 1270, anarchy ruled. The Árpád line died out in 1301 with the death of Andrew III, who left no heir, leading to a period of great upheaval.

MEDIEVAL BUDAPEST

The struggle for the Hungarian throne after the death of Andrew III involved several European dynasties, but it was Charles Robert (Károly Róbert) of the French House of Anjou who finally won out (with the pope's blessing) in 1307 and was crowned in Buda two years later. He didn't stay there long though; until his death in 1342, Charles Robert ruled from a palace he built on the Danube at Visegrád, 42km to the northwest. Buda would not play a leading role in history for another five decades, but after that it would never look back. In the meantime, Pest had started to develop as a town of wealthy and independent burghers; by 1406 it had its own royal charter and full independence from Buda.

Under Charles Robert's son and successor, Louis the Great (Nagy Lajos; r 1342–82), the kingdom returned to a policy of conquest. A brilliant military strategist, Louis acquired territory in the Balkans as far as Dalmatia and Romania and, through an alliance, as far north as Poland, where he was crowned king in 1370. But his successes were short-lived as the menace of the Ottoman Turks had appeared on the horizon.

As Louis had no sons, one of his daughters, Mary (Mária; 1382–87), succeeded him. This was deemed to be unacceptable by the barons, who rose up against the 'petticoat throne' and had Mary's husband, Sigismund (Zsigmond; r 1387–1437) of Luxembourg, crowned king. Sigismund's exceptionally long reign brought peace at home, and there was a great flowering of Gothic art and architecture. Sigismund enlarged the Royal Palace on Castle Hill, founded a university at Óbuda (1389), oversaw the construction of the first pontoon bridge over the Danube – until then the only way to cross the river was by ferry – and set national standards of measurement, including the 'Buda pound' (490g) for weight and the 'Buda icce' (about 0.85L) for liquids. But despite these advances and his enthronement as Holy Roman Emperor in 1433, Sigismund was unable to stop the march of the Turks up through the Balkans.

An alliance between Poland and Hungary in 1440 gave the former the Hungarian crown. When Vladislav I (Úlászló), son of the Polish Jagiellonian king, was killed fighting the Turks at Varna (in today's Bulgaria) in 1444, János Hunyadi was made regent. A Transylvanian general born of a Wallachian (Romanian) father, János Hunyadi began his career at the court of Sigismund. His victory over the Turks at Belgrade (Hungarian: Nándorfehérvár) in 1456 checked the Ottoman advance into Hungary for 70 years and assured the coronation of his son Matthias (Mátyás), the greatest ruler of medieval Hungary.

Matthias (r 1458–90), nicknamed 'the Raven' (Corvinus) from his coat of arms, wisely maintained a mercenary force of up to 10,000 soldiers through taxation of the nobility, and this 'Black Army' (one of the first standing armies in Europe) conquered Moravia, Bohemia and even parts of lower Austria. Not only did Matthias Corvinus make Hungary one of central Europe's leading powers, but under his rule Buda enjoyed something of a golden age and for the first time became the true focus of the nation. His second wife, Beatrix, the daughter of

1541	1566	1686
Buda Castle falls to the Ottomans; Hungary is partitioned and shared by three separate groups: Turks, the Habsburgs and the Transylvanian princes.	Miklós Zrínyi and his 2500 soldiers make their heroic sally at Szigetvár Castle; Sultan Suleiman I dies in battle.	Austrian and Hungarian forces backed by the Polish army liberate Buda from the Turks, though little of the castle is left standing.

the king of Naples, brought artisans from Italy who completely rebuilt, extended and fortified the Royal Palace in the Renaissance style. The Corvina Library of more than 2000 codices and incunabula was second only to the library in the Vatican.

But while Matthias busied himself with centralising power for the crown in the capital, he ignored the growing Turkish threat. His successor Vladislav II (Úlászló; r 1490–1516) was unable to maintain even royal authority as the members of the diet, which met to approve royal decrees, squandered royal funds, sold off the royal library and expropriated land. In May 1514 what had begun as a crusade organised by the power-hungry archbishop of Esztergom, Tamás Bakócz, turned into an uprising against the landlords by peasants who rallied near Pest under their leader, György Dózsa.

The revolt was repressed by Transylvanian leader John Szapolyai (Zápolyai János) in a manner considered brutal even by the standards of the Middle Ages. Some 70,000 peasants were tortured and executed, as was Dózsa himself. The retrograde Tripartitum Law that followed in 1522 codified the rights and privileges of the barons and nobles, and reduced the peasants to perpetual serfdom. By the time Louis II (Lajos) took the throne in 1516 at the tender age of nine, he couldn't rely on either side.

THE BATTLE OF MOHÁCS

The defeat of Louis' ragtag army by the Ottoman Turks at Mohács in 1526 is a watershed in Hungarian history. On the battlefield near this small town in Southern Transdanubia, some 195km south of Budapest, a relatively prosperous and independent Hungary died, sending the nation into a tailspin of partition, foreign domination and despair that would be felt for centuries.

It would be unfair to put all the blame on the weak and indecisive teenager Louis or on his commander-in-chief Pál Tomori, the archbishop of Kalocsa. Bickering among the nobility and the brutal crackdown of the Dózsa uprising a dozen years earlier had severely weakened Hungary's military power, and there was virtually nothing left in the royal coffers. By 1526 Ottoman sultan Suleiman the Magnificent (r 1520–66) had taken much of the Balkans, including Belgrade, and was poised to march on Buda and then Vienna with a force of up to 90,000 men.

Unable – or, more likely, unwilling – to wait for reinforcements from Transylvania under the command of his rival John Szapolyai, Louis rushed from Buda with a motley army of just over 25,000 men of mixed nationalities to battle the Turks and was soundly thrashed in less than two hours. Along with bishops, nobles and an estimated 18,000 soldiers, the king himself was killed – crushed by his horse while trying to retreat across a stream.

The Turks then turned north, sacking and burning Buda before retreating. John Szapolyai, who had sat out the battle in the castle at Tokaj with forces of up to 13,000, was crowned king three months later but, despite grovelling before the Turks and kissing the sultan's hand, he was never able to exploit the power he had so desperately sought.

TURKISH OCCUPATION

After the Turks returned and occupied Buda in 1541, Hungary was divided into three parts. The central section, with Buda – Budun to the Turks – as the provincial seat, went to the Ottomans while parts of Transdanubia and what is now Slovakia were governed by the Austrian House of Habsburg and assisted by the Hungarian nobility based at Bratislava (Hungarian: Pozsony).

1699	1703–11	1795
Peace with the Turks is signed by Austria, Poland, Venice and Russia at Karlowitz (now Sremski Karlovci in Serbia); Austria receives large accessions of territory in Hungary and Transylvania.	Ferenc Rákóczi II fights and loses a war of independence against the Habsburgs; he is given asylum in Thrace by the Turkish Sultan Ahmet III.	Seven pro-republican Jacobites, including the group's leader Ignác Martonovics, are beheaded at Vérmező in Buda for plotting against the Habsburg throne.

BUDUN: BUDA ALATURKA

The Turkish occupation of Hungary was marked by constant fighting among the three divisions: Catholic 'Royal Hungary' was pitted not only against the Muslim Turks but the Protestant Transylvanian princes as well. Although Habsburg Hungary enjoyed something of a cultural renaissance during this period, the Turkish-occupied part and Buda itself suffered greatly, with many people fleeing the town to Pest.

The Turks did little building in Buda (or Budun as they called it), apart from several bathhouses still extant, including the Király and Rudas, dervish monasteries and tombs, and city walls and bastions; for the most part, they used existing civic buildings for administration and converted churches into mosques. Matthias Church (see p64) on Castle Hill, for example, was hastily turned into the Büyük Cami, or 'Great Mosque', and the heart of the Royal Palace became a gunpowder store and magazine. Contemporary accounts suggest that what had been a central European town now appeared to be a Balkan one, with copperware shops lining Kasandzhilar yolu – perhaps a transliteration of Kazancilar yolu (Earners St) – today's I Szentháromság utca on Castle Hill. The nearby church of St Mary Magdalene, of which only the tower still stands (see p65), was shared by both Catholics and Protestants who fought bitterly for every square centimetre of space. It seems it was the Muslim Turks who had to keep the peace among the Christians.

But direct contact between Hungarians and Turks was generally minimal and usually only involved the collection of taxes. A colourful Hungarian expression recalls those times. *Hátravan még a feketeleves* literally means 'Still to come is the black soup', but suggests something painful is about to happen. Apparently, after a meal the new Turkish 'hosts' would serve their Hungarian 'guests' an unknown beverage – coffee – which meant it was time to talk about money.

The principality of Transylvania prospered as a vassal state of the Ottoman Empire. This division of the country would remain in place for almost a century and a half.

Turkish power began to wane in the 17th century, especially after the Turkish attempt to take Vienna was soundly defeated. In 1686, with the help of the Polish army, some 45,000 Austrian and Hungarian forces advanced down both banks of the Danube from Štúrovo (Hungarian: Párkány), now in Slovakia, to liberate Buda. An imperial army under Eugene of Savoy wiped out the last Turkish army in Hungary at the Battle of Zenta (now Senta in Serbia) 11 years later. Peace was signed with the Turks at Karlowitz (now Sremski Karlovci in Serbia) in 1699.

THE HABSBURGS

The expulsion of the Turks did not result in a free and independent Hungary. Buda and the rest of the country were under military occupation and governed from Bratislava, and the policies of the Catholic Habsburgs' Counter-Reformation and heavy taxation further alienated the nobility. In 1703, the year in which both Buda and Pest regained their privileges as royal free towns, Transylvanian prince Ferenc Rákóczi II raised an army of Hungarian mercenaries *(kuruc)* against the Habsburgs. The war dragged on for eight years, during which time the rebels 'deposed' the Austrians as Hungary's rulers. But superior imperial forces and lack of funds forced the *kuruc* to negotiate a separate peace with Vienna behind Rákóczi's back. The 1703–11 War of Independence had failed, but Rákóczi was the first leader to unite Hungarians against the Habsburgs.

Though the armistice had brought the fighting to an end, Hungary was now a mere province of the Habsburg empire. Its main cities – Buda, Pest and Óbuda – counted a total of just over 12,000 people. With the ascension of Maria Theresa to the throne in 1740, the Hungarian nobility pledged their 'lives and blood' to her at the diet in Bratislava in exchange for concessions.

1838	1848–49	1867
Devastating Danube flood takes a heavy toll, with three-quarters of the homes in Pest washed away and some 150 people drowned.	War of Independence; Sándor Petőfi dies fighting, Lajos Batthyány and 13 of his generals are executed for their roles, and leader Kossuth goes into exile.	Act of Compromise creates Dual Monarchy of Austria (the empire), based in Vienna, and Hungary (the kingdom), with its seat at Budapest.

Thus began the period of enlightened absolutism that would continue under her son, Joseph II, the 'hatted king' (so-called because he was never crowned in Hungary), who ruled for a decade from 1780. By then the population of Buda and Pest had almost tripled to 35,000 – a significant number, even in the sprawling Habsburg empire.

Under the reigns of both Maria Theresa and Joseph, Hungary took great steps forward economically and culturally, though the first real moves towards integration with Austria had also begun. Buda effectively became the German-speaking town of Ofen and the city's first newspaper – in German, of course – was established in 1730. Funded by the grain and livestock trades, Pest began to develop outside the city walls. In 1749 the foundations for a new palace were laid in Buda, the university was moved from Nagyszombat (now Trnava in Slovakia) to Buda in 1777 and seven years later Joseph ordered the government to move from Bratislava to Buda, the nation's new administrative centre.

Joseph's attempts to modernise society by dissolving the all-powerful (and corrupt) monastic orders, abolishing serfdom and replacing 'neutral' (but archaic) Latin with German as the official language of state administration (1781–85) were opposed by the Hungarian nobility, and the king rescinded some of these reforms on his deathbed.

Dissenting voices could still be heard, and the ideals of the French Revolution of 1789 began to take root in certain intellectual circles in Budapest. In 1795 seven republican Jacobites were beheaded at Vérmező (Blood Meadow; Map p62) in Buda for plotting against the crown.

By 1800 Pest, with a population of about 30,000, was the nation's most important commercial centre while Buda, with 24,000 people, remained a royal garrison town and grew under the eye of the monarch. But 90% of the national population worked the land, and it was primarily through agriculture that modernisation would come to Hungary.

Liberalism and social reform found their greatest supporters among certain members of the aristocracy in Pest. A prime example was Count István Széchenyi (1791–1860), a true Renaissance man known as 'the greatest Hungarian', who advocated the abolition of serfdom and returned much of his own land to the peasantry, proposed the first permanent link between Buda and Pest (Chain Bridge) and oversaw the regulation of the Danube as much for commerce and irrigation as for safety (see the boxed text, opposite).

The proponents of gradual reform were quickly superseded, however, by a more radical faction demanding more immediate action. The group included such men as Miklós Wesselényi, Ferenc Deák and the poet Ferenc Kölcsey, but the predominant figure was Lajos Kossuth (1802–94). It was this dynamic lawyer and journalist who would lead Hungary to its greatest ever confrontation with the Habsburgs.

THE 1848–49 WAR OF INDEPENDENCE

The Habsburg empire began to weaken as Hungarian nationalism increased early in the 19th century. The Hungarians, suspicious of Napoleon's policies, ignored appeals by France to revolt against Vienna, and the Austrians introduced certain reforms in the 1830s: the replacement of Latin, the official language of administration, with Hungarian; a law allowing serfs alternative means of discharging their feudal obligations of service; and increased Hungarian representation in the Council of State in Vienna.

The reforms carried out were too limited and far too late, however, and the diet became more defiant in its dealings with the crown. At the same time, the wave of revolution sweeping Europe

1896	1918	1919
Millennium of the Magyar conquest of the Carpathian Basin is marked by a major exhibition in City Park that attracts four million people over six months.	Austria-Hungary loses WWI in November and the political system collapses; Hungary declares itself a republic under the leadership of Count Mihály Károlyi.	Béla Kun's Republic of Councils, the world's second Communist government after the Soviet Union's, lasts for five months and Kun is driven into exile by the Romanian army.

IN FOR THE COUNT

The contributions that Count István Széchenyi made to his city and his country were enormous and extremely varied. In his seminal 1830 work *Hitel* (meaning 'credit' and based on *hit*, or 'trust'), he advocated sweeping economic reforms and the abolition of serfdom (he himself had distributed the bulk of his property to landless peasants two years earlier). The Chain Bridge, the design of which Széchenyi helped push through parliament, was the first permanent link between Buda and Pest, and for the first time everyone – nobles included – had to pay a toll to use it.

Széchenyi was instrumental in straightening the serpentine Tisza River, which rescued half of Hungary's arable land from flooding and erosion, and his work made the Danube navigable as far as the Iron Gates in Romania. He arranged the financing for Hungary's first railway lines (from Budapest north and east to Vác and Szolnok, and west to Bécsújhely, now Wiener Neustadt in Austria) and launched the first steam transport on the Danube and Lake Balaton. A lover of all things English, Széchenyi got the upper classes interested in horse racing, with the express purpose of improving breeding stock for farming. A large financial contribution made by Széchenyi led to the establishment of the nation's prestigious Academy of Science on V Roosevelt tér.

Széchenyi joined the revolutionary government in 1848, but political squabbling and open conflict with Vienna caused him to lose control and he suffered a nervous breakdown. Despite a decade of convalescence in an asylum, Széchenyi never fully recovered and, tragically, he took his own life in 1860.

For all his accomplishments, Széchenyi's contemporary and fellow reformer, Lajos Kossuth, called him 'the greatest Hungarian'. This dynamic but troubled visionary retains that accolade to this day.

spurred on the more radical faction. On 3 March 1848 Kossuth, who had been imprisoned by the Habsburgs at I Táncsics Mihály utca 9 (see p67) on Castle Hill for three years (1837–40), made a fiery speech in Parliament demanding an end to feudalism. On 15 March a group calling itself the Youth of March led by the poet Sándor Petőfi, who read out his poem *Nemzeti Dal* (National Song) on the steps of the Hungarian National Museum (Map pp102–3), took to the streets of Pest with hastily printed copies of their Twelve Points to press for radical reforms and even revolution.

The frightened government in Vienna quickly approved plans for a new Hungarian ministry responsible to the diet, led by the liberal Lajos Batthyány and to include Deák, Kossuth and Széchenyi. The Habsburgs also reluctantly agreed to abolish serfdom and proclaim equality under the law. But when the diet voted to raise a local army, Habsburg patience began to wear thin.

In September 1848 Habsburg forces launched an attack on Hungary at Pákozd, on the northern shore of Lake Velence, some 55km southwest of Budapest, and Batthyány's government was dissolved. The Hungarians hastily formed a national defence commission and moved the government seat to Debrecen in the east, where Kossuth was elected leader. In April 1849 the Parliament declared Hungary's full independence and the Habsburgs were 'dethroned' for the second time.

The new Habsburg emperor, Franz Joseph (r 1848–1916), was not at all like his feeble-minded predecessor, Ferdinand V, and quickly took action. He sought the assistance of Russian tsar Nicholas I, who obliged with 200,000 troops; Franz Joseph then began appointing a series of heads of government who were inflexible on the national question. Support for the revolution was already waning, however, particularly in areas of mixed population where the Magyars were seen as oppressors. Weak and vastly outnumbered, the rebel troops were defeated by August 1849 and martial law was declared.

A series of brutal reprisals ensued. Summary executions of 'spies' (most of them simply army deserters) took place in the gardens of the National Museum. Batthyány was executed in Pest, 13

1920	1931	1939
Treaty of Trianon carves up much of central Europe, reducing historical Hungary by almost two-thirds and enlarging the ethnic Hungarian populations in Romania, Yugoslavia and Czechoslovakia.	Strongman Miklós Horthy declares martial law in the face of economic unrest; suspected Communists are rounded up, imprisoned and, in some cases, executed.	Nazi Germany invades Poland; Britain and France declare war on Germany two days later.

of his generals (the so-called Martyrs of Arad) were incarcerated and shot in Romania. (Petőfi had died in battle in July of that year and Kossuth was already in exile in Turkey.) Habsburg troops then went around the country systematically blowing up castles and fortifications lest they be used by resurgent rebels.

THE DUAL MONARCHY

Hungary was again merged into the Habsburg empire as a vanquished province and 'neo-absolutism' was the order of the day. Hungarian war prisoners were forced to build the Citadella (p68) atop Gellért Hill to 'defend' the city from further insurrection, but by the time it was ready in 1854 the political climate had changed and the fortress had become obsolete. Passive resistance among Hungarians and disastrous military defeats for the Habsburgs by the French in 1859 and the Prussians in 1866 pushed Franz Joseph to the negotiating table with liberal Hungarians under Deák's leadership.

The result was the Compromise of 1867 (Ausgleich in German, meaning 'balance' or 'reconciliation'), which fundamentally restructured the Habsburg monarchy and created the Dual Monarchy of Austria (the empire) and Hungary (the kingdom) ruled by Emperor/King Franz Josef and the much-beloved Empress Queen Elizabeth (see the boxed text, p96). It was a federated state of two parliaments and two capitals – Vienna and Budapest (the result of the union of Buda, Pest and Óbuda in 1873). Only defence, foreign relations and customs were directed by the old imperial administration in Vienna. Hungary even retained its Honvéd, a type of national guard under the direction of the Hungarian Parliament.

This 'Age of Dualism' would carry on until 1918 and spark an economic, cultural and intellectual rebirth in Budapest – a golden age the likes of which the city has never seen again. Trade and industry boomed, factories were established and the composers Franz (Ferenc) Liszt and Ferenc Erkel were making beautiful music. The middle class – dominated by Germans and Jews in Pest – burgeoned, and the capital entered into a frenzy of building. Much of what you see in Budapest today – from the grand boulevards and their Eclectic-style apartment blocks to the Parliament building, State Opera House and Palace of Art – was built at this time.

The apex of this belle époque was the six-month exhibition in City Park 1896, celebrating the millennium of the Magyar conquest of the Carpathian Basin. Some four million visitors from Hungary and abroad were transported to the fairground on continental Europe's first underground railway (now the M1 or 'little yellow' metro line). By the turn of the 20th century, the population of the 'new' capital had jumped from about 280,000 at the time of the Compromise to 750,000, Europe's sixth-largest city.

But all was not well in the kingdom. The working class, based almost entirely in Budapest, had almost no rights and the situation in the countryside was almost as dire as it had been in the Middle Ages. Despite a new law enacted in 1868 to protect their rights, minorities under Hungarian control (Czechs, Slovaks, Croats and Romanians) were under increased pressure to 'Magyarise' and many viewed their new rulers as oppressors. Increasingly, they worked to dismember the empire.

WWI & THE REPUBLIC OF COUNCILS

On 28 July 1914, a month to the day after the assassination of Archduke Franz Ferdinand, heir to the Habsburg throne, by a Bosnian Serb in Sarajevo, Austria-Hungary declared war on Serbia and entered WWI allied with the German empire. The result of this action was disastrous, with

1941	1944	1945
Hungary joins the Axis led by Germany and Italy against the Allies in WWII, largely in order to recover territories lost according to the terms of the Treaty of Trianon.	Germany invades and occupies Hungary; most Hungarian Jews, who had largely been able to avoid persecution under Horthy, are deported to Nazi concentration camps.	Budapest is liberated by the Soviet army in April, a month before full victory in Europe, with three-quarters of its buildings and all of its bridges in ruins.

widespread destruction and hundreds of thousands killed on the Russian and Italian fronts. At the armistice in 1918 the fate of the Dual Monarchy – and Hungary as a multinational kingdom – was sealed with the despised Treaty of Trianon (see boxed text, p33).

A republic under Count Mihály Károlyi was set up in Budapest five days after the armistice was signed, and the Habsburg monarchy was dethroned for the third and final time. But the fledgling republic would not last long. Rampant inflation, mass unemployment, the occupation and dismemberment of Hungary by the Allies and the victory of the Bolshevik Revolution in Russia all combined to radicalise much of the Budapest working class.

In March 1919 a group of Hungarian Communists led by a former Transylvanian journalist called Béla Kun seized power. The so-called Republic of Councils (*Tanácsköztársaság*) set out to nationalise industry and private property and build a fairer society, but Kun's failure to regain the 'lost territories' (despite getting some land back from Romania and briefly occupying Slovakia) brought mass opposition to the regime and the government unleashed a reign of 'red terror' around the country.

In August Romanian troops occupied the capital, and Kun and his comrades (including Minister of Culture Béla Lugosi, later of *Dracula* fame) fled to Vienna. The Romanians camped out at Oktogon, taking whatever they wanted when they wanted it, and left the city in November – just ahead of Admiral Miklós Horthy, the 'hero of the Battle of Rijeka', mounted on a white steed and leading 25,000 Hungarian troops into what he called *a bűnös város* (the sinful city).

THE HORTHY YEARS & WWII
In the nation's first-ever election by secret ballot in March 1920, Parliament chose a kingdom as the form of state and – lacking a king – elected as its regent Admiral Horthy, who would remain in that position until the penultimate year of WWII. The arrangement even confused US president Franklin D Roosevelt in the early days of the war. After being briefed by an aide on the government and leadership of Hungary, he reportedly said: 'Let me see if I understand you right. Hungary is a kingdom without a king run by a regent who's an admiral without a navy?'

Horthy embarked on a 'white terror' – every bit as brutal as Béla Kun's red one – that attacked Jews, social democrats and Communists for their roles in supporting the Republic of Councils. As the regime was consolidated, it showed itself to be extremely rightist and conservative, advocating the status quo and 'traditional values' – family, state and religion. Though the country had the remnants of a parliamentary system, Horthy was all-powerful, and very few reforms were enacted. On the contrary, the lot of the working class and the peasantry worsened.

One thing everyone agreed on was that the return of the territories lost through the Treaty of Trianon (see the boxed text, p33) was essential for national development. Budapest was swollen with ethnic Hungarian refugees from Romania, Czechoslovakia and the newly formed Kingdom of Serbs, Croats and Slovenes; unemployment skyrocketed and the economy was at a standstill. Hungary obviously could not count on the victors – France, Britain and the US – to help recoup its land; instead, it would have to seek help from the fascist governments of Germany and Italy.

Hungary's move to the right intensified throughout the 1930s, though it remained silent when WWII broke out in September 1939. Horthy hoped an alliance would not mean actually having to enter the war but, after recovering northern Transylvania and part of Croatia with Germany's help, Hungary joined the German- and Italian-led Axis in June 1941. The war was just as disastrous for Hungary as the 1914–18 one had been, and hundreds of thousands of

1946	1949	1956
Hungary experiences the world's worst hyperinflation, with notes worth up to 10,000 trillion pengő issued; Liberty Bridge, the first of the spans over the Danube to be rebuilt, reopens.	The Communists, now in complete control, announce the formation of the 'People's Republic of Hungary'; Stalinist show trials of 'Titoists' and other 'enemies of the people' begin in Budapest.	Budapest is in flames after riots in October; Hungary briefly withdraws from the Warsaw Pact and proclaims its neutrality but the status quo is restored and János Kádár installed as leader.

Hungarian troops died while retreating from Stalingrad, where they'd been used as cannon fodder. Realising too late that his country was again on the losing side, Horthy and his prime minister began secret discussions with the Allies.

When Hitler caught wind of this in March 1944 he sent in his army, with Adolf Eichmann in command from the Buda Hills and the Wehrmacht billeted in the Astoria Hotel. Under pressure, Horthy installed Ferenc Szálasi, the deranged leader of the pro-Nazi Arrow Cross Party, as prime minister in October and was then deported to Germany. He later found exile in Portugal, where he died in 1957.

The Arrow Cross Party moved quickly to quash any opposition, and thousands of the country's liberal politicians and labour leaders were arrested. At the same time, its puppet government introduced anti-Jewish legislation similar to that in Germany, and Jews, who lived in fear but were still alive under Horthy, were rounded up into ghettos by Hungarian pro-Nazis. During the summer of 1944, a mere 10 months before the war ended, approximately 450,000 Hungarian Jewish men, women and children – 70% of Hungarian Jewry – were deported to Auschwitz and other labour camps in just over eight weeks, where they either starved to death, succumbed to disease or were brutally murdered by the German fascists and their unsayable henchmen. Many of the Jews who did survive owed their lives to heroic men like Raoul Wallenberg, a Budapest-based Swedish diplomat (see the boxed text, p69) and the Swiss consul, Carl Lutz.

Budapest now became an international battleground for the first time since the Turkish occupation, and the bombs began falling everywhere – particularly around Castle Hill and, in Pest, in the northern and eastern districts of Angyalföld and Zugló, where there were munitions factories. The resistance movement was virtually nonexistent and incidents of sabotage and propaganda activity very few and far between. In fact, what little opposition there was came from the Communists.

By Christmas 1944 the Soviet army had surrounded Budapest. When the Germans and Hungarian Nazis rejected a settlement, the siege of the capital began. By the time the German war machine had surrendered in April 1945, three-quarters of the city's homes, historical buildings and churches had been severely damaged or destroyed. Some 20,000 Hungarian soldiers and 25,000 civilians of Budapest had been killed. As their goodbye gift, the vindictive Germans blew up Buda Castle and knocked out every bridge spanning the Danube.

THE PEOPLE'S REPUBLIC

When free parliamentary elections were held in November 1945, the Independent Smallholders' Party received 57% (245 seats) of the vote. But Soviet political officers, backed by the occupying army, forced three other parties – the Communists, Social Democrats and National Peasants – into a coalition. Limited democracy prevailed, and land-reform laws, sponsored by the Communist minister of agriculture, Imre Nagy, were enacted, wiping away the prewar feudal structure.

Within a couple of years, the Communists were ready to take complete control. After a disputed election was held under a complicated new electoral law in 1947, they declared their candidate, Mátyás Rákosi, the winner. The following year the Social Democrats merged with the Communists to form the Hungarian Workers' Party.

In 1948 Rákosi, a big fan of Stalin, began a process of nationalisation and unrealistically fast industrialisation at the expense of agriculture – a kind of Hungarian 'Great Leap Forward'. Peasants were forced into collective farms, and all produce had to be delivered to state warehouses. A network of spies and informers exposed 'class enemies' such as Cardinal József Mindszenty

1958	1963	1968
Imre Nagy and others are executed by the Communist regime for their role in the uprising and buried in unmarked graves in Budapest's New Municipal Cemetery.	Amnesty is extended to those involved in the 1956 Uprising by the Communist government after a UN resolution condemning the suppression of the rebellion is struck from the agenda.	Plans for a liberalised economy are introduced in an attempt to overcome the inefficiencies of central planning but are rejected as too liberal by conservatives.

NEVER! SAY NEVER!

In June 1920, scarcely a year and a half after the treaty ending WWI was signed, the victorious Allies drew up a postwar settlement under the Treaty of Trianon at Versailles, near Paris, that enlarged some countries, truncated others and created several 'successor states'. As one of the defeated enemy nations and with large numbers of minorities clamouring for independence within its borders, Hungary stood to lose more than most. And it sure did. It was reduced to 40% of its historical size and, while it was now a largely uniform, homogeneous state, for millions of ethnic Hungarians in Romania, Yugoslavia and Czechoslovakia, they were now the minority.

'Trianon' became the singularly most hated word in Hungary, and 'Nem, Nem, Soha!' (No, No, Never!) the rallying cry during the interwar years. Indeed, one of my university professors, the heroic Polish 'righteous gentile' Jan Karski, saw these words spelled out in a flowerbed in front of the Parliament building in Budapest when he travelled through the Hungarian capital on a secret mission shortly after the outbreak of WWII. Many of the problems the *diktátum* created remained in place for decades, and it has coloured Hungary's relations with its neighbours for upwards of a century. Hungary has now signed basic treaties with fellow EU members Romania and Slovakia renouncing all outstanding territorial claims, but the issue of ethnic Hungarian minority rights in those countries causes bilateral tensions to flare up from time to time.

(see the boxed text, p90) to the secret police, the ÁVO (ÁVH after 1949), who interrogated them at their headquarters at VI Andrássy út 60 (now the House of Terror; p94) in Pest and sent them to trial at the then Military Court of Justice (Map p62) on II Fő utca in Buda. Some were executed; many more were sent into internal exile or condemned to labour camps. It is estimated that during this period up to 25% of the adult population of Budapest faced police or judicial proceedings.

Bitter feuding within the party began, and purges and Stalinist show trials became the order of the day. László Rajk, the Communist minister of the interior (which also controlled the secret police), was arrested and later executed for 'Titoism'; his successor János Kádár was jailed and tortured. In August 1949 the nation was proclaimed the 'People's Republic of Hungary'. In the years that followed – among the darkest and bleakest in Budapest's history – apartment blocks, small businesses and retail outlets were expropriated by the state.

After the death of Stalin in March 1953 and Khrushchev's denunciation of him three years later, Rákosi's tenure was up and the terror began to abate. Under pressure from within the party, Rákosi's successor, Ernő Gerő, rehabilitated Rajk posthumously and readmitted Nagy, who had been expelled from the party a year earlier for suggesting reforms. But Gerő was ultimately as much a hardliner as Rákosi had been and, by October 1956 during Rajk's reburial, murmured calls for a real reform of the system – 'socialism with a human face' – were already being heard.

THE 1956 UPRISING

The nation's greatest tragedy – an event that for a while shook the world, rocked international Communism and pitted Hungarian against Hungarian – began in Budapest on 23 October 1956 when some 50,000 university students assembled at II Bem József tér in Buda, shouting anti-Soviet slogans and demanding that Nagy be named prime minister. That night a crowd pulled down and sawed into pieces the colossal statue of Stalin on Dózsa György út on the edge of City Park (Városliget; Map p108), and shots were fired by ÁVH agents on another group

1978	1988	1989
The Crown of St Stephen is returned to Hungary from the US, where it had been held at Fort Knox in Kentucky since the end of WWII.	János Kádár is forced to retire in May after more than three decades in power; he dies and is buried in Budapest's Kerepesi Cemetery the following year.	Communist monopoly on power is relinquished and the national borders are opened; Imre Nagy is reburied in Budapest; Republic of Hungary is declared.

gathering outside the headquarters of Hungarian Radio (see p106) on VIII Bródy Sándor utca in Pest. In the blink of an eye, Budapest was in revolution.

The next day Nagy formed a government while János Kádár was named president of the Central Committee of the Hungarian Workers' Party. At first it appeared that Nagy might be successful in transforming Hungary into a neutral, multiparty state. On 28 October the government offered an amnesty to all those involved in the violence and promised to abolish the ÁVH. On 30 October demonstrators stormed Communist Party headquarters at VIII Köztársaság tér 26–27 (now offices of the 'reformed' MSZP; Map pp102–3), dragging out and shooting members of the secret police. On 31 October hundreds of political prisoners were released, and widespread (and often times quite violent) reprisals against ÁVH agents began. The next day Nagy announced that Hungary would leave the Warsaw Pact and declare its neutrality.

At this, Soviet tanks and troops crossed into Hungary and within 72 hours began attacking Budapest and other centres. Kádár, who had slipped away from Budapest to join the Russian invaders, was installed as leader.

Fierce street fighting continued for several days. Fighting was especially heavy in and around Corvin tér, VIII József körút and the nearby Kilián army barracks on IX Üllői út in Pest, and II Széna tér in Buda – encouraged by Radio Free Europe broadcasts and disingenuous promises of support from the West, which was embroiled in the Suez Canal crisis at the time. When the fighting was over, 25,000 people were dead. Then the reprisals – the worst in the city's history – began. An estimated 20,000 people were arrested and 2000 – including Imre Nagy and his associates in 1958 – were executed. Another 250,000 refugees fled to Austria. The government lost what little credibility it had ever had and the city many of its most competent and talented citizens. As for the physical scars, just look around you in some of the older parts of Pest: the bullet holes and shrapnel damage on the exterior walls still cry out in silent fury.

HUNGARY UNDER KÁDÁR

After the revolt, the ruling party was reorganised as the Hungarian Socialist Workers' Party, and Kádár, now both party president and premier, launched a program to liberalise the social and economic structure based on compromise. (His most quoted line was 'Whoever is not against us is for us' – a reversal of the Stalinist adage that stated 'Those not for us are against us'.) In 1968 he and the economist Rezső Nyers unveiled the so-called New Economic Mechanism (NEM) to introduce elements of a market to the planned economy. But even this proved a step too far for many party conservatives. Nyers was ousted and the NEM all but abandoned.

Kádár managed to survive that power struggle unscathed and went on to introduce greater consumerism and market socialism. By the mid-1970s Hungary was light years ahead of any other Soviet-bloc country in its standard of living, freedom of movement and opportunities to (softly) criticise the government. Budapesters may have had to wait seven years for a Lada car or 12 for a telephone, but most could at least enjoy access to a second house in the countryside and a decent material life. The 'Hungarian model' attracted both Western attention and investment.

But things began to sour in the 1980s. The Kádár system of 'goulash socialism', which had seemed 'timeless and everlasting' (as one writer in Budapest put it), was incapable of dealing with such 'unsocialist' problems as unemployment, soaring inflation and the largest per-capita

1990	1991	1994
The centrist MDF wins the first free elections in 43 years in April; Árpád Göncz is chosen the republic's first president in August.	Last Soviet troops leave Hungarian soil in June – two weeks ahead of schedule; parliament passes the first act dealing with the return of property seized under Communist rule since 1949.	Socialists win the general election decisively and form a government under Gyula Horn for the first time since the changes of 1989.

foreign debt in Eastern Europe. Worse, Kádár and the 'old guard' refused to hear talk about party reforms. In June 1987 Károly Grósz took over as premier, and less than a year later Kádár was booted out of the party and forced to retire.

THE END OF AN ERA

A group of reformers, including Nyers, Imre Pozsgay, Miklós Németh and Gyula Horn, took control. Party conservatives at first put a lid on any real change by demanding a retreat from political liberalisation in exchange for their support of the new regime's economic policies. But the tide had turned.

Throughout the summer and autumn of 1988, new political parties were formed and old ones revived. In January 1989 Pozsgay, second-guessing what was to come as Mikhail Gorbachev launched sweeping reforms in the Soviet Union, announced that the events of 1956 had been a 'popular insurrection' and not the 'counter-revolution' that the regime had always dubbed it. In June 1989 some 250,000 people attended ceremonies marking the reburial of Imre Nagy and other victims of 1956 in Budapest's New Municipal Cemetery (see p105).

In July 1989, again at Pozsgay's instigation, Hungary began to demolish the electrified wire fence separating it from Austria. The move released a wave of East Germans holidaying in Hungary into the West and the opening attracted thousands more. The collapse of the Communist regimes around the region was now unstoppable. What Hungarians call *az átkos 40 év*, 'the accursed 40 years', had come to a withering, almost feeble, end.

THE REPUBLIC OF HUNGARY REBORN

At its party congress in February 1989, the ruling Hungarian Socialist Workers' Party changed its name to the Hungarian Socialist Party (MSZP) and later in the year agreed to surrender its monopoly on power, paving the way for free elections in the spring of 1990. In a volte-face being seen more and more in the region, the party now advocated social democracy and a free-market economy. Most voters saw the party leaders as evil, two-faced despots who had just changed their outfit; hollow promises were not enough to shake off the stigma of four decades of autocratic rule. On 23 October 1989, the 33rd anniversary of the 1956 Uprising, the nation once again became the Republic of Hungary.

The 1990 election was won by the centrist Hungarian Democratic Forum (MDF), which advocated a gradual transition to capitalism and was led by a softly spoken former museum curator, József Antall. The social-democratic Alliance of Free Democrats (SZDSZ), which had called for much faster change, came in a distant second with 18% of the vote. As Gorbachev looked on, Hungary changed political systems as if it were clothing and the last Soviet troops left Hungarian soil in June 1991. Street names in Budapest such as Lenin körút and Marx tér ended up on the rubbish tip of history, and monuments to 'glorious workers' and 'esteemed leaders' were packed off to a socialist-realist theme park now called Memento Park (p80).

In coalition with two smaller parties – the Independent Smallholders (FKgP) and the Christian Democrats (KDNP) – the MDF provided Hungary with sound government during its difficult transition to a full market economy. Those years saw Hungary's neighbours to the north (Czechoslovakia) and south (Yugoslavia) split along ethnic lines; Prime Minister Antall did little to improve Hungary's relations with Slovakia, Romania or Yugoslavia by claiming to be the 'emotional and spiritual' prime minister of the large Magyar minorities in those countries.

1995	1999	2000
Árpád Göncz of the SZDSZ, arguably the most popular politician in Hungary, is elected for a second (and, by law, final) five-year term as president of the republic.	Hungary becomes a fully fledged member of NATO, along with the Czech Republic and Poland; NATO aircraft heading for Kosovo begin using Hungarian airfields.	Ferenc Mádl, the nominee of the Fidesz-MPP and FKgP coalition government, is elected the second president of the republic to succeed Árpád Göncz.

Despite initial successes in curbing inflation and lowering interest rates, a host of economic problems slowed the pace of development, and the government's laissez-faire policies did not help. Even more than most Hungarians, Budapesters had unrealistically expected a much faster improvement in their living standards. Indeed, according to a poll taken in mid-1993, 76% of respondents were 'very disappointed' with the results.

In the May 1994 elections the MSZP, led by Gyula Horn, won an absolute majority in Parliament. This in no way implied a return to the past, and Horn was quick to point out that it was in fact his party that had initiated the whole reform process in the first place. (As foreign minister in 1989, Horn had played a key role in opening the border with Austria.)

THE ROAD TO EUROPE

After its dire showing in the 1994 elections, the Federation of Young Democrats (Fidesz), which until 1993 had limited membership to those aged under 35 in order to emphasise a past untainted by Communism, privilege and corruption, moved to the right and added the extension 'MPP' (Hungarian Civic Party) to its name to attract the support of the burgeoning middle class. In the 1998 vote, during which it campaigned for integration with Europe, Fidesz-MPP won by forming a coalition with the MDF and the agrarian conservative FKgP. The party's youthful leader, Viktor Orbán, was named prime minister. Hungary became a fully fledged member of NATO the following year.

Despite the astonishing economic growth and other gains made by the coalition government, the electorate grew increasingly hostile to Fidesz-MPP's – and Orbán's – strongly nationalistic rhetoric and perceived arrogance. In April 2002 the largest turnout of voters in Hungarian history unseated the government in a closely fought election and returned the MSZP, allied with the SZDSZ, to power under Prime Minister Péter Medgyessy, a free-market advocate who had served as finance minister in the Horn government. Hungary, with nine other so-called accession countries, was admitted into the EU in May 2004. Just three months later, Hungary experienced the first collapse of a government in its postwar history. Amid revelations that he had served as a counterintelligence officer in the late 1970s and early '80s while working in the finance ministry, and with the government's popularity at a three-year low, Medgyessy was forced to resign. Sports Minister Ferenc Gyurcsány of the MSZP was named prime minister.

HOME AT LAST

Gyurcsány was reappointed prime minister in April 2006 after the electorate gave his coalition 55% of 386 parliamentary seats. He immediately began a series of austerity measures to tackle Hungary's budget deficit, which had reached a staggering 10% of the GDP. But in September in an incident that could have been scripted by the courtiers of Louis XIV's Versailles, just as these unpopular steps were being put into place an audiotape recorded shortly after the election at a closed-door meeting of the prime minister's cabinet had Gyurcsány confessing that the party had 'lied morning, evening and night' about the state of the economy since coming to power and now had to make amends. Gyurcsány refused to resign, and public outrage led to a series of demonstrations near the Parliament building in Budapest, culminating in widespread rioting that marred the 50th anniversary of the 1956 Uprising.

Since then, sometimes violent demonstrations have become a regular feature on the streets of Budapest, especially during national holidays. The radical right-wing nationalist party Jobbik

2004	2006	2008
Hungary is admitted to the EU along with nine other new member-nations, including neighbouring states Slovakia and Slovenia, with Romania following three years later.	Socialist Ferenc Gyurcsány is re-elected as prime minister; Budapest is rocked by antigovernment riots during the 50th anniversary celebrations of the 1956 Uprising.	Government loses key referendum on health-care reform; SZDSZ quits coalition, leaving the socialists to form a minority government; Hungary is particularly hard hit by the global 'credit crunch'.

Magyarországért Mozgalom (Movement for a Better Hungary) and its uniformed militia arm, Magyar Gárda (Hungarian Guard), have been at the centre of many of these demonstrations and riots. Many Hungarian people are deeply concerned with the rise in the activities and increased popularity of the extreme right.

Gyurcsány, who could be called Rasputin for his ability to survive near-death blows, had his head on the block again in March 2008 when the opposition forced through a referendum on the government's health-care reform program. The referendum was soundly defeated and the SZDSZ quit the coalition, leaving Gyurcsány to head a feeble minority government until general elections scheduled for 2010.

At the time of writing, Hungary, once the success story of Eastern Europe, was still reeling from the fallout of worldwide economic collapse. Overborrowed and overspent, the country had been especially hard hit and, with such unlikely fellow travellers as Iceland, Belarus and Pakistan, had just a week before Republic Day approached the International Monetary Fund for an economic bailout. It felt like a century – not less than two decades – had passed since the heady moments of 23 October 1989 when the republic of Hungary had re-emerged phoenix-like from the ashes of Communism.

ARTS & ARCHITECTURE

The arts in Budapest have been both stunted and spurred on by the pivotal events in the nation's history. King Stephen's conversion to Catholicism brought Romanesque and Gothic art and architecture, while the Turkish occupation nipped most of Budapest's nascent Renaissance in the bud. The Habsburgs opened the doors to baroque influences. The arts thrived under the Dual Monarchy, through truncation brought by the Trianon Treaty and even under fascism. The early days of Communism brought socialist-realist art celebrating wheat sheaves and muscle-bound steelworkers to a less-than-impressed populace, but much money was spent on music and 'correct art' such as classical theatre.

While the artistic, cultural and literary hypertrophy of Budapest is indisputable, it would be foolish to ignore folk art when discussing fine arts here. The two have been inextricably linked for several centuries and have greatly influenced one another. The music of Béla Bartók and the ceramic sculptures of Margit Kovács are deeply rooted in traditional Hungarian culture, for example. Even the architecture of the Secession (p47) incorporated many folk elements. The best place in Budapest to see this type of art is the Ethnography Museum (p87).

MUSIC

Hungary has made many contributions to the world of classical music, but one person stands head and shoulders above the rest: Franz (or Ferenc) Liszt (1811–86). He established the Academy of Music (p156) in Budapest and lived in a four-room 1st-floor apartment on VI Vörösmarty utca (see p95) from 1881 until his death. Liszt liked to describe himself as 'part Gypsy', and some of his works, notably the 20 *Hungarian Rhapsodies,* do in fact echo the traditional music of the Roma people.

Ferenc Erkel (1810–93), who taught at the Academy of Music from 1879 to 1886 and was the State Opera House's first musical director, is the father of Hungarian opera. Two of his works – the stirringly nationalistic *Bánk Bán,* based on József Katona's play of that name, and *László Hunyadi* – are standards at the State Opera House (p161).

Béla Bartók (1881–1945) and Zoltán Kodály (1882–1967), both long-term residents of Budapest (their former residences are now museums; see p80 and p96), made the first systematic study of Hungarian folk music, travelling and recording throughout the Magyar linguistic region during 1906. Both integrated some of their findings into their own compositions – Bartók in *Bluebeard's Castle,* for example, and Kodály in his *Peacock Variations.*

Imre Kálmán (1882–1953) was Hungary's most celebrated composer of operettas. The *Queen of the Csárdás* and *Countess Marica* are two of his most popular works and standard fare at the Budapest Operetta (p161).

The most prestigious orchestras are the Budapest-based Hungarian National Philharmonic Orchestra and the Budapest Festival Orchestra, which has been voted by the London-based music magazine *Gramophone* as one of the world's top 10 symphonies.

top picks

CDS

- *Live at the Liszt Academy* Muzsikás, winners of the 2008 WOMEX award, have been making music for over 35 years now and never sound better than when they join forces with warbler Marta Sebestyén.
- *Psyché* Gutsy Beáta Pálya's award-winning third album combines folk, Gypsy music and jazz backed by her own quintet.
- *Romano Trip: Gypsy Grooves from Eastern Europe* This CD from the incomparable Romano Drom is where Roma folk meets world music, with an electronic twist. Unmissable.
- *A Sip of Story* Eclectic early offering in English from multifaceted alt rock sextet Quimby.
- *We Strike!* Latest and most political effort yet from Anima Sound System, Hungary's premier electronic band, mixing Western beats with East European tonal flavours.
- *With the Gypsy Violin Around the World: Sándor Déki Lakatos & His Gypsy Band* No one's Hungarian musical education is complete without this compilation, the epitome of saccharine *csárdás* music.

When discussing folk music, it is important to distinguish between 'Gypsy' music and Hungarian folk music. Gypsy music as it is known and heard in Hungarian restaurants from Budapest to Boston is urban schmaltz and based on recruiting tunes called *verbunkos*, played during the Rákóczi independence wars. At least two fiddles, a bass and a cymbalom (a curious stringed instrument played with sticks) are de rigueur. You can hear this saccharine *csárda*-style (Hungarian-style restaurant/inn) music at hotel restaurants throughout Budapest or get hold of a recording by Sándor Déki Lakatos and his band.

To confuse matters, real Roma – as opposed to Gypsy – music traditionally does not use instruments but is sung a cappella. Some modern Roma music groups – Kalyi Jag (Black Fire), Romano Drom (Gypsy Road) and Romani Rota (Gypsy Wheels) – have added guitars, percussion and even electronics to create a whole new sound.

Hungarian folk musicians play violins, zithers, hurdy-gurdies, bagpipes and lutes on a five-tone diatonic scale. Watch out for Muzsikás; Marta Sebestyén; Ghymes, a Hungarian folk band from Slovakia; and the Hungarian group Vujicsics, which mixes elements of South Slav music. Another folk musician with eclectic tastes is the Paris-trained Beáta Pálya, who combines such sounds as traditional Bulgarian and Indian music with Hungarian folk. Attending a *táncház* (literally 'dance house'; p42) is an excellent way to hear Hungarian folk music and even to learn to dance.

Traditional Yiddish music is not as well known as the Gypsy and Roma varieties but it is of similar origin, having once been closely associated with central European folk music. Until WWI, *klezmer* dance bands were led by the violin and cymbalom, but the influence of Yiddish theatre and the first wax recordings inspired the inclusion of the clarinet. *Klezmer* music is currently going through something of a renaissance in Budapest (see the boxed text, p160).

Pop music is as popular here as anywhere – indeed, Budapest has one of Europe's biggest pop spectacles, the annual Sziget Music Festival (p17). It boasts more than 1000 performances over a week and attracts an audience of up to 400,000 people.

ARCHITECTURE

You won't find as much Romanesque and Gothic architecture in Budapest as you will in, say, Prague – the Mongols, Turks and Habsburgs destroyed most of it – but the Royal Palace incorporates many Gothic features and the *sedile* (niches with seats) at the entranceways in many of the houses in the Castle District, most notably on I Úri utca and I Országház utca, are pure Gothic. The chapels in the Inner Town Parish Church (p84) have some fine Gothic and Renaissance tabernacles, and you can't miss the Renaissance stonework – along with the Gothic wooden sculptures and panel paintings and late-Gothic triptychs – at the Hungarian National Gallery (p61).

Baroque architecture abounds in Budapest; you'll see examples of it everywhere. St Anne's Church (p66) on I Batthyány tér in Buda and the Óbuda Parish Church (Map p74) on III Flórián tér are fine examples of ecclesiastical baroque, while the Citadella (p68) on Gellért Hill in Buda and the municipal council office (Map p85) on V Városház utca in Pest are baroque in its civic or secular form.

RUBIK CUBES, BIROS, VITAMIN C & ZSA ZSA

It is not enough to be Hungarian – one must also have talent.

Slogan spotted in a Toronto employment office in the early 1960s

The contributions made by Hungarians in a number of fields – from films and toys to science and fine art – both at home and abroad have been enormous, especially when you consider the nation's relatively small size and population. The following is a list of people whom you may not have known were Hungarian or of Magyar ancestry. Should you want an even longer list, consult *Eminent Hungarians* by Ray Keenoy, which looks at 'heroes and scoundrels, titans of commerce and saints of science'.

Biro, Laszlo (Bíró József László; 1899–1985) Inventor of the ballpoint pen, patented in Paris in 1938.

Brassaï (Halász Gyula; 1899–1984) Hungarian-born French poet, draftsman, sculptor and photographer, known for his dramatic photographs of Paris by night.

Capa, Robert (Friedmann Endre Ernő; 1913–54) One of the greatest war photographers and photojournalists of the 20th century.

Cukor, George (Cukor György; 1899–1983) Legendary New York–born film producer/director (*The Philadelphia Story,* 1940).

Curtis, Tony (Bernard Schwartz; 1925–) Evergreen American actor (*Spartacus,* 1960) and painter.

Eszterhas, Joe (Eszterhás József; 1944–) American scriptwriter (*Basic Instinct,* 1989).

Gabor, Eva (Gábor Éva; 1919–95) American actress chiefly remembered for her starring role as a New York city socialite and her comical life on a farm in the 1960s TV series *Green Acres;* younger sister of Zsa Zsa.

Gabor, Zsa Zsa (Gábor Sári; 1917–) Ageless-ish American starlet of grade BBB films and older sister of Eva.

Houdini, Harry (Weisz Erich; 1874–1926) American magician and celebrated escape artist.

Howard, Leslie (Steiner László; 1893–1943) Quintessential English actor most famous for his role in *Gone with the Wind* (1939).

Lauder, Estée (Josephine Esther Mentzer; 1908–2004) American fragrance and cosmetics baroness.

Liszt, Franz (Liszt Ferenc; 1811–86) Piano virtuoso and composer.

Lorre, Peter (Löwenstein László; 1904–64) American actor born in what is now Slovakia and usually typecast as a sinister foreigner.

Lugosi, Béla (Blaskó Béla Ferenc Dezső; 1882–1956) The film world's only *real* Dracula – and minister of culture under the Béla Kun regime (see p30).

Newman, Paul (1925–2008) Much-loved and now missed American actor, film director and entrepreneur born of a Hungarian Jewish father.

Rubik, Ernő (1944–) Inventor of the hottest toy of the 1980 Christmas season – an infuriating plastic cube with 54 small squares that when twisted out of its original arrangement has 43 quintillion variations.

Soros, George (Schwartz György; 1930–) Billionaire financier and philanthropist.

Szent-Györgyi, Dr Albert (1893–1986) Nobel Prize–winning biochemist who discovered vitamin C.

Vasarely, Victor (Vásárhelyi Győző; 1906–97) Hungarian-born French painter of geometric abstractions and the 'father of op art'.

The Romantic Eclectic style of Ödön Lechner (Applied Arts Museum; p101) and Hungarian Secessionist or art nouveau (see p47) brought unique architecture to Hungary at the end of the 19th century and the start of the 20th.

Modern architecture in Budapest is almost completely forgettable – with the one notable exception of Imre Makovecz, who has developed his own 'organic' style using unusual materials like tree trunks and turf, and whose work can be seen at the Makovec office building at VIII Szentkirályi utca 18 (Map pp102–3) and the spectacular funerary chapel with its reverse vaulted ceiling at the Farkasréti Cemetery (Map p82) located in district XII. The National Theatre (p105), designed by Mária Siklós in 2002 in the 'Eclectic' style to mirror other great Budapest buildings of that style, is nothing short of a disaster.

PAINTING & SCULPTURE

Distinctly Hungarian art didn't come into its own until the mid-19th century, when Mihály Pollack, József Hild and Miklós Ybl began changing the face of Budapest. The Romantic Nationalist School of heroic paintings, best exemplified by Bertalan Székely (1835–1910), who painted much of the interior of Matthias Church (p64), and Gyula Benczúr (1844–1920), gratefully gave way to the realism of Mihály Munkácsy (1844–1900), who received a state funeral in Hősök tere. But the greatest painters from this period were Kosztka Tivadar Csontváry (1853–1919) and József Rippl-Rónai (1861–1927), both habitués of Café Japan (see the boxed text, p147), whose works are on display at the Hungarian National Gallery (p61).

The 20th-century painter Victor Vasarely (1908–97), the so-called 'father of op art', has his own museum (p75) in Óbuda, as does the contemporary sculptor Imre Varga (see p75). Other sculptors to keep an eye out for include Pál Pátzay (1896–1979), who created *The Serpent Slayer* in Szent István Park (p98), and Zsigmond Kisfaludi Strobl (1884–1975), who sculpted the much loved Liberty Monument (p68) on Gellért Hill.

LITERATURE

Sándor Petőfi (1823–49), who led the Youth of March through the streets of Pest in 1848 (see p28), is Hungary's most celebrated and widely read poet; a line from his work *National Song* became the rallying cry for the 1848–49 War of Independence, in which Petőfi fought and died. A deeply philosophical play called *The Tragedy of Man* by his colleague, Imre Madách (1823–64), published a decade after Hungary's defeat in the War of Independence, is still considered to be the country's greatest classical drama. Madách did not participate in the war due to illness but was imprisoned in Pest for assisting Lajos Kossuth's secretary in 1852.

Hungary's defeat by the Habsburgs in 1849 led many writers to look to historical Romanticism for comfort and inspiration: winner, heroes and knights in shining armour became popular subjects. Petőfi's comrade-in-arms, János Arany (1817–82), whose name is synonymous with impeccable Hungarian and who edited two Pest literary journals in the 1860s, wrote epic poetry (including the *Toldi Trilogy*) and ballads.

Another friend of Petőfi, the prolific novelist Mór Jókai (1825–1904), who divided his time between his villa in XII Költő utca in Buda and his summer retreat at Balatonfüred on Lake Balaton, wrote of heroism and honesty in such wonderful works as *The Man with the Golden Touch* and *Black Diamonds*. This 'Hungarian Dickens' still enjoys widespread popularity. Another perennial favourite, Kálmán Mikszáth (1847–1910), wrote satirical tales such as *The Good Palóc People* and *St Peter's Umbrella*, in which he poked fun at the declining gentry. Apparently the former US president Theodore Roosevelt enjoyed the latter work so much that he insisted on visiting the ageing novelist in Budapest during a European tour in 1910.

Zsigmond Móricz (1879–1942), one of the cofounders of the influential literary magazine *Nyugat* (West; 1908), was a very different type of writer. His works, in the tradition of the

top picks

BOOKS

- **Homage to the Eighth District** (Giorgio and Nicola Pressburger, 1990) Poignant account of life in what was a Jewish working-class section of Budapest during and after WWII by twin brothers who emigrated to Italy in 1956.
- **The Hungarian Girl Trap** (Ray Dexter, 2006) Insightful personal account of life in modern-day Budapest for an expat who, like so many others before him, falls in love with a beautiful Hungarian girl.
- **The Paul Street Boys** (Ferenc Molnár, 1906) Turn-of-the-century novel about boys growing up in the tough Józsefváros district, which can be read both as a youth novel and a biting satire on European nationalism at the turn of the 20th century.
- **Prague** (Arthur Phillips, 2002) Cleverly titled debut novel – it takes place in Budapest and the title supposedly refers to the desire by many of the book's characters to live in the 'more' bohemian paradise of the Czech capital – by a young expat American that focuses on life in Budapest in the first years after the changes from a Communist past.
- **Under the Frog** (Tibor Fischer, 2001) Amusing account of the antics of two members of Hungary's elite national basketball team in Budapest from WWII to the 1956 Uprising.

French naturalist Émile Zola (1840–1902), examined the harsh reality of peasant life in late-19th-century Hungary. His contemporary, Mihály Babits (1883–1941), poet and the editor of *Nyugat*, made the rejuvenation of Hungarian literature his lifelong work.

Two other important names of this period are the poet and short-story writer Dezső Kosztolányi (1885–1936), who met his lifelong friend Babits at university in Pest, and the novelist Gyula Krúdy (1878–1933), who lived in Óbuda and liked the bone marrow on toast as served at Kéhli (p129) so much that he included a description of it in his *The Adventures of Sinbad*.

Two 20th-century poets are unsurpassed in Hungarian letters. Endre Ady (1877–1919), who is sometimes described as the successor to Petőfi, was a reformer who ruthlessly attacked the complacency and materialism of Hungary at that time, provoking a storm of protest from right-wing nationalists. He died in his flat on V Veres Pálné utca in Pest at the age of 42. The work of the socialist poet Attila József (1905–37), who was raised in the slums of Ferencváros, expressed the alienation felt by individuals in the modern age; his poem 'By the Danube' is brilliant even in translation.

Very popular worldwide is the work of the late Sándor Márai (1900–89), whose crisp, spare style has single-handedly encouraged worldwide interest in Hungarian literature.

Among Hungary's most important contemporary writers are Imre Kertész (1929–), György Konrád (1933–), Péter Nádas (1942–) and Péter Esterházy (1950–). Konrád's *A Feast in the Garden* (1985) is an almost autobiographical account of the fate of the Jewish community in a small eastern Hungarian town. *A Book of Memoirs* by Nádas concerns the decline of Communism and is written in the style of Thomas Mann. In *The End of a Family Story*, Nádas uses a child narrator as a filter for the adult experience of 1950s Communist Hungary. Esterházy's *Celestial Harmonies* (2000) is a partly autobiographical novel that paints a favourable portrait of the protagonist's father. His subsequent *Revised Edition* (2002) is based on documents revealing his father to have been a government informer during the Communist regime. Oops.

Novelist and Auschwitz survivor Kertész won the Nobel Prize for Literature in 2002, the first time a Hungarian had ever gained that distinction. Among his novels available in English are *Fatelessness* (1975), *Detective Story* (1977), *Kaddish for an Unborn Child* (1990) and *Liquidation* (2003). Hungary's foremost female contemporary writer, Magda Szabó, died in 2007 at age 90. Her best-known works are *Katalin Street* (1969) and *The Door* (1987), a compelling story of a woman writer and the symbiotic relationship she has with her housekeeper.

CINEMA

Cuts in state funding for films have limited the production of new Hungarian films to under 30 a year, but there are a handful of good (and even great) ones being made in what is still one of the more dynamic film-making countries in the region. For classics, look out for films by Oscar-winning István Szabó *(Sweet Emma, Dear Böbe, The Taste of Sunshine)*, Miklós Jancsó *(Outlaws)* and Péter Bacsó *(The Witness, Live Show)*.

Péter Timár's *Csinibaba* is a satirical look at life – and film production quality – during Communism. *Zimmer Feri*, set on Lake

top picks

FILMS

- *Children of Glory* (Sazabadság, szerelem; Krisztina Goda, 2006) Somewhat clichéd but moving docudrama about the 1956 Uprising in Budapest through the eyes of a player on the Olympic water polo team.
- *Kontroll* (Inspection; Nimród Antal, 2003) Hungarian-American director Antal's high-speed romantic thriller set almost entirely in the Budapest metro in which assorted outcasts, lovers and dreamers meet and interact.
- *Ein Lied von Liebe und Tod* (Gloomy Sunday; Rolf Schübel, 1999) German director Schübel's romantic drama is set in a Budapest restaurant just before the Nazi invasion and revolves around a song called 'Gloomy Sunday' that was so morose it had people committing suicide in Budapest.
- *Evita* (Alan Parker, 1996) You'd never know it, but that Buenos Aires cathedral in Parker's peon to Madonna is the Basilica of St Stephen, the grand, tree-lined boulevard Andrássy út and the swarthy horse guards belong to the Hungarian mounted cavalry.
- *Moszkva Tér* (Ferenc Török, 2001) Comic tale of Buda high-school boys in 1989 oblivious to the important events taking place around them.
- *Napoléon* (Yves Simoneau, 2002) This epic French film about the life of the *empereur* starring Gérard Dépardieu, Isabella Rossellini and John Malkovich is the most expensive European production to be filmed in Budapest to date.

Balaton, pits a young practical joker against a bunch of loud German tourists; the typo in the title is deliberate. Timár's *6:3* takes viewers back to that glorious moment when Hungary defeated England in football (p169). Gábor Herendi's *Something America* is the comic tale of a filmmaking team trying to profit from an expatriate Hungarian who pretends to be a rich producer.

Of more recent vintage is Hungarian-American director Nimród Antal's stunning *Kontroll*. And if it's unusual you want, try *Hukkle* by György Pálfi, a curious film where a bizarre cacophony of hiccups, belches, buzzing and grunting replaces dialogue. Kornél Mundruczó's recent award-winning *Delta* is the brooding tale of a man's return to his home in Romania's Danube Delta and his complex relationship with his half-sister.

DANCE

There are two ballet companies based in Budapest, though the best in the country is the Győr Ballet from Western Transdanubia. For modern dance, however, the capital is *the* centre (see p159).

Groups such as the State Folk Ensemble perform essentially for tourists throughout the year; instead, visit a *táncház* (folk music and dance workshop; see p159), an excellent way to hear Hungarian folk music and to learn traditional dance. It's all good fun and they're relatively easy to find, especially in Budapest where the dance house revival began in the 1970s.

ENVIRONMENT

THE LAND

Pollution has been a large and costly problem for Budapest. Air pollution has long been a problem due to outdated and inefficient coal-fired power plants and the amount of nitrogen oxide produced by the nation's ancient car fleet. This has created sulphur dioxide and acid rain that has threatened the flora and fauna of the Buda Hills to the west and the Börzsöny and Pilis Hills to the north and northwest.

In the past decade, however, there has been a marked improvement in both the public's awareness of environmental issues and the government's dedication to environmental safety. This has largely been due to the creation of the Ministry of Environment and Water, and the introduction and implementation of EU regulations. Many of the plants have been shut down in recent years, resulting in the reduction of the country's sulphur dioxide emissions by a third. Additionally, the government has taken the country's cars to task, forcing many polluting autos off the road and introducing lead- and sulphur-free petrol.

Hungary produces around 80 million tonnes of waste annually, down from just over 100 million tonnes at the turn of the century. Despite the government's push to place recycling stations across the country and clean up waste landfills, not a great amount of waste is recycled. Just over 14% of household rubbish is recycled and a further 6% is incinerated – the rest goes into the ground. Approximately 4000 recycling collection points – 600 of them in Budapest – have been introduced in recent years.

REVERSE ORDER

Following a practice unknown outside Asia, Hungarians reverse their names in all uses, and their 'last' name (or surname) always comes first. For example, John Smith is never János Kovács to Hungarians but Kovács János, while Elizabeth Taylor is Szabó Erzsébet and Francis Flour is Liszt Ferenc.

Most titles also follow the structure: Mr John Smith is Kovács János úr. Many women follow the practice of taking their husband's full name. If Elizabeth were married to John, she might be Kovács Jánosné (Mrs John Smith) or, increasingly popular with professional women, Kovácsné Szabó Erzsébet.

To avoid confusion, all Hungarian names in this guide are written in the usual Western manner – Christian name first – including the names of museums, theatres etc if they are translated into English. Budapest's Arany János Színház is the János Arany Theatre in English. Addresses are always written in Hungarian as they appear on street signs, however: Kossuth Lajos utca, Rákóczi Ferenc tér etc.

WATCH OUR LIPS

Local gadfly Erik D'Amato, founder/owner of Caboodle (www.caboodle.hu), Hungary's best English-language portal with daily news, features and events, has been a thorn in the side and the foot and other bits of the anatomy of the Hungarian establishment since 2004. Among other sites, Caboodle links to the incomparable Pestiside (www.pestiside.hu), variously subtitled 'The Daily Dish of Cosmopolitan Budapest' and 'The International Voice of Underground Hungary'. But what's the guy or gay in the street thinking? What are those half-dozen big questions on every Budapesters' lips? We asked Erik.

- WHO do you know who can help me get a no-strings government grant?
- WHAT is the deal with my foreigner neighbour always smiling at me in the elevator, even though I never smile back?
- WHEN did the damn Slovaks get all rich and respectable, and how can we stop it?
- WHERE can I get my girlfriend a Louis Vuitton bag other than on Andrássy út, even if it's not any cheaper, because I just can't see buying something like this in Budapest?
- WHY do all these Westerners think force-feeding geese is so bad when it's needed to make goose-liver pâté and many other health foods?
- HOW much worse can the economic hell we've been living in for years possibly get?

GREEN BUDAPEST

Budapest and vicinity counts a total of eight protected landscape areas and 31 nature conservation areas. The largest area within the city proper encompasses the Buda Hills, the lungs of the city and a 10,500-hectare protected area of dolomite and limestone rocks, steep ravines, rocky grasslands and more than 150 caves. Eagle Hill (Sashegy), a 12-hectare conservation area in south Buda, harbours both cold-resistant and heat-seeking dolomite flora as well as snake-eyed skinks.

The most impressive natural area near the capital, however, is the 603.15 sq km Danube-Ipoly National Park taking in the Börzsöny and Pilis Hills on opposite sides of the Danube to the north and northeast. Among some of the Pilis' botanical attractions are endangered Pannonian fennel and the dolomite flax, with its waxy yellow flowers. The flora and fauna of the Börzsöny Hills is more diverse; some 70 protected plant species and more than 100 bird species have been recorded here.

GOVERNMENT & POLITICS

NATIONAL GOVERNMENT

Hungary's revised 1989 constitution provides for a parliamentary system of government. The unicameral assembly sits in the Parliament building and consists of 386 members (about 10% of whom are women at present, including the house speaker) chosen for four years in a complex, two-round system that balances direct ('first past the post') and proportional representation. Of the total, 176 MPs enter Parliament by single-member constituency elections, 152 on the basis of 20 district lists and 58 on the basis of national lists. The prime minister is head of government. The head of state, the president, is elected by the assembly for a term of five years.

For a party to win a mandate to enter Parliament, it must obtain at least 5% of valid votes cast on regional party lists. In the most recent election (April 2006), only four parties were seated in the National Assembly: the ruling socialist MSZP (Hungarian Socialist Party) in coalition with the liberal SZDSZ (Alliance of Free Democrats) with 210 seats and the centre-rightist Fidesz-MPP (Alliance of Young Democrats-Hungarian Civic Party) in alliance with the KDNP (Christian Democratic People's Party) and the conservative MDF (Hungarian Democratic Forum) making up the opposition (176 seats). The SZDSZ quit the coalition in April 2008, leaving Prime Minister Gyurcsány at the head of a minority government with only 190 seats.

LOCAL GOVERNMENT

Budapest is governed by a municipal council (*fővárosi önkormánzat*), whose 66 members are elected to four-year terms and whose leader is the lord mayor (*főpolgármester*). The current mayor, SZDSZ liberal Gábor Demszky, won his fifth term in office in October 2006 after his party and its coalition partners, the MSZP socialists, received just under 47% of the popular vote, his narrowest margin since local elections resumed in 1990. The next elections are due in October 2010.

MEDIA

As in most European countries, printed news has strong political affiliations in Hungary. Almost all the major broadsheets have left or centre-left leanings, with the exception of the conservative *Magyar Nemzet* (Hungarian Nation).

The most respected publications are the weekly news magazine *Heti Világgazdaság* (World Economy Weekly), known as HVG ('ha-gay-vay'), and the former Communist Party mouthpiece *Népszabadság* (People's Freedom). The latter, a daily broadsheet, is now completely independent and had until recently the highest paid circulation of any Hungarian newspaper. It has now been overtaken by *Blikk*, a trashy tabloid that focuses on sport, stars and sex – not necessarily in that order. Specialist publications include the weekly intellectual *Élet és Irodalom* (Life and Literature), the satirical biweekly *Hócipő* (Snowshoe) and the mass-circulation daily *Nemzeti Sport* (National Sport). For information on Budapest's English-language print media see p212.

Magyar Televízió (MTV) controls two channels, recently rebranded as M1 and M2. The third public service station, Duna TV, which was launched in 2004, is independent of MTV. The two main commercial channels are TV2, which airs the ever-popular *Megasztár* (a kind of *Pop Idol* knockoff) and prime-time daily soap *Jóban Rosszban* (In Good Times and Bad), and RTL Klub, with the highly successful *Big Brother*-like *Való Világ* (Real World), daily soap opera *Barátok Közt* (Among Friends) and *Legyen Ön Is Milliomos* (Be a Millionaire).

The public Magyar Rádió (MR; Hungarian Radio) has three stations. They are named after famous Hungarians: Lajos Kossuth (jazz and news; 107.8FM), the most popular station in the country; Sándor Petőfi (1960s to 1980s music, news and sport; 94.8FM); and Béla Bartók (classical music and news; 105.3FM). Budapest Rádió, the external arm of Hungarian Radio, broadcasts on 88.1FM.

Juventus (89.5FM), a music station popular with youngsters, claims the second-highest audience in Hungary. Rádió Danubius (103.3FM) is a mixture of popular hits and news. Tilos Rádió Budapest (90.3FM) is an alternative station with excellent music.

FASHION

In general, dress is very casual in Budapest – in summer, daringly brief, even by continental European standards – and many people attend even the opera in denim. Men needn't bother bringing a necktie; it will be seldom – if ever – used.

Like everywhere, Budapest has its own fashion boutiques and home-grown designers. Keep an eye open for funky pieces from local talent Anikó Németh, high-fashion ready-to-wear and accessories from Paris-trained and French-inspired Tamás Náray, and art deco–inspired, very geometric designs from diva Katti Zoób, the first Hungarian designer to show internationally. Making a big splash these days is Lucia S Hegyi, whose own brand Luan by Lucia follows the English line.

For a good overview of what young people are designing and wearing, visit either branch of Retrock (p115), both of which offer a great range of foundation pieces and accessories.

Judging from what's on offer in some of the used or 'second-generation' clothing shops such as Iguana (p120), the popularity of retro (1950s to '70s) and fetishist (leather, military) has yet to wane.

BUDAPEST'S ART
NOUVEAU ARCHITECTURE

Budapest demonstrates a uniquely Hungarian style of art nouveau

Celebrate Hungary's historical heroes at Török Bank House (p51)

Art nouveau architecture and its Viennese variant, Secessionism, abound here; it is Budapest's signature style. Examples can be seen throughout the city: its sinuous curves; flowing, asymmetrical forms; colourful tiles; and other decorative elements stand out like beacons in a sea of refined and elegant baroque and mannered, geometric neoclassical buildings. It is not uncommon to hear visitors to the city gasp in surprise as they round a corner and spot yet another splendid example.

THE BEGINNING & THE END

Art nouveau was both an architectural style and an art form that flourished in Europe and the US from 1890 to around 1910 (or even the outbreak of WWI in 1914). It began in Britain as the Arts and Crafts Movement founded by William Morris (1834–96), and stressed the importance of manual processes and attempted to create a new organic style in direct opposition to the imitative banalities spawned by the Industrial Revolution.

Proponents of the new style deplored the shoddiness of mass-produced machine-made goods, and moved to elevate the decorative arts to the level of fine art by applying the highest standards of craftsmanship and design to everyday objects. Art nouveau designers also believed that all the arts should work in harmony to create what would be called

top picks

LECHNER'S FINEST

- Royal Postal Savings Bank (p88)
- Applied Arts Museum (p101)
- Institute of Geology (Map p51)
- Thonet House (p90)
- Schmidl tomb (p105)

in German *Gesamtkunstwerk,* or 'total work of art'. Buildings, furniture, textiles, clothes and jewellery all conformed to the principles of the art nouveau.

The style soon spread to Europe, where it took on distinctly local and/or national characteristics. In France it became known as art nouveau or Style 1900, in Germany as *Jugendstil* and in Italy as Stile Liberty. The Italians took their name from the London department store, which was born at the turn of the 20th century out of the Arts and Crafts Movement and still peddles those inimitable Liberty silk scarves.

In Vienna, a group of artists called the Secessionists lent its name to the more geometric local style of art nouveau architecture: *Sezessionstil* (Hungarian: *Szecesszió*). In Budapest, the use of traditional facades with allegorical and historical figures and scenes, folk motifs and Zsolnay ceramics, and other local materials led to an eclectic style. Though working within an art nouveau/Secessionist framework, this style emerged as something that was uniquely Hungarian.

Indeed even in far-flung America, a nation not at the vanguard of art at the time, the 21st president, Chester Alan Arthur, wanting to modernise the White House called in the artist and glassmaker Louis Comfort Tiffany to redecorate in the current rage: florid art nouveau. Among Tiffany's contributions was a huge opalescent glass screen in the White House entrance hall.

Fashion and styles changed as whimsically and rapidly at the start of the 20th century as they do today, and by the end of the first decade art nouveau and its variants were considered limited, passé, even tacky. Shortly after his election to the White House in 1901, Theodore Roosevelt issued a brusque order to 'break into small pieces that Tiffany screen'.

Fortunately for the good citizens of Budapest – and us – the economic and political torpor of the interwar period and the 40-year 'big sleep' after WWII left many art nouveau/Secessionist buildings here beaten but standing – a lot more, in fact, than remain in such important art nouveau/Jugendstil centres as Paris, Munich, Brussels and Vienna. As elsewhere at the time in Eastern Europe, the Hungarian communist regime could not afford wholesale demolition of these valuable but decaying buildings but nor could they pay for their upkeep. This has created ongoing problems: late 19th and early 20th century technologies and materials used in applied-arts decoration present special challenges to renovation experts today.

The Institute of Geology (p51) is one of Ödön Lechner's finest and best-preserved designs

Ferenc Liszt Academy of Music (p156)

ÖDÖN LECHNER

Hungarian art nouveau, or Secessionism (or *Szecesszió*) owes its greatest debt to Ödön Lechner (1845–1914), nicknamed 'the Hungarian Gaudí'. Like the great Catalan master, Lechner took an existing style and put his own spin on it, creating something very new and unique for his time and place. Lechner created a true national style, using motifs from Hungarian folk art in the decoration of his buildings as well as incorporating architectural elements from eastern cultures. As a result, his style has become iconic for Budapest. In 2008 Hungary submitted five of his works, including the Applied Arts Museum, the Royal Postal Savings Bank and the Institute of Geology, for inclusion in Unesco's World Heritage List.

Lechner studied architecture at Budapest's József Trade School, precursor to the University of Technology and Economics (BME) in Buda, and later at the Schinkel Academy of Architecture in Berlin. At the start of his career, Lechner worked in the prevailing styles and there were few immediate signs that he would leave such an indelible mark on his city and his epoch. The firm he formed with partner Gyula Pártos in 1869 received a steady flow of commissions during the boom years of the 1870s, when the construction of buildings lining the Pest's ring roads and along the Danube were under way, but like everyone else, they worked in the popular and all-too-common historicist and neoclassical styles.

When Lechner was widowed not long into his marriage, at that age of 30, he left Budapest and travelled to Paris. Between 1875 and 1878 he worked under the French architect Clément Parent on the renovation and redesign of chateaux. At this time he was also influenced by the emerging style of art nouveau, which had not even been named yet.

In 1879 Lechner returned to Budapest and his partnership with Pártos, and began to move away from historicism to more modern ideas and trends. A turning point in his career was his commission for Thonet House, his innovative steel structure that he covered with glazed ceramics from the Zsolnay factory in Pécs.

Lechner ended the partnership in 1896 and took on much more ambitious commissions: the Applied Arts Museum and the Institute of Geology. But not all was right in the world of Hungarian art nouveau. Lechner's Royal Postal Savings Bank building, now often seen as the architect's tour de force, was not well received when completed in 1901 and Lechner never really worked independently on a commission of that magnitude again. Indeed, he and his work had fallen so far from grace that when plans for the new Ferenc Liszt Academy of Music were ready in 1902, construction was delayed for another two years. The Ministry of Culture reportedly said it did not want to waste taxpayers' money on such a 'non-artistic building resembling Lechner's style'. History, of course, would see otherwise.

The Royal Postal Savings Bank (p88) is often considered Lechner's tour de force

The Applied Arts Museum (p101) was a revolutionary design for its time

The Danubius Gellért Hotel (p175) – Budapest's grande dame

HUNGARY MAKES ITS MARK

The first Hungarian architect to look to art nouveau for inspiration was Frigyes Spiegel, who covered traditional facades with exotic and allegorical figures and scenes. At the northern end of VI Izabella utca (at No 94) is the restored Lindenbaum apartment block (Map pp92–3), which was the first in Hungary to use art nouveau ornamentation including suns, stars, peacocks, flowers, snakes and long-tressed nudes.

The master of the style, however, was Ödön Lechner (see the boxed text, opposite), whose most ambitious work in Budapest is the Applied Arts Museum (p101). Purpose-built as a museum (and completed in time for the millenary exhibition in 1896), it was the first in Europe not to be built in a historicist style. Faced and roofed in a variety of colourful Zsolnay ceramic tiles, its turrets, domes and ornamental figures lend it an 'Eastern' or 'Mogul' feel. Lechner's crowning glory, however, is the sumptuous Royal Postal Savings Bank (p88) at V Hold utca 4; a Secessionist extravaganza of floral mosaics, folk motifs and ceramic figures, just off Szabadság tér in Lipótváros and dating from 1901. The bull's head atop the central tower symbolises the nomadic past of the Magyars, while the ceramic bees

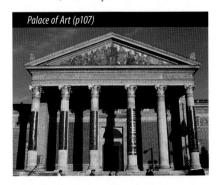

Palace of Art (p107)

The elephants of the City Zoo (p109) have one of the most exotic houses in town

scurrying up the semi-pillars towards their hives represent organisation, industry and economy.

The Ferenc Liszt Academy of Music (p156), designed by Kálmán Giergl and Flóris Korb in 1907, is not so interesting for its exterior as for the decorative elements inside. There's a dazzling art nouveau mosaic called *Art Is the Source of Life* by Aladár Kőrösfői Kriesch, a leader of the seminal Gödöllő Artists' Colony, on the 1st floor landing, and some fine stained glass by master craftsman Miksa Róth, whose home and workshop in central Pest is now a museum (p97). Also take a look at the grid of laurel leaves below the ceiling of the main concert hall, which mimics the ironwork dome of the Secession Building (1897–1908) in Vienna, and the large reflecting sapphire-blue Zsolnay ball finials on the stair balusters.

The Danubius Gellért Hotel (p175), designed by Ármin Hegedűs, Artúr Sebestyén and Izidor Sterk in 1909 and completed in 1918, contains examples of late art nouveau. The thermal spa with its enormous arched glass entrance hall and Zsolnay ceramic fountains in the bathing pools are notable features. The architects were clearly influenced by Lechner but added other elements, including baroque ones.

Very noteworthy indeed is the arcade near V Ferenciek tere called Páriszi Udvar (p90), built in 1909 by Henrik Schmahl. The design contains a myriad of influences – from Moorish Islamic and Venetian Gothic architecture to elements of Lechner's own eclectic style.

Some buildings have got (or are getting) face-lifts and are being used for different purposes. For example, the gemlike Gresham Palace (Map p85) at V Roosevelt tér 5-6, designed by Zsigmond Quittner (1907) with two strikingly decorated inner staircases, stained glass and limestone reliefs, now houses an exquisite five-star hotel (p179). The sumptuous 1915 Bank Palace (Map p85), south of Vörösmarty tér, was home to the Budapest Stock Exchange for 15 years until 2007 and is now being converted into a shopping mall.

IN PURSUIT OF BUDAPEST'S FINEST

One of the joys of exploring the 'Queen of the Danube' is that you'll find elements of art nouveau and Secessionism in the oddest places. A street with a unified image is exceptional in Budapest – keep your eyes open and you'll spot bits and pieces everywhere.

Some people go out of their way for another glimpse of their favourite buildings and details, such as the Institute of Geology (Map p108; XIV Stefánia út 14), designed by Lechner in 1899 and probably his best preserved work; Sándor Baumgarten's 1904 National Institute for the Blind (Map p108; XIV Ajtósi Dürer sor 39); the Philanthia (p90), a flower shop with an exquisite art nouveau interior designed by Kálmán Albert Körössy in 1906; and, almost next door, Lechner's groundbreaking 1890 Thonet House (p90). It is as if they are afraid that these delightful structures – built at a time when all was right with the world in affluent, cosmopolitan Budapest – will wither and disappear unless they are regularly drenched in admiring glances.

Another building worth a look in Belváros is the former Török Bank House (Map p85; V Szervita tér 3), designed by Henrik Böhm and Ármin Hegedűs in 1906. It has an almost totally glass-covered facade and in the upper gable sports a wonderful Secessionist mosaic by Róth called *Patrona Hungariae,* which depicts Hungary surrounded by great Hungarians of the past. Two doors down is Rózsavölgyi House (Map p85; V Szervita tér 5). You would probably never guess it, but this apartment block was built in 1912 and is a wonderful example of early modernism from architect Béla Lajta.

Bedő House (p87), an apartment block deigned by Emil Vidor and completed in 1903, is one of the most intact art nouveau structures in the city. Its exterior decorative features (ironwork gate, maiolica flowers, faces) have been renovated successfully and the interior, which is open to the public, has three floors of period furniture, porcelain, ironwork, paintings and *objets d'art.* On the ground floor you'll find the atmospheric and popular Art Nouveau Café (p149). Ármin Hegedűs' primary school (Map pp92–3; VII Dob utca 85), built in 1906, also has wonderful exterior mosaics depicting contemporary children's games.

The main entrance to the City Zoo (p109) and its renovated Elephant House, designed by Kornél Neuschloss-Knüsli et al in 1912 and fes-

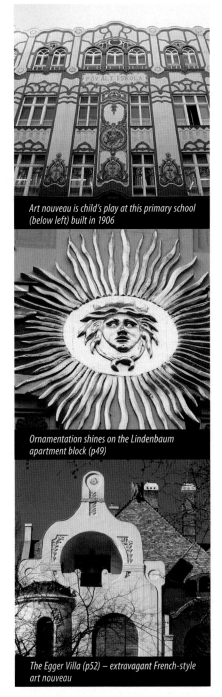

Art nouveau is child's play at this primary school (below left) built in 1906

Ornamentation shines on the Lindenbaum apartment block (p49)

The Egger Villa (p52) – extravagant French-style art nouveau

tooned with Zsolnay ceramic animal heads, are extravagant examples of the influence of the Moorish architecture in vogue in Europe at the time. They are all that is left of an extraordinary collection of exotic buildings that once graced this area of the park. On the other side of the park, the delightful City Park Calvinist Church (Map pp92–3; VII Városligeti fasor 7) is a stunning example of late art nouveau architecture by Aladár Arkay (1913), with carved wooden gates, and stained glass and ceramic tiles on the facade, all designed by the architect himself. And embellishment in the new style was not just reserved for the living; in the Jewish section of the New Municipal Cemetery, the Schmidl tomb (p105),

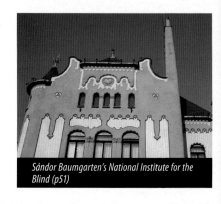

Sándor Baumgarten's National Institute for the Blind (p51)

designed by Lechner and Lajta together in 1903, is a masterpiece of art nouveau, with Jewish and folk elements ornamented with ceramics and mosaics. It's to die for.

The style was also not restricted to public buildings in Budapest, and the affluent districts to the west of City Park are happy hunting grounds for some of the best examples of private residences built in the art nouveau/Secessionist style. The cream-coloured Egger Villa (Map pp92–3; VII Városligeti fasor 24), designed by Emil Vidor in 1902, is among the purest – and most extravagant – examples of French-style art nouveau in the city. On the other side of the road, the green Vidor Villa (Map pp92–3; VII Városligeti fasor 33) with its curious turret was designed by Vidor for his father in 1905, and incorporates any number of European styles in vogue at the time, including French art nouveau and Japanese-style motifs.

Other interesting buildings in this area are Léderer Mansion (Map pp92–3; VI Bajza utca 42), a block with mosaics built by Zoltán Bálint and Lajos Jámbor in 1902, and Sonnenberg Mansion (Map pp92–3; VI Munkácsy Mihály utca 23). Designed by Albert Körössy in 1903 (but with another floor added in the 1960s), it is now the local Budapest headquarters of the MDF political party.

The Gresham Palace (p179) now houses an exquisite five-star hotel

top picks

- **Fishermen's Bastion** (p64) A vantage point on Castle Hill offering the best views of the Danube and the city.
- **Rudas Baths** (p68) Authentically Turkish thermal baths.
- **Royal Postal Savings Bank** (p88) Art nouveau's sinuous curves and asymmetrical forms on display.
- **Andrássy út** (p91) Uber-elegant Unesco World Heritage–listed boulevard.
- **Hungarian State Opera House** (p94) A temple to classical music.
- **Memento Park** (p80) Monumental socialist mistakes on display; a well-manicured trash heap of history.
- **Buda Hills** (p80) A welcome respite from the hot, dusty city, boasting some most unusual forms of transport.
- **Museum of Fine Arts** (p107) Hungary's largest and most outstanding collection of foreign art works.
- **Basilica of St Stephen** (p84) Home to Hungary's most sacred object: the holy right hand of St Stephen.
- **House of Terror** (p94) A startling showcase of Hungary's fascist and Stalinist regimes.

What's your recommendation? www.lonelyplanet.com/budapest

Budapest encompasses some 525 sq km, stretching for about 25km north to south and 29km east to west and divided by the ever-present Danube River. Buda is to the west on the right bank and Pest to the east on the left bank.

> 'While Buda can often feel like a garden, Pest is an urban jungle'

Budapest's borders are Csepel Island in the Danube to the south, the start of the Danube Bend to the north, the Buda Hills to the west and the start of the Great Plain to the east. With few exceptions (the Buda Hills, City Park and some excursions), however, the areas beyond the Nagykörút (literally the 'Big Ring Road') in Pest and west of Moszkva tér in Buda are residential or industrial and of little interest to visitors.

Budapest is a well laid-out city, so much so that it is difficult to get lost here. And public transport is fast, frequent and cheap. For more information on the public transport system, see p204. Travellers can reach the city centre from Budapest's Ferihegy International Airport, 24km southeast of the city centre, by bus and metro, train, minibus or taxi. For details, see p200.

If you look at a map of Budapest you will see that two ring roads – Nagykörút and the semicircular Kiskörút (the 'Little Ring Road') – more or less link all of the most important bridges across the Danube and define central Pest. The Big Ring Road consists of the contiguous Szent István körút, Teréz körút, Erzsébet körút, József körút and Ferenc körút. The Little Ring Road comprises Károly körút, Múzeum körút and Vámház körút. Important boulevards such as Bajcsy-Zsilinszky út, leafy Andrássy út, Rákóczi út and Üllői út fan out from these ring roads.

Buda is dominated by Castle and Gellért Hills; the main square on this side is Moszkva tér. Important roads are Margit körút (the only part of either ring road to cross the river), Fő utca and Attila út on either side of Castle Hill, and Hegyalja út and Bartók Béla út running west and southwest.

Budapest is divided into 23 kerület (districts), which usually also have traditional names, such as Lipótváros (Leopold Town) in district V or Víziváros (Watertown) in district I. The Roman numeral appearing before each street address signifies the district it is in.

So much for the layout, how do Buda and Pest differ for the traveller? Leafy and unpolluted, Buda is more than just a 'pretty face' seen from the Pest side of the Danube. Its more majestic western side fronting the river contains some of Budapest's most important historical landmarks (eg Castle Hill and the Citadella) and museums (eg the National Gallery and the Budapest History Museum) and, to the north, the original Roman settlement at Aquincum.

While Buda can often feel like a garden, Pest is an urban jungle, with a wealth of architecture, museums, historic buildings and broad boulevards that are unmatched on the other side of the Danube. And while there's nothing like the Buda Hills here, there is no shortage of green 'lungs' either – City Park at the end of Andrássy út is the largest park in Budapest and is filled with various sights and diversions.

But the best place in the city to 'get away from it all' is Margaret Island in the middle of the Danube. Neither Buda nor Pest, but easily accessible from either, it has been a 2.5km-long public park since the mid-19th century.

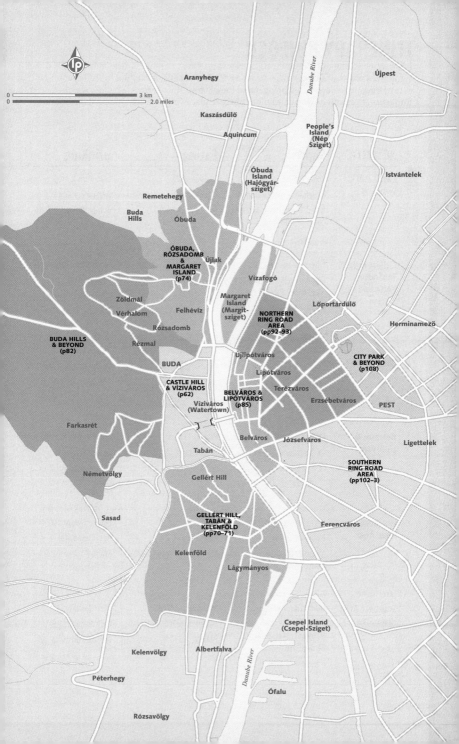

ITINERARY BUILDER

It's easy to see lots of Budapest in a very short time; the city is relatively compact, well-signposted and the public transport system is excellent and cheap. But to really get under the skin of Budapest you need to look beyond the obvious. This Itinerary Builder should help you find a range of both obvious and more obscure places in six different neighbourhoods.

AREA	ACTIVITIES	Sights	Eating	Drinking
	Castle Hill & Víziváros	Royal Palace (p61)	Csalogány 26 (p127)	Café Miró (p145)
		Hospital in the Rock (p64)	Marxim (p128)	Déryné (p146)
		Royal Wine House & Wine Cellar Museum (p65)	Toldi Konyhája (p128)	Bambi Presszó (p146)
	Gellért Hill, Tabán & Kelenföld	Liberty Monument (p68)	Aranyszarvas (p129)	Café Ponyvaregény (p146)
		Semmelweis Museum of Medical History (p72)	Marcello (p129)	Kisrabló Pub (p146)
		Castle Garden Palace (p68)		
	Óbuda, Rózsadomb & Margaret Island	Aquincum Museum (p73)	Kisbuda Gyöngye (p130)	Puskás Pancho (p147)
		Gül Baba's Tomb (p76)	Rozmaring (p130)	Daubner Cukrászda (p147)
		Zsigmond Kun Folk Art Collection (p76)	Nagyi Kifőzdéje (p131)	Poco Loco (p147)
	Belváros & Lipótváros	Parliament (p86)	Fatál (p132)	Gerbeaud Cukrászda (p148)
		Underground Railway Museum (p84)	Kisharang (p134)	Janis Pub (p148)
		Philanthia (p90)	Salaam Bombay (p133)	Montmartre (p149)
	Northern Ring Road Area	Great Synagogue (p96)	Klassz (p136)	Lukács Cukrászda (p150)
		House of Terror (p94)	Kőleves (p138)	Pótkulcs (p149)
		Miksa Róth Memorial House (p97)	Móri Kisvendéglő (p136)	Kiadó Kocsma (p150)
	Southern Ring Road Area	Hungarian National Museum (p101)	Múzeum (p140)	Paris Texas (p152)
		Holocaust Memorial Center (p104)	Fülemüle (p140)	Café Csiga (p152)
		Kerepesi Cemetery (p105)	Pata Negra (p141)	Darshan Udvar (p152)

HOW TO USE THIS TABLE

The table below allows you to plan a day's worth of activities in any area of the city. Simply select which area you wish to explore, and then mix and match from the corresponding listings to build your day. The first item in each cell represents a well-known highlight of the area, while the other items are more off-the-beaten-track gems.

NEIGHBOURHOODS ITINERARY BUILDER

Shopping	Nightlife
Herend (p112)	Matthias Church (p64)
Bortársaság (p113)	National Dance Theatre (p159)
Almárium (p113)	Budavár Cultural Centre (p159)
MOM Park (p114)	Fonó Buda Music House (p159)
	Zöld Pardon (p158)
	WigWam Rock Club (p157)
	Óbuda Society (p157)
	Cha Cha Cha Terasz (p158)
	Dokk Club (p155)
BÁV (p117)	Merlin Theatre (p161)
Holló Atelier (p116)	Gödör (p157)
Valeria Fazekas (p115)	Aranytíz Cultural Centre (p159)
Haas & Czjzek (p118)	Ferenc Liszt Music Academy (p156)
West End City Centre (p118)	Instant (p155)
Treehugger Dan's Bookstore (p119)	Örökmozgó (p161)
Nagycsarnok (p120)	Palace of Arts (p157)
Magyar Pálinka Ház A (p120)	Trafó Bár Tangó (p156)
Iguana (p120)	Cökxpôn (p155)

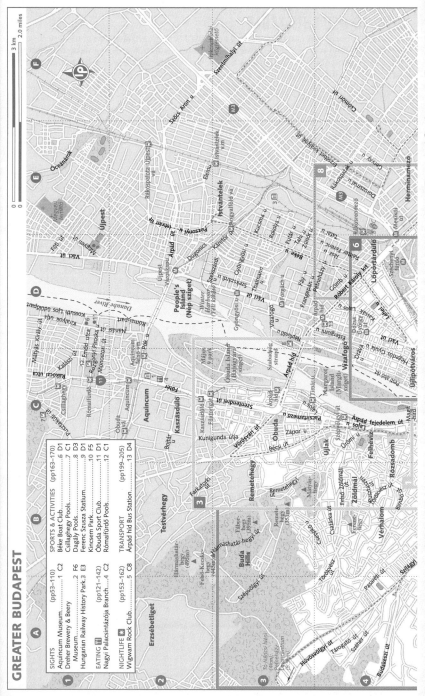

GREATER BUDAPEST

SIGHTS	(pp53–110)
Aquincum Museum................1 C2
Dreher Brewery & Beery
Museum.............................2 F6
Hungarian Railway History Park.3 E3

EATING	(pp121–142)
Nagyi Palacsintázója Branch....4 C2

NIGHTLIFE	(pp153–162)
Wigwam Rock Club.................5 C8

SPORTS & ACTIVITIES	(pp163–170)
Béke Boat Club......................6 D1
Csillaghegy Pools...................7 C1
Dagály Pools.........................8 D3
Ferenc Szusza Statium............9 D1
Kincsem Park........................10 F5
Óbuda Sport Club...................11 D1
Római fürdő Pools..................12 C1

TRANSPORT	(pp199–205)
Árpád híd Bus Station.............13 D4

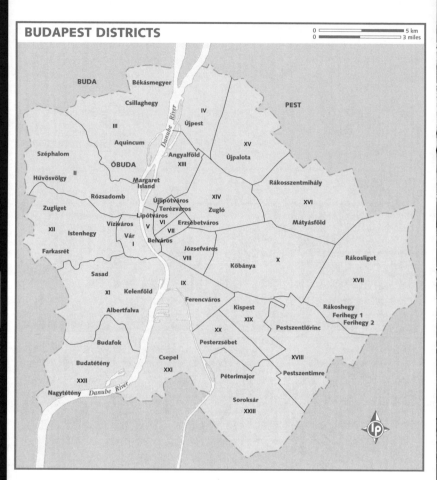

BUDAPEST DISTRICTS

0 |=========| 5 km
0 |=========| 3 miles

BUDA

Békásmegyer

Csillaghegy

III

IV
Újpest

PEST

Aquincum

XV

Széphalom

ÓBUDA

Angyalföld
XIII

Újpalota

II

Hüvösvölgy

Margaret
Island

Rákosszentmihály

Rózsadomb

Újlipótváros

XIV

XVI

Zugliget

Terézváros
Lipótváros

Zugló

Víziváros

V   VI

Erzsébetváros

Mátyásföld

XII

Istenhegy

Vár
I

VII
Belváros

Farkasrét

Józsefváros
VIII

X

Rákosliget

Sasad

Kőbánya

XVII

IX

XI

Kelenföld

Ferencváros

Kispest

Rákoshegy
Feríhegy 1
Feríhegy 2

Albertfalva

XIX

Pestszentlőrinc

Budafok

XX

Pesterzsébet

Budatétény

Csepel

XVIII

XXI

Pestszentimre

XXII

Péterimajor

Nagytétény   Danube River

Soroksár
XXIII

CASTLE HILL & VÍZIVÁROS

Drinking (p145); Eating (p127); Shopping (p112); Sleeping (p174)

Castle Hill (Várhegy), also called the Castle District, is a 1km-long limestone plateau towering 170m above the Danube. It contains Budapest's most important medieval monuments and museums, and is a Unesco World Heritage Site. It is the premier sight in the capital, and with its grand views and so many things to see, you should start here. Below it is a 28km-long network of caves formed by thermal springs, which contain several attractions. They were supposedly used by the Turks for military purposes during the occupation, as air-raid shelters during WWII and as a secret military installation during the Cold War.

The walled area consists of two distinct parts: the Old Town to the north, where commoners lived in the Middle Ages (the present-day owners of the coveted burgher houses here are anything but 'common'); and the Royal Palace, the original site of the castle built in the 13th century, now housing two important museums and a national library to the south.

The easiest way to get to Castle Hill from Pest is to take bus 16 from Deák Ferenc tér to Dísz tér, midway between the Old Town and the Royal Palace. Much more fun, though, is to stroll across Chain Bridge and board the Sikló (adult uphill/downhill ticket 650/550Ft; child 3-14yr flat fare 350Ft; ⏰ 7.30am-10pm, closed 1st & 3rd Mon of each month), a funicular railway built in 1870 that ascends from Clark Ádám tér to Szent György tér near the Royal Palace.

Alternatively, you can walk up the Royal Steps (Király lépcső) that lead northwest from Clark Ádám tér, or the wide staircase that goes to the southern end of the Royal Palace from I Szarvas tér.

Another option is to take metro M2 to Moszkva tér, walk up the steps in the northeastern part of the square and along I Várfok utca to the Vienna Gate (p66); a minibus with a logo of a castle and labelled 'Várbusz' (or 'Dísz tér') follows the same route from the start of Várfok utca. Bus 116 departs from II Fény utca north of Moszkva tér.

Still another way to reach the castle is from I Dózsa tér, serviced by bus 16 from Pest, where you'll find a lift (elevator; 100Ft) that will whisk you up to the Lion Court and National Széchenyi Library (below).

Víziváros (Watertown) is the narrow area between the Danube and Castle Hill that widens as it approaches Óbuda to the north and Rózsadomb (Rose Hill) to the northwest, spreading as far west as Moszkva tér, one of Buda's most important transport hubs. In the Middle Ages those involved in trades, crafts and fishing lived here. Many of the district's churches were used as mosques under the Turks, and baths were built here, including the Rudas (p165) and Király Baths (p164).

You can reach Víziváros on foot from the metro M2 Batthyány tér stop by walking south along the river or via tram 19, which links Batthyány tér with Szent Gellért tér and points beyond. Bus 16 from Deák Ferenc tér stops here on its way to/from Castle Hill and bus 86 links it with Óbuda. Mega-useful trams 4 and 6 terminate at Moszkva tér.

CASTLE HILL

ROYAL PALACE Map p62
Budavári Palota; 🚌 16, 16/a or 116

The enormous palace complex has been razed and rebuilt at least a half-dozen times over the past seven centuries. Béla IV established a royal residence here in the mid-13th century and subsequent kings added on to it. The palace was levelled in the battle to rout the Turks in 1686; the Habsburgs rebuilt it, but spent very little time here. Today the Royal Palace contains two important museums as well as the National Széchenyi Library (p210), which contains codices and manuscripts, a large collection of foreign newspapers and a copy of everything published in Hungary or the Hungarian language. It was founded by Count Ferenc Széchenyi (1754–1820), father of István Széchenyi (p28), who endowed it with 15,000 books and 2000 manuscripts.

There are two entrances to the Royal Palace. The first is via the Habsburg Steps, southeast of Szent György tér and through an ornamental gateway dating from 1903. The other way in is via Corvinus Gate, with its big black raven symbolising King Matthias Corvinus, southwest of the square.

The Hungarian National Gallery (Magyar Nemzeti Galéria; ☎ 201 9082; www.mng.hu; Royal Palace, Wings A, B, C & D; adult/child 800/400Ft; ⏰ 10am-6pm

CASTLE HILL & VÍZIVÁROS

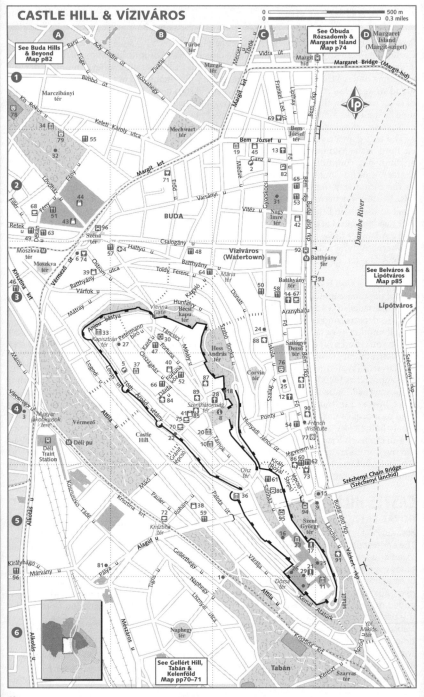

A

See Buda Hills
& Beyond
Map p82

B

C

See Óbuda
Rózsadomb &
Margaret Island
Map p74

D

Margaret
Island
(Margit-sziget)

0 ——— 500 m
0 ——— 0.3 miles

Margaret Bridge (Margit-híd)

BUDA

Vízivárós
(Watertown)

Danube River

Lipótváros

See Belváros &
Lipótváros
Map p85

Castle
Hill

Déli
Train
Station

Széchenyi Chain Bridge
(Széchenyi lánchíd)

French
Institute

Royal

Tabán

See Gellért Hill,
Tabán &
Kelenföld
Map pp70–71

Tue-Sun) is an overwhelming collection spread across four floors that traces Hungarian art from the 11th century to the present. The largest collections include medieval and Renaissance stonework, Gothic wooden sculptures and panel paintings, late-Gothic winged altars, and late Renaissance and baroque art.

The museum also has an important collection of Hungarian paintings and sculpture from the 19th and 20th centuries. Keep an eye open for the overly wrought Romantic Nationalist 'heroic' paintings by Gyula Benczúr, the harrowing depictions of war and the dispossessed by László Mednyánszky, the unique portraits by József Rippl-Rónai, the almost religious canvases by Tivadar Csontváry, the paintings of carnivals by Vilmos Aba-Novák and works by the realist Mihály Munkácsy.

The Budapest History Museum (Budapesti Történeti Múzeum; ☎ 487 8801; www.btm.hu; Royal Palace, Wing E; adult/student & child 1200/600Ft, audio guide 850Ft; ☺ 10am-6pm daily mid-Mar–mid-Sep & Wed-Mon mid-Sep–Oct, to 4pm Wed-Mon Nov–mid-Mar) looks at the 2000 years of the city, on three floors. Restored palace rooms dating from the 15th century can be entered from the basement, where there are three vaulted halls, one with a magnificent Renaissance door frame in red marble bearing the seal of Queen Beatrice and tiles with a raven and a ring (the seal of her husband King Matthias Corvinus), leading to the Gothic Hall, the Royal Cellar and the 14th-century Tower Chapel.

On the ground floor, exhibits showcase Budapest during the Middle Ages, with important Gothic statues of courtiers, squires and saints discovered during excavations in 1974. There are also artefacts recently recovered from a well dating to Turkish times, most notably a 14th-century tapestry of the Hungarian coat-of-arms with the fleur-de-lis of the House of Anjou. The exhibit on the 1st floor – 'Budapest in Modern Times' – traces the history of the city from the

STATUES & MONUMENTS

In the middle of the square facing the entrance to Wing A of the Royal Palace is a statue of a Hortobágy csikós, a Hungarian cowboy in full regalia breaking a mighty *bábolna* steed. The sculpture won international recognition for its creator, György Vastagh, at the Paris World Exhibitions of 1900 and 1901. To the southeast and just in front of Wing C stands the Eugene of Savoya statue (Map p62); he was the Habsburg prince who lived from 1663 to 1736 and wiped out the last Turkish army in Hungary at the Battle of Zenta in 1697. Designed by József Róna 200 years later, it is considered to be the finest equestrian statue in Budapest.

Facing the Royal Palace's large northwestern courtyard is the Romantic-style Matthias Fountain (Mátyás kút; Map p62), which portrays the young king Matthias Corvinus in hunting garb. To his right below is Szép Ilona (Beautiful Helen), a protagonist of a Romantic ballad by the poet Mihály Vörösmarty. Apparently the poor girl fell in love with the dashing 'hunter' and, upon learning his true identity and feeling unworthy, she died of a broken heart. The rather smug-looking fellow with the shiny foot below to the left is Galeotto Marzio, an Italian chronicler at Matthias' court. The middle of the king's three dogs was blown up during the war; canine-loving Hungarians – and most of them are – quickly had an exact copy made.

expulsion of the Turks in 1686 to Hungary's entry into the EU. On the 2nd floor the exhibits reach way back – Budapest from prehistoric times to the arrival of the Avars in the late 6th century.

MATTHIAS CHURCH Map p62

Mátyás-templom; ☎ 355 5657; www.matyas-templom.hu; I Szentháromság tér 2; adult/child/family 700/480/1200Ft, audio guide 400Ft; ⏱ 9am-5pm Mon-Sat, 1-5pm Sun; 🚌 16, 16/a or 116
Parts of Castle Hill's landmark church date back some half a millennium, notably the carvings above the southern entrance. But basically the church (so named because King Matthias Corvinus married Beatrice here in 1474) is a neo-Gothic creation designed by the architect Frigyes Schulek in 1896.

The church has a colourful tiled roof and a delicate spire (although a massive protracted US$20 million restoration keeps the landmark tower under wraps). The interior is remarkable for its stained-glass windows, frescoes and wall decorations by the Romantic painters Károly Lotz and Bertalan Székely. There are organ concerts in the church on certain evenings, continuing a tradition that began in 1867 when Franz Liszt's Hungarian Coronation Mass was first played here for the coronation of Franz Joseph and Elizabeth as king and queen of Hungary.

FISHERMEN'S BASTION Map p62

Halászbástya; adult/student & child 400/200Ft; ⏱ 9am-11pm mid-Mar–mid-Oct, free rest of year; 🚌 16, 16/a or 116
The bastion is a neo-Gothic masquerade that most visitors (and Hungarians) believe to be much older. But who cares? It looks medieval and offers among the best views

in Budapest. Built as a viewing platform in 1905 by Frigyes Schulek, the bastion's name was taken from the medieval guild of fishermen responsible for defending this stretch of the wall. The seven gleaming white turrets represent the Magyar tribes that entered the Carpathian Basin in the late 9th century. In front of the bastion is an ornate equestrian monument to St Stephen by sculptor Alajos Stróbl.

BUDA CASTLE LABYRINTH Map p62

Budavári Labirintus; ☎ 212 0287; www.labirintus.com; I Úri utca 9; adult/child/student/family 1500/600/1100/3400Ft; ⏱ 9.30am-7.30pm; 🚌 16, 16/a or 116
This 1200m-long cave system some 16m under the Castle District, looks at how the caves have been used since prehistoric times in five separate labyrinths encompassing nine halls. It's all good fun and a relief from the heat on a hot summer's day – it's always 20°C down here – but it can get pretty scary if you lose your way. After 6pm the visit is by lamp.

HOSPITAL IN THE ROCK Map p62

Sziklakórház; ☎ 06 30 689 8775; www.hospitalintherock.com; I Lovas út 4/c; adult/student & child/family 2000/1000/5000Ft; ⏱ 10am-7pm Tue-Sun; 🚌 16, 16/a or 116
Part of the Castle Hill caves network, this newly opened attraction was used extensively during the siege of Budapest during WWII. It contains original medical equipment as well as some 70 wax figures and is visited on a guided half-hour tour. More interesting is the hour-long 'full tour' (3000/1500/7000Ft), which includes a walk through a Cold War–era nuclear bunker.

MUSEUM OF MILITARY HISTORY
Map p62

Hadtörténeti Múzeum; ☎ 325 1600; www.hm-him
.hu, in Hungarian; I Tóth Árpád sétány 40; adult/
student & child/family 700/350/1400Ft; ☟ 10am-
6pm Tue-Sun Apr-Sep, to 4pm Tue-Sun Oct-Mar;
🚌 16, 16/a or 116

Loaded with weaponry dating from before the Turkish conquest, the Museum of
Military History also does a good job with
uniforms, medals, flags and battle-themed
fine art. Exhibits focus particularly on the
1848–49 War of Independence and the
Hungarian Royal Army under the command
of Admiral Miklós Horthy (1918–43). Outside is a mock-up of the electrified fence
that once separated Hungary from Austria.

MARY MAGDALENE TOWER Map p62

Magdolna-torony; I Kapisztrán tér; 🚌 16, 16/a or 116
The big steeple on the south side of Kapisztrán tér, opposite the Military History Museum and visible for kilometres to the west
of Castle Hill, is the reconstructed spire of
an 18th-century church. The church, once
reserved for Hungarian speakers in this
district (German speakers worshipped at
Matthias Church), was used as a mosque
during the Turkish occupation and was
destroyed in an air raid in 1944.

GOLDEN EAGLE PHARMACY
MUSEUM Map p62

Arany Sas Patika; ☎ 375 9772; www.semmelweis
.museum.hu; I Tárnok utca 18; adult/student & child
500/250Ft; ☟ 10.30am-6pm Tue-Sun mid-Mar–Oct,
to 4pm Tue-Sun Nov–mid-Mar; 🚌 16, 16/a or 116
Just north of Dísz tér on the site of Budapest's first pharmacy (1681), this branch of
the Semmelweis Museum of Medical History (p72)
contains an unusual mixture of displays,
including a mock-up of an alchemist's
laboratory with dried bats and tiny croco-
diles in jars, and a small 'spice rack' used by
17th-century travellers for their daily fixes
of curative herbs.

ROYAL WINE HOUSE & WINE CELLAR
MUSEUM Map p62

Királyi Borház és Pincemúzeum; ☎ 267 1100;
www.kiralyiborok.com; I Szent György tér, Nyugati
sétány; adult/child 900/500Ft; ☟ noon-8pm;
🚌 16, 16/a or 116
Housed in what once were the royal cellars
below Szent György tér dating back to the
13th century, this new 1400-sq-metre attraction offers the chance of a crash course in
Hungarian viticulture in the heart of the Castle District. Tastings cost 1350/1800/2700Ft
for three/four/six wines. You can also elect
to try various types of Hungarian cham-
pagne and fruit brandy (pálinka).

MEDIEVAL JEWISH PRAYER HOUSE
Map p62

Középkori Zsidó Imaház; ☎ 225 7816; I Táncsics
Mihály utca 26; adult/student 250/250Ft; ☟ 10am-
5pm Tue-Sun May-Oct; 🚌 16, 16/a or 116
With parts dating from the late 14th century, this ancient house of worship contains
documents and items linked to the Jewish
community of Buda, as well as Gothic stone
carvings and tombstones. But it's tiny and
of only limited interest even to the faithful.

TELEPHONY MUSEUM Map p62

Telefónia Múzeum; ☎ 201 8188; www.postamuz
eum.hu; I Úri utca 49; adult/student & child/family
500/250/1000Ft; ☟ 10am-4pm Tue-Sun;
🚌 16, 16/a or 116
This museum, set within a lovely backstreet
garden, documents the history of the
telephone in Hungary since 1881, when
the world's first switchboard – a Rotary 7A1
still working and the centrepiece of the
exhibition – was set up in Budapest. Other
exhibits pay tribute to Tivadar Puskás, a
Hungarian associate of Thomas Edison,
and of the latter's fleeting visit to Budapest
in 1891. Enter from Országház utca 30 on
Saturday and Sunday.

VÍZIVÁROS
CLARK ÁDÁM TÉR Map p62
🚌 16 or 86
'Adam Clark Sq' is named after the 19th-
century Scottish engineer who supervised
the building of the Széchenyi Chain Bridge (p68),
leading from the square, and who designed
the tunnel (alagút) under Castle Hill, which
took just eight months to carve out of
the limestone in 1853. What looks like an
elongated concrete doughnut hidden in
the bushes to the south is the 0km stone. All
Hungarian roads to and from the capital
are measured from this spot.

FŐ UTCA Map p62
🚌 86
Fő utca is the arrow-straight 'Main St'
running from Clark Ádám tér through

Víziváros; it dates from Roman times. At the former Capuchin church (I Fő utca 30-32), used as a mosque during the Turkish occupation, you can see the remains of an Islamic-style ogee-arched door and window on the southern side. Around the corner there's the seal of King Matthias Corvinus – a raven with a ring in its beak – and a little square with the delightful Lajos Fountain (Lajos kútja; 1904) called Corvin tér. The Eclectic building on the north side at No 8 is the Buda Concert Hall (p160), which was renovated in 2007.

To the north the Iron Stump (Vastuskó; cnr I Vám utca & Iskola utca) is the odd-looking tree trunk into which itinerant artisans and merchants would drive a nail to mark their visit.

Batthyány tér, a short distance to the northeast, is the centre of Víziváros and the best place to take pictures of the photogenic Parliament building across the river. In the centre of this rather shabby square is the entrance to both metro M2 and the HÉV suburban line to Szentendre. On the southern side is the 18th-century baroque Church of St Anne (Szent Ana templom; ☎ 201 6364; I Batthyány tér 7), with one of the most eye-catching interiors of any church in Budapest.

A couple of streets north is Nagy Imre tér, with the former Military Court of Justice (II Fő utca 70-78) on the northern side. Imre Nagy and others were tried and sentenced to death here in 1958 for their role in the uprising two years before (p33). It was also the site of the notorious Fő utca prison, where many other victims of the regime were incarcerated and tortured.

The Király Baths (p164), parts of which date from 1580, are one block to the north. Across pedestrianised Ganz utca is the Greek Catholic Chapel of St Florian (Szent Flórián kápolna; II Fő utca 88), built in 1760 and dedicated to the patron saint of fire-fighters.

FOUNDRY MUSEUM Map p62
Öntödei Múzeum; ☎ 201 4370; www.omm.hu, in Hungarian; II Bem József utca 20; adult/student & child/family 400/200/1100Ft; ☼ 9am-5pm Tue-Sun; ☒ 4 or 6

This museum – a lot more interesting than it sounds – is housed in the Ganz Machine Works foundry that was in use until the 1960s, and the massive ladles and cranes still stand, anxiously awaiting employment. Alas, time has frozen them. The exhibits also include cast-iron stoves, bells and street furniture.

MILLENNIUM PARK Map p62
Millenáris Park; ☎ 336 4000; www.millenaris.hu; II Kis Rókus utca 16-20; ☼ 6am-1am; Ⓜ M2 Moszkva tér, ☒ 4 or 6

Millennium Park is an attractive landscaped complex behind the Mammut shopping mall, comprising fountains, ponds, little bridges, a theatre, a gallery and, for kids, the wonderful Palace of Wonders (Csodák Palotája; www.csodapalota.hu; II Kis Rókus utca 16-20, Bldg D; adult/child/family 1200/1000/3400Ft, with exhibition 1900/1300/4700Ft; ☼ 9am-5pm Mon-Fri, 10am-6pm Sat & Sun). It's an interactive playhouse for children of all ages with 'smart' toys and puzzles, most of which have a scientific bent. Next door in building B is the House of the Future Exhibition (Jövő Háza Kiállítás; adult/child/family 1200/1000/3400Ft, with Palace of Wonders 1900/1300/4700Ft; ☼ 9am-5pm Tue-Fri, 10am-6pm Sat & Sun), which hosts some unusual shows for kids. You can also enter the park from Fény utca 20–22 and Lövőház utca 37.

CASTLE HILL
Walking Tour

1 Vienna Gate Walk up Várfok utca from Moszkva tér to Vienna Gate (Bécsi kapu), the medieval entrance to the Old Town, rebuilt in 1936 for the 250th anniversary of the retaking of the castle from the Turks. It's not so big but loquacious children here are told by their parents: 'Your mouth is as big as the Vienna Gate!'.

2 National Archives The large building to the west of the gate with the superb and very colourful maiolica-tiled roof contains the National Archives (Országos Levéltár), built in 1920. It's not open to the public.

3 Burgher Houses On the west side of Béci kapu tér (Vienna Gate Sq), which was a weekend market in the Middle Ages, there's an attractive group of burgher houses; No 6 has a statue of St Ignatius Loyola, No 7 has four medallions of classical poets and philosophers, and No 8, a curious round corner window.

4 Lutheran Church To the east across the square, a Lutheran church, with the words 'A Mighty Fortress is Our God' written in Hungarian, marks the start of Táncsics Mihály utca.

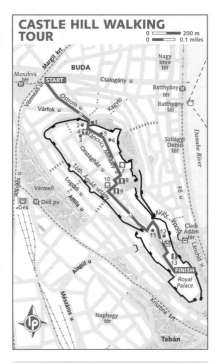

CASTLE HILL WALKING TOUR

0 ———— 200 m
0 ———— 0.1 miles

War of Independence, Lajos Kossuth, was imprisoned from 1837 to 1840.

7 Hilton Budapest The controversial Hilton Budapest (p174), which incorporates parts of a Dominican church dating from the Middle Ages and a baroque Jesuit college, is farther south.

8 I Szentháromság tér Southwest, in the centre of I Szentháromság tér there's a statue of the Holy Trinity (Szentháromság szobor), another one of the 'plague pillars' put up by grateful (and healthy) Buda citizens in the early 18th century. The square is dominated by Castle Hill's two most famous sights: Matthias Church (p64) and Fishermen's Bastion (p64).

9 András Hadik Statue Southwest of I Szentháromság tér is the mounted statue of András Hadik, a Hussar field marshal in the wars against the Turks. If you're wondering why the steed's brass testicles are so shiny, well, it's a student tradition in Budapest to give them a stroke before taking an exam.

10 Ruszwurm Cukrászda For a coffee-and-cake break, try Ruszwurm Cukrászda (p146).

11 Former Ministry of Defence Walking along Úri utca south to Dísz tér you'll come face-to-face with the bombed-out former Ministry of Defence, a casualty of WWII and NATO's supposed nuclear target for Budapest, during the Cold War.

12 Sándor Palace Farther south on the left-hand side is the restored Sándor Palace (Sándor palota), which now houses the offices of the president of the republic and is heavily guarded at all times. Note the wonderful classical reliefs and friezes on the front facade.

13 Statue of the Turul Just south of the upper Sikló (the funicular that runs down to Clark Ádám tér in Víziváros) station, flanking the Habsburg Steps, a 1903 ornamental gateway, is a large statue of the turul, an eagle-like totem of the ancient Magyars erected in 1905. The Sikló goes to I Clark Ádám tér.

WALK FACTS

Start II Moszkva tér
Finish II Clark Ádám tér
Distance 1.2km
Duration 1½ hours
Fuel stop Ruszwurm Cukrászda cafe (p146)

5 Táncsics Mihály utca This narrow utca is full of little houses painted in lively hues and adorned with statues. In many courtyard entrances you'll see *sedilia* – stone niches dating back to the 13th century – which some historians think were used as merchant stalls; others believe servants cooled their heels here while their masters (or mistresses) visited the occupant.

6 Lajos Kossuth Prison Farther along the road to the southeast at Táncsics Mihály utca 9 is the house where the leader of the 1848–49

GELLÉRT HILL, TABÁN & KELENFÖLD

Drinking (p146); Eating (p129); Shopping (p114); Sleeping (p175)

Gellért Hill (Gellért-hegy), a 235m-high rocky hill southeast of the Castle District, is crowned with a fortress of sorts and the Liberty Monument, Budapest's unofficial symbol. You can't beat the views of the Royal Palace or the Danube and its fine bridges from Gellért Hill, and Jubilee Park on the south side is an ideal spot for a picnic. The Tabán, the leafy area between Gellért and Castle Hills, and stretching northwest towards Déli train station, is associated with the Serbs, who settled here after fleeing from the Turks in the early 18th century. Plaques on I Döbrentei utca mark the water level of the Danube during two devastating floods in 1775 and 1838.

The Tabán later became known for its restaurants and wine gardens – a kind of Montmartre for Budapest. Most of these burned to the ground at the turn of the 20th century. All that remains is a lovely little renovated building with a fountain designed by Miklós Ybl in 1878 known as the Castle Garden Palace (Várkert Palota; ☎ 212 1936; I Ybl Miklós tér 9; ☯ 11am-7pm Mon-Fri), which was once a pump house for Castle Hill and is now a conference and events venue and can be inspected on weekdays. The dilapidated steps and archways across the road are all that is left of the Castle Bazaar (Várbazár) pleasure park.

Today Gellért Hill and the Tabán are given over to private homes, parks and a couple of thermal spas that make good use of the hot springs gushing from deep below, including the Gellért Baths (p164) and the fully renovated Rudas Baths (p165). If you don't like getting wet you can try a 'drinking cure' by visiting the pump room (ivócsarnok; ☯ 11am-6pm Mon, Wed & Fri, 7am-2pm Tue & Thu), which is just below the western end of Elizabeth Bridge. A half-litre/litre of the hot, smelly water – meant to cure whatever ails you – is just 50/30Ft.

Kelenföld, the expansive area south of Bartók Béla út, is of special interest to budget travellers for all the cheap seasonal hostel accommodation (see p176).

To reach Gellért Hill from Pest, cross Elizabeth Bridge and take the stairs leading up behind the statue of St Gellért or cross Liberty Bridge and follow Verejték utca through the park starting at the Cave Chapel. Bus 27 runs almost to the top of the hill from Móricz Zsigmond körtér, southwest of the Danubius Gellért Hotel (and accessible on trams 18, 19, 47 and 49).

Gellért tér can be reached from Pest on bus 7 or tram 47 or 49, and from the Buda side on bus 86 and tram 18 or 19. The latter links the metro M2 Batthyány tér stop with Kelenföld train station. Trams 18 and 47 run south along Fehérvári út, useful for several folk-music venues (p159).

BRIDGES & TUNNEL

The city's bridges, both landmarks and delightful vantage points over the Danube, are stitches that have bound Buda and Pest together since well before the two were linked politically in 1873. There are a total of nine spans, including two rail bridges, but the four in the centre stand head and shoulders above the rest. Oh, and there's an all-important (but far less sexy) tunnel running below Castle Hill called, well, Alagút (tunnel).

Margaret Bridge (Margit híd; Map p74) introduces the Big Ring Road to Buda. It is unique in that it doglegs in order to stand at right angles to the Danube at its confluence at the southern tip of Margaret Island. It was originally built by French engineer Ernest Gouin in 1876; the branch leading to the island was added in 1901. It is currently closed and undergoing extensive renovations.

Széchenyi Chain Bridge (Széchenyi lánchíd; Map p62), a twin-towered structure to the south, is the city's oldest and arguably its most beautiful bridge. It is named in honour of its initiator, István Széchenyi (p28), but was built by a Scotsman named Adam Clark. When it opened in 1849, Chain Bridge was unique for two reasons: it was the first permanent dry link between Buda and Pest; and the aristocracy – previously exempt from all taxation – had to pay the toll.

Elizabeth Bridge (Erzsébet híd; Map pp70–1), a gleaming white (though rather generic-looking) suspension bridge farther downstream, enjoys a special place in the hearts of many Budapesters as it was the first newly designed bridge to reopen after WWII in 1964 (the original span, erected in 1903, was too badly damaged to rebuild). Boasting a higher arch than the others, it offers dramatic views of both Castle and Gellért Hills and, of course, the more attractive bridges to the north and south.

Liberty Bridge (Szabadság híd; Map pp70–1), opened for the millenary exhibition in 1896, has a fin-de-siècle cantilevered span. Each post of the bridge, which was originally named after Habsburg emperor Franz Joseph, is topped by a mythical turul bird (p66) ready to take flight. It was rebuilt in the same style in 1946.

RAOUL WALLENBERG: RIGHTEOUS GENTILE

The former Swedish embassy (Map pp70–1; Minerva utca 3a/b; 🚌 27) on Gellért Hill bears a plaque attesting to the heroism of Raoul Wallenberg – together with Carl-Ivan Danielsson (1880–1963) and Per Anger (1913–2002) – a Swedish diplomat and businessman who rescued as many as 35,000 Hungarian Jews during WWII; one of 21,300-odd Gentiles (non-Jews) who either saved Jews during the Holocaust or came to their defence by putting their own lives at risk (these people are honoured as a group at Yad Vashem, a museum dedicated to the Holocaust in Jerusalem, where they are represented by a row of trees called the 'Avenue of the Righteous among Nations').

Wallenberg began working in 1936 for a trading firm whose owner was a Hungarian Jew. In July 1944 the Swedish Foreign Ministry, at the request of Jewish and refugee organisations in the US, sent 32-year-old Wallenberg on a rescue mission to Budapest as an attaché to the embassy there. By that time almost half a million Jews in Hungary had been sent to Nazi death camps in Germany and Poland.

Wallenberg immediately began issuing Swedish safe-conduct passes (called 'Wallenberg passports') from the Swedish embassy. He also set up a series of 'safe houses' flying the flag of Sweden and other neutral countries where Jews could seek asylum. He even followed German 'death marches' and deportation trains, distributing food and clothing and actually pulling some 500 people off the cars along the way.

When the Soviet army entered Budapest in January 1945, Wallenberg went to report to the authorities, but in the wartime confusion was arrested for espionage and sent to Moscow. In the early 1950s, responding to reports that Wallenberg had been seen alive in a labour camp, the Soviet Union announced that he had in fact died of a heart attack in 1947. Several reports over the next two decades suggested Wallenberg was still alive, but none was ever confirmed. Many believe Wallenberg was executed by the Soviets, who suspected him of spying for the US.

Wallenberg has been made an honorary citizen of the US, Canada, Israel and, most recently (in 2003), the city of Budapest.

CITADELLA Map pp70-1
www.citadella.hu; ⏰ 24hr; 🚌 27

The Citadella atop Gellért Hill is a fortress that never did battle. Built by the Habsburgs after the 1848–49 War of Independence to defend the city from further insurrection, by the time it was ready in 1851 the political climate had changed and the Citadella had become obsolete. Today the Citadella contains some big guns and dusty displays in the central courtyard, the rather hokey 1944 Bunker Waxworks (1944 Bunkér Panoptikum; ☎ 466 5794;

STATUES

Looking down on Elizabeth Bridge from Gellért Hill is the St Gellért monument (Map pp70–1); to an Italian missionary invited to Hungary by King Stephen to convert the natives. The monument marks the spot where the bishop was hurled to his death in a spiked barrel in 1046 by pagan Hungarians resisting the new faith.

To the north of the bridge and through the underpass is a Queen Elizabeth statue (Map pp70–1), for the Habsburg empress and Hungarian queen. Consort to Franz Joseph, 'Sissi' was much-loved by the Magyars because, among other things, she learned to speak Hungarian. She was assassinated by an Italian anarchist in Geneva in 1898 (see the boxed text, p96, for more on Sissi).

admission 1200Ft; ⏰ 9am-7pm) inside a bunker used during WWII and a rundown hotel-cum-hostel (p175).

LIBERTY MONUMENT Map pp70-1
Szabadság-szobor; 🚌 27

The lovely lady with the palm frond, proclaiming freedom throughout the city from atop Gellért Hill, is just east of the Citadella. Standing 14m high, she was erected in 1947 in tribute to the Soviet soldiers who died liberating Budapest in 1945. But the victims' names (previously in Cyrillic letters on the plinth) and the statues of the Soviet soldiers were removed in 1992 and sent to what is now called Memento Park (p80). In fact, the monument had been designed by the politically 'flexible' sculptor Zsigmond Kisfaludi Strobl (p40) much earlier for the ultraright government of Admiral Miklós Horthy. After the war, when procommunist monuments were in short supply, Kisfaludi Strobl passed it off as a memorial to the Soviets. Today the monument is dedicated to 'Those who gave up their lives for Hungary's independence, freedom and prosperity'.

If you walk west for a few minutes along Citadella sétány north of the fortress, you'll come to a lookout at arguably the best vantage point in Budapest.

GELLÉRT HILL, TABÁN & KELENFÖLD

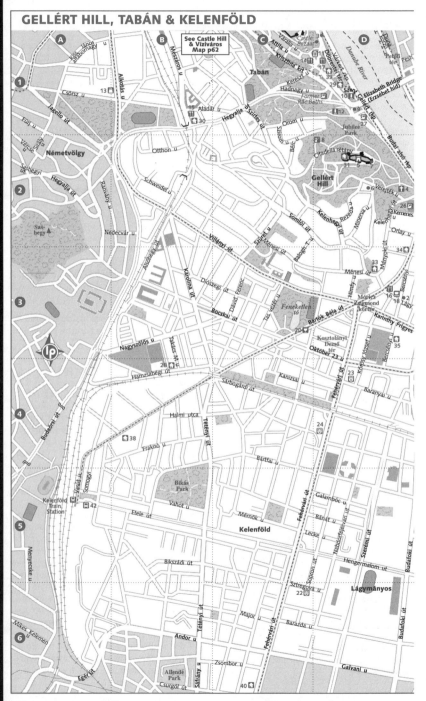

See Castle Hill & Víziváros Map p62

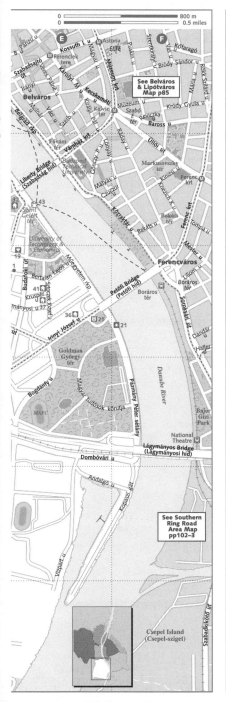

CAVE CHAPEL Map pp70-1

Sziklakápolna; ☎ 385 1529; XI Szent Gellért
rakpart 1; 🕒 9am-8pm; 🚊 47 or 49

This chapel is on a small hill directly north
of the landmark art nouveau Gellért Hotel
(1918; p175). The chapel was built into
a cave in 1926 and was the seat of the
Pauline order until 1951 when the priests
were arrested and imprisoned by the
communists and the cave was sealed off. It
was reopened and reconsecrated in 1992.
Behind the chapel there is a monastery,
with neo-Gothic turrets that are visible
from Liberty Bridge.

SEMMELWEIS MUSEUM OF MEDICAL HISTORY pp70-1

Semmelweis Orvostörténeti Múzeum; ☎ 201 1577;
www.semmelweis.museum.hu; I Apród utca 1-3;
adult/child 700/350Ft; 🕒 10.30am-6pm Tue-Sun
mid-Mar–Oct, to 4pm Tue-Sun Nov–mid-Mar; 🚊 19

This museum traces the history of medicine
from Graeco-Roman times, through medical tools and implements and photographs;
yet another antique pharmacy also makes
an appearance. Ignác Semmelweis (1818–
65), the 'saviour of mothers', who discovered the cause of puerperal (childbirth)
fever, was born in this house and much is
made of his life and works.

Drinking (p147); Eating (p129); Sleeping (p177)

Ó means 'ancient' in Hungarian; as its name suggests, Óbuda is the oldest part of Buda. The Romans established Aquincum, a key military garrison and civilian town north of here at the end of the 1st century AD (p21), and it became the seat of the Roman province of Pannonia Inferior in AD 106. When the Magyars arrived, they named it Buda, which became Óbuda when the Royal Palace was built on Castle Hill and turned into the real centre.

Aquincum, the most complete Roman civilian town in Hungary and now a museum, had paved streets and fairly sumptuous single-storey houses with courtyards, fountains and mosaic floors, as well as sophisticated drainage and heating systems. Not all that is apparent today as you walk among the ruins, but you can see its outlines as well as those of the big public baths, market, an early Christian church and a temple dedicated to the god Mithra, the chief deity of a religion that once rivalled Christianity in its number of believers (p75).

Most visitors on their way to Szentendre (p188) on the Danube Bend are put off by what they see of Óbuda from the highway or the HÉV commuter train. Prefabricated housing blocks seem to go on forever, and the Árpád Bridge flyover splits the heart of the old district (Flórián tér) in two. But behind all this are some of the most important Roman ruins in Hungary, noteworthy museums and small, quiet neighbourhoods that still recall *fin-de-siècle* Óbuda.

You can reach Óbuda on the HÉV commuter train – get off at the Árpád híd stop – from Batthyány tér, which is on the M2 metro line, or on bus 86 from Fő utca and other points along the Danube on the Buda side. You can reach Aquincum on the HÉV (Aquincum stop) or on bus 34 or 106 from Szentlélek tér. For Rózsadomb use trams 4 or 6 from Pest and change to bus 11 or tram 17, depending on your destination.

Neither Buda nor Pest, Margaret Island (Margit sziget) in the middle of the Danube was the domain of one religious order or another until the Turks came and turned what was then called the Island of Rabbits into – appropriately enough – a harem. It's been a public park open to everyone since the mid-19th century. Like the Buda Hills, the island is a recreational rather than educational experience.

Cross over to Margaret Island from Pest or Buda via trams 4 or 6. Bus 26 covers the length of the island as it makes the run between Nyugati train station (Nyugati pályaudvar) and Árpád Bridge bus station. Cars are allowed on Margaret Island from Árpád Bridge only as far as the two big hotels at the northeastern end; the rest is reserved for pedestrians and cyclists.

ÓBUDA

AQUINCUM MUSEUM Map pp58-9

Aquincumi Múzeum; ☎ 250 1650, 430 1081; www .aquincum.hu; III Szentendrei út 139; summer adult/student & child/family 1200/960/2000Ft, winter 800/400/1600Ft; ⏰ park 9am-6pm Tue-Sun May-Sep, to 5pm Tue-Sun 15-30 Apr & Oct, museum 10am-6pm Tue-Sun May-Sep, to 5pm Tue-Sun 15-30 Apr & Oct, to 4pm Nov–mid-Apr; HÉV Aquincum, 🚍 34 or 106
The new purpose-built Aquincum Museum, on the western edge of what remains of the Roman civilian settlement, puts the ruins in perspective, with a vast collection of coins and wall paintings. Look out for the replica of a 3rd-century portable organ called a hydra (and the mosaic illustrating how it was played) and the mock-up of a Roman bath. Most of the big sculptures and stone sarcophagi are outside to the left of the old museum building or behind it in the lapidary.

Across the road to the northwest, on Szentendrei út, is the Roman Civilian Amphitheatre (Római polgári amfiteátrum; admission free), about half the size of the one reserved for the military (see p76). Much is left to the imagination, but you can still see the small cubicles where lions were kept and the 'Gate of Death' to the west through which slain gladiators were carried.

KISCELLI MUSEUM & MUNICIPAL PICTURE GALLERY Map p74

Kiscelli Múzeum; ☎ 388 8560, 250 0304; www .btm.hu; III Kiscelli utca 108; adult/student & child/family 700/350/1100Ft; ⏰ 10am-6pm Tue-Sun Apr-Oct, to 4pm Nov-Mar; 🚋 17, 🚍 106
Housed in an 18th-century monastery, later a barracks that was badly damaged in WWII and again in 1956, this museum contains two excellent sections. The Contemporary City History Collection (Újkori Várostörténeti Gyűjtemény) in which you'll

ÓBUDA, RÓZSADOMB & MARGARET ISLAND

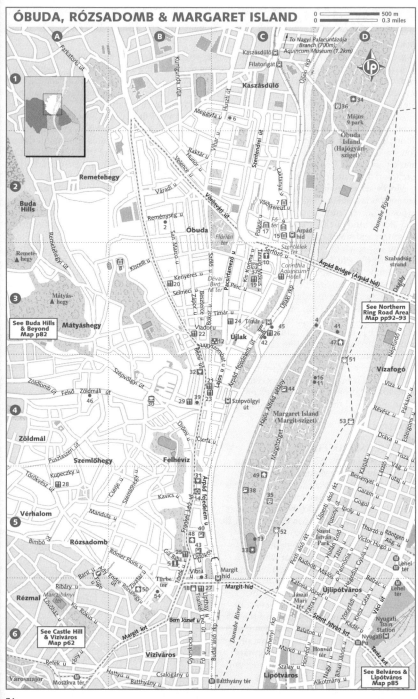

find a complete 19th-century apothecary moved here from Kálvin tér; a wonderful assembly of ancient signboards advertising shops and other trades; and rooms (both public and private) furnished in Empire, Biedermeier and art nouveau furniture and bric-a-brac. The Municipal Picture Gallery (Fővárosi Képtár), with its impressive collection of art works by József Rippl-Rónai, Lajos Tihanyi, István Csók and Béla Czóbel (among others) is upstairs.

VASARELY MUSEUM Map p74

☎ 388 7551; www.vasarely.tvn.hu; III Szentlélek tér 6; adult/student & child 600/300Ft; ☿ 10am-5.30pm Tue-Sun; 🚌 86
In the crumbling Zichy Mansion, this museum contains the works of Victor Vasarely

(or Vásárhelyi Győző before he emigrated to Paris in 1930), the late 'father of op art'. The works, especially ones such as *Tlinko-F* and *Ibadan-Pos-*, are excellent and fun to watch as they 'swell' and 'move' around the canvas. We love *Ganz*.

IMRE VARGA EXHIBITION HOUSE
Map p74

Varga Imre Kiállítóháza; ☎ 250 0274; www .budapestgaleria.hu; III Laktanya utca 7; adult/child 500/250Ft; ☿ 10am-6pm Tue-Sun; 🚌 86
Part of the Budapest Gallery (p78), this exhibition space includes sculptures, statues, medals and drawings by octogenarian Varga, one of Hungary's foremost sculptors. Like others before him, notably Zsigmond Kisfaludi Strobl (p40), Varga seems to have

MITHRA & THE GREAT SACRIFICE

What little is known of Mithra, the god of justice and social contract, has been deduced from reliefs and icons found in sanctuaries and temples, like the one found at Aquincum. Most of these portray Mithra clad in a Persian-style cap and tunic, sacrificing a white bull in front of Sol, the sun god. Grain and grapes sprout from the bull's blood, and animals from its semen. Sol's wife Luna, the moon, begins her cycle and time is born.

Mithraism, the worship of the god Mithra, originated in Persia. It was a mysterious religion with its devotees (mostly males) sworn to secrecy. As Roman rule extended into the west, the religion became extremely popular with traders, imperial slaves and mercenaries of the Roman army; it spread rapidly throughout the empire in the 2nd and 3rd centuries AD. In fact, Mithraism was the principal rival of Christianity until Constantine came to the throne in the 4th century.

Mithraism and Christianity were close competitors partly because of the striking similarity in many of their rituals. Both involve the birth of a deity on winter solstice (around 25 December), shepherds, death and resurrection and a form of baptism. Devotees knelt when they worshipped and a common meal – a 'communion' of bread and water – was a regular feature of both liturgies.

sat on both sides of the fence politically for decades – sculpting Béla Kun and Lenin as dextrously as he did St Stephen, Béla Bartók and even Imre Nagy (see p89 and p80). But his work always remains fresh and is never derivative.

ROMAN MILITARY AMPHITHEATRE
Map p74

Római Katonai Amfiteátrum; III Pacsirtamező utca; admission free; ☉ 24hr; HÉV Tímár utca, 🚌 86
Built in the 2nd century for the Roman garrisons, this amphitheatre about 800m south of Flórián tér could accommodate up to 15,000 spectators and was larger than the Colosseum in Rome. The rest of the military camp extended north to Flórián tér. Archaeology and classical-history buffs taking bus 86 to Flórián tér should descend at III Nagyszombat utca. HÉV passengers should get off at Tímár utca.

ÓBUDA MUSEUM Map p74

☎ 250 1020; www.obudaimuzeum.hu, in Hungarian; III Fő tér 1; adult/student & child 300/200Ft; ☉ 10am-5pm Tue-Sun; 🚌 86
Sharing the same building as the Vasarely Museum (p75), but with its entrance facing the inner courtyard, this museum contains a motley assortment of exhibits related to Óbuda's past: the interior of a three-room 19th-century farmhouse from Békásmegyer, the output of master cooper Simon Tóbiás and toys through history.

ZSIGMOND KUN FOLK ART COLLECTION Map p74

Kun Zsigmond Népművészeti Gyűjtemény; ☎ 368 1138; www.obudaimuzeum.hu, in Hungarian; III Fő tér 4; adult/child 300/200Ft; ☉ 2-6pm Tue-Fri, from 10am Sat & Sun; 🚌 86
This charming branch of the Óbuda Museum displays a collection of folk art amassed by a wealthy ethnographer in his 18th-century town house. Most of the pottery and ceramics are from Mezőtúr near the Tisza River, but there are also some rare Moravian and Swabian pieces as well as Transylvanian furniture and textiles. The attendants are very proud of the collection so be prepared for some lengthy explanations. And don't ask about the priceless tile stove that a workman knocked over a couple of years back (unless you want to see a grown man cry).

HERCULES VILLA Map p74

Herkules Villa; ☎ 250 1650; III Meggyfa utca 19-21; admission free; ☉ 10am-6pm Tue-Sun May-Sep, to 5pm Tue-Sun 15-30 Apr & Oct; 🚌 86
Hercules Villa, in the middle of a vast housing estate northwest of Fő tér, is the name given to some reconstructed Roman ruins. The name is derived from the astonishing 3rd-century floor mosaics of Hercules' exploits found in what was a Roman villa. Phone in advance; visits are usually by pre-arrangement only.

RÓZSADOMB

FRANKEL LEÓ ÚT Map p74

🚌 86, 🚃 17
At Bem József tér, Fő utca turns into Frankel Leó út, a tree-lined street of antique shops and boutiques. At its southern end is the Lukács Baths (p165), which caters to older and quite serious thermal enthusiasts. A short distance north and tucked away in an apartment block is the Újlaki Synagogue (Újlaki zsinagóga; ☎ 326 1445; II Frankel Leó út 49), built in 1888 on the site of an older prayer house and the only functioning synagogue left on the Buda side.

GÜL BABA'S TOMB Map p74

Gül Baba türbéje; ☎ 326 0062; II Türbe tér 1; adult/child/student 500/250/400Ft; ☉ 10am-6pm Mar-Oct, to 4pm Nov-Feb; 🚃 4, 6 or 17
This reconstructed tomb contains the remains of one Gül Baba, an Ottoman Dervish who took part in the capture of Buda in 1541 and is known in Hungary as the 'Father of Roses'. The tomb is a pilgrimage place for Muslims, especially from Turkey, and you must remove your shoes before entering. To reach the tomb from Török utca, which runs parallel to Frankel Leó út, walk west along steep, cobbled Gül Baba utca to the set of steps just past house No 16. You can also get here from Mecset utca, which runs north from Margit utca.

MARGARET ISLAND

Like the Buda Hills, Margaret Island (Margit sziget) is not overly endowed with important sights and landmarks. Instead, the island is a great spot for sports and other activities, and you could spend the entire day here cycling, swimming or just pampering yourself at the

SAINT MARGARET

St Margaret, canonised in 1943, commands something of a cult following in Hungary. According to the story, her father, King Béla IV, promised to commit Margaret to a life of devotion in a nunnery if the Mongols were driven from the land. They were and – at nine years of age – she entered a Dominican convent (p78). Still, she seemed to enjoy it – if we're to believe the *Lives of the Saints* – especially the mortification-of-the-flesh parts.

Danubius Grand Hotel Margitsziget (p164), one of the most modern spas in Budapest.

Margaret Island has two popular swimming pools on its western side. For more information on these, see p165.

WATER TOWER & OPEN-AIR THEATRE
Map p74
Víztorony; 🚌 26
Erected in 1911 in the north-central part of the island, the octagonal water tower rises 66m above the open-air theatre (szabadtéri színpad; ☎ 340 4883), which is used for opera, plays and concerts in summer. The tower contains the Lookout Gallery (Kilátó Galéria; ☎ 340 4520; adult/child 300/200Ft; 🕐 11am-7pm May-Oct). Climbing the 153 steps will earn you a stunning 360-degree view of the island, Buda and Pest.

SÉTACIKLI Map p74
☎ 06 30 966 6453; 3-speed per half-hr/hr/day 450/650/1900Ft, pedal coach for 3/5 people per hr 1900/2900Ft; 🕐 9am-dusk
You can hire a bicycle from one of several stands, including this place, which is on the western side just before the athletic stadium as you walk from Margaret Bridge.

BRINGÓHINTÓ Map p74
☎ 329 2073; www.bringohinto.hu; mountain bike per half-hr/hr 590/990Ft, pedal coach for 4 people per half-hr/hr 1680/2680Ft, inline skates 980/1680Ft; 🕐 8am-dusk
This place rents out equipment from the refreshment stand near the Japanese Garden (p79) in the northern part of the island.

ÓBUDA
Walking Tour
1 Flórián tér Begin this walking tour of Óbuda in Flórián tér, which is split in two

by the Árpád Bridge flyover and encircled by mammoth housing blocks. It is not the best introduction to the neighbourhood, but it remains the district's historic centre.

2 Thermae Maiores Baths Museum
Roman objects discovered in the area (many, sadly, now vandalised and graffitied) are on display in the subway below Flórián tér and in the adjacent underground Thermae Maiores Baths Museum (Thermae Maiores Fürdő Múzeum; ☎ 250 1650; admission free; 🕐 10am-6pm Tue-Sun May-Sep, to 5pm Tue-Sun 15-30 Apr & Oct). There are more Roman ruins, including a reconstructed temple, in the park above the subway.

3 Óbuda Parish Church Dominating the easternmost side of III Flórián tér is the yellow baroque Óbuda Parish Church (Óbudai plébániatemplom; III 168 Lajos utca), which was built in 1749 and dedicated to Sts Peter and Paul. There's a lovely rococo pulpit inside.

4 Former Óbuda Synagogue To the southeast of the church, the large neoclassical building beside the landmark Corinthia Aquincum Hotel is the former Óbuda Synagogue

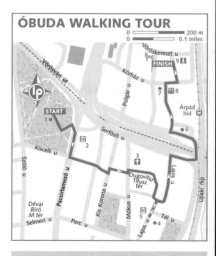

ÓBUDA WALKING TOUR

WALK FACTS
Start III Flórián tér
Finish III Fő tér
Distance 1km
Duration One hour
Fuel stop Új Sípos Halászkert (p130)

(Óbudai zsinagóga; III Lajos utca 163), dating from 1821. It now houses sound studios for Hungarian TV (MTV).

5 Budapest Gallery Opposite the synagogue, the Budapest Gallery (Budapest Galéria; ☎ 388 6771; www .budapestgaleria.hu; III Lajos utca 158; adult/child 400/200Ft; ☺ 10am-6pm Tue-Sun), hosts some interesting avant-garde exhibitions. It also has a standing exhibit of works by Pál Pátzay (p40), whose sculptures can be seen throughout the city.

6 Szentlélek tér Tiny Szentlélek tér (Holy Spirit Sq), a transport hub east of Flórián tér, contains two of Óbuda's most important museums (the Vasarely and Óbuda; see p75 and p76, respectively). To reach it, walk north on Budai alsó rakpart and under the flyover.

7 Fő tér Contiguous to Szentlélek tér is Fő tér (Main Sq), a quiet restored square of baroque houses, public buildings and restaurants.

8 Új Sípos Halászkert If the weather is fine, take advantage of outdoor seating with a bowl of fish soup at Új Sípos Halászkert (p130).

9 Imre Varga Outdoor Sculptures A very short distance northeast of Fő tér, you'll see a group of outdoor sculptures by Imre Varga. They portray four rather worried-looking women holding umbrellas in the middle of the street.

MARGARET ISLAND
Walking Tour

1 Gasztró Hús-Hentesáru Before setting out, visit Gasztró Hús-Hentesáru (p131) opposite the tram stop (4 or 6) on Margaret Bridge to stock up on edibles as the catering options are limited on the island.

2 Centennial Monument In the flower-bedded roundabout 350m north of the tram stop (4 or 6) on Margaret Bridge, is the Centennial Monument (Centenariumi emlékmű), unveiled in 1973 for the 100th anniversary of the union of Buda, Pest and Óbuda. That was an entirely different era in Budapest, and the sculptor filled the strange split cone with all sorts of socialist and nationalist symbols.

3 Margitszigeti Krisztályvíz The Romans used the thermal springs bubbling below the island both as drinking water and therapy and

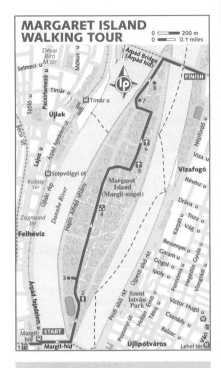

so do modern Magyars. Margitszigeti Krisztályvíz (Margaret Island Crystal Water), one of the more popular brands of mineral water in Hungary, is sourced and bottled here.

4 Franciscan Church & Monastery Just before the Palatinus swimming complex (and almost in the exact centre of the island) are Franciscan church and monastery (Ferences templom és kolostor) ruins, including a late 13th–century tower and wall. The summer residence built here by Habsburg archduke Joseph when he inherited the island in 1867 was later converted into a hotel that ran until 1949.

5 Dominican Convent Due east is the 13th-century former Dominican convent (Domonkos kolostor), built by Béla IV, where

WALK FACTS

Start Margaret Bridge
Finish Árpád Bridge
Distance 3km
Duration Two hours
Fuel stop Gasztró Hús-Hentesáru (p131)

St Margaret (1242–71; see the boxed text, p77) lived, from age nine. A red-marble sepulchre cover surrounded by a wrought-iron grille marks her original resting place, there's also a much visited brick shrine with ex-votives a short distance to the southeast.

6 Premonstratensian Church Some 200m north is the reconstructed Romanesque Premonstratensian Church (Premontre templom), dedicated to St Michael and originally dating back to the 12th century. Its 15th-century bell mysteriously appeared one night in 1914 under the roots of a walnut tree knocked over in a storm. It was prob-ably buried by monks during the Turkish invasion.

7 Japanese Garden The attractive Japanese Garden (Japánkert), at the northwestern end of the island, has koi, carp and lily pads in its ponds, as well as bamboo groves, a small wooden bridge and a waterfall.

8 Musical Fountain The raised gazebo to the north is called the Musical Fountain (Zenélőkút), a replica of one in Transylvania. A tape plays chimes and snatches of a folk song on the hour. From here, walk to Árpád Bridge and the bus 26 stop to Pest (no tram stop here).

BUDA HILLS & BEYOND

Eating p131; Sleeping p177

With 'peaks' exceeding 500m, a comprehensive system of trails and no lack of unusual conveyances to get you there and around, the Buda Hills (Budai-hegység) are the city's playground, and they're a welcome respite from hot, dusty Pest in the warmer months. Indeed, some well-heeled Budapest families have summer homes here. If you're planning to do some hiking here, take along Cartographia's 1:25,000 *A Budai-hegység* map (No 6; 990Ft), available from bookshops throughout the city. Apart from the Béla Bartók Memorial House (below), there are very few sights per se, though you might want to 'explore' one of the hills' caves (p168).

With all the unusual transport options, heading for the hills is more than half the fun. From Moszkva tér metro station on the M2 line in Buda, walk westward along Szilágyi Erzsébet fasor for 10 minutes (or take tram 18 or 56 for two stops) to the circular Hotel Budapest at II Szilágyi Erzsébet fasor 47. Directly opposite is the terminus of the Cog Railway (Fogaskerekű vasút; ☎ 355 4167; www.bkv.hu; Szilágyi Erzsébet fasor 14-16; admission 1 BKV ticket; ☼ 5am-11pm). Built in 1874, the cog climbs for 3.6km in 14 minutes some three or four times an hour to Széchenyi-hegy (427m), one of the prettiest residential areas in Buda.

At Széchenyi-hegy, you can stop for a picnic in the attractive park south of the old-time station or board the narrow-gauge Children's Railway (Gyermekvasút; ☎ 397 5394; www.gyermekvasut.hu; adult/child 1 stop 450/250Ft, entire line 600/300Ft), two minutes to the south on Hegyhát út. The railway (with eight stops) was built in 1951 by Pioneers (socialist Scouts) and is now staffed entirely by schoolchildren aged 10 to 14 – the engineer excepted. The little train chugs along for 12km, terminating at Hűvösvölgy. Departure times vary widely depending on the day of the week and the season – consult the website – but count on one every hour or so between 9am or 10am and 5pm or 6pm. The line is closed on Monday from September to April.

There are walks fanning out from any of the stops along the Children's Railway line or you can return to Moszkva tér on tram 56 from Hűvösvölgy. A more interesting way down, however, is to get off at János-hegy, the fourth stop and the highest point (527m) in the hills. The 23.5m-tall lookout (101 steps!), from where you can see the Slovakia Tratra Mountains on a clear day, was designed in 1910 by Frigyes Schulek, the same architect who did the neo-Gothic Matthias Church (p64) and Fishermen's Bastion (p64). About 700m to the east is the chairlift (libegő; ☎ 394 3764; adult/child 500/400Ft; ☼ 9.30am-5pm mid-May–mid-Sep, 10am-4pm mid-Sep–mid-May, closed 2nd & 4th Mon of every month), which will take you down 1040m at 4km/h to Zugligeti út. From here bus 291 returns to Moszkva tér.

BÉLA BARTÓK MEMORIAL HOUSE

Map p82

Bartók Béla Emlékház; ☎ 394 2100; www.bartok museum.hu; II Csalán út 29; adult/child 800/500Ft; ☼ 10am-5pm Tue-Sun; 🚌 5 or 29

North of Szilágyi Erzsébet fasor but still very much in the Buda Hills, this is the house where the great composer resided from 1932 until 1940, when he emigrated to the US. Among other things on display is the old Edison recorder (complete with wax cylinders) that Bartók used to record Hungarian folk music in Transylvania, as well as furniture and other objects he collected.

MEMENTO PARK off Map pp58-9

☎ 424 7500; www.mementopark.hu; XXII Balatoni út 16-18; adult/student & child 1500/1000Ft; ☼ 10am-dusk; 🚌 150 from XI Kosztolány Dezsö tér in south Buda

Home to almost four dozen statues, busts and plaques of Lenin, Marx, Béla Kun and 'heroic' workers such as have ended up on trash heaps in other former socialist countries, the recently renamed Memento Park, 10km southwest of the city centre, is a mind-blowing place to visit. Ogle the socialist realism and try to imagine that at least four of these monstrous relics were erected as recently as the late 1980s; a few, including the Béla Kun memorial of our 'hero' in a crowd by fence-sitting sculptor Imre Varga (see p75) were still in place when this author moved to Budapest in early 1992. New attractions here are the replicated remains of Stalin's boots, all that was left after a crowd pulled the enormous statue down from its plinth on XIV Dózsa György út during the 1956 Uprising; and an exhibition centre in an old barracks with displays on the events of 1956, the changes since 1989 and a documentary film

BUDAPEST ABCS & 123S FOR KIDS

Former long-term Budapest resident and journalist Judy Finn had a lot more than excess baggage when she returned to the Hungarian capital in the summer of 2008 for a six-month family visit with her Hungarian-born physician husband. In hand (and tow and underfoot) was a trio of kids aged six and under who had been a mere gleam in their parents eyes when they left for America. Boy, was she about to see Budapest in a new light…

Judy took valuable time out to give some invaluable insider's tips – based on plenty of trial and error, she says – to have your kids enthusing about Budapest as much as you will:

Baths

Even young children will respect the grandeur of the Széchenyi (p165) and Gellért Baths p164), perfect for year-round fun with multiple indoor and outdoor pools. Gellért has a wave pool, Szécsenyi has a whirlpool. Dagály (p166) and Palatinus (p166) have vast lawns for a longer time with the kids on a summer day. Just one? I'd pick the Szécsenyi.

Culture

The Natural History Museum (p101), Transport Museum (p110) and Palace of Wonders (p66) all have hands-on displays geared for young visitors. The Hungarian National Gallery (p61), Applied Arts Museum (p101) and Vasarely Museum (p75) are adult-themed but the art content, the buildings themselves and/or the location combine to appeal to the young. The Hungarian Railway History Park (p97) is the grandpapa of museums for kids, with vintage locomotives to clamber about. In the high season, there are cars and trains to ride and drive.

Playgrounds

There are great playgrounds on XIII Margaret Island (Map p74), about 50m northeast of the fountain at the southern end; on III Hajógyári Island (Map p74), also called Óbuda Island, about 200m along the main road; and in XIII Szent István Park (Map pp92–3). Good-to-know-about playgrounds are at VII Hunyadi tér (Map pp92–3), VII Almássy tér (Map pp92–3), and V Hild tér (Map p85). All are pretty central to the tourist track, except for Hajógyári Island but the HÉV will get you to the island's foot bridge.

Entertainment

We like live music, dancing, cool venues and outdoor events in any combination and we'll stay for the first set of any live act at any bar. The children's dance houses (táncházak) have instructors, and live folk musicians provide the tunes. We watch the calendars at the Budavár Cultural Centre (p159) and the Municipal Cultural House (p159), especially for the bands, Muszikás and Fakutya. The marionette and other puppet shows at the Budapest Puppet Theatre (p161) had all of my kids, even the baby, fully mesmerised for the whole show.

Eating

Now that dining is a major family affair/effort, I tend to go for the hearty Hungarian meals served at sturdy wood-topped tables in places such as Fatál (p132). Kéhli (p129) has not changed since the days of literary great, Krúdy Gyula, and the live gypsy musicians add to the chaotic feast. Outdoor dining anywhere is a serious plus. Bagolyvár (p142) has a wonderful garden dining area. Remíz (p131) has a playground in its garden. Restaurants usually do not have a set children's menu but will split the adult portion. We satisfy our crystal and glitz urges at the over-the-top coffeehouses for our sweets and treats breaks: Lukács (p150), Gerbeaud (p148) and New York Café (p151). The Gellért Hotel (p175) has a beautiful cafe. The be-all-and-end-all for kids is the dessert bar at the Budapest Marriott Hotel (Map p85). One price and as many cakes as you want. The view of the Danube, the Castle, and Chain Bridge is perfection from here.

Shopping

Shearling vests from kiosks at the entrance to City Park (Map p108) are a good buy; my three-year-old still takes her nap on her shearling mat. An older child might enjoy reading Géza Gádonyi's *Eclipse of the Crescent Moon* to glean a little Hungarian history. Look for Kaláka CDs for kids' music – it won't drive you cuckoo if you want to bring home a bit of Hungarian language for your kids. We got the whole range of Disney DVDs in Hungarian while here, and *Vuk*, *Dr Bubó*, and *Ugrifules* are Hungarian classic cartoons that the kids love. We've added to our collection of hand-painted Easter eggs and special Christmas ornaments and bought eclectic tea party sets this trip. Also, though not special to Budapest, bath bombs from Lush (p117) are the perfect way to wind down your kids after a hectic day. In fact, jump in yourself. You deserve a rest.

An interview with former long-term Budapest resident and journalist Judy Finn

BUDA HILLS & BEYOND

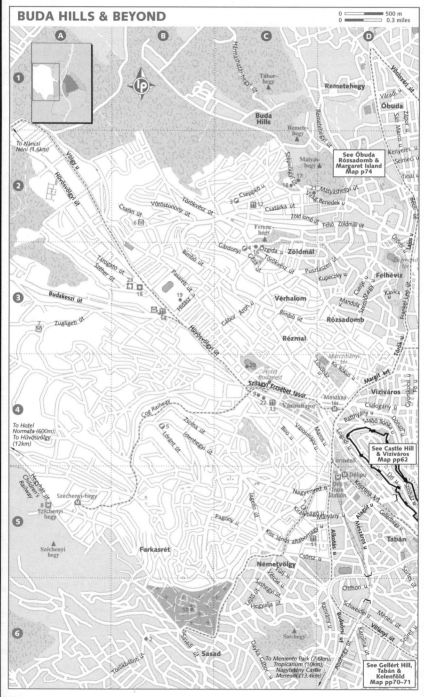

0 — 500 m
0 — 0.3 miles

See Óbuda Rózsadomb & Margaret Island Map p74

See Castle Hill & Víziváros Map pp62

See Gellért Hill, Tabán & Kelenföld Map pp70–71

with rare footage of secret agents collecting information on 'subversives'.

To reach this socialist Disneyland, take tram 19 from I Batthyány tér in Buda, tram 47 or 49 from V Deák Ferenc tér in Pest or bus 7 or 173 from V Ferenciek tere in Pest to XI Kosztolány Dezsö tér in southern Buda and board city bus 150 (25 minutes, every 20 to 30 minutes) for the park.

An easier (though more expensive) way to go is via the park's direct bus (with park admission adult/child return 3950/2450Ft), which departs from in front of the Le Meridien Budapest Hotel (p178) on Deák Ferenc tér at 11am year-round, with an extra departure at 3pm in July and August.

NAGYTÉTÉNY CASTLE MUSEUM
off Map pp58-9

Nagytétényi Kastélymúzeum; ☎ 207 5462, 207 0005; www.nagytetenyi.hu; XXII Kastélypark utca 9-11; adult/student & child/family from 600/300/1200Ft; 🕐 10am-6pm Tue-Sun Apr-Oct, 10am-6pm Fri-Sun Nov-Mar; 🚌 33 from XI Móricz Zsigmond körtér in south Buda

In a baroque mansion in deepest south Buda, this branch of the Applied Arts Museum (p101) traces the development of European furniture – from the Gothic to Biedermeier styles (approximately 1450 to 1850) – with some 300 items on display in more than two dozen rooms.

TROPICARIUM off Map pp58-9

☎ 424 3053; www.tropicarium.hu; XXII Nagytétényi út 37-45; adult/child/senior & student 1900/1200/1300Ft; 🕐 10am-8pm; 🚌 33 from XI Móricz Zsigmond körtér in south Buda

This vast aquarium complex at the Campona shopping mall in south Buda measures 3000 sq metres and is apparently the largest in central Europe. Don't expect just to see snazzy neon-coloured tropical examples, however; this place prides itself on its local specimens too. *Fogas* (pike-perch native to Balaton), anyone?

NEIGHBOURHOODS BUDA HILLS & BEYOND

BELVÁROS & LIPÓTVÁROS

Drinking (p147); Eating (p132); Shopping (p114); Sleeping (p178)

Belváros (Inner Town) is the heart of Pest and contains the most valuable commercial real estate in the city. The area north of busy Ferenciek tere is particularly full of flashy boutiques and well-touristed bars and restaurants; you'll usually hear more German, Italian, Spanish and English spoken here than Hungarian. The neighbourhood to the south was once rather studenty, quieter and much more local. Now much of it is reserved for pedestrians, and there is no shortage of trendy shops and cafes here too.

Belváros contains four important 'centres': V Deák Ferenc tér, a busy square in the northeast corner of the Inner Town – the only place where all three metro lines (M1/2/3) converge, it's also accessible by trams 47 and 49; touristy V Vörösmarty tér, which is on the M1 metro at the northern end of V Váci utca; V Ferenciek tere on metro M3, which divides the Inner Town at Szabadsajtó út (Free Press Ave) and can be reached from Pest on bus 7; and V Egyetem tér (University Sq), a five-minute walk south along V Károly Mihály utca from Ferenciek tere and 250m northwest of Kálvin tér on the M3 metro along leafy V Kecskeméti utca.

North of Belváros, Lipótváros (Leopold Town) is full of offices, government ministries, 19th-century apartment blocks and grand squares. Its confines are, in effect, Szent István körút to the north, V József Attila utca to the south, the Danube to the west and, to the east, V Bajcsy-Zsilinszky út, the arrow-straight boulevard that stretches from central Deák Ferenc tér to Nyugati tér, where Nyugati train station is located.

Best transport options for the Lipótváros are metro stops Deák Ferenc tér (M1/2/3) and Kossuth Lajos tér (M2). Buses are 15 and 115 and trams 47 and 49 for the southern areas and 4 and 6 for the northern bits.

BELVÁROS

INNER TOWN PARISH CHURCH Map p85
Belvárosi plébániatemplom; ☎ 318 3108; V Március 15 tér 2; ☼ 9am-7pm; ⓟ 2

On the eastern side of Március 15 tér, now uncomfortably close to the Elizabeth Bridge flyover, is where a Romanesque church was first built in the 12th century within a Roman fortress. You can still see a few bits of the fort, Contra Aquincum, in the small park to the north. The present church was rebuilt in the 14th and 18th centuries, and you can easily spot Gothic, Renaissance, baroque and even Turkish elements.

UNDERGROUND RAILWAY MUSEUM
Map p85
Földalatti Vasúti Múzeum; ☎ 461 6500; 1 BKV ticket or adult/child 270/220Ft; ☼ 10am-5pm Tue-Sun; Ⓜ M1/2/3 Deák Ferenc tér

In the pedestrian subway beneath V Deák Ferenc tér and next to the main ticket window, the Underground Railway Museum traces the history of the capital's three (and soon to be four!) underground lines, and displays plans for the future. Much emphasis is put on the little yellow metro (M1), Continental Europe's first underground railway, which opened for the millenary celebrations in 1896 and was completely renovated for the millecentenary 100 years later. In fact, the museum is housed in a stretch of tunnel that once formed part of the M1 line until it was diverted in 1955.

LIPÓTVÁROS

BASILICA OF ST STEPHEN Map p85
Szent István Bazilika; ☎ 311 0839, 338 2151; V Szent István tér; ☼ 7am-7pm; Ⓜ M2 Arany János utca

Budapest's neoclassical cathedral was built over the course of half a century and completed in 1905. Much of the interruption had to do with the fiasco in 1868 when the dome collapsed during a storm, and the structure had to be demolished and rebuilt from the ground up. The basilica is rather dark and gloomy inside, but take a trip to the top of the dome (adult/child 500/400Ft; ☼ 10am-4.30pm Apr & May, 9.30am-6pm Jun-Aug, 10am-5.30pm Sep & Oct), which can be reached by lift and 146 steps and offers one of the best views in the city.

To the right as you enter the basilica is a small treasury (kincstár; adult/child 400/300Ft; ☼ 9am-5pm Apr-Sep, 10am-4pm Oct-Mar) of ecclesiastical objects. Behind the main altar and to the left is the basilica's major draw card: the Holy Right Chapel (Szent Jobb kápolna; ☼ 9am-4.30pm Mon-Sat, from 1pm Sun May-Sep, 10am-4pm Mon-Sat, 1-4.30pm Sun Oct-Apr). It contains the Holy Right (also known as the Holy Dexter),

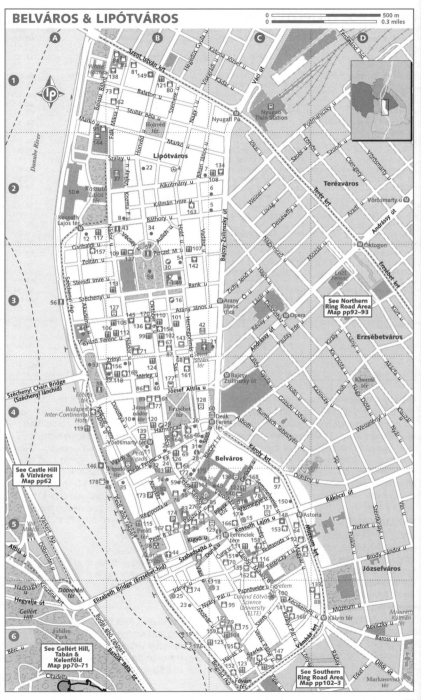

0   500 m
0   0.3 miles

Danube River

Szent István krt
Hegedüs Gyula u
Katona József u
Visegrádi u
Kádár u
Vám u

White House
138
81 149
121
80
73
62
Balaton u
Stollár Béla u
Honvéd tér
Markó u
Markó u
Balassi Bálint u
Falk Miksa u
Honvéd u
Nyugati Pu
Nyugati Train Station
Pozsonyi u
Eötvös u
Szondi u
Csengery u
Vörösmarty u
91
144
Szalay u
50
Kossuth Lajos tér
22
4
Bihari János u
134
108
7
Lipótváros
37
Alkotmány u
6
Terézváros
Weiner L u
Lovag u
Dessewffy u
Aradi
Vörösmarty
Andrássy út
Kossuth Lajos tér
12 117
43
34
Garibaldi u
157
109
137
Zoltán u
54
30
58
107
142
Steindl Imre u
113
Bajcsy-Zsilinszky út
Kálmán Imre u
Báthory u
Nádor u
Vécsey u
Aulich u
Hold u
Vadász u
Perczel M u
8
163
5
56
Széchenyi rkp
Akadémia u
Széchenyi u
Szent István tér
127
145 170
106 105
136
112
99
102
67
Október 6 u
Arany János u
Hercegprímás u
Sas u
16
101
151
143
42
Bank u
Zichy Jánó u
Hild tér
Nagymező u
Mozsár u
Arany János utca
Opera
Révay u
Paulay Ede u
Dalszínház u
Andrássy út
Liszt Ferenc tér
See Northern Ring Road Area Map pp92–93
Erzsébetváros
Király u
Eötvös tér
Budapest Inter-Continental Hotel
119
Zrínyi u
59
156
38
118
124
171
Mérleg u
86
40
89
77
József Attila u
József nádor u
128
60
Dorottya u
Vigadó tér
Vigadó u
Pesti
Deák Ferenc u
10
139
146
178
Harmincad u
120
29
146
Erzsébet tér
Deák Ferenc tér
Deák Ferenc tér
Belváros
Vörösmarty tér
Bárczy István
11
26
165 46
31
69
126
28
172
164
130
168
97
Károly krt
Dohány u
Rákóczi út
Astoria
Kálvin Károly Gyula u
Holló u
Rumbach Sebestyén u
Gerlóczy u
Kazinczy u
Dob u
Nagy Diófa u
Wesselényi u
Nyár u
Klauzál tér
Síp u
Erzsébetváros
Kisn Diófa u
Csányi u
Akácfa u
Osvát u
35
173
59
14
Apácza Csere János u
Petőfi tér
Régiposta u
83 27
174
178
Párizsi u
Kígyó u
115
Petőfi S u
Vámház krt
Ferenciek tere
Kossuth Lajos u
Szabadsajtó út
Veres Pálné u
Curia u
Ferenczy István u
Reáltanoda u
Magyar u
Károlyi Mihály u
148
150
153
64
92
Múzeum krt
Trefort u
Bródy Sándor u
Józsefváros
Mikszáth Kálmán
Múzeum
Reviczky u
Baross u
Szentkirályi u
Puskin u
Ötpacsirta u
See Castle Hill & Víziváros Map pp62
Széchenyi Chain Bridge (Széchenyi lánchíd)
Ybl Miklós tér
Várkert rkp
Döbrentei u
Attila u
Hadnagy u
Krisztina krt
Döbrentei tér
Hegyalja út
Gellért Hill
Jubilee Park
Bérc u
See Gellért Hill, Tabán & Kelenföld Map pp70–71
Citadella
Elizabeth Bridge (Erzsébet híd)
Budai alsó rakpart
Pesti alsó rakpart
Belgrád rakpart
Bartók Béla út
18
74
3
25
23
95
141
160
88
135
Papnövelde u
Egyetem tér
Loránd Eötvös Science University (ELTE)
Kálvin tér
Ólloi út
Ferenc krt
Ráday u
Markusovszky tér
Vámház krt
Sörház u
Molnár u
Irányi u
Nyáry Pál u
Veres Pálné u
76
129
166
151
155
135
162
65
70
94
144
79
104
159
125
176
19
155
123
98
147
152
Fővám tér
See Southern Ring Road Area Map pp102–3

85

BELVÁROS & LIPÓTVÁROS

the mummified right hand of St Stephen and an object of great devotion. It was returned to Hungary by Habsburg empress Maria Theresa in 1771 after it was discovered in a monastery in Bosnia. Like the Crown of St Stephen (see the boxed text, p88), it too was snatched by the bad guys after WWII but was soon, er, handed over to the rightful (ugh) owners.

PARLIAMENT Map p85

Országház; ☎ 441 4904, 441 4415; V Kossuth Lajos tér 1-3, Gate X; admission for EU citizens free, others adult/student & child 2520/1260Ft; ☽ 8am-6pm Mon & Wed-Fri, to 4pm Sat, to 2pm Sun May-Sep, 8am-4pm Mon & Wed-Sat, to 2pm Sun Oct-Apr; Ⓜ M2 Kossuth Lajos tér

The parliament building, designed by Imre Steindl and completed in 1902, has 690 sumptuously decorated rooms but you'll only get to see three on a guided tour of the North Wing: the main staircase and landing, where the Crown of St Stephen (see the boxed text, p88), the nation's most

important national icon, is on display, along with the ceremonial sword, orb and the oldest object among the coronation regalia, the 10th-century Persian-made sceptre with a crystal head depicting a lion; the Loge Hall; and the Congress Hall, where the House of Lords of the one-time bicameral assembly sat until 1944. The building is a blend of many architectural styles (neo-Gothic, neo-Romanesque, neobaroque) and overall works very well. Unfortunately, what

top picks

IT'S FREE

- Parliament (left; for EU citizens)
- Kerepesi Cemetery (p105)
- Basilica of St Stephen (p84)
- Hungarian Electrical Engineering Museum (p96)
- MNB Visitor Centre (p89)

was spent on the design wasn't matched in the building materials. The ornate structure was surfaced with a porous form of limestone that does not resist pollution very well. Renovations began almost immediately after it opened and will continue until the building crumbles. Members of parliament sit in the National Assembly Hall in the South Wing from February to June, and September to December. You can join a tour in any of eight languages – they depart continually in Hungarian, but the English-language ones are at 10am, noon and 2pm. To avoid disappointment, book ahead in person.

ETHNOGRAPHY MUSEUM Map p85

Néprajzi Múzeum; ☎ 473 2400; www.neprajz.hu; V Kossuth Lajos tér 12; adult/student & child/family 800/400/1300Ft; ⏰ 10am-6pm Tue-Sun; Ⓜ M2 Kossuth Lajos tér

Visitors are offered an easy introduction to traditional Hungarian life at this sprawling museum opposite the parliament building

with thousands of displays in 13 rooms on the 1st floor. The mock-ups of peasant houses from the Őrség and Sárköz regions of Western and Southern Transdanubia are well done, and there are also some priceless objects collected from Transdanubia. On the 2nd floor, most of the temporary exhibitions deal with other peoples of Europe and farther afield: Africa, Asia, Oceania and the Americas. The building itself was designed in 1893 to house the Supreme Court; note the ceiling fresco in the lobby of *Justice* by Károly Lotz.

BEDŐ HOUSE Map p85

Bedő-ház; ☎ 269 4622; www.magyarszecessziohaza.hu; V Honvéd utca 3; adult/student & child 1000/600Ft; ⏰ 10am-5pm Tue-Sat; Ⓜ M2 Kossuth Lajos tér

Just around the corner from Kossuth Lajos tér is this stunning art nouveau apartment block deigned by Emil Vidor and built in 1903. Now a shrine to Hungarian Secessionist interiors, its three floors are crammed

THE CROWN OF ST STEPHEN

Legend tells us that it was Asztrik, the first abbot of the Benedictine monastery at Pannonhalma in Western Trans-danubia, who presented a crown to Stephen as a gift from Pope Sylvester II around AD 1000, thus legitimising the new king's rule and assuring his loyalty to Rome over Constantinople. It's a nice story but has nothing to do with the object on display in the parliament building. That two-part crown, with its characteristic bent cross, pendants hanging on either side and enamelled plaques of the Apostles, dates from the 12th century. Regardless of its provenance, the Crown of St Stephen has become the very symbol of the Hungarian nation.

The crown has disappeared several times over the centuries – purloined or otherwise – only to reappear later. During the Mongol invasions of the 13th century, the crown was dropped while being transported to a safe house, giving it that slightly skewed look. More recently, in 1945, Hungarian fascists fleeing ahead of the Soviet army took the crown to Austria. Eventually it fell into the hands of the US army, which transferred it to Fort Knox in Kentucky. In January 1978 the crown was returned to Hungary with great ceremony – and relief. Because legal judgments had always been handed down 'in the name of St Stephen's Crown' it was considered a living symbol and thus to have been 'kidnapped'.

with furniture, porcelain, ironwork, paintings and objets d'art. The lovely Art Nouveau Café (p149) is on the ground floor.

HUNGARIAN MUSEUM OF TRADE & TOURISM Map p85

Magyar Kereskedelmi és Vendéglátóipari Múzeum; ☎ 375 6249; www.mkvm.hu; V Szent István tér 15; adult/child/family 600/300/1200Ft; ☷ 11am-7pm Wed-Sun; Ⓜ M2 Arany János utca

A shadow of what it was when based on Castle Hill, this museum deals almost exclusively in temporary exhibitions, and serves as an educational centre for schools and those in the catering and hospitality trade. Only one small room of restaurant items, tableware, advertising and packing contains remnants of the original collection. Bring it back, we say.

ROOSEVELT TÉR Map p85

🚌 16 or 105, 🚃 2

Named in 1947 after the long-serving (1933–45) American president, Roosevelt tér sits at the foot of Chain Bridge and offers among the best views of Castle Hill in Pest.

On the southern end of the square is a statue of Ferenc Deák, the Hungarian minister largely responsible for the Compromise of 1867, which brought about the Dual Monarchy of Austria and Hungary (p30). The statue on the western side is of an Austrian and a Hungarian child holding hands in peaceful bliss. The Magyar kid's hair is tousled and he is naked; the Osztrák is demurely covered by a bit of the patrician's robe and his hair neatly coifed.

The art nouveau building with the gold tiles to the east is the Gresham Palace (V Roosevelt tér 5-6), built by an English insurance company in 1907. It now houses the sumptuous Four Seasons Gresham Palace Hotel (p179). The Hungarian Academy of Sciences (Magyar Tudományos Akadémia; V Roosevelt tér 9), founded by Count István Széchenyi, is at the northern end of the square.

SZABADSÁG TÉR Map p85

🚌 15

'Liberty Sq', one of the largest in Budapest, is a few minutes' walk northeast of Roosevelt tér. In the centre is a memorial to the Soviet army, the last of its type still standing in the city.

At the eastern side of the square is the fortresslike US Embassy (V Szabadság tér 12), now cut off from the square by high metal fencing and concrete blocks. It was here that Cardinal József Mindszenty (see boxed text, p90) sought refuge after the 1956 Uprising and stayed for 15 years until departing for Vienna in 1971. The embassy backs onto Hold utca (Moon St), which, until 1990, was named Rosenberg házaspár utca (Rosenberg Couple St) after the American husband and wife Julius and Ethel Rosenberg who were executed as Soviet spies in the US in 1953.

On the same street to the south you'll find the sensational former Royal Postal Savings Bank (V Hold utca 4), a Secessionist extravaganza of colourful tiles and folk motifs built by Ödön Lechner (see the boxed text, p48) in 1901. It is now part of the National Bank of Hungary (Magyar Nemzeti Bank; V Szabadság tér 9) next door, which has reliefs that illustrate trade and commerce through history: Arab camel traders, African rug merchants, Chinese tea salesmen – and the inevitable solicitor witnessing contracts. The MNB Visitor Centre (☎ 428 2752; www.lk.mnb.hu; admission free; 🕑 9am-4pm Mon-Wed & Fri, to 6pm Thu) contains an interesting multimedia exhibition on the history of currency and banking in Hungary, but most people come to gawp at the stunning entrance hall and staircase.

BELVÁROS
Walking Tour

1 Egyetem tér The best place to start walking Belváros is Egyetem tér (University Sq), a five-minute walk south along Károlyi Mihály utca from Ferenciek tere. The square's name refers to the branch of the prestigious Loránd Eötvös Science University (ELTE; V Egyetem tér 1-3).

2 University Church Next to the university building to the west is the lovely baroque 1742 University Church (Egyetemi templom; ☎ 318 0555; V Papnövelde utca 5-7; 🕑 7am-7pm). Over the altar is a copy of the Black Madonna of Częstochowa so revered in Poland. The church is often full of young people.

3 Károly Palace Just north of Egyetem tér, the neoclassical Károly Palace (Károlyi Palota; 1840) houses the Petőfi Literary Museum (Petőfi Irodalmi Múzeum; ☎ 317 3611; www.pim.hu; V Károlyi Mihály utca 16; adult/child/family 480/240/900Ft; 🕑 10am-6pm Tue-Sun). There is also a centre for contemporary literature, a library, concert/lecture hall and terrace restaurant (in the courtyard) here.

4 Serbian Orthodox Church Southwest of Egyetem tér, at the corner of Szerb utca and Veres Pálné utca, stands the Serbian Orthodox church (Szerb ortodox templom; ☎ 337 2970; V Veres Páné utca 19; admission 500Ft; 🕑 9.30am-1pm & 2-5pm), built by Serbs fleeing the Turks in the 17th century. The iconostasis is worth a look.

WALK FACTS
Start V Egyetem tér
Finish V Vörösmarty tér
Distance 1.2km
Duration 1½ hours
Fuel stop Gerbeaud Cukrászda (p148)

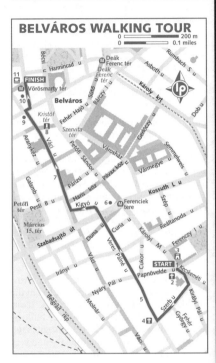

BELVÁROS WALKING TOUR

NEIGHBOURHOODS BELVÁROS & LIPÓTVÁROS

5 Veres Pálné There are a couple of interesting things to see as you walk north along Veres Pálné utca, which runs north to south just west of Egyetem tér. For example, the building at No 19 has bronze reliefs above the 2nd floor illustrating various periods of

STATUES & MONUMENTS

Southeast of V Kossuth Lajos tér is an Imre Nagy statue (Map p85; V Vértanúk tere; Ⓜ M2 Kossuth Lajos tér); he was the reformist communist prime minister executed in 1958 for his role in the Uprising two years earlier (p33). It was unveiled with great ceremony in the summer of 1996.

Farther south from the same square is a monument to Hungarian Jews shot and thrown into the Danube by members of the fascist Arrow Cross Party (p31) in 1944, entitled Shoes on the Danube (Map p85; Cipők a Dunaparton; V Pesti alsó rakpart), by sculptor Gyula Pauer and film director Can Togay. It's a simple affair – 60 pairs of old-style boots and shoes in cast iron, tossed higgledy-piggledy on the bank of the river – but it is one of the most poignant monuments yet unveiled in this city of so many tears.

CARDINAL MINDSZENTY

Born József Pehm in the village of Csehimindszent near Szombathely in western Hungary in 1892, Mindszenty was politically active from the time of his ordination in 1915. Imprisoned under the short-lived regime of communist Béla Kun in 1919 and again when the fascist Arrow Cross came to power in 1944, Mindszenty was made archbishop of Esztergom (and thus primate of Hungary) in 1945, and cardinal the following year.

In 1948, when he refused to secularise Hungary's Roman Catholic schools under the new communist regime, Mindszenty was arrested, tortured and sentenced to life imprisonment for treason. Released during the 1956 Uprising, Mindszenty took refuge in the US embassy on Szabadság tér when the communists returned to power. He would remain there until 1971.

As relations between the Kádár regime and the Holy See began to improve in the late 1960s, the Vatican made several requests for the cardinal to leave Hungary, which he refused to do. Following the intervention of US president Richard Nixon, Mindszenty left for Vienna, where he continued to criticise the Vatican's relations with the regime in Hungary. He retired in 1974 and died the following year. But as he had vowed not to return to Hungary until the last Russian soldier had left Hungarian soil, Mindszenty's remains were not immediately returned to Hungary. However, they were returned in May 1991, which was actually several weeks before that pivotal date.

construction in the capital in the 18th, 19th and early 20th centuries.

6 Páriszi Udvar From Ferenciek tere, cross over Szabadsajtó utca and walk through the 1909 Parisian-style arcade Páriszi Udvar (Parisian Court; V Ferenciek tere 5) to tiny Kigyó utca; pedestrian Váci utca, the capital's premier – and most expensive – shopping street, with designer clothes, expensive jewellery shops, pubs and some bookshops, is immediately to the west.

7 Váci utca Many of the buildings on narrow Váci utca, which ran the length of Pest in the Middle Ages, are worth a closer look. Thonet House (V Váci utca 11/a) is a masterpiece built by Ödön Lechner in 1890. Florist-cum-gift shop Philanthia (V Váci utca 9) has an original – and very rare – art nouveau interior.

8 Fishergirl Fountain Just off Váci utca in Kristóf tér is the little Fishergirl Fountain dating from the 19th century and complete with a ship's wheel that actually turns. On the square is a brick outline of the foundations of Vác Gate (Váci kapu), once part of the old city wall.

9 Bank Palace A short distance to the northwest is the sumptuous Bank Palace (Bank Palota; V Deák utca 5), built in 1915 and the home of the Budapest Stock Exchange for 15 years until 2007. It is now being converted into a shopping gallery called Váci 1.

10 Vörösmarty tér Váci utca empties into Vörösmarty tér, a large square of smart shops, galleries, cafes and a smattering of artists who will draw your portrait or caricature. In the centre is a statue of the 19th-century poet after whom Vörösmarty tér was named. The first station of the little yellow metro line M1 is also here.

11 Gerbeaud Cukrászda At the northern end of Vörösmarty tér is Gerbeaud Cukrászda (p148).

NORTHERN RING ROAD AREA

Drinking (p149); Eating (p135); Shopping (p118); Sleeping (p180)

Szent István körút, the northernmost stretch of the Big Ring Road in Pest, runs in a westerly direction from Nyugati tér to Margaret Bridge and the Danube. It's an interesting street to stroll along, with many fine Eclectic-style buildings erected in the last part of the 19th century and decorated with Atlases, reliefs and other details. Don't hesitate to explore the inner courtyards here and farther on – if Dublin is celebrated for its doorways and London for its squares, Budapest is known for its lovely *udvarok* (courtyards).

The area north of Szent István körút is known as Újlipótváros (New Leopold Town) to distinguish it from Lipótváros (Leopold Town) to the south of the Big Ring Road. (Archduke Leopold was the grandson of Habsburg empress Maria Theresa.) It is a wonderful neighbourhood with tree-lined streets, antique shops, boutiques and a few cafes, and is best seen on foot (p97). It was upper middle class and Jewish before the war, and many of the 'safe houses' organised by the Swedish diplomat Raoul Wallenberg (see boxed text, p69) during WWII were here. A street named after this heroic man, two blocks to the north, bears a commemorative plaque.

You can reach Jászai Mari tér, at the western end of Szent István körút, on tram 4 or 6 from either side of the river or via tram 2 from the Inner Town in Pest. The eastern end of the boulevard is best reached by metro (M3 Nyugati pályaudvar). Újlipótváros is served by buses 15 and 115 and trolleybuses 75 and 76.

Teréz körút carries on from Szent István körút after Nyugati train station, which is on the M3 metro. The neighbourhood on either side of this section of the ring road – district VI – is known as Terézváros (Teresa Town) and was named in honour of Maria Teresa. It extends as far as VI Király utca and the start of VII Erzsébet körút. Trams 4 and 6 serve the neighbourhood.

Andrássy út, listed as a Unesco World Heritage Site, starts a short distance north of Deák Ferenc tér and stretches for 2.5km to the northeast, ending at Hősök tere and Városliget, Pest's sprawling 'City Park'. Andrássy út is such a pretty boulevard and there's so much to enjoy en route that the best way to see it is on foot (p98), though the M1 metro runs beneath Andrássy út from Deák Ferenc tér as far as the City Park if you tire out.

The Big Ring Road slices district VII, also called Erzsébetváros (Elizabeth Town), in half between two busy squares: Oktogon and Blaha Lujza tér. The eastern side is rather rundown, with little of interest to travellers except the Keleti train station on Baross tér. The western side, bounded by the Little Ring Road, has always been predominantly Jewish, and this was the ghetto where Jews were forced to live behind wooden fences when the Nazis occupied Hungary in 1944.

Oktogon is on the M1 metro line and Blaha Lujza tér on the M2. You can also reach this area via trams 4 and 6 from both Buda and the rest of Pest.

SZENT ISTVÁN KÖRÚT & TERÉZVÁROS

NYUGATI TRAIN STATION Map pp92-3

Nyugati pályaudvar; VI Teréz körút 55-57; Ⓜ M3 Nyugati pályaudvar

The large iron and glass structure on Nyugati tér (known as Marx tér until the early 1990s) is the Nyugati train station, built in 1877 by the Paris-based Eiffel Company. In the early 1970s a train actually crashed through the enormous glass screen on the main facade when its brakes failed, coming to rest at the 4 and 6 tram line. The old dining hall on the south side now houses one of the world's most elegant McDonald's.

HOUSE OF HUNGARIAN PHOTOGRAPHERS Map pp92-3

Magyar Fotográfusok Háza; ☎ 473 2666; www .maimano.com; VI Nagymező utca 20; adult/senior & student/family 700/300/1500Ft; ☻ 2-7pm Mon-Fri, 11am-7pm Sat & Sun; Ⓜ M1 Opera

The House of Hungarian Photographers is an extraordinary venue in the city's theatre district with top-class photography exhibitions. It is in delightful Mai Manó Ház, which was built in 1894 as a photo studio.

NORTHERN RING ROAD AREA

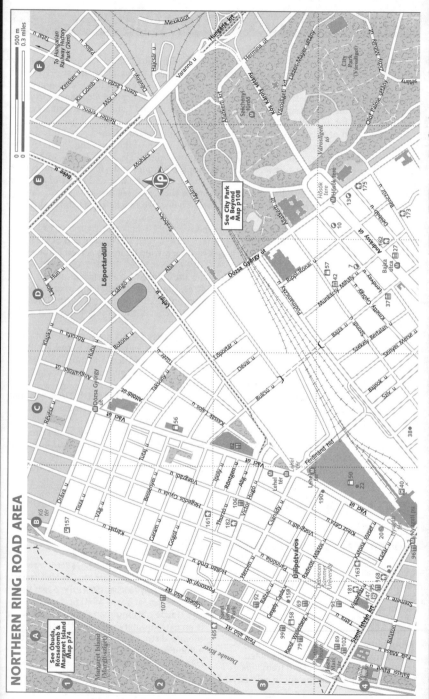

See Óbuda, Rózsadomb & Margaret Island Map p74

See City Park & Beyond Map p108

To Hungarian Railway History Park (2km)

Margaret Island (Margit-sziget)

Danube River

Újlipótváros

Lipótváros

0 500 m
0 0.3 miles

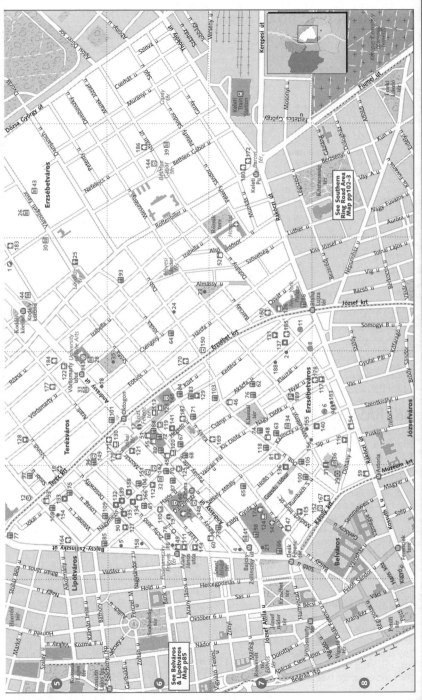

See Southern
Ring Road Area
Map pp102–3

See Belváros
& Lipótváros
Map p85

NORTHERN RING ROAD AREA

INFORMATION

Austrian Consulate	1 D5
AvoComp	(see 82)
BKV Lost & Found Office	2 C7
British Chamber of Commerce in Hungary	3 B4
Budatours	4 B7
Cartographia	5 B6
Chatman Internet	6 C8
Croatian Consulate	7 D4
Discover Budapest	(see 19)
Electric Cafe	8 D7
Express	9 C8
French Consulate	10 E4
Great Synagogue	(see 29)
Mosómata	(see 165)
Narancs	11 D7
Post Office	12 B5
Serbian Consulate	13 E4
SOS Dent	14 B7
Teréz Patika	15 B5
Térképkirály	16 B6
Tourinform Oktogon Branch	17 C6
Treehugger Dan's Bookstore	18 C5
Treehugger Dan's Bookstore Branch	19 B6
Vist@netcafe	20 B4
Vista	21 B7
Vodafone	22 B4

SIGHTS & ACTIVITIES (pp55–110)

Alamássy tér	23 D6
Art Nouveau Primary School	24 D6
City Park Calvinist Church	25 D5
Egger Villa	26 E5
Ferenc Hopp Museum of East Asian Art	27 D4
Franz Liszt Memorial Museum	28 C5
Great Synagogue	29 B8
György Ráth Museum	30 D5
Holocaust Memorial	31 B8
House of Hungarian Photographers	32 B6
House of Terror	33 C5
Hungarian Electrical Engineering Museum	34 C7
Hungarian State Opera House	(see 146)
Hunyadi tér	35 C6
Jewish Museum	36 C8
Léderer Mansion	37 D4
Lindenbaum Apartment Block	38 C4
Miksa Róth Memorial House	39 E6
Nyugati Train Station	40 B4
Postal Museum	41 B7
Sonnenberg Mansion	42 D4
Vidor Villa	43 E5
Zoltán Kodály Memorial Museum	44 D5

SHOPPING (pp111–120)

Alexandra	45 C6
Billerbeck	46 C7
Billerbeck Branch	47 B7
Concerto Hanglemezbolt	48 C7
Haas & Czjzek	49 B6
Írok Boltja	50 C6
Jajcica	51 D7
Játékszerek Anno	52 B5
Libri Könyvpalota	53 C8
Liszt Ferenc Zebneműbolt	54 C6
Mountex	55 C2
Museum of Fine Arts Office	56 D4
Pendragon	57 A3
Tisza Cipő	58 B8
Wave Music	59 B7
West End City Centre	60 B4

EATING (pp121–142)

Artesano	61 B6
Bangla Büfé	62 C7
Carmel Pince	63 C7
City Maharaja	64 D6
Donatella's Kitchen	65 B7
Durcin	66 B7
Falafel Faloda	67 C6
Ferenc József Sőrőző	68 C6
Firkász	69 A3
Főzelék Faló	70 B6
Frici Papa Kifőzdéje	71 C6
Giero	72 C6
Goa	73 B7
Hanna	74 C7
Holly	75 B5
Kádár	76 C7
Kaiser's Supermarket	77 B5
Kinai-Koreai Étterem	78 B5
Kiskakukk	79 A3
Klassz	80 C6
Kőleves	81 C7
Lehel Csarnok	82 C3
M Restaurant	83 C6
Magdalena Merlo	84 C6
Marquis de Salade	85 B5
Match Supermarket	86 D7
Match Supermarket	87 B6
Menza	88 C6
Mézes Kuckó	89 A4
Mini Coop	90 B6
Mosselen	91 A4
Móri Kisvendéglő	92 A3
Napfényes Ízek	93 D6
Napos Oldal	94 C5
Okay Italia	95 A4

Map key continued page 95

ANDRÁSSY ÚT & SURROUNDS

HUNGARIAN STATE OPERA HOUSE Map pp92-3

Magyar Állami Operaház; ☎ 332 8197; www
.operavisit.hu; VI Andrássy út 22; adult/student
2600/1400Ft; ⏱ English-language tours 3pm &
4pm; Ⓜ M1 Opera

The neo-Renaissance Hungarian State
Opera House, among the city's most beautiful buildings, was designed by Miklós Ybl
in 1884. If you cannot attend a concert
or an opera, join one of the guided tours.
Tickets are available from the souvenir shop
inside the main entrance to the left.

HOUSE OF TERROR Map pp92-3

Terror Háza; ☎ 374 2600; www.terrorhaza.hu; Andrássy út 60; adult/child 1500/750Ft; ⏱ 10am-6pm
Tue-Fri, to 7.30pm Sat & Sun; Ⓜ M1 Vörösmarty utca
This startling museum is housed in what
was once the headquarters of the dreaded
ÁVH secret police (see p32). The building has
a ghastly history, for it was here that many
activists of every political persuasion that
was out of fashion before and after WWII
were taken for interrogation and torture.
The walls were apparently double thickness
to mute the screams. A plaque on the outside of this house of shame reads in part:
'We cannot forget the horror of terror, and
the victims will always be remembered'.

The museum focuses on the crimes and
atrocities committed by both Hungary's
fascist and Stalinist regimes in a permanent
exhibition called Double Occupation. But
the years after WWII leading up to the 1956
Uprising get the lion's share of the exhibition space (almost three-dozen spaces
on three floors). The tank in the central
courtyard is a jarring introduction and the
wall outside displaying many of the victims'
photos speaks volumes. Even more harrowing are the reconstructed prison cells (col-
lectively called the 'gym') and the final Hall
of Tears gallery. The excellent audio guide
costs 1300Ft.

ASIAN ART MUSEUMS Map pp92-3
Ⓜ M1 Bajza utca

There are two fine museums within easy walking distance of one another in the Andrássy út area devoted to Asian arts and crafts. The **Ferenc Hopp Museum of East Asian Art** (Hopp Ferenc Kelet-Ázsiai Művészeti Múzeum; ☎ 322 8476; www.hoppmuzeum.hu; VI Andrássy út 103; adult/child 600/300Ft; ☻ 10am-6pm Tue-Sun) is housed in the former villa of its benefactor and namesake. Founded in 1919, the museum has six rooms showing an important collection of Chinese and Japanese ceramics, porcelain, textiles and sculpture, Indonesian wayang puppets and Indian statuary as well as lamaist sculpture and scroll paintings from Tibet. The Ferenc Hopp Museum's temporary exhibits are shown at the **György Ráth Museum** (Ráth György Múzeum; ☎ 342 3916; VI Városligeti fasor 12; adult/child 400/250Ft; ☻ 10am-6pm Tue-Sun) in an art nouveau residence a few minutes' walk southwards down Bajza utca.

FRANZ LISZT MEMORIAL MUSEUM
Map pp92-3

Liszt Ferenc Emlékmúzeum; ☎ 322 9804; www.lisztmuseum.hu; VI Vörösmarty utca 35; adult/child 600/300Ft; ☻ 10am-6pm Mon-Fri, 9am-5pm Sat; Ⓜ M1 Vörösmarty utca

This small but perfect museum is housed in the Old Music Academy, where the great composer lived in a 1st-floor apartment for five years until his death in 1886. The four rooms are filled with his pianos (including a tiny glass one), the composer's table, portraits and personal effects. Concerts (included in the entry fee) are sometimes held here on Saturday at 11am.

POSTAL MUSEUM Map pp92-3
Postamúzeum; ☎ 269 6838; www.postamuzeum.hu; VI Andrássy út 3; adult/child/family 500/250/1000Ft; ☻ 10am-6pm Tue-Sun; Ⓜ M1 Bajcsy-Zsilinszky út

The Postal Museum exhibits the contents of original 19th-century post offices – old uniforms and coaches, those big curved brass horns etc – which probably won't do much for you. But the museum is housed in the seven-room apartment of a wealthy late-19th-century businessman and is among the best-preserved in the city. Even the communal staircase and hallway are richly decorated with fantastic murals.

ZOLTÁN KODÁLY MEMORIAL MUSEUM Map pp92-3

Kodály Zoltán Emlékmúzeum; ☎ 352 7106; www.kodaly.hu; VI Kodály körönd 1; adult/child 240/120Ft; ✆ 10am-4pm Wed, to 6pm Thu-Sat, to 2pm Sun; Ⓜ M1 Kodály körönd

In the flat facing magnificent Kodály körönd, where the great composer lived from 1924 until his death in 1967, is the Zoltán Kodály Memorial Museum, with four rooms bursting with furniture, furnishings and other personal items. One room is devoted to Kodály's manuscripts.

ERZSÉBETVÁROS

GREAT SYNAGOGUE Map pp92-3

Nagy zsinagóga; ☎ 413 5500; VII Dohány utca 2-8; adult/student & child 1600/750Ft; ✆ 10am-6.30pm Mon-Thu, to 2pm Fri, to 5.30pm Sun mid-Apr–Oct, 10am-3pm Mon-Thu, to 2pm Fri, to 4pm Sun Nov–mid-Apr; Ⓜ M2 Astoria

The Great Synagogue is the largest Jewish house of worship in the world outside New York City and can seat 3000. Built in 1859

according to the designs of Frigyes Feszl, the synagogue contains both Romantic-style and Moorish architectural elements. It was renovated largely with private donations, including a cool US$5 million from fragrance and cosmetics baroness Estée Lauder (see the boxed text, p39), in the 1990s.

In an annexe of the synagogue is the Jewish Museum (Zsidó Múzeum; ☎ 342 8949; www .bpjewmus.hu; VII Dohány utca 2), which contains objects related to religious and everyday life and an interesting handwritten book of the local Burial Society from the 18th century. The Holocaust Memorial Room relates the events of 1944–45, including the infamous mass murder of doctors and patients at a hospital on XII Maros utca south of Moszkva tér in Buda.

On the synagogue's north side, the Holocaust Memorial (opposite VII Wesselényi utca 6) stands over the mass graves of those murdered by the Nazis in 1944–45. On the leaves of the metal 'tree of life' are the family names of some of the hundreds of thousands of victims.

HUNGARIAN ELECTRICAL ENGINEERING MUSEUM Map pp92-3

Magyar Elektrotechnikai Múzeum; ☎ 342 5750; www.emuzeum.hu, in Hungarian; VII Kazinczy utca 21; admission free; ✆ 10am-5pm Tue-Fri, 9am-4pm Sat; Ⓜ M2 Astoria

This place doesn't sound like everyone's cup of tea, but the white-coated staff are very

SISSI LOVE

The Hungarian love affair with Elizabeth of Bavaria, the consort of Franz Joseph and namesake of Erzsébetváros (Elizabeth Town), affectionately known as Sissi, continues unabated well over a century after her death. Is it her much ballyhooed free spirit? Her somewhat exaggerated role in forging the Compromise of 1867? Her clear dislike for court life at the Hofburg in Vienna (every time she went back she seemed to get sick)? Maybe. But most important was her patriotism.

Although German by birth, Sissi loved Hungary above her homeland and her adopted Austria, learned Hungarian fluently and worked hard at being queen. Sissi spent much time at her summer residence in Gödöllő (p191), northeast of Budapest, and there you'll find a Romantic-style painting of the young queen performing the ultimate Hungarian corporal work of mercy: repairing the coronation robe of King Stephen with a needle and thread.

Sissi's privileged life was not without its share of tragedies. Her distaste for the rigid etiquette of the Habsburg court offended Viennese high society and she frequently withdrew, travelling abroad for long stretches of time. Her obsessive attention to her appearance drove her to what is now recognised as anorexia. And she never recovered from the death of her 30-year-old son, Crown Prince Rudolf, who committed suicide in 1889.

Even Sissi's own untimely death was tragic for several reasons. In 1898, when in her 60th year, Sissi was stabbed to death by an anarchist named Luigi Lucheni as she walked along the promenade of Lake Geneva. Had the union of Austria and Hungary – the Compromise of 1867 – instilled such wrath in the young Italian that he sought to commit the ultimate act of vengeance on one of its supposed perpetrators? Hardly. 'I wanted to kill a royal,' said Lucheni, when questioned by the authorities. 'It did not matter which one.' What a scoundrel.

WORTH THE TRIP

Hungarian Railway History Park

This mostly outdoor museum (Magyar Vasúttörténeti Park; Map pp58-9; ☎ 450 1497, 428 0180; www.mavnosztal gia.hu; XIV Tatai út 95; adult/child/senior/family 900/300/500/1900Ft; ☼ 10am-6pm Tue-Sun Apr-Oct, to 3pm Tue-Sun Nov-mid-Dec & mid-Mar-Apr; 🚌 30, 30/a, 🚋 14) contains more than 100 locomotives (most of them still working) and an exhibition on the history of the railroad in Hungary. There's a wonderful array of hands-on activities – mostly involving getting behind the wheel – for kids. From late March to October a special train leaves Nyugati train station for the park at 10.20am, 11.20am and 1.20pm.

enthusiastic and some of the exhibits are unusual enough for a visit. Its collection of 19th-century generators, condensers, motors and – egad – the world's largest supply of electricity-consumption meters is not very inspiring, but the staff will show you how the alarm system of the barbed-wire fence between Hungary and Austria once worked. There's also a display on the nesting platforms that the electric company kindly builds for storks throughout the country so they won't try to nest on the wires and electrocute themselves. Sizzling stuff.

MIKSA RÓTH MEMORIAL HOUSE
Map pp92-3

Róth Miksa Emlékház; ☎ 341 6789, 413 6147; www.rothmuzeum.hu; VII Nefelejcs utca 26; adult/ senior & student 500/250Ft; ☼ 2-6pm Tue-Sat Sep-Jul; Ⓜ M2 Keleti pályaudvar

This fabulous museum exhibits the work of the eponymous art nouveau stained-glass maker (1865–1944) on two floors of the house and workshop where he lived and worked from 1911 until his death. The master's stunning mosaics are less well known. Roth's dark brown, almost foreboding, living quarters stand in sharp contrast to the lively, technicolour creations that emerged from his workshop.

ÚJLIPÓTVÁROS & SZENT ISTVÁN KÖRÚT

Walking Tour

1 Jászai Mari tér Begin in XIII Jászai Mari tér, which is split in two by the foot of Margaret Bridge on the Pest side. The modern building south of the square, nicknamed the White House (Fehér Ház; V Széchenyi rakpart 19), is the former headquarters of the Central Committee of the Hungarian Socialist Workers' Party. It now contains offices of the members of Parliament.

2 Palatinus House To the north of the square is an elegant apartment block called Palatinus House (Palatinus Ház; XIII Pozsonyi út 2), built in 1912 and facing the Danube. It contains some of the most expensive flats for sale or rent in Budapest.

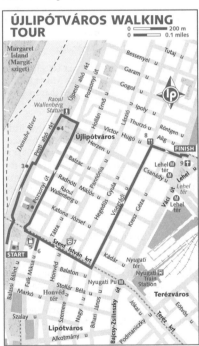

ÚJLIPÓTVÁROS WALKING TOUR

NEIGHBOURHOODS NORTHERN RING ROAD AREA

WALK FACTS

Start XIII Jászai Mari tér
Finish XIII Lehel tér
Distance 2km
Duration Two hours
Fuel stop Troféa Grill (p135)

3 Bauhaus Apartments Along the bank of the river is a rarity for Budapest: a row of Bauhaus apartments. They may not look like much today after decades of bad copies, but they were the bee's knees when they were built in the late 1920s.

4 Szent István Park East of the apartments is Szent István Park, where a statue of Raoul Wallenberg doing battle with a snake (evil) was erected in 1999. It is titled *Kígyóölő* (Serpent Slayer) and replaces one created by sculptor Pál Pátzay that was mysteriously removed the night before its unveiling in 1948.

5 Szőnyi Antikváriuma Return to Szent István körút by walking south along tree-lined Pozsonyi út. Just across the road is the wonderful Szőnyi Antikváriuma (p117), a second-hand and antiquarian bookshop, excellent for browsing – it has old prints and maps in the chest of drawers at the back.

6 Falk Miksa utca The next street on the right and running south, Falk Miksa utca is loaded with pricey antique shops that are great for browsing.

7 Comedy Theatre The attractive little building roughly in the middle of this section of Szent István körút is the Comedy Theatre (Vígszínház; XIII Szent István körút 14), the venue for comedies and musicals. When it was built in 1896, the new theatre's location was criticised for being too far out of the city.

8 Troféa Grill Just up Visegrádi utca is the Troféa Grill (p135), an excellent spot for a blow-out lunch.

9 Lehel Church If you look east down Victor Hugo utca you'll catch sight of the twin spires of the Lehel church (XIII Lehel tér), a 1933 copy of the 13th-century Romanesque church (now in ruins) at Zsámbék, 33km west of Budapest.

ANDRÁSSY ÚT
Walking Tour

Andrássy út splits from Bajcsy-Zsilinszky út about 200m north of V Deák Ferenc tér. This section is lined with plane trees – cool and pleasant on a warm day.

1 Drechsler House The first major point is Drechsler House (VI Andrássy út 25) opposite the Opera

House and designed by Ödön Lechner (see the boxed text, p48) in 1882. It once housed the Hungarian State Ballet Institute but has been empty since the late 1990s awaiting its transformation into a hotel.

2 New Theatre For something even more magical, walk down Dalszínház utca to the west to view the New Theatre (Új Színház; VI Paulay Ede utca 35), a Secessionist gem – embellished with monkey faces, globes and geometric designs – that opened as the Parisiana music hall in 1909.

3 Művész Kávéház The old-world cafe Művész Kávéház (p150) is in the next block and an excellent place for a pit stop.

4 Nagymező utca The following cross street is Nagymező utca, 'the Broadway of Budapest', counting a number of theatres, including the Budapest Operetta (p161) at No 17 and, just opposite, the Thália (VI Nagymező utca 22-24), lovingly restored in 1997.

5 Fashion House On the east side of the next block, Fashion House (Divatcsarnok; VI Andrássy út 39), was the fanciest emporium in town when it opened as the Grande Parisienne in 1912. Ceremonial Hall (Díszterem), on the mezzanine floor, positively drips with gilt, marquetry and Károly Lotz frescoes. Currently being redeveloped as a shopping mall, it may be closed when you pass by.

6 Andrássy út 60 Andrássy út meets the Nagykörút – the Big Ring Road – at Oktogon, a busy intersection full of fast-food places, shops, honking cars and pedestrians. Just beyond it, the former secret police building at Andrássy út 60 now houses the House of Terror (p94).

7 Grand Buildings Along the next two blocks you will pass some very grand buildings housing such institutions as the Budapest Puppet Theatre (p161) at No 69, the Hungarian University of Fine Arts (Magyar Képzőművészeti Egyetem; VI Andrássy út 71) founded in 1871, and the headquarters of MÁV (V Andrássy út 73), the national railway.

8 Kodály körönd The next square (more accurately a circus) is Kodály körönd, one of the most beautiful in the city. Some of the facades of the four neo-Renaissance town houses are

ANDRÁSSY ÚT WALKING TOUR

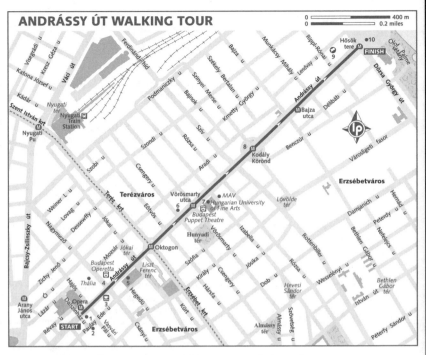

WALK FACTS

Start Opera metro station
Finish VI Hősök tere
Distance 2.5km
Duration 2½ hours
Fuel stop Művész Kávéház (p150)

at least getting a facelift; the one to the south is being converted into a block of flats.

9 Mansions & Embassies The last stretch of Andrássy út, and the surrounding neighbourhood, are packed with stunning old mansions that are among the most desirable addresses in the city. It's no surprise to see that embassies like that of France at VI Lendvay utca 27 and even political parties (eg FIDESZ-MPP at VI Lendvay utca 28) have moved in.

10 Hősök tere Andrássy út ends at Hősök tere (Heroes' Sq), effectively the entrance to City Park. Budapest's most flamboyant monument is in the centre and two of its best exhibition spaces are on either side of the square (see p107).

ERZSÉBETVÁROS
Walking Tour

This walking tour (Map p100) of Erzsébetváros (Elizabeth Town) takes us through the old Jewish Quarter.

1 Ferenc Liszt Music Academy Begin in restaurant- and cafe-packed VI Liszt Ferenc tér, where you'll find the Ferenc Liszt Music Academy (Liszt Zeneakadémia; p156) at the southeastern end. There are always tickets (some very cheap) available to something – perhaps a recital or an early Saturday morning rehearsal.

2 Church of St Teresa If you walk southwest along Király utca you'll pass the Church of St Teresa, built in 1811 and containing a massive neoclassical altar and chandelier.

3 Neo-Gothic House At Király utca 47 (and directly opposite the large Church of St Teresa) is a lovely neo-Gothic house built in 1847 with a protruding window.

4 Klauzál tér The heart of the old Jewish Quarter, Klauzál tér, is a couple of streets southeast over Dob utca. The square and

ERZSÉBETVÁROS WALKING TOUR

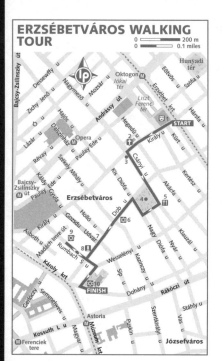

WALK FACTS

Start VI Liszt Ferenc tér
Finish V Károly körút
Distance 1km
Duration One hour
Fuel stop Kádár (p138)

(Ortodox zsinagóga; ☎ 342 1072; VII Kazinczy utca 29-31; admission 800Ft; 🕙 10am-3.30pm Sun-Thu, to noon Fri), which can also be accessed from Dob utca 35, was built in 1913.

7 Gozsdu Udvar The fantastic passage called Gozsdu Udvar (www.gozsduudvar.hu; Dob utca 18) originally built in 1901, has been given a mammoth facelift and once again links Dob utca 16 with Király utca 13 with a 220m-long row of restaurants, shops and private apartments.

8 Monument to Carl Lutz South of the Orthodox Synagogue is an unusual antifascist monument to Carl Lutz (at VII Dob utca 12), a Swiss consul who, like Raoul Wallenberg (see boxed text, p69), provided Jews with false papers in 1944. It portrays an angel on high sending down a long bolt of cloth to a victim.

9 Rumbach Sebestyén utca Synagogue The Moorish Rumbach Sebestyén utca Synagogue (Rumbach Sebestyén utcai zsinagóga; VII Rumbach Sebestyén utca 11; admission 500Ft; 🕙 10am-5.30pm Mon-Fri, to 2.30pm Sat) was built in 1872 by Austrian Secessionist architect Otto Wagner for the conservatives.

10 Great Synagogue No synagogue compares with the Great Synagogue (p96). Another one of its claims to fame is that Theodore Herzl, the father of modern Zionism, was born in a house at the site in 1860.

surrounding streets retain a feeling of prewar Budapest. A continued Jewish presence is still evident – in a kosher bakery (Kazinczy utca 28), the Fröhlich cake shop & cafe (p151), and wigmakers (Kazinczy utca 32 & 36).

5 Kádár Stop at Kádár (p138) on Klauzál tér's northeast corner for refreshments.

6 Orthodox Synagogue There were once a half dozen synagogues and prayer houses in the district, reserved for different sects and ethnic groups (conservatives, Orthodox, Poles, Sephardics etc). The Orthodox Synagogue

SOUTHERN RING ROAD AREA

Drinking (p152); Eating (p139); Shopping (p120); Sleeping (p184)

From Blaha Lujza tér, named after a leading 19th-century stage actress and sheltering one of the liveliest subways in the city – with hustlers, beggars, peasants selling their wares, musicians and, of course, pickpockets – the Big Ring Road runs through district VIII, also called Józsefváros (Joseph Town). The western side of Józsefváros transforms itself from a neighbourhood of lovely 19th-century town houses and villas around the Little Ring Road to a large student quarter. East of the boulevard is the once rough-and-tumble district so poignantly described in the Pressburger brothers' *Homage to the Eighth District* (p40), and where much of the fighting in October 1956 took place (see p33). Today it is being developed at breakneck speed.

The neighbourhood south of Üllői út is Ferencváros (Francis Town), home to the city's most popular football team, Ferencvárosi Torna Club (p169), and many of its tough, green-and-white-clad supporters. There is a tremendous amount of building going on in Ferencváros as well. One highlight of the district is semipedestrianised IX Ráday utca, which leads south from V Kálvin tér and is full of cafes, clubs and restaurants where university students entertain themselves these days.

The Józsefváros and Ferencváros districts are best served by trams 4 and 6. Metro stops include Blaha Lujza tér and Keleti Pályaudvar on the M2 and Kálvin tér and Ferenc Körút on the M3.

JÓZSEFVÁROS

HUNGARIAN NATIONAL MUSEUM
Map pp102-3

Magyar Nemzeti Múzeum; ☎ 338 2122, 317 7806; www.mnm.hu; VIII Múzeum körút 14-16; adult/student & child 1000/500Ft; ☑ 10am-6pm Tue-Sun; Ⓜ M3 Kálvin tér ⓖ 47 or 49

The National Museum (a neoclassical structure, purpose-built in 1847) houses Hungary's most important collection of historical relics. Exhibits trace the history of the Carpathian Basin from earliest times to the end of the Avar period in the early 9th century (on the 1st floor); and the Magyar people and the nation from the conquest of the Carpathian basin to the fall of communism (on the 2nd floor). In the basement, a lapidarium has finds from Roman, medieval and early modern times. Look out for the enormous 3rd-century Roman mosaic from Baláca-puszta, near Veszprém; the crimson silk royal coronation robe (or mantle) stitched by nuns in 1031; a reconstructed 3rd-century Roman villa from Pannonia; the treasury room's Celtic gold jewellery; the stunning baroque library; Beethoven's Broadwood piano; and memorabilia from socialist times.

HUNGARIAN NATURAL HISTORY MUSEUM Map pp102-3

Magyar Természettudományi Múzeum; ☎ 210 1085; www.nhmus.hu; VIII Ludovika tér 2-6; adult/student & child/family 600/300/1500Ft; ☑ 10am-6pm Wed-Mon; Ⓜ M3 Klinikák

Just one metro stop southeast of the Ferenc körút station, the Natural History Museum

has lots of hands-on interactive displays over three floors. The geological park in front of the museum is well designed, the fin whale skeleton in the entrance lobby very impressive and there's an interesting exhibit focusing on both the natural resources of the Carpathian Basin and the flora and fauna of Hungarian legends and tales.

PLANETARIUM Map pp102-3

☎ 263 1811, 265 0725; www.planetarium.hu, in Hungarian; X Népliget; adult/child 1200/990Ft; ☑ shows 9.30am, 11am, 1pm, 2.30pm & 4pm Tue-Sun, plus 5.30pm Tue & Thu; Ⓜ M3 Népliget

Just over the border from Józsefváros in district X' sprawling Népliget (People's Park), this large planetarium has star shows as well as 3-D films and cartoons. It also houses the hokey but perennially popular Laser Theatre (Lézer Színház; p157).

FERENCVÁROS

APPLIED ARTS MUSEUM Map pp102-3

Iparművészeti Múzeum; ☎ 456 5100; www.imm.hu; IX Üllői út 33-37; adult/student & child/family 800/400/1400Ft; ☑ 2-6pm Tue, 10am-6pm Wed & Fri-Sun, 10am-10pm Thu; Ⓜ M3 Ferenc körút

This museum owns a king's ransom of Hungarian furniture dating from the 18th and 19th centuries, art nouveau and Secessionist artefacts, and objects related to the history of trades and crafts (glass making, bookbinding, goldsmithing, leatherwork etc). But only a small part of it forms the 400-piece 'Collectors and Treasures' permanent exhibit on the 1st floor. Most everything else makes

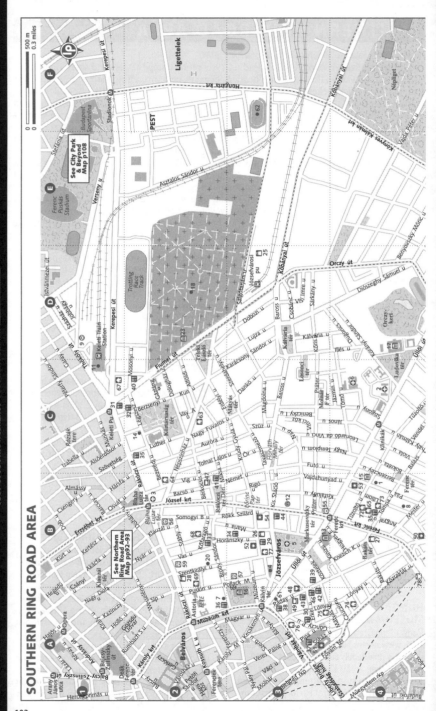

SOUTHERN RING ROAD AREA

See City Park
& Beyond
Map p108

See Northern
Ring Road Area
Map pp92–93

PEST

Ligettelek

Ferenc Puskás
Stadium

Budapest
Sportaréna

Trotting
Race
Track

Kelet Train
Station

Orczy út

Belváros

Józsefváros

0   500 m
0   0.3 miles

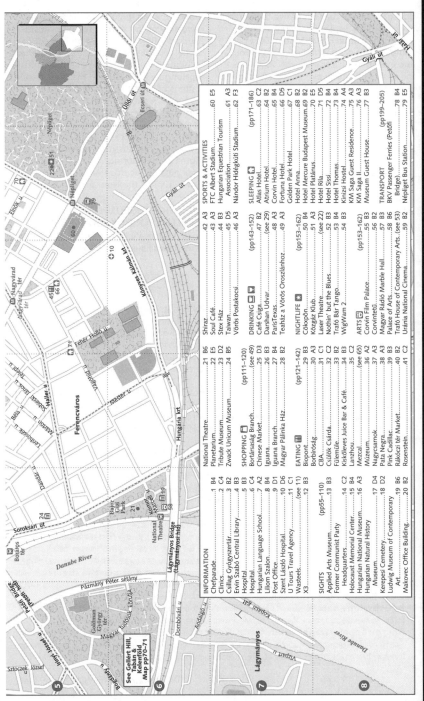

INFORMATION
Chefparade..................................1 B4
Clinics...2 C4
Csillag Gyógyszertár....................3 B2
Ervin Szabó Central Library..........4 B3
Hospital.......................................5 B3
Hospital.......................................6 C4
Hungarian Language School..........7 A2
Liliom Szalon...............................8 B4
Post Office...................................9 D1
Szent László Hospital.................10 D6
U Tours Travel Agency..............11 C1
Wasteels..............................(see 11)
X3...12 B3

SIGHTS (pp55–110)
Applied Arts Museum.................13 B3
Former Communist Party
  Headquarters...........................14 C2
Holocaust Memorial Center........15 B4
Hungarian National Museum.......16 A3
Hungarian Natural History
  Museum....................................17 D4
Kerepesi Cemetery.....................18 D2
Ludwig Museum of Contemporary
  Art...19 B6
Makovec Office Building.............20 B2

National Theatre.........................21 B6
Planetarium................................22 E5
Tribute Museum.........................23 D2
Zwack Unicum Museum.............24 B5

SHOPPING (pp111–120)
Bortársaság Branch...............(see 49)
Chinese Market..........................25 D3
Iguana.......................................26 B3
Iguana Branch...........................27 B4
Magyar Pálinka Ház....................28 B5

EATING (pp121–142)
Biopont.....................................29 B3
Borbíróság.................................30 A3
CBA..31 C1
Csülök Csárda............................32 C2
Fülemüle....................................33 B2
Kisködleves Juice Bar & Café......34 B3
Lanzhou....................................35 C2
Mezcal.................................(see 65)
Múzeum.....................................36 A2
Nagycsarnok..............................37 A3
Pata Negra.................................38 A3
Pink Cadillac..............................39 B3
Rákóczi tér Market......................40 B2
Rosenstein.................................41 C2

Shiraz..42 A3
Soul Café....................................43 A3
Stex Ház....................................44 B3
Taiwan.......................................45 D5
Vörös Postakocsi........................46 A3

DRINKING (pp143–152)
Café Csiga..................................47 B2
Darshan Udvar.....................(see 29)
ParisTexas.................................48 A3
Teaház a Vörös Oroszlánhoz......49 A3

NIGHTLIFE (pp153–162)
Cökxpôn....................................50 B4
Közgáz Klub...............................51 A3
Laser Theatre.......................(see 22)
Nothin' but the Blues.................52 B3
Trafó Bar Tango.........................53 B4
WigWam 2.................................54 B3

ARTS (pp153–162)
Corvin Film Palace......................55 B3
Corvintető..................................56 B2
Magyar Rádió Marble Hall...........57 A3
Palace of Arts.............................58 B6
Trafó House of Contemporary Arts...(see 53)
Uránia National Cinema..............59 B2

SPORTS & ACTIVITIES
FTC Albert Stadium.....................60 E5
Hungarian Equestrian Tourism
  Association...............................61 A3
Nándor Hidegkúti Stadium..........62 F3

SLEEPING (pp171–186)
Atlas Hotel.................................63 C2
Atrium Hotel..............................64 B2
Corvin Hotel...............................65 B4
Fortuna Hotel.............................66 D5
Golden Park Hotel......................67 C1
Hotel Anna.................................68 B2
Hotel Mercure Budapest Museum.69 B2
Hotel Platánus............................70 E5
Hotel Rila...................................71 D5
Hotel Sissi.................................72 B4
Hotel Thomas............................73 B4
Kinizsi Hostel.............................74 A4
KM Saga Guest Residence..........75 A3
KM Saga II.................................76 A3
Museum Guest House.................77 B3

TRANSPORT (pp199–205)
BKV Passenger Ferries (Petőfi
  Bridge)....................................78 B4
Népliget Bus Station...................79 E5

up part of one of the four or five temporary exhibitions on display at any given time. A combined ticket (2500/1250/4500Ft per adult/student or child/family) will get you into everything. It's a novel way to rake in the dosh – just make everything a temporary exhibit. Consider visiting the museum's European furniture exhibit at Nagytétény Castle Museum (p80) instead. The building, designed by Ödön Lechner and decorated with Zsolnay ceramic tiles, was completed for the Millenary Exhibition in 1896.

HOLOCAUST MEMORIAL CENTER
Map pp102-3

Holokauszt Emlékközpont; ☎ 455 3322; www .hdke.hu; IX Páva utca 39; adult 1000Ft, student & child free; ⊗ 10am-6pm Tue-Sun
This centre, housed in a striking modern building in a working-class neighbour-

hood, opened in 2004 on the 60th anniversary of the start of the holocaust in Hungary. Both a museum and an educational foundation, the centre's permanent exhibition traces the rise of anti-Semitism in Hungary from 1938 to the mass deportations of Jews to German death camps in 1944–45. A sublimely restored synagogue, designed by Leopold Baumhorn and completed in 1924, in the central courtyard hosts temporary exhibitions on everything from the Anschluss to the genocide of the Roma people during WWII. An 8m-high wall outside records the names of Hungarian victims of the Holocaust.

LUDWIG MUSEUM OF CONTEMPORARY ART Map pp102-3

Ludwig Kortárs Művészeti Múzeum; ☎ 555 3444; www.ludwigmuseum.hu; IX Komor Marcell utca 1;

GYÖRGY MAKULA

A police captain of Roma origin based in Budapest, György Makula is at the head of a new government initiative to encourage Roma youth to consider a career in law enforcement.

Butcher, baker, candlestick maker… Why should Roma kids want to become a cop? Police work offers them an excellent career opportunity as the education requirements are not particularly demanding. The minimum is a secondary-school diploma, and most Roma kids don't even reach this level. The Ministry of Justice and Law Enforcement is to start a new program where candidates could start police training and then sit their school leaving exams. The key is education.

So how come so many Roma kids miss the boat? The situation for Roma people is bad in Hungary, especially outside Budapest. When the changes came in 1989 the first people to lose their jobs were labourers, those without education, which was most Roma. People are really poor and many people in the countryside can barely afford to support their children much less send them to higher education. Now government funds are focusing on schools that accept more Roma.

Some 200 Roma coppers out of a national force of 38,000. You've got your work cut out for you! There has been prejudice in the police force as elsewhere in Hungary, but it's a two-edged sword. There's bias on both sides. Some Roma cops I have met and questioned have denied their background and have even got angry when I mentioned it. I once spoke to the head of the National Black Police Association in Washington who told me there was a similar problem there in the 1960s and 1970s among black police officers. I truly believe that the most effective way of changing a person's mind is to work with that person. 'Oh my God!' they'll think. 'They're a colleague and Roma and normal.'

What's the background to this bias? Roma have been in Hungary for at least 500 years. In the beginning we were travellers, which of course brought prejudice along with it. Now our concern is the belief that all members of the Roma community are criminals. It's a very real problem borne out by the fact that in the eastern part of Hungary there is a special kind of crime being committed regularly – called 'survival'. People stealing maybe a chicken or some vegetables to survive.

As a Roma police officer, can it be difficult dealing with Roma on the street? Yes, and it's not an uncommon problem. The most important thing is to get the message across. I have various identities. I am a Roma, a Hungarian citizen, a police officer. On the street we are police officers first. Everything else follows.

Is 'Gypsy' the new 'N' word? In my opinion it's OK to use the word Gypsy as it's now been repossessed by us. But Roma is the polite term. The really pejorative word is *cigány* (Hungarian for Gypsy).

Are you hopeful for the future? Things are changing for the positive. Integrated schools will help. But most Roma continue to encounter prejudice in everyday life. 'The job is taken.' 'The flat is rented.' 'We are sold out.' These are things we hear on a regular basis. It can be a lose-lose situation. They say we won't work. We say they won't hire us.

An interview with György Makula, police captain

WORTH THE TRIP

New Municipal Cemetery

This huge city cemetery (Új Köztemető; off Map pp58–9; ☎ 265 2458; X Kozma utca 6; ♡ 8am-7pm; ⓠ 28 or 37), easily reached by tram from Blaha Lujza tér, is where Imre Nagy, prime minister during the 1956 Uprising, and 2000 others were buried in unmarked graves (plots 300–301) after executions in the late 1940s and 1950s. Today, the area has been turned into a moving National Pantheon and is about a 30-minute walk from the entrance; follow the signs pointing the way to '300, 301 parcela'. At peak periods you can take a microbus marked 'temető járat' around the cemetery or hire a taxi at the gate.

Dreher Brewery & Beer Museum

Budapest's – and Hungary's – largest beer maker has a museum (Dreher Sörmúzeum; Map pp58–9; ☎ 432 9700; www.dreherrt.hu; X Jászberényi utca 7-11; adult/senior & student 300/150Ft; ♡ 9am-4pm; Ⓜ M3 Örs vezér tere then ⓠ 161, 161/a or 168/e) at its brewery where you can look at displays of brewing and bottling over the centuries. If you can muster up a group of at least 10, you can take a 1½-hour 'Beer Voyage' (adult/senior & student 1300/650Ft), which includes a tour, a film and a tasting and must be booked in advance on the internet.

adult/student & child 1200/600Ft; ♡ 10am-8pm Tue-Sun; j2 or 24

Housed in the architecturally controversial Palace of Arts (p157) opposite the National Theatre, the Ludwig Museum is Hungary's most important collector and exhibitor of international contemporary art. Works by American, Russian, German and French artists span the past 50 years, while Hungarian, Czech, Slovakian, Romanian, Polish and Slovenian works date from the 1990s onward. The museum also holds frequent, cutting edge, temporary exhibitions.

NATIONAL THEATRE Map pp102-3

Nemzeti Színház; ☎ 476 6800; www.nemzeti szinhaz.hu; IX Bajor Gizi park 1; ⓠ 2 or 24

Perched on the Danube in southwestern Ferencváros, the National Theatre opened in 2002 to much controversy. The design, by architect Mária Siklós, is supposedly 'Eclectic' to mirror other great Budapest buildings (Gellért Hotel, Gresham Palace, Parliament). But in reality it is a pick-and-mix jumble sale of classical and folk motifs, porticoes, balconies and columns that just does not work and certainly will date very fast. But then that's what they said about the much loved parliament building in 1902. The zigguratlike structure outside, whose ramps lead to nowhere, is particularly odd.

ZWACK UNICUM MUSEUM & VISITOR CENTRE Map pp102-3

Zwack Unicum Múzeum és Látogató Központ; ☎ 476 2383; www.zwackunicum.hu; IX Soroksári út 26;

adult/student/senior 1500/850/1250Ft; ♡ 10am-6pm Mon-Fri; ⓠ 2 or 24

If you really can't get enough of Unicum – the thick, brown medicinal-tasting bitter aperitif made from 40 herbs, clocking in at 42% alcohol, supposedly named by Franz Joseph himself (see p144) – visit this very commercial museum tracing the history of the product since it was first made in 1790 and inviting visitors to buy big at its sample store (mintabolt). Enter from Dandár utca.

KEREPESI CEMETERY Map pp102-3

Kerepesi temető; ☎ 323 5100, 314 1269; www .nemzetisirkert.hu; Fiumei út 16; admission free; ♡ 7am-8pm May-Jul, to 7pm Apr & Aug, to 6pm Sep, to 5pm Oct-Mar; ⓠ 24

About 500m southeast of Keleti station is the entrance to Budapest's equivalent of Highgate or Père Lachaise cemeteries. Established in 1847, some of the 3000 gravestones and mausoleums in this 56-hectare necropolis, which is also called the National Graveyard (Nemzeti Sírkert), are worthy of a pharaoh – especially those of statesmen and national heroes such as Lajos Kossuth, Ferenc Deák and Lajos Batthyány. Other tombs are quite moving (eg those of the actress Lujza Blaha and the poet Endre Ady).

Southeast of the main entrance, plot 21 contains the graves of many who died in the 1956 Uprising. Sitting uncomfortably close by is the huge mausoleum for party honchos, including the simple grave of János Kádár, who died in 1989 (see boxed text, p109). Near the main entrance is the Tribute Museum (Kegyeleti Múzeum; ☎ 323 5132; ♡ 10am-3pm Mon-Thu, to 1pm Fri), which looks (grimly, given recent events) at the way of death in Hungary and farther afield (notably Mexico).

JÓZSEFVÁROS & FERENCVÁROS
Walking Tour

1 Rákóczi tér Begin your tour of the traditionally working-class districts of Józsefváros and Ferencváros in VIII Rákóczi tér, the only real square right on the Big Ring Road and as good a place as any to get a feel for these areas.

2 Market Hall Rákóczi tér is the site of a busy market hall (*vásárcsarnok*; p126), erected in 1897 and renovated in the early 1990s after a bad fire.

3 Art Nouveau Building Across József körút, Bródy Sándor utca runs west from Gutenberg tér, where you'll find a lovely art nouveau building at No 4.

4 Former Hungarian Radio headquarters Farther west along VIII Bródy Sándor utca is the recently renovated former Hungarian Radio headquarters (Magyar Rádió; VIII Bródy Sándor utca 5-7), where shots were first fired on 23 October 1956.

5 Italian Institute of Culture Beyond it is the Italian Institute of Culture (VIII Bródy Sándor utca 8), which once housed the erstwhile House of Commons and today appears on the reverse of the 20,000Ft note.

6 Hungarian National Museum Opposite is the Hungarian National Museum (p101). You may enjoy just walking around the museum gardens, laid out in 1856. The column to the left of the main entrance once stood at the Forum in Rome. Look at some of the villas and public buildings on Pollack Mihály tér behind the museum and the white wrought-iron gate in the centre.

7 Ervin Szabó Central Library Walk south to Kálvin tér and follow Baross utca and Reviczky utca eastwards to the Ervin Szabó Central Library (p210), built between 1887 and 1894 and exquisitely renovated in recent years. With its gypsum ornaments, gold tracery and enormous chandeliers, you'll never see another public reading room like it.

8 Biopont Take time out for a refreshment at Biopont (p140) in Darshan Udvar just beyond Mikszáth Kálmán tér.

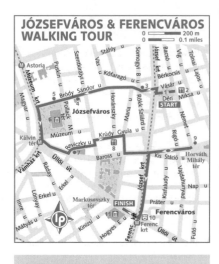

JÓZSEFVÁROS & FERENCVÁROS WALKING TOUR

WALK FACTS

Start VIII Rákóczi tér
Finish Ⓜ M3 Ferenc körút
Distance 3.5km
Duration Three hours
Fuel stop Biopont (p140)

9 Telephone Exchange building Farther east along Baross utca, across the Big Ring Road, the old Telephone Exchange building (VIII Horváth Mihály tér 18), built in 1910, has reliefs of classical figures using the then newfangled invention, the telephone.

10 Corvin Film Palace A restored art deco building, the Corvin Film Palace (Corvin Filmpalota; VIII Corvin köz 1) lies at the southern end of Kisfaludy utca, in the middle of a square flanked by Regency-like houses. This square saw a lot of action during the 1956 Uprising (see p33). Note the two wonderful reliefs outside the cinema and the monument to the *Pesti srácok*, the heroic 'kids from Pest' who fought and died here.

11 Applied Arts Museum West of here is Hungary's answer to London's Victoria and Albert Museum: the Applied Arts Museum (p101), whose central hall of white marble was supposedly modelled on the Alhambra in southern Spain. In fact, the London museum was the inspiration when this museum was founded in 1864.

CITY PARK & BEYOND

Eating (p141); Shopping (p120); Sleeping (p186)

Andrássy út ends at Heroes' Sq (Hősök tere), which effectively forms the entrance to City Park (Városliget). City Park is Pest's green lung, an open space measuring almost a square kilometre that hosted most of the events during Hungary's 1000th anniversary celebrations in 1896. And while it may not compete with the Buda Hills as an escapist's destination, there are more than enough activities and attractions to keep everyone happy.

It's not so cut and dried, but in general museums lie to the south of XIV Kós Károly sétány, the path that runs east–west below the top third of the park. Activities and attractions of a less cerebral nature – the Municipal Great Circus (p109), Funfair Park (p109), Széchenyi Baths (p165) – are to the north.

City Park is served by two M1 metro stops – Hősök tere and Széchenyi fürdő – as well as by trolleybuses 70, 72, 74, 75 and 79.

MILLENARY MONUMENT Map p108
Ezeréves emlékmű; Ⓜ M1 Hősök tere
In the centre of Hősök tere there is a 36m-high pillar backed by colonnades to the right and left. Topping the pillar is the Angel Gabriel, who is holding the Hungarian crown and a cross. At the base are Árpád and the six other Magyar chieftains who occupied the Carpathian Basin in the late 9th century. The 14 statues in the colonnades are of rulers and statesmen: from King Stephen on the left to Lajos Kossuth on the right. The four allegorical figures atop are (from left to right): Work and Prosperity; War; Peace; Knowledge and Glory.

MUSEUM OF FINE ARTS Map p108
Szépművészeti Múzeum; ☎ 469 7100, 363 2675; www.mfab.hu; XIV Dózsa György út 41; adult/student & child 1200/600Ft; ☼ 10am-5.30pm Tue, Wed & Fri-Sun, to 10pm Thu; Ⓜ M1 Hősök tere
The Museum of Fine Arts, on the northern side of Hősök tere, houses the city's most outstanding collection of foreign art works in a building dating from 1906. The Old Masters collection is the most complete, with thousands of works from the Dutch and Flemish, Spanish, Italian, German, French and British schools between the 13th and 18th centuries, including seven paintings by El Greco. Other sections include Egyptian and Greco-Roman artefacts and 19th- and 20th-century paintings, watercolours, graphics and sculpture, including some important impressionist works. There's usually a couple of excellent temporary exhibitions going on at any given time; a combined ticket (3200/1600Ft per adult/student or child) will get you into everything. Free English-language tours of key galleries depart at 11am Tuesday to Saturday, 2pm Tuesday and Friday, 1pm Wednesday and Thursday and 11am Saturday.

PALACE OF ART Map p108
Műcsarnok; ☎ 460 7000; www.mucsarnok.hu; XIV Dózsa György út 37; adult/student & child/family 1200/600/1800Ft; ☼ 10am-6pm Tue, Wed & Fri-Sun, to 8pm Thu; Ⓜ M1 Hősök tere
The Palace of Art is among the city's largest exhibition spaces and now focuses on contemporary visual arts, with some five to

FOLLOW YOUR NOSE
Budapest is tailor-made for exploring on your own. The streets are well marked, the buses and trams easy to negotiate and the natives friendly (though the language can be pretty daunting). This book is designed to whet your appetite and guide you when you arrive; by all means visit many of the sites and the museums listed in this chapter – they're part of the Budapest package. But at the risk of shooting ourselves in the feet (and fingers), we'd like to remind you that this is a *guidebook*, not a *handbook*. Leave it in your room or backpack from time to time, and wander outside to make your own DIY discoveries. Want to see workaday Pest with real residents? Stay on metro M3 and get off at the Örs vezér tér stop. Street fashion in action? Take the M3 metro in the other direction to Gyöngyösi utca and duck into Duna Plaza, a huge shopping complex with three floors of 120 clothing and shoe shops and a multiplex cinema. Or just go blindly into that great maze of streets and rail lines beyond the Big Ring Road, poking your head into little shops, joining in a game of football (*labdarúgás*) in a park or having a beer in a local pub (*söröző*). Welcome to Budapest. For real.

CITY PARK & BEYOND

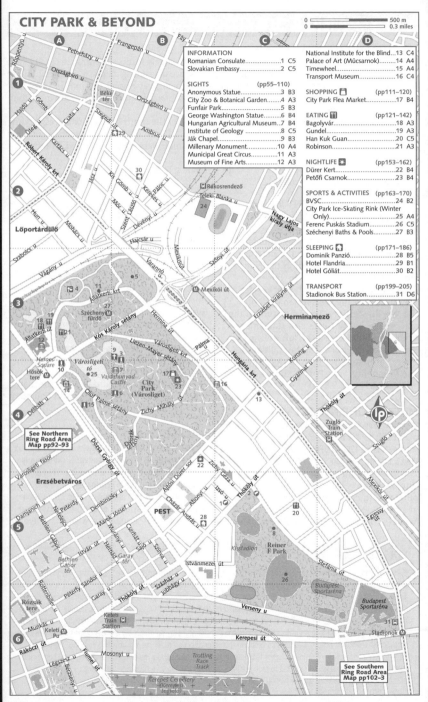

INFORMATION
Romanian Consulate....................1 C5
Slovakian Embassy.....................2 C5

SIGHTS   (pp55–110)
Anonymous Statue.....................3 B3
City Zoo & Botanical Garden.......4 A3
Funfair Park................................5 B3
George Washington Statue.........6 B4
Hungarian Agricultural Museum...7 B4
Institute of Geology 8 C5
Ják Chapel..................................9 B3
Millenary Monument................10 A4
Municipal Great Circus.............11 A3
Museum of Fine Arts................12 A3

National Institute for the Blind...13 C4
Palace of Art (Műcsarnok)........14 A4
Timewheel................................15 A4
Transport Museum....................16 C4

SHOPPING   (pp111–120)
City Park Flea Market...............17 B4

EATING   (pp121–142)
Bagolyvár...................................18 A3
Gundel.......................................19 A3
Han Kuk Guan..........................20 C5
Robinson....................................21 A3

NIGHTLIFE   (pp153–162)
Dürer Kert.................................22 B4
Petőfi Csarnok.........................23 B4

SPORTS & ACTIVITIES   (pp163–170)
BVSC...24 B2
City Park Ice-Skating Rink (Winter
 Only)......................................25 A4
Ferenc Puskás Stadium.............26 C5
Széchenyi Baths & Pools...........27 B3

SLEEPING   (pp171–186)
Dominik Panzió.........................28 B5
Hotel Flandria...........................29 B1
Hotel Góliát...............................30 B2

TRANSPORT   (pp199–205)
Stadionok Bus Station...............31 D6

See Northern
Ring Road Area
Map pp92–93

See Southern
Ring Road Area
Map pp102–3

SHAKE, RATTLE & ROLL

Hungarians are well honed in matters macabre. Who else could – would – have produced the likes of Béla Lugosi and, for that matter, Zsa Zsa Gabor? And matters can often get pretty bony around here. In 1996, for example, the archbishop of Veszprém near Lake Balaton won almost celebrity status by successfully putting King St Stephen's revered right hand (p84) into that of his wife, Queen Gizella (borrowed with much advance planning from the Bavarian city of Passau) – together for the first time in a millennium.

More recently the tales have darkened further. János Kádár, the not-much-lamented former communist leader, had been resting comfortably for some 18 years at Kerepesi Cemetery (p105) when in May 2007 a person or persons unknown crept into the graveyard, unceremoniously broke into his coffin and ran off with comrade Kádár's skull and assorted bones. The perpetrators left behind a note that read: 'Murderers and traitors may not rest in holy ground 1956–2006'. The remains have yet to be found, though we expect the *rendörség* – Bp's boys in blue – and their sniffer dogs are on the scent.

six major exhibitions staged annually. Go for the scrumptious venue alone. Concerts are sometimes staged here as well.

CITY ZOO & BOTANICAL GARDEN
Map p108

Városi Állatkert és Növénykert; ☎ 273 4900; www.zoobudapest.com; XIV Állatkerti körút 6-12; adult/student & child/family 1690/1190/4800Ft; ☺ 9am-6.30pm Mon-Thu, to 7pm Fri-Sun May-Aug, 9am-5.30pm Mon-Thu, to 6pm Fri-Sun Apr & Sep, 9am-5pm Mon-Thu, to 5.30pm Fri-Sun Mar & Oct, 9am-4pm Nov-Feb; Ⓜ M1 Széchenyi fürdő, trolleybus 72

This large zoo and garden, which opened with 500 animals in 1866, has a good collection (big cats, hippopotamuses, polar bear, giraffe), but most visitors come for a glimpse of the calves born in recent years by artificial insemination to Lulu the white rhinoceros. Away from the beasties, have a look at the Secessionist animal houses built in the early part of the 20th century, such as the renovated Elephant House with pachyderm heads in beetle-green Zsolnay ceramic, and the Palm House with an aquarium erected by the Eiffel Company of Paris.

FUNFAIR PARK Map p108

Vidámpark; ☎ 363 8310; www.vidampark.hu; XIV Állatkerti körút 14-16; adult 3700-3900Ft, child (up to 140cm) 2300-2900Ft; ☺ 10am-8pm Jul & Aug, 11am-7pm Mon-Fri, 10am-8pm Sat & Sun May, Jun & Sep, noon-6pm Mon-Fri, 10am-7pm Sat & Sun Apr & Oct, 10am-6pm Sat & Sun Mar; Ⓜ M1 Széchenyi fürdő, trolleybus 72

This luna park on 2.5 hectares dates back to the mid-19th century. There are a couple of dozen thrilling rides, including the heart-stopping Ikarus Space Needle, the looping Star roller coaster (alongside a vintage

wooden one from 1926) and the Hip-Hop freefall tower, as well as go-karts, dodgem cars, a carousel built in 1906 and the new T-Rex dinosaur attraction.

MUNICIPAL GREAT CIRCUS Map p108

Fővárosi Nagycirkusz; ☎ 343 8300; www.circus .hu; XIV Állatkerti körút 7; adult 1500-2400Ft, child 1200-2000Ft; Ⓜ M1 Széchenyi fürdő, trolleybus 72

Europe's only permanent big top has everything one would expect from a circus, including acrobats, dare devils on horseback and ice shows in season. Performances are at 3pm Wednesday to Sunday, with additional shows at 11am and 7pm on Saturday and at 11am Sunday.

HUNGARIAN AGRICULTURAL MUSEUM Map p108

Magyar Mezőgazdasági Múzeum; ☎ 422 0765; www.mmgm.hu; XIV Vajdahunyad sétány; adult/student & child 600/300Ft; ☺ 10am-5pm Tue-Sun Mar-Oct, 10am-4pm Tue-Fri, to 5pm Sat & Sun Nov–mid-Mar; Ⓜ M1 Hősök tere, trolleybus 75 or 79

This rather esoteric museum is housed in the stunning baroque wing of Vajdahunyad Castle. Built for the 1896 millenary celebrations on the little island in the park's lake, the

top picks

BUDAPEST FOR CHILDREN

- Budapest Puppet Theatre (p161)
- Children's Railway (p80)
- Palace of Wonders (p66)
- Funfair Park (left)
- City Zoo & Botanical Garden (left)

STATUES & MONUMENTS

City Park boasts a number of notable statues and monuments. Americans (and collectors of greenbacks) will be amused to see a familiar face in the park south of the lake. The statue of George Washington (Map p108; XIV Washington György sétány) was erected by Hungarian-Americans in 1906. The little church opposite Vajdahunyad Castle is called Ják Chapel (Jáki kápolna; Map p108) because its intricate portal was copied from the 13th-century Abbey Church in Ják in Western Transdanubia. Mass is said here every Sunday at noon.

The statue of the hooded figure south of the chapel is that of Anonymous (Map p108), the unknown chronicler at the court of King Béla III who wrote a history of the early Magyars. Note the pen with the shiny tip in his hand; writers (both real and aspirant) touch it for inspiration.

The Timewheel (Időkerék; Map p108; XIV Felvonulási tér) in 'Procession Sq' on the park's western edge and directly behind the Palace of Art is the world's largest hourglass, standing 8m high and weighing in at 60 tonnes. Unveiled on 1 May 2004 to commemorate Hungary's entry into the EU, it provocatively stands a short distance from the parade grounds of Dózsa György út, where communist honchos once stood to watch May Day processions and where the 25m-tall statue of Joseph Stalin was pulled down by demonstrators on the first night of the 1956 Uprising (p33). The 'sand' (actually grass granules) flows from the upper to lower chamber for one year, finishing exactly at midnight on New Year's Eve, when the wheel is reset to begin its annual flow.

castle was modelled after a fortress in Transylvania – but with Gothic, Romanesque and baroque wings and additions to reflect architectural styles from all over Hungary. Spread over 5200 sq metres of floor space you'll find Europe's largest collection of things agricultural (fruit production, cereals, wool, poultry, pig slaughtering, viticulture etc).

TRANSPORT MUSEUM Map p108

Közlekedési Múzeum; ☎ 273 3840; www.km.iif.hu, in Hungarian; XIV Városligeti körút 11; adult/student & child/family 800/400/1600Ft; ☼ 10am-5pm Tue-Fri, to 6pm Sat & Sun May-Sep, 10am-4pm Tue-Fri, to 5pm Sat & Sun Oct-Apr; trolleybus 72 or 74

The Transport Museum has one of the most enjoyable collections in Budapest and is a great place for kids. In an old and a new wing there are scale models of ancient trains (some of which run), classic late-19th-century automobiles, sailing boats and lots of those old wooden bicycles called 'bone-shakers'. There are a few hands-on exhibits and lots of show-and-tell from the attendants. Outside are pieces from the original Danube bridges that were retrieved after the bombings of WWII, and a cafe in an old MÁV coach.

SHOPPING

top picks

- **BÁV** (p117)
- **Magma** (p116)
- **Holló Atelier** (pp116)
- **Valeria Fazekas** (p115)
- **Pintér Antik** (pp117)
- **Bortársaság** (pp113)
- **Retrock** (pp115)
- **Mester Pálinkák** (pp118)
- **Szőnyi Antikváriuma** (p117)
- **Kieselbach Galéria** (p117)

SHOPPING

Shops in Budapest are well stocked and the quality of the products is generally quite high. Traditional markets stand side by side mammoth shopping malls, and old-style umbrella makers can still be found next to cutting-edge fashion boutiques.

Books and folk-music CDs are affordable, and there's an excellent selection, especially of classical music. Traditional items with a Hungarian stamp – now called Hungarica – include folk embroidery and ceramics, pottery, wall hangings, painted wooden toys and boxes, dolls, all types of basketry, and porcelain (especially from Herend and Zsolnay). Feather- or goose-down pillows and duvets (comforters) are of exceptionally high quality and are second only to the Siberian variety.

Foodstuffs that are expensive or difficult to buy elsewhere – goose liver (both fresh and potted), dried forest mushrooms, jam (especially the apricot variety), prepared meats like Pick salami, the many types of paprika – make nice gifts (as long as you're allowed to take them home). Some of Hungary's 'boutique' wines (p144) make excellent gifts; a bottle of six-*puttonyos* Tokaji Aszú honey-sweet dessert wine always goes down a treat. Fruit-flavoured brandy (*pálinka*) is a stronger option.

In the mid-1990s Budapest began to go mall crazy, and at last count the city had upwards of a dozen, both in the centre of town and on the fringes. However, 'mall' may not properly describe what the Hungarians call *bevásárló és szorakoztató központ* (shopping and amusement centres); here you'll find everything from designer salons, traditional shops and dry cleaners to food courts, casinos, cinemas and night clubs. It's a place to spend the entire day, much as you would just about anywhere in the globalised world of the 3rd millennium.

Some people consider a visit to one of Budapest's flea markets – the famous Ecseri Piac (p120) or the smaller one in City Park (p120) – a highlight, not just as a place to indulge their consumer vices but as the consummate Budapest experience. If you don't have time to get to either or it's the wrong day of the week, check any of the BÁV stores (p117).

Shops are generally open from 9am or 10am to 6pm during the week and till 1pm on Saturday.

CASTLE HILL & VÍZIVÁROS

CASTLE HILL

CARILLON FOLK SHOP
Map p62   Folk Art & Souvenirs
☎ 201 6692; Fortuna koz off I Fortuna utca, Hess András tér 4; 🚌 16, 16/a or 116
This long-established shop, conveniently located in the Castle District, sells Hungarica and quality Hungarian handicrafts.

ROYAL WINE HOUSE & CELLAR MUSEUM SHOP
Map p62   Food & Drink
Királyi Borház és Pincemúzeum; ☎ 267 1100; www.kiralyiborok.com; I Szent György tér, Nyugati sétány; 🕑 noon-8pm; 🚌 16, 16/a or 116
This new tourist attraction (p65) in the Castle District with exhibits and tastings also has a huge selection of some 250 still wines, 35 sparkling wines and 35 fruit brandies.

HEREND
Map p62   Porcelain & Glassware
☎ 225 1050; www.herend.com; I Szentháromság utca 5; 🕑 10am-6pm daily Apr-Oct, 10am-6pm Mon-Fri, 10am-2pm Sat & Sun; 🚌 16, 16/a or 116
For both contemporary and traditional fine porcelain, there is no other place to go but Herend, Hungary's answer to Wedgwood. Among the most popular motifs produced by the company is the Victoria pattern of butterflies and wildflowers designed for the lemon-lipped British queen during the mid-19th century. There's also a more central Belváros branch (Map p85; ☎ 317 2622; V József nádor tér 11; Ⓜ M1 Vörösmarty tér) of this Hungarian icon.

TAXES & REFUNDS
If you're not a resident of the EU, you can get a refund on the ÁFA (VAT or sales tax) you've paid, provided you have spent more than 42,000Ft in any one shop and take the goods out of the country (and the EU) within 90 days. For more information see p214.

VÍZIVÁROS

ALMÁRIUM Map p62 — Antiques

☎ 250 5547; I Attila utca 67; 🚌 5

This wonderful shop near the entrance to the tunnel under Castle Hill sells antique and country Hungarian folk art of every shape and size: mangle boards, wood-carvings, chests etc. But don't expect any bargains. An early 19th-century *tulipán láda* (trousseau chest with tulips painted on it) from Transylvania will cost you as much as 150,000Ft.

BORTÁRSASÁG

Map p62 — Food & Drink

☎ 212 2569; www.bortarsasag.hu; I Batthyány utca 59; 🕑 10am-8pm Mon-Fri, 10am-6pm Sat; Ⓜ M2 Moszkva tér

Once known as the Budapest Wine Society, this place has a half-dozen retail outlets with an exceptional selection of Hungarian wines. No one, but no one, knows Hungarian wines like these guys do. Central for Pest is the *Basilica branch* (Map p85; ☎ 328 0341; V Szent István tér 3; 🕑 noon-8pm Mon-Fri, 10am-4pm Sat; Ⓜ M3 Arany János utca).

HEREND VILLAGE POTTERY

Map p62 — Porcelain & Glassware

☎ 356 7899; II Bem rakpart 37; 🕑 9am-5pm Tue-Fri, 9am-noon Sat; Ⓜ M2 Batthyány tér

An alternative to what some might call overwrought Herend porcelain is the hard-wearing Herend pottery and dishes decorated with bold fruit patterns sold here. You can also enter from II Fő utca 61.

MAMMUT Map p62 — Shopping Mall

☎ 345 8020; www.mammut.hu; II Lövőház utca 2-6; 🕑 8am-11pm; Ⓜ M2 Moszkva tér

The two 'Mammoths' (Mammut I and Mammut II), standing side by side in Buda, are true 'shopping and amusement centres', with almost as many billiard parlours, dance clubs, fitness centres and cafes as shops. They attract the Buda middle class in droves, especially at the weekend.

SPORTHORGÁSZ Map p62 — Sporting Goods

Sport Angler; ☎ 06-70 383 8825; www.sport-horgasz.hu, in Hungarian; II Bem József utca 8; 🕑 9am-5pm Mon-Fri, 9am-1pm Sat; 🚌 86, 🚊 4 or 6

This is the place to come for rods, reels, flies and anything else it takes to get you out fishing.

THE RIGHT WAY

Budapest's antique shops and auction houses are magnets for bargain hunters. Those with a trained eye may find the treasures of tomorrow at some of the modern galleries today, but purchases still require you to reach deep into the pocket – at least for the credit card.

Any item over 100 years old requires a permit from the Ministry of Culture (information hotline ☎ 371 9300) for export; this involves a visit to a museum expert (see below), photos of the piece and a Hungarian National Bank form with proof-of-purchase receipts. Companies that will take care of all this for you and ship the piece(s) include First European Shipping (☎ 06-20 933 5240, 06-30 924 4748; www.firsteuropeanshipping.com) and Move One (☎ 266 0181; www.moveone.info). Be aware that most art shippers won't take a job for under US$450, so if the piece is small enough and not really valuable, consider taking it in your suitcase. First European Shipping quotes a price of about US$950 for obtaining export customs clearance, crating and air-freighting a small chest of drawers to JFK International Airport in New York.

If you're in a DIY mood, the following are the museums and other offices you must contact for valuations and permits in order for your purchase to be allowed out of the country.

Applied Arts Museum (Map pp102–3; ☎ 456 5100; IX Üllői út 33-37) For antique furniture, porcelain, glass and carpets.

Ethnography Museum (Map p85; ☎ 473 2400; V Kossuth Lajos tér 12) For folk art and handicraft items.

Hungarian National Gallery (Map p62; ☎ 201 9082; Wings B & D, Royal Palace, I Szent György tér) For pictorial works by Hungarian artists.

Museum of Fine Arts office (Map pp92–3; ☎ 302 1785; VI Szondi utca 77) For foreign paintings, sculptures and other works of art.

National Széchenyi Library (Map p62; ☎ 224 3700; Wing F, Royal Palace, I Szent György tér) For books, printed matter, written music, hand-written items older than 50 years.

GELLÉRT HILL, TABÁN & KELENFÖLD

MOM PARK Map pp70-1   Shopping Mall

☎ 487 5501; www.mompark.hu; XII Alkotás út 53; ⊗ 7am-midnight Mon-Sat 8am-9pm Sun; 🚋 61
South Buda's biggest mall has both office and retail space, including a nine-screen cinema, recreation centre, in-house brewery and German-style *bierhaus*.

BELVÁROS & LIPÓTVÁROS

BELVÁROS

KÖZPONTI ANTIKVÁRIUM
Map p85   Antiquarian & Secondhand Books

☎ 317 3514; V Múzeum körút 13-15; ⊗ 10am-6.30pm Mon-Fri, 10am-2pm Sat; Ⓜ M2 Astoria
For antique and secondhand books in Hungarian, German and English, try the 'Central Antiquarian'. Established in 1885, it is the largest antique bookshop in Budapest.

MÚZEUM ANTIKVÁRIUM
Map p85   Antiquarian & Secondhand Books

☎ 317 5023; V Múzeum körút 35; ⊗ 10am-6pm Mon-Fri, 10am-2pm Sat; Ⓜ M3 Kálvin tér
Just opposite the Hungarian National Museum is this well-stocked bookshop with both used and antique volumes in a Babel of languages, including English.

RED BUS SECONDHAND BOOKSTORE
Map p85   Antiquarian & Secondhand Books

☎ 337 7453; www.redbusbudapest.hu; V Semmelweis utca 14; ⊗ 11am-6pm Mon-Fri, 10am-2pm Sat; Ⓜ M1/2/3 Deák Ferenc tér

Below the popular hostel (p179) of the same name, this shop has a good selection of used English-language books.

DUNAPARTI AUCTION HOUSE & GALLERY Map p85   Antiques & Auction House

Dunaparti Aukciósház és Galéria; ☎ 266 8374; www.auctiongallery.hu; V Váci utca 36; ⊗ 10am-6pm Mon-Sat; Ⓜ M3 Ferenciek tere
The ' Inner Town Auction House' usually has themed auctions (jewellery, artwork and graphics, silver and sculpture) at 5pm on Monday from September to June and is open for viewing throughout the week.

BALOGH KESTYŰ ÜZLET
Map p85   Fashion & Clothing

☎ 266 1942; V Haris köz 2; ⊗ 11am-6pm Mon-Fri, 10.30am-1pm Sat; Ⓜ M3 Ferenciek tere
If he can have a pair of bespoke shoes from Vass (opposite), why can't she have a pair of custom-made gloves lined with cashmere? You'll get them here at the 'Balogh Gloves Shop' – and there's any number of materials to choose from for men too, including shearling-lined leather gloves.

BYBLOS Map p85   Fashion & Clothing

☎ 377 1908; www.byblos.hu; V Deák Ferenc utca 17; ⊗ 10am-7pm Mon-Sat, 10am-5pm Sun; Ⓜ M1/2/3 Deák Ferenc tér
Anchor tenant of the pedestrianised thoroughfare that so desperately wants to be called 'Fashion Street', this ultraelegant establishment owned by Hungarian-American movie mogul Andrew G Vajna has both casual wear and formal attire for both men and women from international designers as well as its own youth-oriented Byblos Blu line.

CHINA IN HUNGARY

Herend porcelain is among the finest of all goods produced in Hungary and makes a wonderful gift or memento. The stuff also has a long and fascinating pedigree.

A terracotta factory set up at Herend (p194) in 1826 began producing porcelain 13 years later under Mór Farkasházi Fischer of Tata, Western Transdanubia. Initially specialising in copying and replacing nobles' broken chinaware settings imported from Asia, it soon began producing its own patterns; many, like the Rothschild bird and *petites roses*, were inspired by Meissen and Sèvres designs from Germany and France. The famous Victoria pattern of butterflies and wild flowers was made especially for Queen Victoria after she admired a display of Herend pieces at the Great Exhibition in London in 1851.

To avoid bankruptcy in the 1870s, the Herend factory began mass production; tastes ran from kitschy pastoral and hunting scenes to the ever-popular animal sculptures with the distinctive scale-like triangle patterns. In 1993, three-quarters of the factory was purchased by its 1500 workers and became one of the first companies in Hungary privatised through an employee stock-ownership plan. The state owns the other quarter.

ECLECTICK Map p85   Fashion & Clothing
☎ 266 3341; www.eclectick.hu; V Irányi utca 20; 10am-7pm Mon-Fri, 11am-5pm Sat; Ⓜ M3 Ferenciek tere

Just opposite the Centrál Kávéház (p148), local designer Edina Farkas' boutique mostly sells her own innovative creations but also stocks clothing and accessories by Aquanauta, Camou, Balkan Tango, Heart and Roll, Red Aster, PUCC, Kriszta Marosi and Kati Nádasdi.

MANU-ART Map p85   Fashion & Clothing
☎ 266 8136; www.manu-art.hu; V Károly körút 10; ⊗ 10am-6pm Mon-Fri, 10am-2pm Sat; Ⓜ M2 Astoria

This small shop is stuffed to the gills with brightly coloured T-shirts, bags and sink-in beanbag chairs produced by local designers. And you can tick the green box – most of the materials used are cotton, hemp and linen.

NÁRAY TAMÁS Map p85   Fashion & Clothing
☎ 266 2473; V Károlyi Mihály utca 12; ⊗ 10am-6pm Mon-Wed & Fri, noon-8pm Thu, 10am-2pm Sat; Ⓜ M3 Ferenciek tere

The principal outlet for one of Hungary's most celebrated and controversial designers, the Paris-trained Tamás Náray (p44) stocks elegant ready-to-wear fashion and accessories for women and also accepts tailoring orders.

RETROCK Map p85   Fashion & Clothing
☎ 06-30 678 8430; V Ferenczy István utca 28; ⊗ 10.30am-7pm Mon-Fri, 10.30am-3.30pm Sat; Ⓜ M3 Ferenciek tere

This ultra-hip establishment has streetwear and accessories from mostly local designers inspired by street art, music and retro fashion. For fashion, go round the corner to the more recent Retrock Deluxe (☎ 06-30 556 2814; V Henszlmann Imre utca 1; Ⓜ M3 Kálvin tér), which sells limited edition designer clothes for men and women and keeps the same hours.

VALERIA FAZEKAS Map p85   Fashion & Clothing
☎ 337 5320; www.valeriafazekas.com; V50 Design Art Studio, V Vári utca 50; ⊗ 10am-6pm Mon-Fri, 10am-4pm Sat; Ⓜ M3 Ferenciek tere

Are they hats or is it art? We'll say both. Some of the limited headgear in a wide range or colours and fabrics on offer in

CLOTHING SIZES

Women's clothing

Aus/UK	8	10	12	14	16	18
Europe	36	38	40	42	44	46
Japan	5	7	9	11	13	15
USA	6	8	10	12	14	16

Women's shoes

Aus/USA	5	6	7	8	9	10
Europe	35	36	37	38	39	40
France only	35	36	38	39	40	42
Japan	22	23	24	25	26	27
UK	3½	4½	5½	6½	7½	8½

Men's clothing

Aus	92	96	100	104	108	112
Europe	46	48	50	52	54	56
Japan	S		M	M		L
UK/USA	35	36	37	38	39	40

Men's shirts (collar sizes)

Aus/Japan	38	39	40	41	42	43
Europe	38	39	40	41	42	43
UK/USA	15	15½	16	16½	17	17½

Men's shoes

Aus/UK	7	8	9	10	11	12
Europe	41	42	43	44½	46	47
Japan	26	27	27½	28	29	30
USA	7½	8½	9½	10½	11½	12½

Measurements approximate only; try before you buy

this small gem of a boutique are out of this world (or at least on their way). Designer/artist Fazekas also does scarves and stylish tops.

VASS Map p85   Fashion & Clothing
☎ 318 2375; www.vass-cipo.hu; V Haris köz 2; ⊗ 10am-6pm Mon-Fri, 10am-2pm Sat; Ⓜ M3 Ferenciek tere

A traditional shoemaker that stocks both ready-to-wear and cobbles to order, Vass has a reputation that goes back to 1896, and some people travel to Hungary just to have their footwear made here.

VOODOO BILLY Map p85   Fashion & Clothing
☎ 266 7414; V Károly körút 10; ⊗ 10am-7pm Mon-Fri, 10am-2pm Sat; Ⓜ M2 Astoria

Rockabilly, psychobilly, Voodoo Billy – looks like the '50s on acid to us. But you'll find some pretty unique clothes and accessories (including jewellery) at this cage-like shop on the Little Ring Road.

ARTEN STÚDIÓ Map p85 — Fine Art

☎ 266 3127; V Váci utca 25; ⏰ 10am-6.30pm Mon-Fri, 10am-6pm Sat; Ⓜ M3 Ferenciek tere

This fine-art gallery is somewhat commercial with lots of bric-a-brac but also shows works by such important contemporary Hungarian artists as Tibor Fazakas and Gábor Krüzsely. Enter from Pesti Barnabás utca.

FOLKART CENTRUM
Map p85 — Folk Art & Souvenirs

☎ 318 4697; V Váci utca 58; ⏰ 10am-7pm; Ⓜ M1/2/3/Deák Ferenc tér, 🚌 15 or 115

Also called 'Népművészet', this is a large shop where everything Magyar – whether made here or in China – is available, from embroidered waistcoats and tablecloths to painted eggs and plates. The staff are helpful and will advise. A similar place but even bigger is the Folkart Kézművészház (Folk Artisan House; Map p85; ☎ 318 5143; V Régi Posta utca 12; ⏰ 10am-7pm; Ⓜ M3 Ferenciek tere) further north on the same street.

HOLLÓ ATELIER Map p85 — Folk Art & Souvenirs

☎ 317 8103; V Vitkovics Mihály utca 12; ⏰ 10am-6pm Mon-Fri, 10am-2pm Sat; Ⓜ M1/2/3 Deák Ferenc tér

Off the northern end of Váci utca, this shop has attractive folk art with a modern look and remains a personal favourite place to shop for gifts and gewgaws.

INTUITA Map p85 — Folk Art & Souvenirs

☎ 266 5864; V Váci utca 67; ⏰ 11am-6pm; 🚌 15 or 115

You're not about to find painted eggs and *pálinka* here, but it's chock-a-block with modern Hungarian crafted items such as hand-blown glass, jewellery, ceramics and bound books.

STREETS AHEAD

Some streets or areas in Budapest specialise in certain goods or products. For example, antique shops line V Falk Miksa utca (Map p85, B1) in Pest and, to a lesser extent, II Frankel Leó út (Map p62, C3) in Buda. Along V Múzeum körút (Map p85, C5) in Pest you'll find a string of antiquarian and secondhand bookshops. Central (and very high-rent) V Váci utca (Map p85, B5) is chock-a-block with both top-end boutiques and tourist schlock both north and south of Szabadsajtó utca.

CADEAU Map p85 — Food & Drink

☎ 317 7127; www.cukraszok.hu, in Hungarian; V Veres Pálné utca 8; ⏰ 10am-6pm Mon-Fri, 10am-2pm Sat; Ⓜ M3 Ferenciek tere

'Death by chocolate' has arrived in Budapest by way of Gyula, a city in Hungary's southeastern corner, where the delectable handmade bonbons are made and served at the celebrated Százéves Cukrászda (Century Cake Shop).

SZÁMOS MARCIPÁN Map p85 — Food & Drink

☎ 317 3643; www.szamosmarcipan.hu; V Párizsi utca 3; ⏰ 10am-7pm; Ⓜ M3 Ferenciek tere

'Many Kinds of Marzipan' sells just that – in every shape and size imaginable. Its ice cream (140Ft per scoop) – among the best in town – is another major draw here.

MAGMA Map p85 — Household Goods

☎ 235 0277; www.magma.hu; V Petőfi Sándor utca 11; ⏰ 10am-5pm Mon-Fri, 10am-3pm Sat; Ⓜ M3 Ferenciek tere

This showroom in the heart of the Inner Town focuses on Hungarian design and designers exclusively – with everything from glassware and porcelain to textiles and furniture.

RÓZSAVÖLGYI ÉS TÁRSA Map p85 — Music

☎ 318 3312; V Szervita tér 5; ⏰ 9.30am-7pm Mon, Tue, Thu & Fri, 10am-7pm Wed, 10am-5pm Sat; Ⓜ M1/2/3 Deák Ferenc tér

This music shop is a good choice for CDs and tapes of traditional folk and classical music. It also has a good selection of sheet music.

BABAKLINIKA Map p85 — Toys

☎ 267 2445; V Múzeum körút 5; ⏰ 10am-5pm Mon-Fri; Ⓜ M2 Astoria

Just down the road from the Astoria metro station, the 'Doll Clinic' specialises in selling (and repairing) handmade dolls and teddy bears.

LIPÓTVÁROS

ANNA ANTIKVITÁS Map p85 — Antiques

☎ 302 5461; V Falk Miksa utca 18-20; ⏰ 10am-6pm Mon-Fri, 10am-1pm Sat; 🚊 4 or 6

Anna is the place to go if you're in the market for embroidered antique tablecloths and bed linen. They're stacked up all over the shop and of very high quality.

BÁV Map p85 Antiques
**Bizományi Kereskedőház és Záloghitel; www.bav
.hu; ☎ 325 2600, 473 0666; XIII Szent István körút 3;
🚋 4 or 6**
This chain of pawn and secondhand
shops, with a number of branches around
town, is always a fun place to comb for
trinkets and treasures, especially if you
don't have time to get to the Ecseri or City
Park flea markets. Check out this branch
for chinaware, textiles and furniture. Other
stores include the Belváros branch (Map p85;
☎ 429 3020; V Bécsi utca 1-3; Ⓜ M1/2/3 Deák Ferenc
tér) for knick-knacks, porcelain, glassware
and artwork and the Buda branch (Map p74;
☎ 315 0417; II Margit körút 4 & II Frankel Leó utca
13; 🚋 4 or 6) for jewellery, lamps and fine
porcelain.

DÁRIUS ANTIQUES Map p85 Antiques
**☎ 311 2603; http://darius.csorge.hu; V Falk Miksa
utca 24-26; 🚋 4 or 6**
This shop, which handles antique furniture,
paintings, glass and porcelain, is among the
best on V Falk Miksa utca and the owner is
particularly knowledgeable and helpful.

PINTÉR ANTIK Map p85 Antiques
**☎ 311 3030, 06-70 553 8267; www.pinterantik
.hu; V Falk Miksa utca 10; Ⓨ 10am-6pm Mon-Fri,
10am-2pm Sat; 🚋 4 or 6**
With a positively enormous antique showroom measuring 1800 sq metres in a series
of cellars near the Parliament building, Pintér
has everything – from furniture and chandeliers to oil paintings and china – and is the
best outfit on Falk Miksa utca for browsing.

SZŐNYI ANTIKVÁRIUMA
Map p85 Antiquarian & Secondhand Books
**☎ 311 6431; www.szonyi.hu; V Szent István körút
3; Ⓨ 10am-6pm Mon-Fri, 9am-1pm Sat; 🚋 4 or 6**
This long-established antiquarian bookshop
has, in addition to old tomes, an excellent
selection of antique prints and maps. Just
open the drawers in the chests at the back
and have a look.

LUSH Map p85 Bath supplies
**☎ 472 0530; www.lush.hu; V Szent István körút
1; Ⓨ 10am-7pm Mon-Wed, 10am-8pm Thu-Fri,
10am-6.30pm Sat, 11am-6.30pm Sun; 🚋 4 or 6**
This offshoot of a British chain has products
derived from essential oils, fruit, vegetables
and even chocolate. Suitable for vegetar-

ians, 100% cruelty-free and ideal for long
soaks in the tub.

BESTSELLERS Map p85 Books
**☎ 312 1295; www.bestsellers.hu; V Október 6
utca 11; Ⓨ 9am-6.30pm Mon-Fri, 10am-5pm Sat,
10am-4pm Sun; Ⓜ M1/2/3/Deák Ferenc tér,
🚌 15 or 115**
Probably the best English-language bookshop in town, with fiction, travel guides
and lots of Hungarica, as well as a large
selection of newspapers and magazines.
Helpful staff are at hand.

**CENTRAL EUROPEAN UNIVERSITY
BOOKSHOP** Map p85 Books
**☎ 327 3096; V Zrínyi utca 12; Ⓨ 10am-7pm
Mon-Fri, 10am-2pm Sat; Ⓜ M1/2/3/Deák Ferenc
tér, 🚌 15 or 115**
The bookshop at Budapest's renowned
Central European University, while moved
to small quarters around the corner, still
has an excellent selection of academic and
business titles with a regional focus.

KATTI ZOÓB Map p85 Fashion & Clothing
**☎ 312 1865; www.kattizoob.hu; V Szent István
körút 17; Ⓨ 10am-6pm Mon-Fri, 10am-1pm Sat;
Ⓜ M3 Nyugati pályaudvar**
Modern art deco–inspired ready-to-wear
and bespoke foundation pieces and accessories from the doyenne of Hungarian
haute couture.

KIESELBACH GALÉRIA Map p85 Fine Art
**☎ 269 3148; www.kieselbach.hu; V Szent István
körút 5; Ⓨ 10am-6pm Mon-Fri, 10am-1pm Sat;
🚋 4 or 6**
This is without a doubt the best source in
the city for Hungarian painting and there
are frequent auctions of both local and
international artworks.

MALATINSZKY WINE STORE
Map p85 Food & Drink
**Malatinszky Kúria; ☎ 317 5919; www.malatinszky
.hu; V József Attila utca 12; Ⓨ 10am-6pm Mon-Fri,
10am-3pm Sat; Ⓜ M1/2/3 Deák Ferenc tér**
Owned and operated by vintner Csaba
Malatinszky, the former sommelier at the
exclusive Gundel restaurant, this shop also
goes by the French name 'La Boutique des
Vins' (The Wine Shop). It has an excellent
selection of high-end Hungarian wines – ask
the staff to recommend a bottle.

top picks

HUNGARICA

- Holló Atelier (p116)
- Herend (p112)
- Mester Pálinkák (below)
- Nagycsarnok (below)
- Intuita (p116)

MESTER PÁLINKÁK Map p85   Food & Drink
☎ 374 0388; www.mesterpalinkak.hu, in Hungarian; V Zrínyi utca 18; ⏰ 10am-6pm Mon-Fri, 10am-2pm Sat; Ⓜ M1/2/3/Deák Ferenc tér, 🚌 15 or 115
If you're into *pálinka*, Hungarian firewater flavoured with everything from apricot and sour cherry to (be still, our collective hearts) raspberry and sloe, choose this new shop that stocks scores of varieties. Service is helpful, advice very sound.

NÁDORTEX Map p85   Household Goods
☎ 317 0030; V József nádor tér 12; ⏰ 9am-5pm Mon-Fri; Ⓜ M1/2/3 Deák Ferenc tér
Goose-feather or down products such as pillows (from 10,800Ft) or duvets (comforters; from 21,600Ft) are of excellent quality in Hungary and a highly recommended purchase. Nádortex, small and monolingual but reliable, has some of the best prices; a pure down 'summer' (ie 500g per sq metre) measuring 200cm x 220cm costs 38,500Ft.

AJKA KRISTÁLY Map p85   Porcelain & Glassware
☎ 317 8133; www.ajka-crystal.hu; V József Attila utca 7; ⏰ 10am-6pm Mon-Fri, 10am-1pm Sat; Ⓜ M1/2/3/Deák Ferenc tér
Established in 1878, Ajka has Hungarian-made lead crystal pieces and stemware. A lot of it is very old-fashioned, but there are some more contemporary pieces worth a second look.

NORTHERN RING ROAD AREA
ÚJLIPÓTVÁROS & TERÉZVÁROS

PENDRAGON Map pp92-3   Books
☎ 340 4426; XIII Pozsonyi út 21-23; ⏰ 10am-6pm Mon-Fri, 10am-2pm Sat; 🚃 4 or 6, trolleybus 75 or 76

This exclusively English-language bookshop, which takes its name from the legend of King Arthur, has an excellent selection of books and guides (including Lonely Planet titles).

WAVE MUSIC Map pp92-3   Music
☎ 331 0718; VI Révay utca 4; ⏰ 11am-7pm Mon-Fri, 11am-3pm Sat; Ⓜ M1 Bajcsy-Zsilinszky út
Wave is another excellent outlet for both Hungarian and international indie guitar music as well as underground dance music.

HAAS & CZJZEK
Map pp92-3   Porcelain & Glassware
☎ 311 4094; www.porcelan.hu; VI Bajcsy-Zsilinszky út 23; ⏰ 10am-7pm Mon-Fri, 10am-3pm Sat; Ⓜ M3 Arany János utca
Just up from Deák Ferenc tér, this chinaware and crystal shop, in situ since 1879, sells Herend and Zsolnay pieces as well as more affordable Hungarian-made Hollóháza and Alföldi porcelain.

WEST END CITY CENTRE
Map pp92-3   Shopping Mall
☎ 238 7777; www.westend.hu; VI Váci út 1-3; ⏰ 8am-11pm; Ⓜ M3 Nyugati pályaudvar
In central Pest, this Goliath of a shopping complex has everything you could possibly want or need, with 400 shops, telecom outlets, casino and poker club, large indoor fountains, ice-skating rink and the 230-room Hilton West End.

MOUNTEX Map pp92-3   Sporting Goods
☎ 239 6050; XIII Váci út 19; ⏰ 10am-7pm Mon-Fri, 10am-2pm Sat; Ⓜ M3 Lehel tér
This huge (though somewhat far-flung) emporium on two levels with branches throughout the city carries all the gear you'll need for camping, hiking, trekking and climbing. In fact, there's a climbing wall (⏰ 8am-10pm Mon-Fri, 10am-8pm Sat & Sun) round the corner should you want to get in a little practice while shopping.

JÁTÉKSZEREK ANNO Map pp92-3   Toys
☎ 302 6234; www.jatekanno.hu; VI Teréz körút 54; ⏰ 10am-6pm Mon-Fri, 9am-1pm Sat; Ⓜ M3 Nyugati pályaudvar
The tiny but exceptional 'Anno Playthings' shop near Nyugati train station sells finely made reproductions of antique wind-up and other old-fashioned toys.

ANDRÁSSY ÚT & SURROUNDS

ALEXANDRA Map pp92-3   Books
☎ 413 6670; www.alexandra.hu, in Hungarian; VI Andrássy út 35; ⏰ 10am-10pm Ⓜ M1 Opera
The schtick at this welcome new addition on Andrássy út is 'books and wine'. The English-language selection of the former is excellent, especially in the art and photo areas while the choice of wine is 100% Hungarian.

ÍRÓK BOLTJA Map pp92-3   Books
Writers' Bookshop; ☎ 322 1645; www.irokboltja .hu, in Hungarian; VI Andrássy út 45; ⏰ 10am-7pm Mon-Fri, 10am-1pm Sat Ⓜ M1 Oktogon, Ⓣ 4 or 6
For Hungarian authors in translation, including many of those mentioned on p40, this is the place to go.

TREEHUGGER DAN'S BOOKSTORE
Map pp92-3   Books
☎ 322 0774; www.treehugger.hu; VI Csengery utca 48; ⏰ 10am-7pm Mon-Fri, 10am-5pm Sat; Ⓜ M1 Oktogon
This new kid on the block has thousands of secondhand English-language books, does trade-ins and serves organic fair-trade coffee. There's also a branch at Discover Budapest (Map pp92–3; ☎ 269 3843; VI Lázár utca 16; ⏰ 9.30am-6.30pm Mon-Fri, 10am-4pm Sat & Sun; Ⓜ M1 Opera).

LISZT FERENC ZENEMŰBOLT
Map pp92-3   Music
☎ 322 4091; VI Andrássy út 45; ⏰ 10am-7pm Mon-Fri, 10am-1pm Sat Ⓜ M1 Oktogon
Next to the Writers' Bookshop, the 'Ferenc Liszt Music Shop' has mostly classical CDs and vinyl as well as sheet music and books of local interest.

top picks

BOOKSHOPS

- Bestsellers (p117)
- Szőnyi Antikváriuma (p117)
- Treehugger Dan's Bookstore (pabove)
- Alexandra (pabove)
- Írók Boltja (above)

ERZSÉBETVÁROS

LIBRI KÖNYVPALOTA Map pp92-3   Books
☎ 267 4844; VII Rákóczi út 12; ⏰ 10am-7.30pm Mon-Fri, 10am-3pm Sat; Ⓜ M2 Astoria
Spread over two floors, the huge 'Book Palace' has a selection of English-language novels, art books, guidebooks, maps, music, and a cafe on the 1st floor. For books in English and other languages specifically on Hungarian subjects, a more useful branch is Libri Stúdium (Map p85; ☎ 318 5680; V Váci utca 22; ⏰ 10am-7pm Mon-Fri, 10am-3pm Sat & Sun; Ⓜ M3 Ferenciek tere).

JAJCICA Map pp92-3   Fashion & Clothing
☎ 321 2081; www.jajcica.hu; VII Dohány utca 94; ⏰ 10am-7pm Mon-Fri, 10am-2pm Sat; trolleybus 74
Whatever your 'drag' of choice happens to be – 1960s camp to leather or military – the folks at this anti-fashion emporium of used and vintage clothes will have you kitted out before you can say 'Trick or Treat'. Their strong point is 1970s retro.

TISZA CIPŐ
Map pp92-3   Fashion & Clothing
☎ 266 3055;; VII Károly körút 1; ⏰ 10am-7pm Mon-Fri, 9am-1pm Sat; Ⓜ M2 Astoria
'What goes around comes around', the old saying tells us and that's certainly true of 'Tisza Shoes' which has metamorphosed as a communist-era producer of forgettable footwear ('since 1971') to uber-trendy trainer manufacturer.

BILLERBECK Map pp92-3   Household Goods
☎ 322 3606; www.billerbeck.hu; VII Dob utca 49; ⏰ 10am-6pm Mon-Fri, 9.30am-1pm Sat; Ⓣ 4 or 6
With several branches around town, Billerbeck has a large selection of feather- and goose-down duvets and other bedding sold by helpful staff. Enter from Akácfa utca. There's also a Király utca branch (Map pp92–3; ☎ 352 0420; VII Király utca 3; Ⓣ 47 or 49), which keeps the same hours.

CONCERTO HANGLEMEZBOLT
Map pp92-3   Music
☎ 268 9631; VII Dob utca 33; ⏰ noon-7pm Mon-Fri; Ⓜ M2 Astoria
For classical CDs and vinyl, try the wonderful 'Concerto Record Shop', which is always full of hard-to-find treasures.

WORTH THE TRIP

Ecseri Piac

Often just called the *piac* (market), this is one of the biggest flea markets (Map pp58–9; ☎ 282 9563; XIX Nagykőrösi út 156; ☺ 8am-4pm Mon-Fri, 6am-3pm Sat, 8am-1pm Sun) in central Europe, selling everything from antique jewellery and Soviet army watches to Fred Astaire–style top hats. Saturday is said to be the best day to go; dealers get there early to search for those proverbial diamonds amidst the rust. Take bus 54 from Boráros tér in Pest or, for a quicker journey, the red-numbered express bus 84E, 89E or 94E from the Határ utca stop on the M3 metro line farther afield in Pest and get off at the Fiume utca stop. Follow the crowds over the pedestrian bridge.

SOUTHERN RING ROAD AREA

IGUANA Map pp102–3 Fashion & Clothing
☎ 317 1627; VIII Krúdy utca 9; ☺ 10am-7pm Mon-Fri, 10am-2pm Sat; ⓡ 4 or 6
Iguana sells vintage leather, suede and velvet pieces from the 1950s, '60s and '70s, plus its own trousers, skirts and shirts. There's also a Ferencváros branch (Map pp102–3; ☎ 215 3475; IX Tompa utca 1 Ⓜ M3 Ferenc körút), which keeps the same hours.

CHINESE MARKET Map pp102-3 Flea Market
VIII Kőbányai út 21-23; ☺ 6am-6pm; ⓡ 28
The popular name for what is actually called Józsefvárosi Piac (Józsefváros Market), this is the place to come if you don't feel like doing the laundry and want to replace the wardrobe cheaply. It's chock-a-block with clothing made in China and Vietnam at ultra-bargain prices (not to mention cosmetics, cigarettes and liquor of dubious provenance). There are some decent (read authentic) Asian food stalls here too, especially the noodle ones.

NAGYCSARNOK Map pp102-3 Folk Art & Souvenirs; Food & Drink
IX Vámház körút 1-3; ☺ 6am-5pm Mon, 6am-6pm Tue-Fri, 6am-2pm Sat; ⓡ 47 or 49

top picks

FASHIONISTA SHOPS

- Valeria Fazekas (p115)
- Retrock (pp115)
- Vass (pp115)
- Tisza Cipő (p119)
- Katti Zoób (pp117)

The 'Great Market' is Budapest's biggest food market but, because it has been attracting tourists ever since it was renovated for the millecentenary in 1996, it now has dozens of stalls on the 1st floor selling Hungarian folk costumes, dolls, painted eggs, embroidered tablecloths, carved hunting knives and so on. At the same time, gourmets will appreciate the Hungarian and other treats available on the ground floor at a fraction of what they would cost in the shops on nearby Váci utca – shrink-wrapped and potted foie gras and goose-liver pâté (2600/4900Ft for 100/200g), a good selection of dried mushrooms, garlands of dried paprika (600Ft to 800Ft), souvenir sacks and tins of paprika powder (290Ft to 650Ft), and as many kinds of honey (850Ft to 1250Ft) and types of wine as you'd care to name.

MAGYAR PÁLINKA HÁZ A
Map pp102-3 Food & Drink
Hungarian Pálinka House; ☎ 338 4219; www.magyarpalinkahaza.hu; VIII Rákóczi út 17; ☺ 9am-7pm Mon-Sat; Ⓜ M2 Astoria
This large shop a short distance from Astoria stocks hundreds of varieties of *pálinka*, a kind of eau de vie flavoured with a number of varied fruits and berries.

CITY PARK & BEYOND

CITY PARK FLEA MARKET
Map p108 Flea Market
Városligeti Bolhapiac; ☎ 363 3730, 251 7266; www.bolhapiac.com; XIV Zichy Mihály út; ☺ 7am-2pm Sat & Sun; ⓡ 1, trolleybus 72 or 74
This is a huge outdoor flea market – a kind of Hungarian boot or garage sale – held next to the Petőfi Csarnok (p157) in City Park. The usual stuff is on offer – from old records and draperies to candles, honey and herbs. Sunday is the better day.

EATING

top picks

EATING

Much has been written about Hungarian food over the years – some of it true, an equal part downright false. It certainly is the bright point among the cuisines of Eastern Europe, but it is decidedly not one of the world's three essential styles of cooking (after French and Chinese) that many here would have you believe. Hungarian cooking has had many outside influences but has changed relatively little over the centuries. And while the cuisine makes great use of paprika, even the spice's hottest variety (called *csípős*) is pretty tame stuff; a taco with salsa or chicken vindaloo will taste a lot more 'fiery' to you.

In spite of all this, Budapest has been currently undergoing something of a restaurant revolution in recent years. Stodgy and heavy main dishes are being 'enlightened', brought up to date and rechristened as *kortárs magyar konyha* (modern Hungarian cuisine) at many midrange and upmarket restaurants. Just as important, a number of vegetarian (or partially meatless) restaurants have opened up and more 'regular' restaurants have a greater selection of 'real' vegetarian dishes – not just fried cheese and stuffed mushroom caps. And ethnic food – from Middle Eastern and Greek to Indian and Chinese – has become very popular. It all makes a very nice change from the not-too-distant days when munching on a cheeseburger at McDonald's was an attractive alternative to tussling with an overcooked Wiener schnitzel (*bécsiszelet*) in yet another smoky *vendéglő* (small restaurant).

You'll find branches of all the international fast-food places in Budapest; Oktogon is full of them. But when looking for something cheap and cheerful, try an old-style *önkiszolgáló* (self-service restaurant), the mainstay of workers in the old regime and fast disappearing.

Even more interesting places for local colour and better value in the long run are the wonderful little restaurants called *étkezdék,* canteens not unlike British 'cafs' that serve simple but very tasty Hungarian dishes that change daily.

Traditional coffee houses and newly popular teahouses are primarily known for hot drinks, but they also serve cakes and other sweets, and sometimes light meals as well. These are listed in the Drinking chapter (p144).

HISTORY

Budapest's reputation as a food capital dates largely from the late 19th and the first half of the 20th centuries. During the heady period following the promulgation of the Dual Monarchy in 1867 and right up until WWII, food became a passion among well-to-do Budapesters, and writers and poets were generous in their praise of it. This was the 'gilded age' of the famous chef Károly Gundel and the confectioner József Dobos, and of Gypsy violinists such as Jancsi Rigo and Gyula Benczi, when nothing was too extravagant. The world took note and Hungarian restaurants sprouted up in cities across the world – including a 'Café Budapest' in Boston, Massachusetts – complete with imported Gypsy bands and waiters who sounded like Béla Lugosi.

Budapest's gastronomic reputation lived on during the chilly days of Communism, most notably because the food was so bad everywhere else in the region. Indeed, Hungarian cuisine was, as one observer noted, 'a bright spot in a culinary black hole'. But most of the best chefs, including Gundel himself, had voted with their feet and left the country in the 1950s, when restaurants were put under state control. The reputation and the reality of food in Budapest had diverged.

Although still relatively inexpensive by European standards, and served in huge portions, Hungarian food today remains heavy and, at times, it can be unhealthy. Meat, sour cream and animal fat abound and, except in season, *saláta* (salad) means a plate of pickled vegetables. Things are changing in the Hungarian capital, however, with more and more vegetarian and ethnic choices available.

STAPLES & SPECIALITIES
Bread & Noodles

It is said that people here will 'eat bread with bread', and leftover bread (*kenyér*) has been used to thicken soups and stews since at least the reign of the 15th-century medieval king Matthias, while *kifli* (crescent-shaped rolls) gained popularity during the Turkish occupation. But, frankly, bread available commercially in Budapest is not as memorable as the flour-based *galuska* (dumplings) and *tarhonya* (barley-shaped egg pasta) served with *pörkölt*, *paprikás* and *tokány* (see below).

Soups

Most Hungarian meals start with *leves* (soup). This is usually something relatively light like *gombaleves* (mushroom soup) or *húsgombócleves* (tiny liver dumplings in broth). More substantial soups are beef *gulyásleves* (see below) and *bableves*, a thick bean soup usually made with meat, which are sometimes eaten as a main course. Another favourite is *halászlé* (fisherman's soup), a rich soup of poached carp, fish stock, tomatoes, green peppers and paprika.

Meat & Fish

People here eat an astonishing amount of meat, and 'meat-stuffed meat' is a dish not unknown on Budapest menus. Pork, beef, veal and poultry are the meats most commonly consumed and they can be breaded and fried, baked, turned into some paprika-flavoured concoction or simmered in *lecsó*, a tasty mix of peppers, tomatoes and onions (and one of the few Hungarian sauces here that does not include paprika).

A typical menu will have up to 10 pork and beef dishes, a couple of fish ones and usually only one poultry dish. Goose legs and livers and turkey breasts – though not much else of either bird – make an appearance on most menus. Lamb and mutton are rarely eaten here.

Freshwater fish, such as the indigenous *fogas* (great pike-perch) and the smaller *süllő* from Lake Balaton, and *ponty* (carp) from rivers and streams, is plentiful but often overcooked.

Paprika

Many dishes are seasoned with paprika, a spice as Magyar as St Stephen's right hand (p84). Indeed, not only is this 'red gold' used in cooking but it also appears on restaurant tables as a condiment beside the salt and pepper shakers. It's generally quite a mild spice and used predominantly with sour cream or in *rántás*, a heavy roux of pork fat and flour added to cooked vegetables. *Töltött*, things stuffed with meat and/or rice, such as cabbage or peppers, are cooked in *rántás* as well as in tomato sauce or sour cream.

There are four major types of meat dishes containing paprika. The most famous is *gulyás* (or *gulyásleves*), a thick beef soup cooked with onions, cubed potatoes and paprika, and usually eaten as a main course. *Pörkölt*, or 'stew', is closer to what foreigners call 'goulash'; the addition of sour cream, a reduction in paprika and the use of white meat such as chicken makes the dish *paprikás*. *Tokány* is similar to *pörkölt* and *paprikás* except that the meat is cut into strips, black pepper is on equal footing with the paprika, and bacon, sausage or mushrooms are added as flavouring agents.

Vegetables

Fresh salad is often called *vitamin saláta* here and is generally available when lettuce is in season; almost everything else is *savanyúság* (literally 'sourness'), which can be anything from mildly sour-sweet cucumbers, pickled peppers and very acidic-tasting sauerkraut. It may seem an acquired taste, but such things actually go very well with heavy meat dishes.

Boiled or steamed *zöldség* (vegetables), when they are available, are 'English-style' (*angolos zöldség*). The traditional way of preparing vegetables is in *főzelék*, where peas, green beans, lentils, marrow or cabbage are fried or boiled and then mixed into a roux with milk. This dish, which is sometimes topped with a few slices of meat, is enjoying a major comeback at 'retro-style' eateries.

Desserts

People here love sweets. Complicated pastries such as *Dobos torta*, a layered chocolate and cream cake with a caramelised brown sugar top, and the wonderful *rétes* (strudel), filled with poppy seeds, cherry preserves or *túró* (curd or cottage cheese), and *piték* (fruit pies) are usually consumed mid-afternoon in one of Budapest's ubiquitous *cukrászdák* (cake shops or pâtisseries). Desserts more commonly found on restaurant menus include *Somlói galuska*, sponge cake with chocolate and whipped cream, and *Gundel palacsinta* (flambéed pancake with chocolate and nuts).

CELEBRATING WITH FOOD

Traditional culture, particularly where it involves food, is not exactly thriving in Hungary, though a popular event for Budapesters with ties (however tenuous) to the countryside is the *disznótor*, the slaughtering

A MAGYAR MATCH MADE IN HEAVEN

The pairing of food with wine is as great an obsession in Budapest as it is in Paris. Everyone agrees that sweets like strudel go very well indeed with a glass of Tokaji Aszú, but what is less appreciated is the wonderful synergy that this wine enjoys with savoury foods like foie gras and cheeses such as Roquefort, Stilton and gorgonzola. A bone-dry Olaszrizling from Badacsony is a superb complement to any fish dish, but especially *fogas* (pike-perch indigenous to Lake Balaton). Dry Furmint goes well with *harcsa* (catfish). Villány sauvignon blanc is excellent with creamy and salty goat's cheese.

It would be a shame to 'waste' a big wine like a Vili Papa Cuvée on traditional but simple Hungarian dishes like *gulyás* or *pörkölt;* save it for a more meaty dish and try Kékfrankos or Szekszárd Kadarka with these simpler dishes. Cream-based dishes stand up well to late-harvest Furmint, and pork dishes are nice with new Furmint or any type of red, especially Kékfrankos. Try Hárslevelű with poultry.

of a pig – a butcher does it – followed by an orgy of feasting and drinking. The celebration can even boast its own dish: *disznótoros káposzta,* which is stuffed cabbage served with freshly made sausages. Wine festivals, now mostly commercial events with rock bands and the like, occur during the harvest in September and October, and are always a good excuse for getting sloshed. The most important one is the Budapest International Wine Festival (www.winefestival.hu) held in the Castle District in September.

ETIQUETTE

By and large people in Budapest tend to meet their friends and entertain outside of their homes at cafes and restaurants. If you are invited to a local person's home, bring a bunch of flowers or a bottle of good local wine (see p144).

Drinking is an important part of social life in the capital of a country that has produced wine and fruit brandies for thousands of years. Consumption is high at an annual 13.6L of alcohol per person; only citizens of Luxembourg and Ireland drink more alcohol per capita in Europe. Alcoholism in Hungary is not as visible to the outsider as it is, say, in Poland or Russia, but it's there nonetheless; official figures suggest that a full 10% of the population are fully fledged alcoholics. There is little pressure for others (particularly women) to drink, however, so if you really don't want that glass of apricot brandy that your host has handed you, refuse politely.

It is said that Hungarians don't clink glasses when drinking beer because that's how the Habsburgs celebrated the defeat of Lajos Kossuth in the 1848–49 War of Independence (see p28), but most Magyars say that's codswallop.

WHEN & WHERE TO EAT

Hungarians are not for the most part big eaters of *reggeli* (breakfast), preferring a cup of tea or coffee with an unadorned bread roll at the kitchen table or on the way to work. As it is a meal at which most Magyars hardly excel, expect the worst of hotel breakfasts – ersatz coffee, weak tea, unsweetened lemon water for 'juice', tiny triangles of processed 'cheese' and stale bread. You may be pleasantly surprised, though.

Ebéd (lunch), eaten at around 1pm, was once the main meal of the day and might still consist of two or even three courses. *Vacsora* (dinner or supper) is less substantial when eaten at home, often just sliced meats, cheese and some pickled vegetables.

It's important to know the different styles of eateries to be found in Budapest. An *étterem* is a restaurant with a wide-ranging menu, sometimes including international dishes. A *vendéglő* or *kisvendéglő* is smaller and is supposed to serve inexpensive regional dishes or 'home cooking', but the name has become 'cute' enough for a lot of places to use it indiscriminately. An *étkezde* or *kifőzde* is something like a diner, smaller and cheaper than a *vendéglő* and often with counter seating. The term *csárda* originally referred to a country inn with a rustic atmosphere, Gypsy music and hearty local dishes. Now any place that hangs up a couple of painted plates and strings a few strands of dry paprika on the wall is a *csárda*.

A *bisztró* is a much cheaper sit-down place that is often *önkiszolgáló* (self-service). A *büfé* is cheaper still with a very limited menu, where you eat while standing at counters. A *presszó* is a very simple establishment (sometimes just a kiosk) selling coffee, alcohol and a few basic snacks.

A *hentesáru bolt* (butcher shop) in Budapest sometimes has a *büfé* selling cooked *kolbász* (sausage), *virsli* (frankfurters), *hurka* (blood sausage or liverwurst), roast chicken, bread and pickled vegetables. Point to what you want; the staff will weigh it all and hand you a slip of paper with the price. You usually pay at the *pénztár* (cashier) and hand the stamped receipt back to the staff for your food. You pay for everything here, including a slice of rye bread and a dollop of mustard for your sausage.

A food stall, known as a *Laci konyha* (literally, 'Laci's kitchen') or *pecsenyesütő* (roast oven), can often be found near markets or train stations. One of the more popular traditional snacks is *lángos*, deep-fried dough with various toppings (usually cheese and sour cream).

VEGETARIANS & VEGANS
Such a carnivorous place has always been suspicious of nonmeat-eaters but things are changing. If you can't find a vegetarian restaurant in the neighbourhood, you'll have to make do with what's on the regular menu or shop for ingredients in the markets. The selection of fresh vegetables and fruit is not great in the dead of winter, but come spring and a cycle of bounty begins: from strawberries and raspberries and cherries through all the stone fruits to apples and pears and nuts. Large supermarket chains such as Kaiser's, Match and Rothschild usually sell takeaway salads in plastic containers.

In restaurants, vegetarians can usually order *gombafejek rántva* (fried mushroom caps), pasta and noodle dishes with cheese, such as *túrós csusza* and *sztrapacska*, and any number of types of *főzelék*, Hungary's unique 'twice-cooked' vegetable dishes.

Other vegetarian dishes include *gombaleves* (mushroom soup), *gyümölcsleves* (fruit soup) in season, *rántott sajt* (fried cheese) and *sajtos kenyér* (sliced bread with soft cheese). *Bableves* (bean soup) usually – but not always – contains meat. *Palacsinta* (pancakes) may be savoury and made with *sajt* (cheese) or *gomba* (mushrooms), or sweet and prepared with *dió* (nuts) or *mák* (poppy seeds).

COOKING COURSES
For the capital of a country laying claims to such a sophisticated cuisine, cooking courses are pretty thin on the ground. The best-known cookery school dealing with foreigners is Chefparade (Map pp102–3; ☎ 210 6042; www.chefparade.hu;

IX Páva utca 13; Ⓜ M3 Ferenc körút) in Ferencváros. Course dates vary – consult the website – but they usually run from 10am to 1pm, including visiting a market and preparing a four-course lunch, and cost €50 per person. Courses at other times and of a longer duration can be organised in advance.

PRACTICALITIES
Opening Hours
Most restaurants are open from 10am or 11am to 11pm or midnight; if there are no times listed under a particular entry in this chapter, you can assume the place will be open between those hours. It's always best to arrive by 9pm or 10pm (at the latest), though, to ensure being served.

How Much?
Very roughly, a two-course sit-down meal for one person with a drink for under 3000Ft in Budapest is 'budget' (though you can eat 'cheaply' for less than that). A 'moderate' meal will cost up to 6500Ft. There's a big jump to an 'expensive' meal (6500Ft to 10,000Ft), and 'very expensive' is anything above that. Most restaurants offer an excellent-value *menü* (set menu) of two or three courses at lunch.

Booking Tables
It is advisable to book tables at medium-priced to expensive restaurants any time but especially at the weekend.

Tipping
The way you tip in restaurants here is unusual. You never leave the money on the table – that is considered both stupid and rude – but tell the waiter how much you're paying in total. If the bill is, say, 2700Ft, you're paying with a 5000Ft note and you think the waiter deserves a gratuity of around 10%, first ask if service

is included (some Budapest restaurants now add it to the bill automatically, which makes tipping unnecessary). If it isn't, tell the waiter you're paying 3000Ft or that you want 2000Ft back.

It is not unknown for waiters to try to rip you off once they see you are a foreigner. They may try to bring you an unordered dish or make a 'mistake' when tallying the bill. If you think there's a discrepancy, ask for the menu and check the bill carefully. If you've been taken for more than 15% or 20% of the bill, call for the manager. Otherwise, just don't leave a tip.

Self-Catering

Budapest counts some 20 large food markets, most of them in Pest. The vast majority are closed on Sunday, and Monday is always very quiet and only some stalls will be staffed. Supermarkets and 24-hour shops called 'non-stops' that sell everything from cheese and cold cuts to cigarettes and beer abound on both sides of the Danube. Fresh food is generally sold by weight or by piece (*darab*). When ordering by weight, you specify by kilos or *deka* (decagrams – 50dg is equal to 500g or 0.5kg, or a little more than 1lb).

BUDA
One of the largest and most central food markets in Buda is the **Fény utca market** (Map p62; II Fény utca; ☽ 6am-6pm Mon-Fri, to 2pm Sat; Ⓜ M2 Moszkva tér) next to the Mammut shopping mall (p113).

A conveniently located nonstop in Buda is the **Nonstop Büfé** (Map p62; I Attila utca 57; ☽ 24hr; ⓺ 5), which also serves prepared foods for takeaway round the clock.

Artigiana Gelati (Map p62; ☎ 212 2439; XII Csaba utca 8; per scoop 220Ft; ☽ 10.30am-7.30pm Tue-Sun; Ⓜ M2 Moszkva tér), we're told by readers, sells the best shop-made ice cream and sorbet in Buda, and with flavours like fig, pomegranate and gorgonzola-walnut, they're also the most unusual.

PEST
Two of the most central (though not necessarily the most colourful) markets are **Rákóczi tér market** (Map pp102–3; VIII Rákóczi tér 8; ☽ 6am-4pm Mon, to 6pm Tue-Fri, to 1pm Sat; ⓺ 4 or 6) and, near V Szabadság tér, the smaller **Hold utca market** (Map p85; V Hold utca 11; ☽ 6am-5pm Mon, 6.30am-6pm Tue-Fri, 6.30am-2pm Sat; Ⓜ M3 Arany János utca).

One of Pest's more interesting traditional markets, **Lehel Csarnok** (Map pp92–3; XIII Lehel tér;

☽ 6am-6pm Mon-Fri, to 2pm Sat, to 1pm Sun; Ⓜ M3 Lehel tér) is housed in a hideous boat-like structure designed by László Rajk, son of the Communist minister of the interior executed for 'Titoism' in 1949. Apparently this is his revenge.

Nagycsarnok (Great Market; Map p102–3; IX Vámház körút 1-3; ☽ 6am-5pm Mon, to 6pm Tue-Fri, to 2pm Sat; ⓺ 47 or 49) is Budapest's biggest market, though it has become a bit of a tourist trap since it was renovated for the millecentenary celebrations in 1996. Still, plenty of locals head here for fruit and vegetables, deli items, fish and meat. For details see p120.

Large supermarkets are everywhere in central Pest, including **Match** (Map pp92–3; VIII Rákóczi út 50; ☽ 6am-9pm Mon-Fri, 7am-8pm Sat, 7am-3pm Sun; Ⓜ M3 Blaha Lujza tér) facing Blaha Lujza tér, with an **Opera branch** (Map pp92–3; VI Andrássy út 30; ☽ 7am-9pm Mon-Fri, to 6pm Sat, 8am-1pm Sun; Ⓜ M1 Opera) at the corner with VI Nagymező utca; **Kaiser's** (Map pp92–3; VI Nyugati tér 1-2; ☽ 7am-8pm Mon-Fri, to 4pm Sat, 8am-1pm Sun; Ⓜ M3 Nyugati pályaudvar), opposite Nyugati train station; and **Rothschild** (Map pp92–3; VI Teréz körút 19; ☽ 24hr; ⓺ 4 or 6), open round-the-clock near Oktogon and with an **Újlipótváros branch** (Map pp92–3; XIII Szent István körút 4; ☽ 6am-10pm Mon-Fri, 8am-8pm Sat, 9am-7pm Sun; ⓺ 4 or 6) carrying a good supply of kosher products. An even bigger choice is available at **Rothschild Kóser Bolt** (Rothschild Kosher Store; Map pp92–3; Dob utca 12; ☽ 9am-6pm Mon-Thu, to 2pm Fri; ⓺ 47 or 49).

There are convenience stores open very late or even 24 hours throughout Pest, including the **CBA** (Map pp102–3; VIII Baross tér 3; ☽ 6am-midnight Mon-Fri, 7am-midnight Sat & Sun; Ⓜ M2 Keleti pályaudvar) opposite Keleti train station; and the **Mini Coop** (Map pp92–3; VI Nagymező utca 50; ☽ 6am-10pm Mon-Thu, to 11pm Fri & Sat, 7am-10pm Sun; Ⓜ M1 Opera).

T Nagy Tamás (Big Tom; Map p85; ☎ 317 4268; V Gerlóczy utca 3; ☽ 9am-6pm Mon-Fri, 9am-1pm Sat; Ⓜ M1/2/3 Deák Ferenc tér), Budapest's best cheese shop, stocks more than 200 varieties of Hungarian and imported cheeses. In summer ask for the *kecskesajt* (goat's cheese).

Mézes Kuckó (Honey Nook; Map pp92–3; XIII Jászai Mari tér 4; ☽ 10am-6pm Mon-Fri year-round, 9am-1pm Sat Oct-May; ⓺ 4 or 6) is the place to go if you've got the urge for something sweet; its nut-and-honey cookies (200Ft per 10dg) are to die for. A colourfully decorated *mézeskalács* (honey cake; 400Ft to 750Ft) in the shape of a heart makes a lovely gift.

CASTLE HILL & VÍZIVÁROS

The Castle District is a picturesque and romantic neighbourhood in which to break bread, but most of the restaurants up here are overrated and overpriced. A better idea is to take the Sikló (funicular; see p61) down to Víziváros and choose from the embarrassment of recommended eateries on or just off I Fő utca.

CASTLE HILL

CAFÉ PIERROT
Map p62   Hungarian, International €€€
☎ 375 6971; I Fortuna utca 14; starters 2790-4190Ft, mains 4190-5790Ft; ☒ 11am-midnight; 🚌 16, 16/a or 116
This very stylish and long-established cafe-cum-bar-cum-restaurant is one of the very few places to be recommended on Castle Hill. The decor is, well – what else? – clownish and there's live piano music nightly. The food is Hungo-hybrid and quite good, the staff are exceptionally friendly and the clientele overwhelmingly appreciative Japanese.

RIVALDA
Map p62   International €€€
☎ 489 0236; I Színház utca 5-9; starters 2200-2950Ft, mains 3100-5600Ft; ☒ 11.30am-11.30pm; 🚌 16, 16/a or 116
An international cafe-restaurant in a former convent next to the National Dance Theatre with international favourites, Rivalda has a thespian theme, delightful garden courtyard and excellent service. This is the second of very few places we'd choose to visit in the generally touristy and expensive Castle District. The menu changes frequently and the wine list is among the best.

VÖRÖS ÖRDÖG
(Map p62)   Hungarian €€
%214 3798; I Országház utca 20; starters 1200-2800Ft, mains 2700-3400Ft; h11am-10pm; g16 or 116)
The 'Red Devil' is a relatively inexpensive eatery on Castle Hill with a cellar, a delightful courtyard and traditional Hungarian dishes like pörkölt (what you would call goulash).

FORTUNA ÖNKISZOLGÁLÓ
Map p62   Hungarian, Self-Service €
Fortune Self-Service Restaurant; ☎ 375 6071; I Fortuna utca 4; soups 300-450Ft, mains 700-950Ft; ☒ 11.30am-2.30pm Mon-Fri; 🚌 16, 16/a or 116

You'll find cheap and quick weekday lunches in a place you'd least expect it – the Castle District – at this very basic but clean and cheerful self-service restaurant. Reach it via the stairs on the left side as you enter the Fortuna Passage.

VÍZIVÁROS

KACSA
Map p62   Hungarian €€
☎ 201 9992; II Fő utca 75; starters 2500-4900Ft, mains 3800-5000Ft; ☒ noon-1am; 🚌 86
The 'Duck' is the place to go, well, 'quackers', though you need not restrict yourself to the eight dishes with a bill (4400Ft to 5100Ft). It's a fairly elegant place dating back 100 years, with art on the walls and piano and violin music in the evening, so dress appropriately. Fresh ingredients but somewhat stuffy service and pricey wines.

LE JARDIN DE PARIS
Map p62   French €€
☎ 201 0047; II Fő utca 20; starters 1900-3500Ft, mains 2200-4700Ft; ☒ noon-midnight; 🚌 86
A regular haunt of staff from the French Institute across the road (who should know their cuisine française), the 'Parisian Garden' is housed in a wonderful old townhouse with interesting reliefs on the facade and abutting an ancient castle wall. The back garden is a delight in the warmer months. Set lunch is a snip at 1500Ft for two courses.

CSALOGÁNY 26
Map p62   International €€
☎ 201 7892; I Csalogány utca 26; starters 1200-1800Ft, mains 2800-4000Ft; ☒ noon-3pm & 7pm-midnight Tue-Sat; Ⓜ M2 Batthyány tér
Judged by Hungary's most respected food guide to be the best restaurant in Budapest (the chef hails from Lou Lou, p133), this new institution with the unimaginative name and decor turns its imagination to its superb food. Try the tenderloin of mangalica (a kind of pork) with Puy lentils (2800Ft) or the Australian lamb shoulder with polenta (4000Ft). A two-/three-course set lunch is a budget-extolling 1200/1400Ft.

SEOUL HOUSE
Map p62   Korean €€
☎ 201 9607; I Fő utca 8; soups 500-1400Ft, mains 2300-4800Ft; ☒ noon-3pm & 6-11pm Mon-Sat; 🚌 86
This place serves pretty excellent Korean food, from barbecue grills (2900Ft to 4800Ft) to kimchi (pickled spicy cabbage) dishes. Not the most atmospheric place in

town and service is Pyongyang grim but, well, that makes it all very authentic.

PATER MARCUS Map p62 — Belgian €€

☎ 212 1612; I Apor Péter utca 1; starters 790-1890Ft, mains 1190-2490Ft; ☯ noon-midnight; 🚍 86

Located 50m from Chain Bridge, this basement pub-restaurant done up like a monastery is short on monks but heavy on mussels and fries. Try one of the nine flavoured Belgian beers on offer; there's another 100 brews available by the bottle. The two-course set lunch (2100Ft) is good value.

SZENT JUPÁT Map p62 — Hungarian, Late Night €€

☎ 212 2923; II Dékán utca 3; soups 390-660Ft, mains 1490-3380Ft; ☯ noon-2am Sun-Thu, to 4am Fri & Sat; Ⓜ M2 Moszkva tér

This is the classic late-night choice for solid Hungarian fare – consider splitting a dish with a friend – though there's half a dozen vegetarian choices as well. It's just north of Moszkva tér and opposite the Fény utca market – enter from II Retek utca 16 – so within easy striking distance of both Buda and Pest.

MONGOLIAN BARBECUE Map p62 — Asian €€

☎ 212 1859; XII Márvány utca 19/a; buffet before/after 5pm & weekends 2990/4990Ft; ☯ noon-5pm & 6pm-midnight; 🚍 105, 🚋 61

Just south of Moszkva tér, this is one of those all-you-can-eat pseudo-Asian places where you choose the raw ingredients and legions of cooks stir-fry it for you. The difference here is that as much beer, wine and sangria you can sink is included in the price. During summer there's also seating in an attractive, tree-filled courtyard.

ÚJ LANZHOU Map p62 — Chinese €

☎ 201 9247; II Fő utca 71; rice & noodle dishes 1290-1690Ft, mains 1190-3290Ft; ☯ noon-11pm; 🚍 86

A lot of people say this is the most authentic Chinese restaurant in Budapest. We're still out to lunch on the matter, frankly, but we like the hot and sour soup (320Ft), the relatively large choice of vegetarian dishes and stylish surrounds.

TOLDI KONYHÁJA
Map p62 — Hungarian, Étkezde €

☎ 214 3867; I Batthyány utca 14; starters 250-590Ft, mains 920-1590Ft; ☯ 11am-4pm Mon-Fri; 🚍 39

This little eatery just west of Fő utca is the place to come if you're in search of Hungarian comfort food at lunchtime on weekdays. Unusually for this kind of place, 'Toldi's Kitchen' has on offer about a half-dozen *real* vegetarian dishes (890Ft to 1130Ft) to choose from.

MARXIM Map p62 — Italian €

☎ 316 0231; II Kis Rókus utca 23; pizza 750-1390Ft, pasta 790-990Ft; ☯ noon-1am Mon-Thu, to 2am Fri & Sat, 6pm-1am Sun; Ⓜ M2 Moszkva tér

A short walk – naturally – from Moscow Sq, this odd place is a hang-out for teens who have added a layer of their own graffiti to the Communist memorabilia and kitsch, a joke that is now two decades old and kinda not funny. OK, we all know Stalin *szuksz*, but it's still a curiosity for those who appreciate the Kremlin, ÁVO, Yuri Gagarin, Red October pizzas and the campy Stalinist decor. It also serves not-often-seen *lepények* (pies stuffed with meat or cheese; 650Ft to 920Ft).

ÉDEN Map p62 — Vegetarian €

☎ 06-20 337 7575; I Iskola utca 31; soups 450-550Ft, mains 790-990Ft; ☯ 8am-9pm Mon-Thu, to 6pm Fri, 11am-9pm Sun; 🚍 86

Now in a new location in an early-19th-century townhouse just below Castle Hill, this self-service place offers stodgy but healthy vegetarian platters and ragouts (no fat, preservatives, MSG, white sugar etc). Seating is in the main dining room on the ground floor or, in warmer months, in the atrium courtyard. The small Éden Veggie Express (☎ 06-20 775 1167; V Kristóf tér 2; dishes 590-950Ft; ☯ 11.30am-8pm Mon-Thu, to 6pm Fri; Ⓜ M1 Vörösmarty tér) is just south of Vörösmarty tér in Pest.

NAGYI PALACSINTÁZÓJA
Map p62 — Hungarian, Late Night €

Granny's Palacsinta Place; ☎ 201 5321; I Hattyú utca 16; set menus 760-950Ft; ☯ 24hr; Ⓜ M2 Moszkva tér

Granny's Palacsinta Place serves Hungarian pancakes – both the savoury (240Ft to 620Ft) and sweet (130Ft to 640Ft) varieties – round the clock and is always packed. There are other 24-hour branches in Buda (Map p62; ☎ 212 4866; I Batthyány tér 5; Ⓜ M2 Batthyány tér), Óbuda (Map pp58–9; ☎ 212 4866; III Szentendrei út 131; 🚍 34 or 106) and Pest (Map p85; ☎ 411 0721; V Petőfi Sándor tér 17–19; Ⓜ M1/2/3 Deák Ferenc tér).

GELLÉRT HILL, TABÁN & KELENFÖLD

Second only to eating atop Castle Hill is dining down looking up. The Tabán, an area once known for its jolly outdoor cafes and wine gardens – a kind of Montmartre for Budapest – still has some wonderful places in which to eat and drink (p146), as does the northern end of Kelenföld.

TABÁNI TERASZ Map pp70-1   Hungarian €€€
☎ 201 1086; I Apród utca 10; starters 1950-2980Ft, mains 2600-4900Ft; ⏰ noon-midnight; 🚌 86
This delightful terrace and cellar restaurant below Buda Castle takes a somewhat modern look at Hungarian cuisine, with less calorific dishes, and an excellent wine selection. The candlelit cellar is very atmospheric in winter. Set lunch is a snip at around 1800Ft.

ARANYSZARVAS Map pp70-1   Hungarian €€
☎ 375 6451; I Szarvas tér 1; starters 1200-3200Ft, mains 1950-3650Ft; ⏰ noon-11pm; 🚌 86
Set in an 18th-century inn literally at the foot of Castle Hill, the 'Golden Stag' serves up – guess what? – game dishes. The covered outside terrace is a delight in summer and the views upward fantastical, but leaf-chewers should give this place a wide berth and head for nearby Éden (see opposite).

DAIKICHI (Map pp70-1   Japanese €€
☎ 225 3965; I Mészáros utca 64; dishes 1600-3600Ft; ⏰ noon-3pm & 5-10pm Tue-Sat, noon-9pm Sun; 🚌 8, 112 or 178
Everyone's favourite Japanese find on the Buda side, this minuscule eatery serves up decent soba noodles and seafood dishes.

MARCELLO Map pp70-1   Italian €
☎ 466 6231; XI Bartók Béla út 40; pizza 850-980Ft, pasta 1080-1550Ft, mains 2000Ft; ⏰ noon-10pm Mon-Sat; 🚋 47 or 49
A perennial favourite with students from the nearby university since it opened almost two decades ago, this father-and-son-owned operation just down the road from XI Gellért tér offers reliable Italian fare at affordable prices. The salad bar (small/large 980/680Ft) is good value and the lasagne (1200Ft) is legendary in these parts.

ÓBUDA, RÓZSADOMB & MARGARET ISLAND

The catering options in these neighbourhoods offer a very wide choice. Some of the little neighbourhood eateries of Óbuda are so long established they make a cameo in Hungarian literature, while one of the fine-dining restaurants atop posh Rózsadomb is probably the best known restaurant in the city. Margaret Island, for the most part, is reserved for picnickers and other self-caterers.

VADRÓZSA Map p74   Hungarian, International €€€€
☎ 326 5817; II Pentelei Molnár utca 15; starters 2680-5450Ft, mains 4750-7680Ft; ⏰ noon-3pm & 7pm-midnight; 🚌 91 or 291
Housed in a beautiful neo-Renaissance villa on Rózsadomb, the 'Wild Rose' remains one of the swishest (and most expensive) restaurants in Buda after four decades in operation. It's filled with roses, antiques and soft piano music. You can order off the menu (fish and game dishes are especially good), or choose from the cart of raw ingredients and specify the style.

KÉHLI Map p74   Hungarian €€€
☎ 368 0613; III Mókus utca 22; starters 1090-3990Ft, mains 1990-6290Ft; ⏰ noon-11.30pm; HÉV Árpád híd, 🚌 86)
A self-consciously rustic but stylish place in Óbuda, Kéhli has some of the best traditional Hungarian food in town. In fact, one of Hungary's best-loved writers, the novelist Gyula Krúdy (1878–1933), who lived in nearby Dugovits Titusz tér and whose statue greets you outside the restaurant, moonlighted as a restaurant critic and enjoyed Kéhli's bone marrow on toast (990Ft as an entrée) so much that he included it in one of his novels.

top picks

OLD-STYLE HUNGARIAN RESTAURANTS

- Móri Kisvendéglő (p136)
- Kádár (p138)
- Nagyi Kifőzdéje (p131)
- Toldi Konyhája (popposite)
- Fülemüle (pp140)

MALIGÁN Map p74 Hungarian, Wine €€€

☎ 240 9010; III Lajos utca 38; starters 1300-2800Ft, mains 3650-4900Ft; ⏰ noon-2pm & 6-10pm Tue-Sat; 🚌 86

This wine-cellar restaurant in Óbuda has become a firm favourite, and nothing is more enjoyable than eating course after course of extremely well-prepared modern Hungarian cuisine with 4cL of excellent wine recommended by the waiter-somme-lier. Try the roast duck stuffed with foie gras (2800Ft) or the beef cheeks braised in red wine (3600Ft).

KISBUDA GYÖNGYE Map p74 Hungarian €€€

☎ 368 6402; III Kenyeres utca 34; starters 1680-3380Ft, mains 1880-4680Ft; ⏰ noon-midnight Mon-Sat; 🚌 160 or 260, 🚋 17

A traditional and very elegant Hungarian restaurant in Óbuda, where the antiques-cluttered dining room and attentive service manage to create a *fin-de-siècle* atmos-phere. Try the excellent goose liver special-ity plate with a glass of Tokaj (3380Ft) or a much more pedestrian dish like *csirke paprikás* (chicken paprika; 2680Ft), which still manages to be out of this world.

ÚJ SÍPOS HALÁSZKERT

Map p74 Hungarian €€

New Piper Fisher's Garden; ☎ 388 8745; III Fő tér 6; starters 1100-2300Ft, mains 1900-4100Ft; ⏰ noon-midnight; 🚌 86

This lovely, very traditional restaurant faces (and, in the warmer weather, has outside seating in) Óbuda's most beautiful and historic square. Try the signature *halászlé* (fish soup; 1100Ft to 2200Ft), which comes in various guises. As the restaurant's motto puts it so succinctly: *Halászlében verhetetlen* (You can't beat fish soup).

LEROY CAFÉ Map p74 International €€

☎ 439 1698; III Bécsi út 63; starters 1280-2150Ft, mains 1650-2980Ft; ⏰ 11.30am-midnight; 🚌 86

Like the other branches of the Leroy chain, this cafe-restaurant serves international cui-sine that is not especially inspired but is of a certain standard – and it's there in Óbuda just when you've ordered one too many pints of Dreher. Pasta dishes (1650Ft to 2150Ft) are always a good blotter. The large terrace fills up (and stays that way) very early in the warm weather. Two-course weekday lunches are a big draw at only 1250Ft.

ROZMARING Map p74 Hungarian €€

☎ 367 1301; III Árpád fejedelem útja 125; starters 990-1850Ft, mains 1450-3950Ft; ⏰ noon-11pm Mon-Sat, to 9pm Sun; HÉV Tímár utca

You probably wouldn't want to come all the way up to this part of Óbuda just for the food (it's mostly average Hungarian at best) but the flower-bedecked, covered terraces at this 'garden restaurant' that look out onto the Danube and the western side of Margaret Island, with the water tower just visible above the trees, are a delight in warm weather and well worth the schlep.

MAHARAJA Map p74 Indian €€

☎ 250 7544; III Bécsi út 89-91; starters 500-1850Ft, mains 1400-4300Ft; ⏰ noon-11pm; 🚋 17

This Óbuda institution was the first Indian restaurant to open in Budapest. It special-ises in northern Indian dishes, especially tandoori (1600Ft to 4300Ft). It's never been the best subcontinental eatery in town, but it does manage some kick-ass samosas. There's a branch called City Ma-haraja (Map pp92-3; ☎ 351 1289; VII Csengery utca 24; open noon to 11pm; 🚋 4 or 6) in Pest's Erzsé-betváros.

WASABI Map p74 Japanese €€

☎ 430 1056; III Szépvölgyi út 15; lunch Mon-Fri/Sat & Sun 3990/4990Ft, dinner 4990Ft; ⏰ 11am-11pm; 🚌 86

This sushi restaurant with a central con-veyor belt has more than five dozen items to choose from and the decor is dark, minimalist and very cool. There's also a Pest branch (Map pp92-3; ☎ 374 0008; VI Podman-iczky utca 21; ⏰ 11.30am-11.30pm; Ⓜ M3 Nyugati pályaudvar).

MENNYEI ÍZEK

Map p74 Korean, Chinese €

☎ 388 6430; Pacsirtamező utca 13; dishes 880-1980Ft; ⏰ noon-10pm; 🚌 86

That's 'Celestial Tastes' to you... This little Korean-Chinese hole in the wall in Óbuda serves excellent and very cheap dishes such as spicy pork with eggplant (1880Ft) and there are lots of vegetarian dishes such as wild mountain vegetables with kimchi (1880Ft). Weekday set lunches cost 990Ft and 1490Ft. It's a great place for refuelling to/from Aquincum.

NAGYI KIFŐZDÉJE

Map p74   Hungarian, Étkezde €

☎ 326 2060; Frankel Leó út 36; starters 790-990Ft, mains 990-1100Ft; ⏰ 11.30am-5pm; 🚋 4, 6 or 17
Our favourite new home-style eatery serving Hungarian comfort food in Buda is 'Granny's Canteen' just opposite the Lukács Baths (p165). It's worth a visit for the retro decor alone.

GASZTRÓ HÚS-HENTESÁRU

Map p74   Hungarian, Butcher's Shop €

☎ 212 4159; II Margit körút 2; dishes from 350Ft; ⏰ 7am-6pm Mon, 6am-7pm Tue-Fri, 6am-1pm Sat; 🚋 4 or 6
Opposite the first stop of trams 4 and 6 on the west side of Margaret Bridge, this place with the unappetising name of 'Gastro Meat and Butcher Products' is a traditional butcher shop also serving cooked sausages and roast chicken to be eaten in situ, which is common in Hungary.

BUDA HILLS & BEYOND

Visitors to Budapest head for the hills for a variety of reasons. There's great hiking, a couple of trip-worthy sights and a plethora of unusual forms of transport that everyone from age nine to 90 enjoys riding (see p80). Locals go for the same reasons and more. Some of the restaurants up here have become legends in their own lunchtime.

FUJI JAPÁN Map p82

Japanese €€€

☎ 325 7111; II Csatárka út 54; starters 800-1300Ft, mains 1800-6800Ft; ⏰ noon-11pm; 🚌 29
Above Rózsadomb (pretty much the top shelf of Budapest) in district II, and on the corner of Zöld lomb utca and Zöldkert út, Fuji is a long way to schlep for sushi and sashimi (1900Ft to 5800Ft per piece) and other Japanese dishes like sukiyaki. But this is the most authentic Japanese game in town, judging from the repeat clientele who nip in regularly for noodles and more.

ARCADE BISTRO Map p82

International €€

☎ 225 1969; XII Kiss János altábornagy utca 38; starters 950-2450Ft, mains 2600-4500Ft; ⏰ noon-midnight Mon-Sat, to 4pm Sun; 🚌 105
This family-run eatery in Buda's well-heeled district XII, southwest of the Déli train station, has superb and very creative international cuisine, a much coveted leafy terrace

set between two converging roads, and seamless service. There's a good wine list.

REMÍZ Map p82

Hungarian, International €€

☎ 275 1396; II Budakeszi út 5; starters 1480-2980Ft, mains 2220-4560Ft; ⏰ 11am-11pm; 🚌 22, 🚋 56
Next to a remíz (tram depot) in the Buda Hills, this virtual institution remains popular for its reliable food (try the grilled dishes, especially the ribs; 2180Ft to 2980Ft), competitive prices and verdant garden terrace. Portions are huge, service flawless.

NÁNCSI NÉNI Off Map p82

Hungarian €€

Auntie Nancy; ☎ 397 2742; II Ördögárok út 80; soups & starters 750-1500Ft, mains 2350-3200Ft; ⏰ noon-midnight; 🚋 56
Auntie Náncsi (any loopy old lady in Hungarian) is a perennial favourite with Hungarians and expats alike, and very much of a sound mind. Housed in a wood-panelled cabin in Hűvösvölgy, the restaurant specialises in game in autumn and winter. In

top picks

FOOD & WINE BOOKS

- *Culinaria Hungary* (Aniko Gegely et al, 2000) This beautifully illustrated 320-page tome on all things involving Hungarian food, from soup to nuts and more, is as prized for its recipes as the history and traditions it describes.
- *Gundel's Hungarian Cookbook* (Károly Gundel, 2008) Reissued quintessential reference in the Hungarian kitchen by the chef and epicure who ran his eponymous restaurant in City Park from 1910 until it was nationalised in 1949. The book has the advantage of listing all dishes bilingually.
- *Hungary: Its Fine Wines & Winemakers* (David Copp, 2006) More entertaining but also less serious than Alex Liddell's *The Wine of Hungary* is this large-format book with lots of photographs.
- *Food Wine Budapest: The Terroir Guides* (Carolyn Bánfalvi, 2008) Comprehensive and detailed overview of the dining and drinking scene in Budapest that will take you to a lot more places than we have space for here.
- *The Wines of Hungary* (Alex Liddell, 2003) For a look not just at Hungarian wines themselves but the whole picture, this no-nonsense guide is ideal.

summer it's the lighter fare and garden seating that attract.

MUGHAL SHAHI Map p82 — Pakistani €

☎ 202 4488; XII Városmajor utca 57; starters 200-800Ft, mains 900-2900Ft; ⏰ 11.30am-10pm Mon-Sat; 🚌 28 or 128

Yum, yum… Authentic (and cheap) Pakistani fare on the way up to the Buda Hills (of all places). Pakistani dishes are usually hotter and spicier and somewhat more salty than their Indian equivalents. The only downside here is that it doesn't sell alcohol, though you can BYOB.

BELVÁROS & LIPÓTVÁROS

Central Pest offers a much wider range of restaurants than Buda – especially when it comes to things like ethnic cuisine. Not always as sophisticated as those across the Danube, eateries on this side are often more relaxed and – it must be said – hipper and up to date.

BELVÁROS

SPOON Map p85 — International €€€

☎ 411 0933; off V Vigadó tér 3; starters 1990-3290Ft, mains 3660-5990Ft; ⏰ noon-midnight; 🚋 2

If you like the idea of dining on the high waters but still remaining tethered to the bank (just in case), Spoon's for you. It serves international fusion cuisine amid bright and breezy surrounds and the choices for vegetarians are great. You can't beat the views of the castle and Chain Bridge.

KÁRPÁTIA Map p85 — Hungarian €€€

☎ 317 3596; V Ferenciek tere 7-8; starters 1900-4800Ft, mains 3500-5900Ft; ⏰ 11am-11pm; Ⓜ M3 Ferenciek tere

A veritable palace of *fin-de-siècle* design dating back more than 130 years that has to be seen to be believed, the 'Carpathia' serves almost modern Hungarian and Transylvanian specialities in both a restaurant and less-expensive *söröző* (brasserie), and there is a lovely covered garden terrace. This is one place to hear authentic *csárdás* Gypsy music, played nightly from 6pm to 11pm.

PESTI LAMPÁS

Map p85 — Hungarian, International €€€

☎ 266 5482; V Károlyi Mihály utca 12; starters 1300-2650Ft, mains 2350-5450Ft; ⏰ 10am-midnight Mon-Fri, noon-midnight Sat, 5pm-midnight Sun; Ⓜ M3 Ferenciek tere, 🚌 15 or 115

The light leads the way (we're being figurative here) to the 'Pest Lantern', a stunning new restaurant and coffee house in the university district. The place beckons not so much for the food (though it is very good) but for its location in a renovated mansion near ELTE university. It has a wonderful terrace in the palace courtyard open in the warmer months and the menu has lots of options for vegetarians (1450Ft to 1950Ft).

ÓCEÁN BÁR & GRILL Map p85 — Seafood €€€

☎ 266 1826; V Petőfi tér 3; starters 1950-3900Ft, mains 2300-5290Ft; ⏰ noon-midnight; 🚋 2

We'd like to say this place has made quite a splash in Budapest but we're afraid we'd be arrested by the pun police. Still, it's making waves with its fresh seafood sourced from Scandinavia, congenial decor and wonderful fishmonger and delicatessen (enter from Régiposta utca; open from 10am to 9pm Tuesday to Saturday). We'll come back for the seafood linguine (4690Ft) and the boiled lobster (2650Ft per 100g), but we do wish they'd remove that aquarium (or at least the Nemo residing therein).

TRATTORIA TOSCANA Map p85 — Italian €€

☎ 327 0045; V Belgrád rakpart 13; starters 1100-2990Ft, mains 2390-4590Ft; ⏰ noon-midnight; 🚋 15, 🚋 2

Hard by the Danube, this trattoria serves rustic and very authentic Italian and Tuscan food, including pasta e fagioli (890Ft), a hearty soup of beans and fresh pasta, and a wonderful Tuscan farmer's platter (2350Ft) of prepared meats. The pizza and pasta dishes (1650Ft to 3890Ft) are excellent too.

FATÁL Map p85 — Hungarian €€

☎ 266 2607; V Váci utca 67; soups 720-1090Ft, mains 2680-3390Ft; ⏰ 11.30am-2am; 🚋 47 or 49

No, this is not what you risk when visiting this place. Fatál might be a tourist trap but it serves massive Hungarian meals on a *fatál* (wooden platter) or in iron cauldrons in three rustic rooms. And follow the rules:

bring your appetite and its friends; avoid the noisy backroom; and book in advance.

BANGKOK HOUSE Map p85 Thai €€
☎ 266 0584; V Só utca 3; soups & starters 650-2250Ft, mains 1950-3550Ft; ☷ noon-11pm; ▣ 47 or 49
Bangkok House is done up in kitsch, Asian-esque decor that recalls takeaway places around the world. The Thai and Laotian-inspired dishes are acceptable, though, and service all but seamless. A lunch menu (1300Ft to 1500FT) is available from noon to 4pm.

TAVERNA PIREUS REMBETIKO
Map p85 Greek €€
☎ 266 0292; V Fővám tér 2-3; starters & snacks 390-2990Ft, mains 1890-4990Ft; ☷ noon-midnight; ▣ 47 or 49
Directly opposite the Nagycsarnok (Great Market) at the foot of Liberty Bridge, this place serves reasonably priced and pretty authentic Greek fare. Rembetiko is a folk music school and a style of traditional Greek music; unfortunately, what you'll hear here is canned.

SUSHI AN Map p85 Japanese €€
☎ 317 4239; V Harmincad utca 4; sushi per piece 400-700Ft, hand rolls 1000-2000Ft, sets 2900-3700Ft; ☷ noon-10pm; Ⓜ M1/2/3 Deák Ferenc tér
This tiny sushi bar next to the British embassy in central Pest is great for reasonably priced sushi and sashimi but even better for Japanese sets served with miso soup. But there's not much more room in here than space to swing the proverbial cat.

MOMOTARO RAMEN Map p85 Asian €
☎ 269 3802, 06-30 999 5102; V Széchenyi utca 16; noodles & dumplings 800-1800Ft, mains 1500-3600Ft; ☷ 11am-10pm; ▣ 15, ▣ 2
This is a favourite pit stop for noodles – especially the soup variety – and dumplings when pálinka and other lubricants have been a-flowing the night before. But it's also good for more substantial dishes.

VAPIANO Map p85 Italian €
☎ 411 0864; V Bécsi utca 5; salads & starters 650-1750Ft, pizza & pasta 1200-1950Ft; Ⓜ M1 Vörösmarty tér

A very welcome addition to the Inner Town is this pizza and pasta bar where everything is prepared on-site. You'll be in and out in no time but the taste will certainly linger. It caters mostly to office workers in the centre.

CAFÉ ALIBI Map p85 International €
☎ 317 4209; V Egyetem tér 4; salads 1190-1490Ft, sandwiches 990-1250Ft; ☷ 8am-9pm Mon-Wed, to 10pm Thu-Sat, 9am-9pm Sun; Ⓜ M3 Ferenciek tere
This cafe-restaurant in the heart of university land also does more substantial mains (1290Ft to 1590Ft) and even the occasional set dinner paired with Hungarian wines (8990Ft). But we come here for late breakfast (till noon), snacks (650Ft to 1190Ft) and light meals.

LIPÓTVÁROS

LOU LOU Map p85 French €€€
☎ 312 4505; V Vigyázó Ferenc utca 4; starters 1800-3200Ft, mains 2300-6400Ft; ☷ noon-3pm & 7-11pm Mon, 11am-3pm & 6pm-midnight Tue-Fri, 7-11pm Sat; ▣ 15, ▣ 2
One of the most popular places with expatriate français in Budapest, and said to be chasing Bp's first Michelin star, this lovely bistro with its signature antique rocking horse has excellent daily specials. Try the smoked duck breast (4400Ft) or the scrumptious grilled scallops (6400Ft).

TOM-GEORGE Map p85 International €€€
☎ 266 3525; V Október 6 utca 8; starters 1650-3500Ft, mains 2900-5800Ft; ☷ noon-midnight; ▣ 15
You got to hand it to these guys. They've set a standard for Budapest and stuck to it – for years now OK, it's uber-trendy and could be in London or New York, but the service is great, decor très contemporain and there's something here for everyone – from modern Hungarian and Kobe beef (12,900Ft) to sushi (290Ft to 2440Ft) and even Indian dishes. This ain't fusion, it's confusion. Set lunch is 1250Ft and 2250Ft.

SALAAM BOMBAY Map p85 Indian €€
☎ 411 1252; V Mérleg utca 6; starters 950-1590Ft, mains 2190-3990Ft; ☷ noon-3pm & 6-11pm; ▣ 15, ▣ 2
If you're hankering for a fix of authentic curry or tandoori in a bright, upbeat environment,

look no further than this attractive eatery just east of Roosevelt tér. Don't believe us? Even staff from the Indian embassy are said to come here regularly. As would be expected, there's a large choice of vegetarian dishes (950Ft to 1990Ft).

CAFÉ KÖR Map p85 International €€

☎ 311 0053; V Sas utca 17; salads 910-1590Ft, mains 1560-4190Ft; ⏱ 10am-10pm Mon-Sat; 🚊 15 or 115

Just behind the Basilica of St Stephen, the 'Circle Café' is a great place for a light meal at any time, including breakfast (150Ft to 780Ft) till noon. Salads, desserts and daily specials are usually very good.

IGUANA Map p85 Mexican €€

☎ 331 4352; V Zoltán utca 16; starters 890-1990Ft, mains 1390-3990Ft; ⏱ 11.30am-12.30am; Ⓜ M2 Kossuth Lajos tér, 🚊 15

Iguana serves decent enough Mexican food (not a difficult task in this cantina desert), but it's hard to say whether the pull is the chilli (1390Ft to 2290Ft), the enchilada and burrito combination *platos* (plates; 1990Ft to 2390Ft), the fajitas (2390Ft to 3390Ft) or the frenetic and boozy 'we-party-every-night' atmosphere with its canned music.

GASTRONOMIA POMO D'ORO
Map p85 Italian €

☎ 374 0288; V Arany János utca 9; dishes 1830-3090Ft; ⏱ 9am-10pm Mon-Sat; 🚊 15, 🚋 2

Next door to a much more extravagant (and expensive) trattoria bearing the same name, this Italian delicatessen/caterer has a small dining area on the 1st floor where you can choose from a small selection of dishes or sample cheese and prepared meats by the 100g measure (490Ft to 890Ft). Excellent value.

HUMMUS BAR Map p85 Middle Eastern €

☎ 302 1385, 06-70 932 8029; V Alkotmány utca 20; dishes 600-1500Ft, ⏱ 11am-10pm Mon-Sat, noon-10pm Sun; Ⓜ M2 Kossuth Lajos tér

If you're looking for vegetarian food on the, err, hoof, this is the place to go for mashed chickpeas blended with sesame-seed paste, oil and lemon juice. Enjoy it au naturel (we mean the hummus) on pita or in a dish with accompaniments such as mushrooms or felafel.

top picks

ASIAN RESTAURANTS

- Új Lanzhou (p128)
- Salaam Bombay (p133)
- Seoul House (pp127)
- Bangla Büfé (p138)
- Wasabi (pp130)

KISHARANG Map p85 Hungarian, Étkezde €

☎ 269 3861; V Október 6 utca 17; soups 400-500Ft, mains 540-1250Ft; ⏱ 11.30am-8pm Mon-Fri, to 4.30pm Sat & Sun; 🚊 15 or 115

The centrally located 'Little Bell' is an *étkezde* that is on the top of the list with students and staff of the nearby Central European University. The daily specials are something to look forward to and the retro decor is fun.

GOVINDA Map p85 Vegetarian €

☎ 269 1625; V Vigyázó Ferenc utca 4; soups 450Ft, dishes 230-490Ft; ⏱ 11.30am-8pm Mon-Fri, noon-9pm Sat; 🚊 15, 🚋 2

This basement restaurant northeast of the Chain Bridge serves wholesome salads, soups and desserts as well as a daily set menu plate (large/small 1850/1550Ft). It's also a centre for yoga (see p166) and alternative health remedies.

ALSO RECOMMENDED

Bisztro Oregano (Map p85; ☎ 269 3273; V Október 6 utca 15; sandwiches 900-1100Ft, salads 1200-1800Ft; ⏱ 8am-8pm Mon-Fri; 🚊 15 or 115) This brightly coloured cafe is a modern take on a Hungarian *önkiszolgáló* (self-service restaurant) where, along with light meals available throughout the day, including breakfast (750Ft to 950Ft), main dishes are sold by weight (220Ft per 100g).

Szeráj (Map p85; ☎ 311 6690; XIII Szent István körút 13; dishes 450-1400Ft, ⏱ 9am-4am Mon-Thu, to 5am Fri & Sat, to 2am Sun; 🚋 4 or 6) A very inexpensive self-service Turkish place for *lahmacun* (Turkish 'pizza'; 450Ft) and felafel (900Ft) and kebabs (700Ft), with up to a dozen varieties on offer, and open late.

Pick Ház (Map p85; ☎ 331 7783; V Kossuth Lajos tér 9; sandwiches & salads 140-180Ft, mains 210-580Ft; ⏱ 8am-4pm Mon-Fri; Ⓜ M2 Kossuth Lajos tér) Next to M2 Kossuth Lajos tér metro station, this self-service eatery is above the famous salami manufacturer's central showroom opposite the Parliament building.

NORTHERN RING ROAD AREA

This large area, stretching from the northern reaches of the Danube to central Blaha Lujza tér, captures a tremendous amount of eateries – from silver-service on or just off the Big Ring Road of Szent István körút, Teréz körút and Erzsébet körút to the Jewish *étkezdék* of the so-called Ghetto and backstreet Indian messes. This area is a paradise for self-caterers (see p126).

ÚJLIPÓTVÁROS & TERÉZVÁROS

FIRKÁSZ
Map pp92-3 — Hungarian €€

☎ 450 1118; Tátra utca 18; starters 1490-2490Ft, mains 2590-4990Ft; ⊗ noon-midnight; 🚌 15 or 115
Set up by former journalists, Firkász, a retro Hungarian restaurant with lovely old mementos on the walls, great home-style cooking and a good wine list, has been one of our favourite Hungarian eateries for years. But when we last visited we were sorely disappointed with our dishes and the cavalier service. Bad night? In solidarity, we'll give the 'Hack' a second chance. Lunch is good value at 1250Ft and 1450Ft.

MOSSELEN
Map pp92-3 — Belgian €€

☎ 452 0535; XIII Pannónia utca 14; starters 1195-2190Ft, mains 2790-4190Ft; ⊗ noon-midnight; 🚌 15 or 115
This pleasant 'Belgian beer cafe' in Újlipótváros serves Belgian (and some Hungarian) specialities, including its namesake, those much-loved bivalves, prepared in several different ways. There's a wide selection of Belgian beers, including some two-dozen fruit-flavoured ones.

ZSÁKBAMACSKÁHOZ
Map pp92-3 — Hungarian €€

☎ 354 1810; VI Lovag utca 3; starters 1450-2850Ft, mains 1950-4850Ft; 5pm-midnight Mon-Fri, noon-midnight Sat & Sun; Ⓜ M3 Arany János utca
'At the Cat in the Bag', an attractive basement restaurant just north of the theatre district, serves up Hungarian and Transylva-

nian specialities by the cartload; don't leave your appetite behind. Best of all, there's no hokey Gypsy music to distract you from the matter at hand.

TROFÉA GRILL
Map pp92-3 — International, Buffet €€

☎ 270 0366; XIII Visegrádi utca 50/a; lunch/dinner Mon-Thu 2999/3999Ft, lunch & dinner Fri-Sun 4299Ft; ⊗ noon-midnight Mon-Fri, 11.30am-midnight Sat, 11.30am-9pm Sun; Ⓜ M3 Lehel tér
This is the place to head when you really could eat a horse (which might be found sliced on one of the tables). It's an enormous buffet of more than 100 cold and hot dishes over which diners swarm like bees while observed by the cooks from their kitchen. There's also a Buda branch (Map p74; ☎ 438 9090; I Margit körút 2; lunch Monday to Friday 3399Ft, Saturday and Sunday 4999Ft, dinner Monday to Thursday 4499Ft, Friday to Sunday 4999Ft; 🚉 4 or 6), where the opening times are the same but the prices higher.

VOGUE
Map pp92-3 — South Slav €€

☎ 350 7000, 06-30 942 5027; XIII Újpesti alsó rakpart 1; starters 1090-2100Ft, mains 1650-3900Ft; ⊗ 11am-1am; 🚌 115 or 133, trolleybus 76
This fine old vessel moored off XIII Szent István Park in Újlipótváros and opposite the eastern side of Margaret Island has fine views south to Margaret and Chain bridges, and (unusually) you can also take in both sides of the river. The food is Serbian and other South Slav – *čevapčiči* (spicy meatballs) and *pljeskavica* (spicy meat patties; both 2490Ft) and *ražnjiči* (shish kebab; 2800Ft) – always grilled and always in large portions.

MARQUIS DE SALADE
Map pp92-3 — International €€

☎ 302 4086; VI Hajós utca 43; soups & salads 800-2500Ft, mains 2400-3400Ft; ⊗ noon-midnight; Ⓜ M3 Arany János utca, trolleybuses 72 or 73
This basement restaurant is a strange hybrid of a place, with dishes from Russia and Azerbaijan as well as Hungary. There are lots of quality vegetarian choices, too. And, by the way, it's not just about *salade*.

OKAY ITALIA
Map pp92-3 — Italian €€

☎ 349 2991; XIII Szent István körút 20; pizza 1590-2050Ft, pasta 1190-1980Ft, mains 1890-3310Ft; ⊗ 11am-midnight Mon-Fri, noon-midnight Sat & Sun; 🚉 4 or 6

This perennially popular eatery is run by Italians and does serve a full range of dishes but most people come for the pasta and pizza. There is a much classier (and more expensive) Pest branch (Map pp92–3; ☎ 332 6960; V Nyugati tér 6; starters 1690-2690Ft, mains 1990-3490Ft; M M3 Nyugati pályaudvar) up the ring road opposite the Nyugati train station.

POZSONYI KISVENDÉGLŐ

Map pp92-3   Hungarian €

☎ 787 4877; XIII Radnóti Miklós utca 38; starters 750-1700Ft, mains 1050-1800Ft; ⏱ 9am-midnight Mon-Sat, 10am-9am Sun; trolleybus 75 or 76
Visit this neighbourhood restaurant on the corner of Pozsonyi út for the ultimate local Budapest experience: gargantuan portions of standard Hungarian favourites, rock-bottom prices and a cast of local characters. There's a bank of tables on the pavement in summer and simple set weekday menus for 650Ft.

MÓRI KISVENDÉGLŐ

Map pp92-3   Hungarian Jewish, Étkezde €

☎ 349 8390; XIII Pozsonyi út 39; dishes 520-1350Ft; ⏱ 10am-5pm Mon-Thu, to 3pm Fri; trolleybus 75 or 76
Probably the most popular of its type, with some of the best home-cooked food in Budapest, this simple borozó (wine bar) and restaurant a short walk north from Szent István körút serves home-cooked Hungarian Jewish food. But, as the owner would like to warn our 'dear readers', get here by 3pm if you want to taste the famous főzelék vegetables (see p123).

HOLLY Map pp92-3   Hungarian, Étkezde €

☎ 353 3064; VI Lovag utca 22; dishes 390-850Ft; ⏱ 11.30am-4pm Mon-Fri; 🚃 4 or 6
This very popular étkezde is an excellent place for lunch or a very early evening meal. There are daily specials and the menu changes every week.

NAPOS OLDAL Map pp92-3   Vegetarian €

☎ 354 0048; VI Jókai utca 7-8; dishes 260-380Ft; ⏱ 10.30am-9pm Mon-Fri, 10am-1.30pm Sat; M M1 Oktogon, 🚃 4 or 6
This tiny cafe-restaurant inside a health-food shop on the 'Sunny Side' of the street serves up shop-made salads, pastries and hot soups.

ALSO RECOMMENDED

Kiskakukk (Map pp92–3; ☎ 450 0829; XIII Pozsonyi utca 12; starters 1490-1750Ft, mains 1950-2950Ft; ⏱ noon-midnight; 🚃 4 or 6, trolleybus 75 or 76) This ever-so traditional Hungarian eatery has been serving up gulyás leves (hearty beef soup; 650Ft) and stuffed cabbage (1850Ft) since the year before WWI broke out. It's tried and tested and remains true.

Parázs Presszó (Map pp92–3; ☎ 950 3770; VI Szobi utca4; Thai starters 1350-1820Ft, Thai mains 1450-2850Ft; ⏱ noon-1am Mon-Thu, 11am-2am Fri & Sat, noon-1am Sun; 🚃 4 or 6) A presszó (coffee shop) on the wrong side of the tracks serving Thai and Hungarian food? We're sticking to the former and wishing them the best of luck.

ANDRÁSSY ÚT & SURROUNDS
GOA

Map pp92-3   Hungarian, International, Fusion €€€

☎ 302 2570; VI Andrássy út 8; starters 1350-2150Ft, mains 3450-5600Ft; ⏱ noon-midnight; M M1 Bajcsy-Zsilinszky út
This anchor tenant on Budapest's most beautiful boulevard serves excellent, innovative Asian-esque fusion food (try the prawns, though the salads – 1350Ft to 2950Ft – are excellent too). The wood-and-fabric decor is soft and welcoming, and we love eating outdoors on a summer's evening (despite the toxic traffic fumes). The only downside is the 'attitude' on the staff. As one diner put it, 'They're waiters, not celebrities'.

KLASSZ Map pp92-3   Hungarian, Wine €€

☎ no phone; www.klassz.eu; VI Andrássy út 41; starters 1590-1890Ft, mains 1490-3580Ft; ⏱ 11.30am-11pm Mon-Sat, to 6pm Sun; M M1 Oktogon
Probably our favourite restaurant in Budapest at the moment, Klassz is mostly about wine – Hungarian to be precise – and here you can order by the 10cL measure from an ever-changing list of up to four-dozen wines to sip and compare. The food is of a very high standard, with foie gras in its various avatars and native mangalica pork permanent fixtures on the menu, as well as more unusual (and fleeting) dishes like Burgundy-style leg of rabbit (2390Ft) and lamb trotters with vegetable ragout. Reservations are not accepted; just show up and wait.

MENZA Map pp92-3 Hungarian €€

☎ 413 1482; VI Liszt Ferenc tér 2; starters 1290-1590Ft, mains 1890-2490Ft; ⊗ 10am-1am; Ⓜ M1 Oktogon, 🚋 4 or 6

This stylish Hungarian restaurant on Budapest's most lively square takes its name from the Hungarian for a drab school canteen – something it is anything but. Book a table if you can; it's always packed with diners who come for its simply but perfectly cooked Hungarian classics with a modern twist and chilled atmosphere. Weekday two-course set lunches are a mere 890Ft.

PESTI VENDÉGLŐ Map pp92-3 Hungarian €€

☎ 266 3227; VI Paulay Ede utca 5; starters 1690-2200Ft, mains 1790-2990Ft; ⊗ 11am-11pm; Ⓜ M1/2/3 Deák Ferenc tér

Here is a great choice for someone trying traditional Hungarian specialities for the first time. This very popular upbeat and nicely decorated family-run eatery close to central Deák tér offers a lighter take on standard Hungarian favourites, and the staff are very welcoming and helpful.

GIERO Map pp92-3 Hungarian €

☎ 344 4726; VI Paulay Ede utca 58; set meals 1400-2000Ft; ⊗ 10am-late; M1 Oktogon

We won't say anything about the food beyond that it comes out of the kitchen on a plate, it's stodgy and there's lots of it. And the choice of wine depends on what wasn't drunk by customers and musicians the night before. But you come here primarily to listen to Gypsy music as Roma musicians play it when they're off duty from playing that saccharine junk at the top-end hotels.

NAPFÉNYES ÍZEK

Map pp92-3 Hungarian Vegetarian €

☎ 351 5649; VII Rózsa utca 39; starters 450-690Ft, mains 1390-1890Ft; ⊗ 10am-10.30pm Mon-Fri, noon-10.30pm Sat & Sun; Ⓜ M1 Kodály körönd, trolleybus 73 or 76

'Sunny Tastes' is a bit out of the way (though not if you're staying on or near Andrássy út), but the wholesome foods and the speciality cakes are worth the trip. There is an organic shop where you can stock up on both packaged and baked goods, including excellent cakes. Set lunches are a bargain at 600Ft to 1100Ft.

top picks

RESTAURANTS WITH GARDEN SEATING

- Le Jardin de Paris (p127)
- Robinson (pp141)
- Náncsi Néni (pp131)
- Rozmaring (pp130)
- Rivalda (pp127)

ERZSÉBETVÁROS

DONATELLA'S KITCHEN

Map pp92-3 Italian €€€

☎ 878 0515; VI Király utca 30-32; starters 1250-1750Ft, mains 2650-4500Ft; ⊗ noon-midnight; Ⓜ M1/2/3 Deák Ferenc tér

Black is apparently the new black at this uber-trendy New York–style restaurant directed by Italian chef Donatella Zampoli. The service might be a bit attitudinous and the chandeliers made of (plastic) antlers a bit scary but we'll come back for the excellent pizzas (around 2000Ft), more substantial Italian mains and stylish crowd.

ARTESANO Map pp92-3 Spanish €€

☎ 688-1696; VI Ó utca 24-26; starters 1400-1800Ft, mains 2400-4800Ft; ⊗ noon-midnight Mon-Sat; Ⓜ M3 Arany János utca

This is an excellent choice for a stylish but affordable meal of tapas or more substantial Spanish dishes such as the cold Iberian plate (2500Ft) or paella (2900Ft), which comes in various guises. It's a wonderful find in an area overrun by low-quality tourist dives.

CARMEL PINCE Map pp92-3 Jewish, Kosher €€

☎ 322 1834; VII Kazinczy utca 31; starters 1100-2900Ft, mains 2500-4800Ft; ⊗ noon-11pm Sun-Fri; trolleybus 74

With kosher restaurants of any sort at something of a premium in Budapest, the Carmel's metamorphosis from ethnic Jewish to a bona-fide glatt kosher eatery is more than welcome. Try any of its authentic Ashkenazi specialities such as gefilte fish (1700Ft), matzo ball soup (1000Ft), chopped chicken liver (2500Ft) and a *cholent* (hearty brisket and bean casserole; 3000Ft) almost as good as the one Aunt

Goldie used to make. There's live *klezmer* (Jewish folk music; 2000Ft) at 7.30pm on Thursday.

KŐLEVES Map pp92-3 — Hungarian €€
☎ 322 1011, 06-20 213 5999; Kazinczy utca 35 & Dob utca 26; soups 650-1490Ft; mains 1280-3680Ft; ☽ noon-midnight; 🚊 4 or 6, trolleybus 74

Always buzzy and lots of fun, the 'Stone Soup' attracts a young crowd with its delicious matzo ball soup (large/small 960/670Ft), tapas (890Ft to 1110Ft), lively decor and, of course, reasonable prices. It's a great place to try Hungarian food for the first time.

M RESTAURANT Map pp92-3 — Hungarian €€
☎ 322 3108; VII Kertész utca 48; starters 600-1400Ft; mains 1500-2600Ft; ☽ 6pm-midnight; 🚊 4 or 6

What started life a few years back looking a lot more *menza* (drab school canteen) than it does now, M has evolved into a stylish place (love walls lined with brown wrapping paper and the graphics), with an ever-changing menu of Hungarian dishes with a French twist. The atmosphere is so chilled it's almost comatose.

MAGDALENA MERLO
Map pp92-3 — Hungarian, Italian €€
☎ 322 3278; VII Király utca 59/b; starters 620-1190Ft; mains 1490-2490Ft; ☽ 10am-midnight; 🚊 4 or 6

Conveniently catty-cornered to the Ferenc Liszt Academy of Music, this down-home eatery serves an odd mix of Hungarian as well as pizza (1090Ft to 1590Ft) and pasta (1290Ft to 1800Ft) dishes. What's more, since it was the Svejk (from Jaroslav Hašek's satirical novel *The Good Soldier Svejk*) for many years, it has retained a page of 'nostalgic' Czech and Slovak dishes (740Ft to 1990Ft), including specialities like Slovakian cabbage soup and *sztrapacska* (noodles with cheese) for those who can't let go of the memories.

SPINOZA CAFÉ
Map pp92-3 — Hungarian, Jewish €€
☎ 413 7488; VII Dob utca 15; starters 590-690Ft; mains 1690-2490Ft; ☽ 11am-11pm; 🚊 47 or 49

This attractive cafe-restaurant in the Jewish district has become a personal favourite both for meals and as a chill-out zone. The venue includes an art gallery and theatre,

where concerts by the Pannónia Klezmer Band (see p160) and other events take place from September to May, along with a restaurant and coffee house. There's live music Tuesday to Saturday from around 7pm. The food is mostly Hungarian/Jewish nonkosher comfort food. Remember: the play's the thing.

SHALIMAR Map pp92-3 — Indian €€
☎ 352 0297; VII Dob utca 50; starters 610-880Ft; mains 1680-2290Ft; ☽ noon-4pm & 6pm-midnight; 🚊 4 or 6

Here since forever, Shalimar serves tandoori, tikka and kebab dishes from an open kitchen that taste like they've come via southern Hungary (there's got to be paprika in there somewhere) rather than the subcontinent, but at least it's a fix when you need it most. We're told the chef's from Nepal, which may explain the hybrid tastes. Still the mutton biryani (2190Ft) is a force to be reckoned with and the choice of vegetarian dishes (1050Ft to 1750Ft) is plentiful.

HANNA Map pp92-3 — Jewish, Kosher €
☎ 342 1072; VII Dob utca 35; soups & salads 350-600Ft; mains 1300-2000Ft; ☽ 8am-10pm Sun-Fri, 11am-2pm Sat; 🚊 4 or 6

Housed upstairs in an old school in the Orthodox Synagogue complex, this simple eatery is as soulless as the devil himself, but if you answer to a Higher Authority on matters culinary it is another option for kosher food. On Sabbath, you order and pay for meals in advance.

KÁDÁR Map pp92-3 — Hungarian, Étkezde €
☎ 321 3622; X Klauzál tér 9; soups 620-660Ft; mains 950-1800Ft; ☽ 11.30am-3.30pm Tue-Sat; 🚊 4 or 6

Located in the heart of the Jewish district, still called the Ghetto by local residents, Kádár is probably the most popular and authentic *étkezde* you will find in town and attracts punters with its ever-changing menu. Be advised that it usually closes for most of the month of August.

BANGLA BÜFÉ Map pp92-3 — Bangladeshi €
☎ 266 3674, 06-30 480 6279; Akácfa utca 40; starters 250-590Ft; mains 790-1190Ft; ☽ noon-11pm Sat-Thu, 2.30-11pm Fri; 🚊 4 or 6, trolleybus 74

This place started up by a Bangladeshi expatriate has as authentic samosas

HUNGARY'S RED GOLD

Paprika, the 'red gold' (*piros arany*) so essential to many Hungarian dishes, is cultivated primarily on the southern reaches of Hungary's Great Plain, mostly around the cities of Szeged and Kalocsa. About 10,000 tonnes of the spice are produced annually, 55% of which is exported. Hungarians themselves consume about 0.5kg of the spice per capita every year.

Opinions vary on how and when the *Capsicum annum* plant first arrived in Hungary – from India via Turkey and the Balkans or from the New World – but mention of it is made in Hungarian documents dating from the 16th century.

There are many types of fresh or dried paprika available in Budapest's markets and shops, including the rose, apple and royal varieties. But as a ground spice it is most commonly sold as *csípős* (hot), *erős* (strong) and *édes* (sweet) paprika.

Capsicum annum is richer in vitamin C than citrus fruits, and it was during experimentation with the plant that Dr Albert Szent-Györgyi of Szeged first isolated the vitamin. He was awarded the Nobel Prize for medicine in 1937.

(390Ft), chicken and lamb biryani (790Ft to 1050Ft) and dhal (490Ft) as you'll find in Budapest. It's simple but the food is very tasty indeed.

FALAFEL FALODA
Map pp92-3   Vegetarian, Middle Eastern €
☎ 351 1243; VI Paulay Ede utca 53; small/large sandwiches 460/760Ft, salads 650-820Ft; ⏰ 10am-8pm Mon-Fri, to 6pm Sat; trolleybus 70 or 78

This inexpensive place just south of Budapest's theatre district has Israeli-style nosh. You pay a fixed price to stuff a piece of pita bread or fill a plastic container from a great assortment of salads. It also has a good variety of soups (380Ft to 420Ft).

FRICI PAPA KIFŐZDÉJE
Map pp92-3   Hungarian, Étkezde €
☎ 351 0197; VI Király utca 55; soups 339-529Ft, mains 399-699Ft; ⏰ 11am-9pm Mon-Sat; 🚋 4 or 6

'Papa Frank's Canteen' is larger and more modern than most *étkezde* in Budapest. Excellent *főzelék* dishes are around 340Ft. We love the funny old murals of Pest in days of yore.

SOHO PALACSINTABÁR
Map pp92-3   Hungarian €
☎ 311 0838; VI Nagymező utca 21; savoury pancakes 310-690Ft, sweet pancakes 115-210Ft; ⏰ 11am-1am Sun-Wed, 24hr Thu-Sat; Ⓜ M1 Opera

It may not be as popular as the Nagyi Palacsintázója chain (see p128), but the Soho can provide a fix of *palacsinta* (Hungarian-style pancakes) till the wee hours just as effortlessly. Try the more unusual pancake varieties like Mexican. It's open nonstop from Thursday to Sunday morning.

DURCIN
Map pp92-3   Sandwiches €
☎ 267 9624; VI Bajcsy-Zsilinszky út 7; sandwiches 159-299Ft; ⏰ 8am-6pm Mon-Fri, to 2pm Sat, to noon Sun; Ⓜ M1/2/3 Deák Ferenc tér

This is the place to go for bite-sized open-face sandwiches and mini pizzas (239Ft to 259Ft). There are several other outlets, including a Lipótváros branch (Map p85; ☎ 332 9348; V Október 6 utca 15; 🚌 15 or 115) as well as a Buda branch (Map p62; ☎ 438 3104; II Retek utca 18; Ⓜ M2 Moszkva tér) behind the Mammut shopping mall; both branches are open from 8am to 6pm Monday to Friday and to 1pm on Saturday.

ALSO RECOMMENDED

Ferenc József Söröző (Map pp92-3; ☎ 344 5316; VI Nagymező utca 12; starters 990-1800Ft, mains 1440-3590Ft; ⏰ 11am-1am Mon-Sat, 1pm-1am Sun; Ⓜ M1 Opera) This is another one of those pile-it-on-high Budapest pubs where you'll leave feeling you'll never eat again.

Kinai-Koreai Étterem (Map pp92-3; ☎ 06-30 305 6975; VI Zichy Jenő utca 9; starters 290-1290Ft, mains 1390-1990Ft; ⏰ noon-10pm; Ⓜ M3 Arany János utca) The cleverly named 'Chinese-Korean Restaurant' serves dishes from both great nations but, for the sake of authenticity, veer toward the latter.

Főzelék Faló (Map pp92-3; ☎ 266 6398; VI Nagymező utca 18; dishes 120-580Ft; ⏰ 9am-10pm Mon-Fri, 10am-9pm Sat, 11am-6pm Sun; Ⓜ M1 Opera) Some people say that this *étkezde*, which keeps relatively extended hours and is convenient to the bars of Liszt Ferenc tér and the music academy, is the best in town.

SOUTHERN RING ROAD AREA

Rapid development of districts 8 (Józsefváros) and 9 (Ferencváros) have changed the face of the eating scene here, especially in and around

Ferencváros' IX Ráday utca. The area west of the Hungarian National Museum, particularly VIII Krúdy Gyula utca in Józsefváros, is another happy hunting ground for restaurants, *étkezdék* and cafes.

JÓZSEFVÁROS

MÚZEUM Map pp102-3 Hungarian €€€
☎ 267 0375; VIII Múzeum körút 12; starters 1400-3400Ft, mains 2800-5400Ft; ☽ noon-midnight Mon-Sat; ☷ 47 or 49
This is the place to come if you like to dine in old-world style, with a piano softly tinkling in the background. It's a cafe-restaurant that is still going strong after 125 years at the same location near the Hungarian National Museum. The goose liver parfait (3900Ft) is to die for, and there's a good selection of Hungarian wines.

ROSENSTEIN Map pp102-3 Hungarian, Jewish €€€
☎ 333 3492; VIII Mosonyi utca 3; starters 1300-3000Ft, mains 3700-5500Ft; noon-11pm Mon-Sat; ☷ 24
This is an odd fish: a classy Hungarian place (with Jewish tastes and aromas) and super service in the dark (and rather mean) streets of district VIII just south of Keleti train station. It is family run and has been here for years, so expect everyone to know each other.

FÜLEMÜLE Map pp102-3 Hungarian, Jewish €€
☎ 266 7947; VIII Kőfaragó utca 5; starters 990-2400Ft, mains 1900-4800Ft; ☽ noon-10pm Sun-Thu, to 11pm Fri & Sat; ☷ 7 or 78
This quaint Hungarian restaurant that looks like time stood still just before WWII is quite a find in deepest Józsefváros and well worth the search. Dishes mingle Hungarian and international tastes with some old-style Jewish favourites.

CSÜLÖK CSÁRDA Map pp102-3 Hungarian €€
☎ 210 7897; VIII Berzsenyi utca 4; starters 800-1700Ft, mains 1250-2800Ft; ☽ noon-11pm Mon-Fri, 5-11pm Sat; Ⓜ M2 Keleti pályaudvar
The rough-and-ready 'Pork Knuckle Inn' serves just that (from 1150Ft) and other country specialities in enormous quantities in a cellar restaurant. Slide into one of the wooden booths and order a plate to share before you board your train at the nearby Keleti train station.

STEX HÁZ Map pp102-3 Hungarian, Late Night €€
☎ 318 5716; VIII József körút 55-57; starters 600-2350Ft, mains 990-2850Ft; ☽ 8am-4am Mon-Sat, 9am-2am Sun; Ⓜ M3 Ferenc körút
A big, noisy place that's open almost 24 hours, the Stex is north of the Applied Arts Museum. The menu offers soups, sandwiches, pasta, fish and meat dishes as well as vegetarian choices (750Ft to 890Ft). It transforms into a lively bar late at night. Best of all, there's breakfast (350Ft to 910Ft).

BIOPONT Map pp102-3 Vegetarian €
☎ 266 4601; VIII Krúdy utca 7; soups 425-650Ft, dishes 585-980Ft; ☽ 11am-9pm Mon-Fri, noon-9pm Sat; ☷ 4 or 6
In the Darshan Udvar complex (p152), this is a pleasant place for a meatless organic meal, with all dishes available in both full and half portions. There are also 'bio' pita sandwiches (590Ft to 690Ft) and salads (420Ft) if you just want a snack.

FERENCVÁROS

BORBÍRÓSÁG Map pp102-3 Hungarian, Wine €€€
☎ 219 0902; IX Csarnok tér 5; starters 1750-3250Ft, mains 2250-4250Ft; ☽ noon-11.30pm; ☷ 47 or 49
Some people like the idea of the 'Wine Court' where more than 70 Hungarian wines are available by the glass, and the food, especially game, is taken pretty seriously. Others find the legal theme cutesy in the extreme and the dishes overpriced. We fall into the first camp, but only when we're in the neighbourhood.

SOUL CAFÉ Map pp102-3 International €€
☎ 217 6986; IX Ráday utca 11-13; starters 980-2180Ft, mains 1990-4390Ft; ☽ noon-11.30pm; Ⓜ M3 Kálvin tér
One of the better choices along a street heaving with so-so restaurants and iffy cafes with attitude, the Soul has inventive continental food and decor, and a great terrace on both sides of the street.

VÖRÖS POSTAKOCSI
Map pp102-3 Hungarian €€
☎ 217 6756; IX Ráday 15; starters 1700-2600Ft, mains 1900-4000Ft; ☽ 11.30am-midnight; ☷ 15 or 115
What was for more than three decades a more than forgettable eatery serving Hun-

EATING SOUTHERN RING ROAD AREA

garian stodge and overlooked by all but the bravest or most desperate of diners in Ferencváros has turned into a trendy retro-style Hungarian restaurant with a lively Gypsy band. If you want a take on how modern Hungarians think they used to eat when times were tougher (and less health-conscious), visit the 'Red Postal Coach'.

TAIWAN Map pp102-3   Chinese €€
☎ 215 1236; IX Gyáli út 3/b; starters 545-1080Ft, mains 1720-4500Ft; ☽ noon-11pm; Ⓜ M3 Nagyvárad tér
In the same building as the Fortuna Hotel (p185) in south Ferencváros, this mammoth (and relatively expensive for Budapest) Chinese restaurant – think airline hangar coloured red – may seem a long way to go for a bit of rice but it's one of the few places in Budapest that does decent dim sum.

SHIRAZ Map pp102-3   Middle Eastern €€
☎ 218 0881; IX Ráday utca 21; starters & salads 750-1850Ft, mains 1550-3600Ft; ☽ noon-midnight; 🚌 15 or 115
A Persian restaurant with carpets and hookahs loaded with apple, peach and strawberry tobacco (1490Ft) to lure in the punters (where else in Europe can you smoke indoors?), the Shiraz serves tasty but not particularly substantial dishes. Most are stew-like in form and taste.

PATA NEGRA Map pp102-3   Spanish €€
☎ 215 5616; IX Kálvin tér 8; tapas 350-790Ft, plates 750-2200Ft; ☽ 11am-midnight Mon-Wed, to 1am Thu-Sat, noon-midnight Sun; Ⓜ M3 Kálvin tér
The 'Black Foot' – it's a special kind of Spanish cured ham – is a lovely Spanish tapas bar and restaurant at the (almost) top of trendy Ráday utca; the floor tiles and ceiling fans really help create a mood à la valenciana. There's good cheese and an excellent wine selection, too.

PINK CADILLAC Map pp102-3   Italian €
☎ 216 1412, 06-20 962 6442; IX Ráday utca 22; pizzas 750-2150Ft; ☽ 11am-12.30am; 🚌 15 or 115
More of an upbeat 1950s diner than a pizzeria, the recently redecorated Pink Cadillac still reigns supreme on IX Ráday utca after all this time. If you don't like the surrounds, have your pizza delivered to Paris Texas (p152), the pub next door and

not some one-horse town in the Lone Star State.

ALSO RECOMMENDED

Mezcal (Map pp102–3; ☎ 06-20 428 2872; IX Tompa utca 14; dishes 1590-2390Ft; ☽ noon-midnight Mon-Wed, to 1am Thu-Sat, to 10pm Sun; Ⓜ M3 Ferenc körút) Ferencváros is about the last place you'd expect to find Tex-Mex food, but this bright and upbeat basement cantina serves surprisingly tasty tacos and burritos (1790Ft to 2390Ft) as well as quesadillas (1590Ft to 2190Ft).

Lanzhou (Map pp102–3; ☎ 314 1080; VIII Luther utca 1/b; dishes 1090-1490Ft; ☽ noon-11pm; Ⓜ M2 Keleti pályaudvar) Erstwhile sister to the Új Lanzhou (p128), this place can't even reach that Buda restaurant's knees but it's there when you need a fix of some rice and/or noodles.

Kiskőleves Juice Bar & Café (Map pp102–3; ☎ no phone; VIII Horánszky utca 10; snacks & sandwiches 350-500Ft; ☽ 8am-6pm Mon-Fri; 🚌 4 or 6) This upbeat juice bar and cafe keeps bankers' hours but serves some of the best freshly squeezed juice and java in town.

CITY PARK & BEYOND

The Városliget (City Park) itself offers some wonderful options for dining alfresco in the warmer months. A bit further afield there's no end to the choice of eateries – be it very traditional Hungarian or even hard-to-find ethnic.

ROBINSON Map p108   International €€€
☎ 422 0222; XIV Városligeti tó; starters 2550-3290Ft, mains 3290-5990Ft; ☽ noon-4pm & 6pm-midnight; Ⓜ M1 Hősök tere
Located within leafy City Park, Robinson is the place to secure a table on the lakeside terrace on a warm summer's evening. Starters include sliced goose liver (3290Ft) and grilled duck liver on ginger toast (2890Ft), and mains feature fogas (Balaton pike-perch; 3990Ft), grilled tuna and smoked duck breast cooked on lava stones. It's overpriced but it's all about location, location, location.

HAN KUK GUAN Map p108   Korean €€€
☎ 460 0838; XIV Ilka utca 22; starters 2800-3000Ft, grills 3000-6800Ft; ☽ noon-10pm Mon-Sat; trolleybus 75 or 77
No one is going to be able to tell you what a Korean joint is doing way out in district XIV southeast of City Park, but who cares? It's about as authentic as you'll find. If you can afford it, try one of the barbecues. Otherwise

stick to things like the *pajon* (green onion pancakes) served with seafood or any of the rice and noodle dishes (2600Ft to 3200Ft).

BAGOLYVÁR Map p108   Hungarian €€
☎ 468 3110; XIV Állatkerti út 2; starters 980-2980Ft, mains 2850-4250Ft; ☺ noon-11pm; Ⓜ M1 Hősök tere

With reworked Hungarian classics that make it a winner, the 'Owl's Castle' attracts the Budapest cognoscenti, who leave its sister restaurant, Gundel (see right), next door, to the expense-account brigade. It's staffed entirely by women – in the kitchen, at table, front of house. There's a bargain-basement three-course set menu for 2800Ft.

GUNDEL Map p108   Hungarian €€
☎ 486 4040; XIV Állatkerti út 2; brunch adult/child under 15 5800/2900Ft; ☺ 11.30am-3pm Sun; Ⓜ M1 Hősök tere

Gundel, next to the zoo and directly behind the Museum of Fine Arts, is the city's fanciest (and most famous) restaurant, with a tradition dating back to 1894. Indeed, apparently it still feeds the Habsburgs (or what's left of them) when they're in town. But we've always found Gundel to be vastly overpriced, offering little value for money. Except, that is, for Sunday brunch, a multicourse themed gobble-fest of cold and warm dishes and desserts that changes every week.

top picks

What's your recommendation? www.lonelyplanet.com/budapest

Budapest (and particularly Pest) is loaded with pubs and bars, and there are enough to satisfy every taste. For popular seasonal outdoor venues, beyond the pubs and bars with terraces along VI Liszt Ferenc tér and up and down IX Ráday utca, see the boxed text, p158.

This city has always been as famous as Vienna for its cafes, cake shops and cafe culture; at the start of the 20th century, Budapest counted more than 500 cafes, but by the time of the change in 1989 (ie the collapse of communism) there were scarcely a dozen left. The majority of the traditional cafes are in Pest, but Buda can still lay claim to a handful.

NONALCOHOLIC DRINKS

Most international soft drink brands are available in Budapest, but mineral water (*ásvány víz*) seems to be the most popular libation for teetotallers in cafes, pubs and bars. Fruit juice is usually canned or boxed fruit 'drink' with lots of sugar added, though some of us are addicted to the sour cherry variety.

Budapesters drink a tremendous amount of coffee (*kávé*) – as a single black (*fekete*) or double (*dupla*). *Tejes kávé* (coffee with frothed milk) is closer to what we call cappuccino. 'Cappuccino' here is coffee with whipped cream. Decaffeinated coffee is *koffeinmentes kávé*.

Tea (pronounced *tay*-ah) is not as popular as coffee here; in fact, it can often be difficult to find 'English' tea in small grocery stores, though you'll always be able to choose from a wide range of herbal teas and fruit tisanes. People here never add milk to tea, preferring lemon, honey or even rum.

ALCOHOLIC DRINKS

Hungarians are big drinkers and enjoy a tipple at the drop of a hat (or a forint or a glass). Beer, especially lager, is extremely popular with the young; older folk drink homemade fruit-flavoured brandies, and wine is drunk by everyone.

Beer

Hungary produces a number of its own beers for national distribution; the most common ones are Dreher, Kőbányai and Arany Ászok, all produced by the same Budapest-based brewery. Some, however, are found more commonly in the vicinity of where they are brewed, such as Borsodi near Miskolc, Szalon in Pécs and Soproni. Bottled and canned Austrian, German and Czech beers are readily available. Locally brewed and imported beer in Hungary is almost always lager (*világos sör*), though occasionally you'll come across Dreher Barna, a 'brown' or stout.

Brandy & Liqueur

Pálinka is a strong (usually 40% but sometimes as high as 50%) brandy or eau de vie distilled from a variety of fruits but most commonly from apricots or plums. There are many different types and qualities, but among our favourites are Óbarack, the double-distilled 'Old Apricot'; the kind made with raspberry (*málna*) or blackthorn or sloe (*kökény*) and anything with *kóser* (kosher) on the label, which is always a sign of quality.

Hungarian liqueurs are usually overly sweet and artificial tasting, though the Zwack brand is reliable. Zwack also produces Unicum (see p105), a bitter aperitif that has been around since 1790. Habsburg emperor Joseph II supposedly named it when he first tasted it, exclaiming 'Das ist ein Unikum!' (This is a unique drink!).

Wine

Wine has been produced in Hungary for thousands of years, and it remains very important both economically and socially. You'll find it available by the glass or bottle everywhere in Budapest – at very basic wine bars, in food stalls, restaurants, supermarkets and 24-hour grocery stores – usually at reasonable prices. If you're seriously into wine, visit the speciality wine shops on both sides of the Danube and reviewed in the Shopping chapter.

Before WWII Hungarian wine was much in demand throughout Europe, but with the advent of socialism and mass production, quality went down the drain. Most of what wasn't consumed at home went to the Soviet Union where, frankly, they were prepared to drink anything. Political and economic circumstances provided little incentive to upgrade antiquated standards of winemaking. All of that has changed over the past decade and a number of small- to medium-sized family-owned wineries such as Tiffán, Bock, Szeremley, Thummerer and Szepsy are now producing very fine wines indeed.

When choosing a Hungarian wine, look for the words *minőségi bor* (quality wine) or *különleges minőséű bor* (premium quality wine), Hungary's version of the French quality regulation *appellation controlée*. Generally speaking, vintage (*évjárat*) has become important only recently so should not be much of a concern just yet.

On a wine label the first word of the name indicates where the wine comes from, while the second word is the grape variety (eg Villányi Kékfrankos) or the type or brand of wine (eg Tokaji Aszú, Szekszárdi Bikavér). Other important words that you'll see include: *édes* (sweet), *fehér* (white), *félédes* (semisweet), *félszáraz* (semidry or medium), *pezsgő* (sparkling), *száraz* (dry) and *vörös* (red).

Hungary counts 22 distinct wine-growing areas in Transdanubia, the Balaton region, the Northern Uplands and on the Great Plain. They range in size from tiny Somló in Western Transdanubia, to the vast vineyards of the Kunság on the Southern Plain, with its sandy soil nurturing more than a third of all the vines growing in the country.

Of course it's all a matter of taste, but the most distinctive red wines come from Villány and Szekszárd in Southern Transdanubia and the best dry whites are produced around Lake Balaton and in Somló. The reds from Eger, especially Bikavér (Bull's Blood), and the sweet whites from Tokaj are much better known abroad, however.

WHERE TO DRINK

A *kávéháv* is literally a 'coffee house' – ie a cafe – and the best place to stop if you just want something hot or nonalcoholic and cold. An *eszpresszó,* along with being a type of coffee, is essentially a coffee house too (also called *presszó*), but it usually also sells alcoholic drinks and light snacks. A *cukrászda* serves cakes, pastries and ice cream as well as hot and cold drinks.

To sample some local brew or vintage try visiting a *söröző,* a pub with draught beer (*csapolt sör*) available on tap; a *borozó,* an establishment (usually a dive) serving wine; or a *pince,* which can be a cellar with beer or wine but usually the latter (also called *bor pince*).

At a pub, beer is served in a *pohár* (0.3L) or a *korsó* (0.4L or 0.5L). In an old-fashioned wine bar, the wine is ladled out by the *deci* (deciliter, 0.1L), but in more modern places it comes by the ill-defined *pohár* (glass).

Old-style cafes, some of which date back as much as a century and a half, abound in Budapest and some of them are classic examples of their type. They were once the centre of social life and in them alliances were formed and momentous events planned and plotted. For more, see the boxed text, p147.

Teahouses serving every imaginable type of exotic tea and tisane have become very trendy in Budapest in recent years and they're often quite stylish places.

HOW MUCH?

A *korsó* of beer will cost anywhere between 350Ft and 600Ft in a bar or pub. A glass of wine starts at around 500Ft and a cocktail costs from 900Ft. Expect to pay 250Ft to 400Ft for a coffee in a cafe. In clubs and chic bars, prices can easily be double this. To hunt down the place with the cheapest drinks, just follow the trail of students to some of those happy hours with reduced-price drinks or two-for-one deals.

For tips on tipping conventions in Budapest, see p125 and p215.

CASTLE HILL & VÍZIVÁROS
CASTLE HILL

OSCAR AMERICAN BAR Map p62 Bar
☎ 212 8017; www.oscarbar.hu, in Hungarian; I Ostrom utca 14; ☽ 5pm-2am Mon-Thu, to 4am Fri & Sat; Ⓜ M2 Moszkva tér

The decor is cinema inspired – film memorabilia on the wood-panelled walls, leather directors chairs – and the beautiful crowd often act like they're on camera. Not to worry, the potent cocktails – from daiquiris and cosmopolitans to mojitos – go down a treat. There's music most nights.

CAFÉ MIRÓ Map p62 Modern Cafe
☎ 201 5573; www.cafemiro.hu, in Hungarian; I Úri utca 30; ☽ 9am-midnight; ◻ 16, 16A or 116

A personal favourite in the Castle District, this bright cafe-restaurant has wrought-iron furniture and local artwork and photography on the walls. Aside from its decent snacks and cakes (360Ft to 390Ft), it does more substantial starters (1790Ft to 2190Ft) and main courses (1990Ft to 2990Ft). There's also a Pest branch called Café Miró Grande (Map pp92–3; ☎ 321 8666; VI Liszt Ferenc tér 9; ☉ 10am-1am; Ⓜ M1 Oktogon).

VÍZIVÁROS

LÁNCHÍD SÖRÖZŐ Map p62   Bar
☎ 214 3144; I Fő utca 4; ☉ 11am-1am; 🚌 86, 🚊 19

The 'Chain Bridge Pub', at the southern end of Fő utca, has a wonderful retro Magyar feel to it, with old movie posters and advertisements on the walls and red-checked cloths on the tables. Friendly service too.

BAMBI PRESSZÓ Map p62   Modern Cafe
☎ 213 3171; II Frankel Leó út 2-4; ☉ 7am-10pm Mon-Fri, 9am-9pm Sat & Sun; 🚌 86

The words 'Bambi' and 'modern' do not make comfortable bedfellows; nothing about this place (named after a communist-era soft drink) has changed since the 1960s. And that's just the way we (and the rest of the crowd here) like it. Surly, set-it-down-with-a-crash service completes the distorted picture.

DÉRYNÉ Map p62   Modern Cafe
☎ 225 1407; www.cafederyne.hu; I Krisztina tér 3; ☉ 8am-midnight Sun-Wed, to 1am Thu-Sat; 🚌 5

What was until not too long ago a very untouristed traditional cafe near the entrance to the Alagút (the tunnel running under Castle Hill) has metamorphosed into a beautiful cafe-bar-bistro with excellent breakfast (950Ft to 1250Ft) and more substantial meals (starters 590Ft to 2690Ft, mains 1490Ft to 4190Ft) throughout the day.

ANGELIKA KÁVÉHÁZ
Map p62   Traditional Cafe
☎ 225 1653; www.angelikacafe.hu; I Batthyány tér 7; ☉ 9am-midnight Mon-Sat, to 11pm Sun; Ⓜ M2 Batthyány tér

Angelika is a charming cafe – this time attached to an 18th-century church – with a raised terrace. The more substantial dishes (salads 1390Ft to 2290Ft, sandwiches 1190Ft to 1390Ft) are just so-so; come here for the cakes (320Ft to 390Ft) and the views across the square to the Danube and Parliament.

AUGUSZT CUKRÁSZDA
Map p62   Traditional Cafe
☎ 316 3817; II Fény utca 8; ☉ 10am-6pm Tue-Fri, from 9am Sat; Ⓜ M2 Moszkva tér

Tucked away behind the Fény utca market and Mammut shopping mall (p113), this is the original Auguszt cafe (there are newer branches) and only sells its own shop-made cakes (200Ft to 500Ft), pastries and biscuits. There's limited seating on the 1st floor.

RUSZWURM CUKRÁSZDA
Map p62   Traditional Cafe
☎ 375 5284; www.ruszwurm.hu; I Szentháromság utca 7; ☉ 10am-7pm; 🚌 16, 16/a or 116

This diminutive cafe is the perfect place for coffee and cakes (200Ft to 550Ft) in the Castle District, though it can get pretty crowded. Indeed, in high season it's almost always impossible to get a seat.

GELLÉRT HILL, TABÁN & KELENFÖLD

KISRABLÓ PUB Map pp70-1   Bar
☎ 209 1588; XI Zenta utca 3; ☉ 11am-2am Mon-Sat; 🚊 18, 19, 47 or 49

Close to the Budapest University of Technology and Economics (BME) and to many of the summer hostels (see p172) mentioned in this guide, the 'Little Pirate' is, not surprisingly, very popular with students. But don't be misled – it's an attractive and well-run place with decent food (salads 1290Ft to 1680Ft, pasta 1200Ft to 1890Ft) available.

ROLLING ROCK CAFÉ Map pp70-1   Bar
☎ 385 3348; www.caferollingrock.hu, in Hungarian; XIII Bartók Béla út 76; ☉ 11am-3am; 🚊 18, 19, 47 or 49

Should you find yourself near Buda's Fenéketlen-tó (Bottomless Lake) and would like a drink or three, you could do worse than this place: a revamped pub where the local young bloods gather for libations, Tex-Mex grub and (more often than not) live music.

CAFÉ PONYVAREGÉNY
Map pp70-1   Modern Cafe
☎ 209 5255; XI Bercsényi utca 5; ☉ 10am-midnight Mon-Sat, 2-10pm Sun; 🚊 18, 19, 47 or 49

MY CAFE, MY CASTLE

Cafe life has a longer (and arguably more colourful) history in Budapest than in virtually any other city in Europe. The Turks introduced coffee to the Hungarians (who first called it 'black soup') in the early 16th century, and the coffee house was an essential part of the social scene here long before it had even made an appearance in Vienna or Paris. In the final decades of the Austro-Hungarian empire, Budapest counted some 600 cafes.

Budapest cafes of the 19th century were a lot more than just places to drink coffee that was 'black like the devil, hot like hell and sweet like a kiss', as they used to say. They embodied the progressive liberal ideal that people of all classes could mingle under one roof, and acted as an incubator for Magyar culture. Combining the neighbourliness of a local pub, the bonhomie of a gentlemen's club and the intellectual activity of an open university, coffee houses were places to relax, gamble, work, network, do business and debate. As the writer Dezső Kosztolányi put it in his essay *Budapest, City of Cafés*: 'Az én kávéházam, az én váram' (My cafe is my castle).

Different cafes catered to different groups. Actors preferred the Pannónia and businessmen the Orczy, while cartoonists frequented the Lánchíd and stockbrokers the Lloyd. But the two most important in terms of the city's cultural life were the Japán and the New York.

The Café Japán at VI Andrássy út 45 (today the Írók Boltja; p119) was a favourite haunt of artists and architects and attracted the likes of Kosztka Tivadar Csontváry, József Rippl-Rónai, Pál Merse Szinyei and Ödön Lechner. The New York Café (p151), which opened in 1894 at VII Erzsébet körút 9-11 and quickly became the city's most celebrated literary cafe, hosted virtually every Hungarian writer of note at one time or another – from Kosztolányi and Endre Ady to Gyula Krúdy and Ferenc Molnár. Molnár, playwright-in-residence at the Comedy Theatre, famously threw the key to the New York into the Danube the night the cafe opened so that it would never close. And that's just what it did, remaining open round the clock 365 days a year for decades.

But all good things must come to an end, and the depression of the 1930s, WWII and the dreary days of communism conspired against grand old cafes in favour of the cheap (and seldom cheerful) *eszpresszó* (coffee shop). By 1989 and the return of the Republic of Hungary only about a dozen remained.

Nowadays you're more likely to find young Budapesters drinking a beer or a glass of wine at one of the new modern cafes. It's true – the cafe *is* very much alive in Budapest. It's just reinvented itself, that's all.

The 'Pulp Fiction' is a great new place that's supposed to be a local secret but, alas, is no longer. The old beans and fringed lampshades are a nice touch and the coffee (200Ft to 700Ft) is some of the best in town. Chilled clientele.

ÓBUDA, RÓZSADOMB & MARGARET ISLAND

POCO LOCO Map p74   Bar
☎ 438 3227; www.pocoloco.hu, in Hungarian; II Frankel Leó út 51; ⏰ 11.30am-midnight; 🚊 17
At the corner of Harcsa utca and Frankel Leó út on the way to Óbuda, this one-time seamy place has cleaned up its act but still remains interesting. It doubles as a restaurant too. There's wi-fi throughout.

PUSKÁS PANCHO Map p74   Bar
☎ 333 5656; www.symbolbudapest.hu; III Bécsi út 56; ⏰ 11.30am-midnight; 🚊 17
Buda's newest sports pub is just one of seven bars and restaurants in the enormous Symbol complex in Óbuda. Should

you tire of the place, the world's, well, your oyster.

DAUBNER CUKRÁSZDA
Map p74   Traditional Cafe
☎ 335 2253; www.daubnercukraszda.hu; II Szépvölgyi út 50; ⏰ 9am-7pm Tue-Sun; 🚌 65
It may seem quite a journey for your *Sachertorte* and you can only stand and nibble on the hoof here, but Daubner gets rave reviews from locals and expats alike as the best shop for cakes (250Ft to 400ft) in Buda.

BELVÁROS & LIPÓTVÁROS
BELVÁROS

ACTION BÁR Map p85   Bar
☎ 266 9148; www.action.gay.hu; V Magyar utca 42; ⏰ 9pm-4am; Ⓜ M3 Kálvin tér
Action is where to head if you want just that (though there's a strip show at midnight and an extra one at 2am on Friday, which may distract). Take the usual precautions and don't forget to write home.

JANIS PUB Map p85 Bar

☎ 266 2619; www.janispub.hu; V Királyi Pál utca 8; ☺ 4pm-2am Mon-Thu, 4pm-3am Fri & Sat, 6pm-midnight Sun; Ⓜ M3 Kálvin tér

Close to the university, this ever-popular pub is a shrine to the late, great singer Janis 'Pearl' Joplin, which, according to the pub's publicity blurb, 'makes the traditional 'Irish pub' spirit unique' (we don't get it either). But it's always a good place to stop for a quick one or two on the way to somewhere else.

GERLÓCZY KÁVÉHÁZ Map p85 Modern Cafe

☎ 501 4000; www.gerloczy.hu; V Gerlóczy utca 1; ☺ 7am-11pm; 🚊 47 or 49

This wonderful retro-style cafe looks out onto one of Pest's most attractive little squares and serves excellent breakfast (600Ft to 2000Ft) and light meals (1720Ft to 2450Ft), including a cheese plate sent over from the excellent T Nagy Tamás (p126) cheese shop around the corner.

1000 TEA Map p85 Teahouse

☎ 337 8217; www.1000tea.hu, in Hungarian; V Váci utca 65; ☺ noon-9pm Mon-Sat; 🚌 15 or 115

In a small courtyard off lower Váci utca, this is the place if you want to sip a soothing blend made by tea-serious staff, and lounge on pillows in a Japanese-style tearoom. You can also sit on the tea chests and sip in the courtyard. There's a shop here too.

CENTRÁL KÁVÉHÁZ Map p85 Traditional Cafe

☎ 266 2110; www.centralkavehaz.hu; V Károlyi Mihály utca 9; ☺ 8am-midnight; Ⓜ M3 Ferenciek tere

This grande dame of a traditional cafe is still jostling to reclaim her title as the place to sit and look intellectual in Pest, after reopening a few years ago following extensive renovations. It serves meals as well as lighter fare, such as sandwiches (1000Ft) and omelettes (from 1490Ft) and, of course, cakes and pastries (390Ft to 800Ft).

GERBEAUD CUKRÁSZDA

Map p85 Traditional Cafe

☎ 429 9000; www.gerbeaud.hu; V Vörösmarty tér 7-8; ☺ 9am-9pm; Ⓜ M1 Vörösmarty tér

Founded in 1858, Gerbeaud has been the most fashionable meeting place for the city's elite on the northern side of Pest's busiest square since 1870. Along with exquisitely prepared cakes and pastries (410Ft to 1150Ft), it serves continental breakfasts (2950Ft) and sandwiches (1550Ft to 2950Ft). A visit is mandatory.

LIPÓTVÁROS

BECKETTS IRISH BAR Map p85 Bar

☎ 311 1033; www.becketts.hu; V Alkotmány utca 20; ☺ noon-1am Sun-Thu, to 3am Fri & Sat; Ⓜ M3 Nyugati pályaudvar

Of the capital's ubiquitous 'Irish' pubs, this is arguably the best (and definitely the largest) of the lot, with all-day breakfasts (2500Ft) as well as sandwiches (950Ft), pizzas (1750Ft to 1950Ft) and salads (1900Ft). The cocktail bar in the rear is an additional plus.

FEHÉR GYŰRŰ Map p85 Bar

☎ 312 1863; V Balassi Bálint utca 27; ☺ 3pm-midnight Mon-Thu, 3pm-1am Fri & Sat, 5pm-midnight Sun; 🚊 2, 4 or 6

The 'White Ring' has always been a firm favourite and, frankly, it's never been clear why. Perhaps it's because it is opposite the so-called White House (p97) and it's always fun to play 'spot the MP'. More likely it's because there are so few pubs in this area.

LE CAFE M BAR Map p85 Bar

☎ 312 1436; www.lecafem.com; V Nagysándor József utca 3; ☺ 4pm-4am Mon-Fri, from 6pm Sat & Sun; Ⓜ M3 Arany János utca

Our favourite (err, actually, just about the only) neighbourhood gay bar in Budapest has super-cool decor (bye bye draped muslin and Greek statues), friendly staff and internet access for 300/500Ft per half-/full hour for a little cruising while you're cruising.

TERV ESZPRESSZÓ Map p85 Bar

☎ 269 3132; V Nádor utca 19; ☺ 9am-midnight Mon-Sat, 10am-11pm Sun; Ⓜ M1/2/3/Deák Ferenc tér, M3 Arany János utca

'Plan' (as in 'Five-Year') is a retro-style cafe-bar on two levels decorated with photographs of Hungarian athletes, politicians, actors and so on from the 1950s and '60s. Unlike a lot of such places, the theme doesn't get old in a half-hour and it's a useful place for a quick beer or coffee on the way down to Váci utca.

FARGER KÁVÉ Map p85 — Modern Cafe

☎ 373 0078; www.farger.hi; V Zoltán utca 18; ⏰ 7am-8pm Mon-Fri, 9-4pm Sat & Sun; Ⓜ M2 Kossuth Lajos tér

This modern and – thanks to some ingenious 'urban gardening' – leafy cafe has two major draws: its first-rate views of Szabadság tér from the window seats and terrace and the free wi-fi throughout.

MONTMARTRE Map p85 — Modern Cafe

☎ 301 8765; V Zrínyi utca 18; ⏰ 9am-1am; Ⓜ M3 Arany János utca

This very unpretentious cafe and art gallery just down the road from the Basilica of St Stephen is always fun, especially on the nights when there is live Latino and jazz. The welcome here is always warm.

NEGRO CAFÉ Map p85 — Modern Cafe

☎ 302 0136; V Szent István tér 11; ⏰ 8am-1am Sun-Thu, to 2.30am Fri & Sat; Ⓜ M3 Arany János utca

This sleek and very stylish cafe with the non-PC name and stunning views of the basilica attracts a well-heeled crowd dressed to the nines (or did we see 10s too?) and sipping from an impressive cocktail menu. Breakfasts, served till noon daily, are a snip at 690Ft to 1590Ft.

ART NOUVEAU CAFÉ Map p85 — Traditional Cafe

☎ 06-30 685 5153; V Honvéd utca 3; ⏰ 8am-6pm Mon-Fri, from 9am Sat; Ⓜ M2 Kossuth Lajos tér

This small but comfortable cafe on the ground floor of delightful Bedő House (p87) is tailor-made for fans of the Secessionist style. The cakes (290Ft to 370Ft) are pretty average though.

ELSÖ PESTI RÉTESHÁZ Map p85 — Traditional Cafe

☎ 428 0135; www.reteshaz.com; V Október 6 utca 22; ⏰ 9am-11pm Mon-Fri, from 11am Sat & Sun; Ⓜ M1/2/3/Deák Ferenc tér ☐ 15 or 115

It may be a bit overdone (think Magyar Disneyland, with olde worlde counters, painted plates stuck on the walls and curios embedded in Plexiglass washbasins) but the 'First Strudel House of Pest' is just the place to taste this Hungarian stretched pastry (240Ft to 290Ft) filled with apple, cheese, poppy seeds or sour cherry.

SZALAI CUKRÁSZDA

Map p85 — Traditional Cafe

☎ 269 3210; V Balassi Bálint utca 7; ⏰ 9am-7pm Wed-Mon; ☐ 2

This humble cake shop in Lipótváros just north of parliament probably has the best cherry strudel (from 310Ft) in the capital, though its cream cakes also go down a treat.

NORTHERN RING ROAD AREA
ÚJLIPÓTVÁROS & TERÉZVÁROS

BOX UTCA Map pp92-3 — Bar

☎ 354 1444; www.origo.hu/boxutca, in Hungarian; VI Bajcsy-Zsilinszky út 21; ⏰ noon-midnight Sun-Thu, to 2am Fri & Sat; Ⓜ M2 Arany János utca

This swish new sports bar and restaurant (think 'ring' not 'gift' when you say 'box' – it's owned by local pugilist István 'Ko-Ko' Kovács) has screens aplenty for all events and a lovely street-side terrace open in the warmer months.

CAPTAIN COOK PUB Map pp92-3 — Bar

☎ 269 3136; VI Bajcsy-Zsilinszky út 19/a; ⏰ 10am-1.30am Mon-Sat, from 2pm Sun; Ⓜ M2 Arany János utca

There's not much to say about the CC except that it enjoys an enviable location diagonally opposite the basilica, the terrace is a delight in the warm weather, there are four beers on tap and the staff are welcoming and friendly. And for us, that's sufficient.

PICASSO POINT Map pp92-3 — Bar

☎ 06-20 342 1446; www.picassopoint.hu, in Hungarian; VI Hajós utca 31; ⏰ 5pm-2am Mon-Thu, to 4am Fri & Sat; Ⓜ M3 Arany János utca

A stalwart of the Budapest entertainment scene, Picasso Point is a laid-back place for a drink, listening to canned blues and jazz and meeting people.

PÓTKULCS Map pp92-3 — Bar

☎ 269 1050; www.potkulcs.hu; VI Csengery utca 65/b; ⏰ 5pm-1.30am Sun-Wed, to 2.30am Thu-Sat; Ⓜ M3 Nyugati pályaudvar

The 'Spare Key' is a wonderful little drinking venue, with a varied menu of live music from 9.30pm most nights, *táncház* (dance house; p42) at 8pm every Tuesday and an astrology night on Monday. The small central courtyard is a wonderful place to chill out in summer.

CAFÉ EKLEKTIKA Map pp92-3 Modern Cafe
☎ 266 1226; VI Nagymező utca 30; ◷ noon-midnight; Ⓜ M1 Opera, trolleybuses 70 or 78
While there are no specifically lesbian bars in Budapest, Café Eklektika – love the name and the concept – comes the closest and attracts a very mixed, gay-friendly crowd. Lots of canned jazz and the like.

ANDRÁSSY ÚT & SURROUNDS

KIADÓ KOCSMA Map pp92-3 Bar
☎ 331 1955; VI Jókai tér 3; ◷ 10am-2am Mon-Fri, from noon Sat & Sun; Ⓜ M2 Oktogon
The 'Pub for Rent' is a great place for a swift pint and a quick bite (salads and pasta dishes, 1000Ft to 1500Ft) a stone's throw – and light years – away from flashy VI Liszt Ferenc tér.

BALLETTCIPŐ Map pp92-3 Modern Cafe
☎ 269 3114; www.balettcipo.hu; VI Hajós utca 14; ◷ 9am-midnight Mon-Thu, noon-1am Fri & Sat, noon-midnight Sun; Ⓜ M1 Opera
The pretty little 'Ballet Slipper' in the theatre district – just behind the Hungarian State Opera House – is a delightful place to stop for a rest and refreshment or to have a light meal (sandwiches and salads 1250Ft to 1750Ft, burritos and fajitas 1450Ft to 1890Ft).

CAFÉ VIAN Map pp92-3 Modern Cafe
☎ 268 1154; VI Liszt Ferenc tér 9; ◷ 9am-1am; Ⓜ M1 Oktogon
This comfortable cafe – all done up in warm tones and serving breakfast all day – remains the anchor tenant on the sunny side of 'the tér' and the court of Pest's arty aristocracy. Indeed, it's got its very own built-in art gallery called Artitude (www.artitude.hu).

CALLAS Map pp92-3 Modern Cafe
☎ 354 0954; wwwcallascafe.hu; VI Andrássy út 20; ◷ 8.30am-midnight Tue-Fri, from 10am Sat & Sun; Ⓜ M1 Opera
With its location hard by the opera house, this place just had to be named in honour of the late (and much lamented) Greek-American soprano. But we come here for the terrace in fine weather, surely the best for people-watching and cruising in town.

INCOGNITO CAFÉ Map pp92-3 Modern Cafe
☎ 342 1471; VI Liszt Ferenc tér 3; ◷ 2pm-1am Sun-Wed, 2pm-3am Thu-Sat; Ⓜ M1 Oktogon
The 'Unknown' is hardly that. It was the first cafe to open on what everyone now calls 'the tér', some 15 years ago and is still going strong in its low-key sort of way.

KÉT SZERECSEN Map pp92-3 Modern Cafe
☎ 343 1984; www.ketszerecsen.hu; VI Nagymező utca 14; ◷ 8am-1am Mon-Fri, from 9am Sat & Sun; Ⓜ M1 Opera
Not on VI Liszt Ferenc tér but close enough, the very relaxed 'Two Moors' serves both main meals (starters from 990Ft to 1790Ft, mains 1980Ft to 3090Ft) and decent breakfasts till 11am every morning.

TEAHÁZ A VÖRÖS OROSZLÁNHOZ
Map pp92-3 Teahouse
☎ 269 0579; VI Jókai tér 8; ◷ 11am-11pm Mon-Sat, from 3pm Sun; Ⓜ M1 Oktogon
This serene place with quite a mouthful of a name (it means 'Teahouse at the Sign of the Red Lion') just north of Liszt Ferenc tér is quite serious about its teas (490Ft to 790Ft). There's also a Ráday utca branch (Map pp102–3; ☎ 215 2101; IX Ráday utca 9), which keeps the same hours.

LUKÁCS CUKRÁSZDA
Map pp92-3 Traditional Cafe
☎ 373 0407; www.lukacscukraszda.com; VI Andrássy út 70; ◷ 9am-8pm Mon-Sat, from 9.30am Sun; Ⓜ M1 Vörösmarty utca
This cafe is dressed up in the finest of decadence – all mirrors and gold – with soft piano music in the background. The selection of cakes (450Ft to 1250Ft) is excellent but expensive. Must be because the chief pâtissier has come all the way from France.

MŰVÉSZ KÁVÉHÁZ
Map pp92-3 Traditional Cafe
☎ 352 1337; VI Andrássy út 29; ◷ 9am-midnight Sun-Wed, to 1am Thu-Sat; Ⓜ M1 Opera
Almost opposite the State Opera House, the 'Artist' is a more interesting place to people-watch (especially from the terrace) though some say its cakes (490Ft to 790Ft) are not what they used to be (though presumably not as far back as 1898 when it opened).

ERZSÉBETVÁROS

CHAMPS SPORT BAR
Map pp92-3   Bar

☎ 413 1655; www.champsbuda.hu; VII Dohány utca 20; ☎ noon-midnight Mon-Thu, to 2am Fri-Sun; Ⓜ M2 Astoria

Established by five Olympic medallists (swimmer, runner, pentathlon, kayaker and racer), Champs is the place for sports fans and the vicarious, with two giant screens and 35 TVs. There's a wide choice of low-fat 'fitness meals' along with the less healthy favourites of armchair athletes. There's also a Buda branch (Map p62; ☎ 201 0569; II Erőd utca 22; 🚋 4 or 6), which keeps the same hours.

COXX MEN'S BAR
Map pp92-3   Bar

☎ 344 4884; www.coxx.hu; VII Dohány utca 38; 🕓 9pm-4am Sun-Thu, to 5am Fri & Sat; 🚎 7

Probably the cruisiest game in town, this boldly named mee(a)t rack has a long brick-lined cellar bar and some significant play areas in back. You might soon find yourself 'behind bars' in more ways than one.

SZIMPLA
Map pp92-3   Bar

☎ 321 9119; www.szimpla.hu; VII Kertész utca 48; 🕓 10am-2am Mon-Fri, noon-2am Sat, noon-midnight Sun; 🚋 4 or 6

This distressed-looking, very unflashy place – the name says it all – remains one of the most popular drinking venues south of VI Liszt Ferenc tér. There are live music evenings Tuesday to Thursday.

VITTULA
Map pp92-3   Bar

☎ 06-20 527 7069; http://klubvittula.blogspot.com; VII Kertész utca 4; 🕓 6pm-dawn Sep-Jun; Ⓜ M2 Blaha Lujza tér

Great (though tiny and very smoky) underground (both senses) bar just off the Big Ring Road, with international performances, cutting-edge DJs and some cheap Slovakian lager.

CASTRO BISZTRÓ
Map pp92-3   Modern Cafe

☎ 215 0814; VII Madách tér 3; 🕓 11am-midnight Mon-Thu, 11am-1am Fri, noon-1am Sat, 2pm-midnight Sun; Ⓜ M1/2/3 Deák Ferenc tér

Now in a new location just off the Little Ring Road, this eclectic place has a mixed clientele, Serbian finger food like čevapčiči (spicy meatballs; 900Ft to 1800Ft) and tasty pljeskavica (meat patties; 1200Ft), wi-fi throughout and the same chilled vibe it had when located on IX Ráday utca.

The street running north from here, Madách Imre út, was originally designed to be as large and grand a boulevard as nearby Andrássy út. But WWII nipped that plan in the bud, and it now ends abruptly and rather self-consciously after just two blocks.

MOZAIK TEAHÁZ
Map pp92-3   Teahouse

☎ 266 7001; www.mozaikteahaz.hu, in Hungarian; VI Király utca 18; 🕓 10am-10.30pm Mon-Fri, from 1pm Sat & Sun; 🚋 4 or 6

An eclectic – note the mosaic of a satyr outside – rarity among Budapest teahouses, with non–New Age music and smoking permitted (for the moment). There are 100 types of tea on offer.

FRÖHLICH CUKRÁSZDA
Map pp92-3   Traditional Cafe

☎ 267 2851; www.frohlich.hu; VII Dob utca 22; 🕓 9am-6pm Mon-Thu, 7.30am-4pm Fri, 10am-6pm Sun; trolleybus 74

This kosher cake shop and cafe in the former ghetto, dating back to 1953, makes and sells old Jewish favourites (180Ft to 350Ft) like flódni (a three-layer cake with apple, walnut and poppy-seed fillings) as well as holiday sweets: for Purim there is kindli (cookies with nuts or poppy seeds) and hamentaschen ('pocket' biscuits filled with nuts and poppy seeds or apricot jam); and for Rosh Hashanah, lekach (honey and nut pastry).

NEW YORK CAFÉ
Map pp92-3   Traditional Cafe

☎ 886 6111; www.boscolohotels.com; VII Erzsébet körút 9-11; 🕓 10am-midnight Mon-Fri, 9am-midnight Sat & Sun; 🚋 4 or 6

This Renaissance-style cafe, considered the most beautiful in the world when it opened in 1895, was the scene of many a literary gathering over the years (see the boxed text, p147). It has now been extensively renovated but, alas, lacks the warmth and erudite crowd of most traditional cafes. Still, the opulence and the history of the New York will impress and it's a great place for a late breakfast (1500Ft to 4800Ft; available till noon).

SOUTHERN RING ROAD AREA

DARSHAN UDVAR Map pp102-3   Bar

☎ 266 5541; www.darshan.hu; VIII Krúdy utca 7;
🕙 11am-midnight; 🚊 4 or 6

This cavernous complex with bar, restaurant and vegetarian cafe has decor that combines Eastern flair with a hippy vibe. It's an easy escape from the bars of VI Liszt Ferenc tér and the dull sophistication of IX Ráday utca, though VIII Krúdy utca has yet to take over as Budapest's next after-hours strip. There are pizzas (1090Ft to 1390Ft) and pasta dishes (990Ft to 1190Ft) as well as more substantial mains (1290Ft to 2550Ft) to accompany the liquid offerings.

PARIS TEXAS Map pp102-3   Bar

☎ 218 0570; IX Ráday utca 22; 🕙 noon-3am;
Ⓜ M3 Kálvin tér

One of the original bars on the IX Ráday utca nightlife strip, this place has a coffee-house feel to it with old sepia-tinted photos on the walls and pool tables downstairs. Nurse a cocktail from the huge list and order a pizza from Pink Cadillac (p141) next door.

CAFÉ CSIGA Map pp102-3   Modern Cafe

☎ 210 0885; VIII Vásár utca 2; 🕙 11am-1pm;
🚊 4 or 6

The 'Snail Cafe' is a very popular, eclectically decorated Irish-owned place just opposite the Rákóczi tér market, attracting a mixed, arty crowd. It does food, too, including an excellent set lunch for 990Ft.

NIGHTLIFE & THE ARTS

top picks

For a city of its size, Budapest has a huge choice of things to do and places to go after dark – from opera and (participatory) folk dancing to live jazz and pulsating clubs with some of the best DJs in the region. It's usually not difficult getting tickets or getting in; the hard part is deciding what to do.

There are no concentrated nightlife areas on the Buda side, unless you count sedate (some might say comatose) and over-priced Castle Hill or the rather dispersed II Moszkva tér (Map p62, A3). The Pest side, on the other hand, has all sorts of strips – from the ultratouristed V Duna korzó (Map p85, B5) along the Danube, with pricey watering holes commanding fine views of Buda Castle, to leafy VI Andrássy út (Map pp92–3, B6). But the two main areas are trendy VI Liszt Ferenc tér (Map pp92–3, C6), where you'll have to duel to the death for a spot under the plane trees, and IX Ráday utca (Map pp102–3, A3), a more subdued semi-pedestrianised street in Józsefváros full of pubs and bars, restaurants and that new breed of modern cafe – all polished chrome, halogen lighting and straight lines. Another place to find these is up-and-coming V Szent István tér behind the renovated Basilica of St Stephen.

Information & Listings

Your best source of information in English for what's on in the city is the freebie Budapest Funzine (www.funzine.hu), published every other Thursday and available at hotels, bars, cinemas and wherever tourists congregate. More comprehensive but in Hungarian only is the freebie PestiEst (www.est.hu, in Hungarian) and the ultra-thorough Pesti Műsor (Budapest Program; www.pestimusor.hu, in Hungarian; 295Ft), with everything from clubs and films to art exhibits and classical music. Both appear weekly on Thursday.

Other freebies include the vastly inferior monthly Budapest Life (www.budapestlife.hu) and the English- and German-language *Programme Magazine in Hungary/in Ungarn*. The free *Koncert Kalendárium,* published monthly (bimonthly in summer), has more serious offerings: classical concerts, opera, dance and the like. A hip little publication with all sorts of insider's tips is the *Budapest City Spy Map.* It's available free at pubs and bars.

For general websites that include lots of information on Budapest nightlife, see p18. For info on clubs, parties, music, DJs and so on check out www.budacast.hu, http://english.mashkulture.net and www.mykunk.com.

Tickets & Reservations

Some of the most useful booking agencies in Budapest are listed here. You can book almost anything online at www.jegymester.hu and www.kulturinfo.hu.

Ticket Express (Map pp92–3; ☎ information 312 0000, bookings 06-30 303 0999; www.tex.hu; VI Andrássy út 18; ☽ 10am-6.30pm Mon-Fri, 10am-3pm Sat; Ⓜ M1 Opera) The largest ticket-office network in the city, with dozens of outlets.

Ticket Pro (Map pp92–3; ☎ 555 5155; www.ticketpro.hu; VII Károly körút 9; ☽ 9am-9pm Mon-Fri, 10am-2pm Sat; Ⓜ M1/2/3 Deák Ferenc tér) This is a smaller, more personable agency, with tickets to plays and shows, concerts and sporting events.

Symphony Ticket Office (Szimfonikus Jegyiroda; Map pp92–3; ☎ 302 3841; VI Nagymező utca 19; ☽ 10am-6pm Mon-Fri, 10am-2pm Sat; Ⓜ M1 Opera) Visit this place for tickets to the philharmonic and other classical-music concerts.

CLUBBING

Budapest offers a club scene unmatched elsewhere in the region and there's everything on offer from underground (in every sense) venues where DJs spin quality retro and indie to enormous meat markets attracting the posh along with porno stars. Like everywhere, clubs in Budapest don't really get off the ground until well after Cinderella's coach has turned into a pumpkin – or later. Not all clubs and music bars in Budapest levy a cover charge but those that do will ask for between 1000Ft and 2500Ft at the door. The trendier (and trashier) places usually let women in for free.

ALTER EGO Map pp92-3

☎ 06-70 345 4302; www.alteregoclub.hu; VI Dessewffy utca 33; ☽ 10pm-5am Fri & Sat; Ⓜ M3 Nyugati pályaudvar, 🚋 4 or 6

This is Budapest's premier gay club, with the chic-est (think attitude) crowd and the best dance music on offer. It can be cruisy, but if you're seriously looking for action, go to the bar of that name (p147).

CINETRIP Map pp70-1
☎ 317 9338, 318 9844; www.cinetrip.hu; admission 5000Ft; ⏲ 9pm-late Saturday; Ⓜ M3 Ferenciek tere
By no means should you miss this regular event at the Rudas Baths (p165), if one is taking place during your visit. It combines partying and dancing with music, film and bathing and is just short of being an all-out orgy. Woohoo! It is usually held monthly from 9pm on Saturday; schedules are available at the box office of the Merlin Theatre (p161).

CÖKXPÔN Map pp102-3
☎ 06 30 826 4804, 06 30 270 8027; www.cokx ponambient.hu; IX Soroksári út 8-10; ⏲ 6pm-2am Sun-Wed, 6pm-4am Thu, 6pm-6am Fri & Sat; 🚊 2, 4 or 6
A club, a live-music venue, a cafe, a theatre, a cultural space almost on Boráros tér in Pest – welcome to the world of esoterica. Making Ambient a philosophy, Cökxpôn (nope, no idea) offers one of the best underground nights out in Budapest.

DOKK CLUB Map p74
☎ 06 30 535 2747, 955 0600; www.dokkdisco.hu, in Hungarian; III Hajógyári-sziget 122; ⏲ 8pm-4am Mon-Thu, 8pm-6am Fri & Sat; HÉV Árpád híd, 🚌 86
One of the perennials in Budapest's ever-changing club scene, Dokk is a cavernous club in a converted warehouse on an island in the Danube. It attracts a well-heeled crowd and employees from the nearby porn-movie studio; it's at its hottest, grinding-est best on a Friday night. Take a taxi, or it's an easy walk over Árpád Bridge from the HÉV or bus stop.

INSTANT Map pp92-3
☎ 06 30 830 8747; www.instant.co.hu; VI Nagymező utca 38; ⏲ 1pm-3am; Ⓜ M1 Opera, trolleybuses 70 or 78
Love, love, love this new 'rubble bar' on Pest's most vibrant nightlife strip and so do all our friends. It's got four bars on two levels with bopping, relaxing and chilling. If you want a taste of things to come and can't wait till lunchtime, head for the ground-floor coffee shop (⏲ 8am-10pm).

KLUB B7 Map pp92-3
☎ 269 0573; www.bseven.hu, in Hungarian; VI Nagymező utca 46-48; ⏲ 5pm-5am Wed-Sat; Ⓜ M1 Opera, trolleybuses 70 or 78)
The biggest club in central Budapest, B7 plays house and R&B classics at full throttle to a crowd that's obviously spent some time deciding what they're wearing tonight. You might try chatting up but forget conversation.

KÖZGÁZ KLUB Map pp102-3
☎ 215 4359, 06 30 992 9644; www.kozgazklub.hu; IX Fővám tér 8; ⏲ 10pm-5am Tue-Sat; 🚊 47 or 49
With few frills and cheap covers, this never-cool club at the Economics University is the pick-up venue of choice for many a student and there's plenty of dance room. Don't hang about if (when) the karaoke kicks in, though.

MERLIN Map p85
☎ 317 9338, 266 0904; www.merlinbudapest .org; V Gerlóczy utca 4; ⏲ 10am-midnight Sun-Thu, 10am-5am Fri & Sat; Ⓜ M1/2/3 Deák Ferenc tér
This venue is one of those something-for-everyone kind of places, with everything from jazz and breakbeat to techno and house. It hosts the biggest names on the international DJ scene passing through Budapest and is most visitors' first port of call.

MORRISON'S 2 Map p85
☎ 374 3329; www.morrisons.hu; V Honvéd utca 40; ⏲ 5pm-4am Mon-Sat; 🚊 4 or 6
Far and away Budapest's biggest party venue, this cavernous cellar club attracts a younger crowd with its four dance floors, half-dozen bars (including one in a covered courtyard) and enormous games room upstairs. Live bands from 9pm to 11pm in the week. No 2's daddy is the much smaller and more sedate Morrison's Opera (Map pp92–3; ☎ 269 4060; VI Révay utca 25; ⏲ 7pm-4am Mon-Sat; Ⓜ M1 Opera), a music pub with a signature red telephone booth all the way from Londontown.

PIAF Map pp92-3
☎ 312 3823; www.piafklub.hu; VI Nagymező utca 25; ⏲ 10pm-6am Sun-Thu, 10pm-7am Fri & Sat; Ⓜ M1 Opera, trolleybuses 70 or 78
Piaf is the place to go when everything else slows down. There's dancing and action well into the new day. There's a piano and

GAY & LESBIAN VENUES

What a difference a couple of decades makes! With only one or two sleazy – actually kind of scary – dives full of Romanian and Transylvanian hustlers less than 20 years ago, Budapest now counts close to two dozen gay venues and can lay claim to being central Europe's gayest city (and, for better or worse, porno capital). For useful websites and organisations, see p208.

Budapest's premier gay club is Alter Ego (p154) but you may not want to fire all your guns at once. Instead, start the evening off at Le Cafe M Bar (p148) and when (not if) you're feeling frisky, head for Action Bár (p147) or CoXx Men's Bar (p151).

Choices are more limited for girlz but there's always Café Eklektika (p149) if you don't mind a mixed but very gay-friendly scene. Living Room (Map p85; ☎ 06 30 992 9932; www.livingroom.hu; V Kossuth Lajos utca 17; ☺ 10pm-5am Wed-Sat; Ⓜ M2 Astoria) usually hosts lesbian parties on the last Saturday of each month. Check with Candy (☎ 06 70 330 0919; www.candybudapest.hu) for dyke parties held at other venues each month.

some louche lounge lizards on the ground floor but most of the fun and the characters – including some professionals – are in the smoky cavern with a dance floor below.

SOHO LONDON Map pp92-3

☎ 354 1096, 06 20 364 6940; www.soholondon.hu, in Hungarian; VI Nagymező utca 31; ☺ pub 11am-11pm Mon-Sat; club 7pm-5am Thu-Sat; Ⓜ M1 Opera, trolleybus 70 or 78

With its art deco neon light outside luring in the punters, Soho is a lively pub for much of the week but goes ballistic from Thursday night, with 'funky' (a Hungarian thing), Latino and '80s pop parties.

TRAFÓ BÁR TANGÓ Map pp102-3

☎ 456 2053, 06 20 414 0322; www.trafo.hu; IX Liliom utca 41; ☺ 6pm-4am; Ⓜ M3 Ferenc körút

One of the hottest cool venues in town, this club in the basement of the Trafó House of Contemporary Arts (p159) attracts arty (ie less booze, more smoke) types and their cohorts and features some of the best DJs in town.

TŰZRAKTÉR Map pp92-3

☎ 06 70 321 3536; www.tuzrakter.hu, in Hungarian; VI Hegedű utca 3; ☺ 3pm-2am; 🚊 4 or 6

Once housed in an abandoned factory building and now in an equally 'distressed' location just off Király utca, this independent community turns werewolf by night with DJs, concerts and parties.

MUSIC
CLASSICAL

The monthly freebie *Koncert Kalendárium* (www.koncertkalendarium.hu) lists all concerts in Budapest, and most nights you'll have several to choose from. As well as the city's

main concert halls listed here, many museums and other venues feature chamber music including, in Pest, the Old Music Academy, where the Franz Liszt Memorial Museum (p95) is housed; Magyar Rádió Marble Hall (Map pp102-3; ☎ 328 8779; VIII Pollack Mihály tér 8; 🚊 47 or 49); and the Hungarian Academy of Sciences (p88). 'Second-tier' venues in Buda include the Budapest History Museum (p65), the Millennium Theatre (p66) and the Béla Bartók Memorial House (p80).

Organ recitals are best heard in the city's churches, including Matthias Church (p61) and St Anne's Church (p65) in Buda and the Basilica of St Stephen (p84) and the Inner Town Parish Church (p84) in Pest.

DUNA PALOTA Map p85

☎ 235 5500; V Zrínyi utca 5; tickets adult 6400-8100Ft, student 5600-7200Ft; 🚊 15 or 115

The elaborate 'Danube Palace' diagonally opposite the main Central European University building hosts light classical music concerts at 8pm on Saturday from May to October.

FERENC LISZT MUSIC ACADEMY Map pp92-3

Liszt Zeneakadémia; ☎ information 462 4636, bookings 342 0179; www.zeneakademia.hu; VI Liszt Ferenc tér 8; tickets 500-6000Ft; ☺ ticket office 2-8pm; Ⓜ M2 Oktogon

A block southeast of Oktogon, what's usually just called the 'music academy' was built in 1907. It attracts students from all over the world and is one of the top venues for concerts. The interior, with large and small concert halls richly embellished with Zsolnay porcelain and frescoes, is worth a look even if you're not attending a performance.

ÓBUDA SOCIETY Map p74

Óbudai Társaskör; ☎ 250 0288; www.obudaitar
saskor.hu; III Kis Korona utca 7; tickets free-3000Ft;
HÉV Tímár utca, 🚌 86
This very intimate venue surrounded by
appalling Óbuda housing estates takes its
music very seriously and hosts recitals and
some chamber orchestras.

PALACE OF ARTS Map pp102-3

Művészetek Palotája; ☎ information 555 3000,
tickets 555 3301; www.mupa.hu; IX Komor Marcell
utca 1; tickets 600-7900Ft; 🕐 ticket office 10am-6pm
Mon-Fri, 11am-7pm Sat & Sun; 🚋 2
The main concert halls at this palatial arts
centre by the Danube and just opposite
the National Theatre are the 1700-seat
National Concert Hall (Nemzeti Hangversenyterem)
and the smaller Festival Theatre (Fesztivál Színház)
accommodating up to 450 people. Both
are purported to have the best acoustics in
Budapest.

ROCK & POP

A38 HAJÓ Map pp70-1

A38 Ship; ☎ 464 3940; www.a38.hu, in Hungarian; XI Pázmány Péter sétány 3-11; 🕐 11am-4pm,
terraces 4pm-4am Tue-Sat; 🚋 4 or 6
Moored on the Buda side just south of
Petőfi Bridge, the A38 is a decommissioned
Ukrainian stone hauler ship from 1968 that
has been recycled as a major live-music
venue. It's so cool it's hot in summer and
the hold, well, rocks throughout the year.

BUDAPEST SPORTARÉNA Map p108

☎ 422 2600; www.budapestarena.hu; XIV Stefánia
út 2; 🕐 ticket office 9am-6pm Mon-Fri, 10am-2pm
Sat; Ⓜ M2 Stadionok
This purpose-built 12,500-seat arena named
after local pugilist László Papp is where
big local and international acts (eg James
Blunt, Beyoncé) perform.

GÖDÖR Map p85

☎ 06 20 201 3868; www.godorklub.hu; V Erzsébet
tér; 🕐 noon-2am Mon-Fri, noon-4am Fri & Sat;
Ⓜ 1/2/3 Deák Ferenc tér
The 'Pit', a city-sponsored cultural centre in
the old bays below Erzsébet tér in central
Pest where international buses used to
drop off and pick up passengers, is a real
mixed bag, offering everything from folk
and world but especially rock and pop.

LASER THEATRE Map pp102-3

Lézer Színház; ☎ 263 0871, 281 2211; www
.lezerszinhaz.hu; X Népliget; adult/child/student
2390/600/1890Ft; 🕐 performances 7.30pm Mon-
Sat; Ⓜ M3 Népliget
At the Planetarium in Népliget, the Laser
Theatre has a mixed bag of video (some
3-D) concerts with laser and canned music
featuring the likes of Madonna, Pink Floyd,
Queen, Mike Oldfield, Vangelis and Enigma,
as well as performances by Carmina Burana.
Kind of low tech and old hat but fun in a
retro kind of way.

PETŐFI CSARNOK Map p108

☎ 363 3730; www.petoficsarnok.hu; XIV Zichy
Mihály út 14; 🕐 ticket office 2-7pm Mon-Fri,
9am-2pm Sat; Ⓜ M1 Széchenyi fürdő, trolleybus
72 or 74
In the southeast corner of City Park, Budapest's main youth centre is this 1250-seat
venue for smaller rock concerts (eg Jethro
Tull) as the hall is intimate enough to get
really close to the performers.

SZIMPLA Map pp92-3

☎ 321 9119; www.szimpl.hu, in Hungarian; VII
Kertész utca 48; 🕐 10am-2am Mon-Fri, noon-2am
Sat, noon-midnight Sun; 🚋 4 or 6
This distressed-looking, very unflashy place
remains one of the most popular drinking
venues south of VI Liszt Ferenc tér, with live
music Tuesday to Thursday evenings.

WIGWAM ROCK CLUB Map pp58-9

☎ 208 5569; www.wigwamrockclub.hu in Hungarian; XI Fehérvári utca 202; 🕐 9pm-5am; 🚋 41
This place is one of the best venues of its
kind and hosts some big-name Hungarian
rock and blues bands on Friday and Saturday
in deepest south Buda. A new branch called
WigWam 2 (Map pp102–3; ☎ 06 70 346 2472, VIII Krúdy
Gyula utca 17; 🕐 6pm-2am Mon-Wed, 6pm-4am Thu-Sat;
🚋 4 or 6) unfortunately keeps the tacky 'cowboy and injun' theme (dead or) alive.

JAZZ & BLUES

COLUMBUS JAZZKLUB Map p85

☎ 266 9013; www.majazz.hu; V Pesti alsó rakpart
at Lánchíd Bridge; 🕐 4pm-midnight; 🚋 2
On a boat moored in the Danube just off the
northern end of V Vigadó tér, this club has
transformed itself from 'just another Irish
pub' to a jazz club of note, with big-name

ATTENDING THE GARDENS

During Budapest's long and often very hot summers, so-called *kertek* (literally 'gardens' but in Budapest any outdoor spot that has been converted into an entertainment zone) empty out even the most popular indoor bars and clubs. These venues, including courtyards and *romkocsmák* (ruin bars) that rise phoenixlike from abandoned buildings, can change from year to year and a definitive list is usually not available until spring. The best single source of information is Caboodle (www.caboodle.hu). Some of the more popular ones in recent years include the following:

Cha Cha Cha Terasz (Map p74; ☎ 06 70 554 0670; www.chachacha.hu; XIII Margit-sziget; ☿ 4pm-late; 🚌 26, 🚊 4 or 6) In the stadium at the southern tip of Margaret Island, Cha Cha Cha Terasz is an attitude-free venue, with eclectic party music and dance space.

Corvintető (Map pp102–3; ☎ 461 0007, 06 20 772 2984; www.corvinteto.com, in Hungarian; VIII Blaha Lujza tér 1-2; ☿ 6pm-5am; Ⓜ M2 Blaha Lujza tér) This 'underground garden above the city' is on the rooftop of the former Corvin department store and has excellent concerts. Enter from a Somogyi Béla utca and take the goods lift to the top floor.

Dürer Kert (Map p108; ☎ 789 4444; www.durerkert.com, in Hungarian; XIV Ajtósi Dürer sor 19-21; ☿ 4pm-5am; 🚊 1, trolleybus 74 or 75) Very relaxed open space on the southwestern edge of City Park; boasts some of the best DJs on the 'garden' circuit.

Holdudvar (Map p74; ☎ 236 0155; www.holdudvar.net; XIII Margit-sziget; ☿ 10am-5am; 🚊 4 or 6) Another popular 'garden club' on Margaret Island, with a relaxed atmosphere but fairly predictable music.

Mokka Cuka (Map p74; ☎ 242 1707; www.mokkacuka.com; III Hajógyári-sziget; ☿ 5pm-5am Wed-Sun; HÉV Filatorigát) On the island that attracts the capital's beautiful people and porn stars and hosts the astonishingly successful Sziget Music Festival (p16) in August, Mokka Cuka is a leading outdoor underground venue showcasing indie DJs.

Mumus (Map pp92–3; nincs@meg.hu; VII Dob utca 18; ☿ 5pm-2am or 3am; 🚊 47 or 49) Everyone's favourite chilled *romkocsma*, the 'bogeyman' transforms from a cavernous vaulted beer hall in the cooler months to a wonderful outdoor *kert* in summer, with its own tree (real), stars (fake) and old oil drums masquerading as tables.

Szimpla Kert (Map pp92–3; ☎ 352 4198; www.szimpla.hu; VII Kazinczy 14; ☿ noon-3am; trolleybus 74) One of the capital's first *kertek*, Szimpla has now winterised (sort of) and opens year-round.

Zöld Pardon (Map pp70–1; ☎ 279 1880; www.zp.hu; XI Goldman György tér 6; ☿ 9am-6am; 🚊 4 or 6) What bills itself as the 'world's longest summer festival' is a rocker's paradise in Buda just south of Petőfi Bridge.

local and international bands. Music starts at 8pm.

JAZZ GARDEN MUSIC CLUB Map p85
☎ 266 7364; www.jazzgarden.hu; V Veres Pálné utca 44/a; ☿ 6pm-1am Sun, Mon, Wed & Thu, 6pm-2am Fri & Sat; 🚊 47 or 49
A sophisticated venue with traditional, vocal and Latin jazz, and odd decor: a faux cellar 'garden' with street lamps and a night 'sky' bedecked with blinking stars. Book a table (starters 1680Ft to 2650Ft, mains 2680Ft to 4180Ft) in the dining room; music starts at 9.30pm and finishes at 12.30am.

NOTHIN' BUT THE BLUES Map pp102-3
☎ 784 7793, 06 20 404 0304; www.bluespub.hu, in Hungarian; VIII Krúdy Gyula utca 6; ☿ 11am-11.30pm Mon-Thu, 11am-4am Fri & Sat, 11am-midnight Sun; 🚊 47 or 49
The oldest blues venue in town, NBB has been wailing for more than 15 years now. The name may be accurate Thursday to Sat-

urday from 8pm when there's always a live strummer or some such but acts vary the rest of the week. Jamming is on Sunday afternoon and open mike on Monday night. Grab the in-house 'beer guitar' and give it a go.

OLD MAN'S MUSIC PUB Map pp92-3
☎ 322 7645; www.oldmans.hu; VII Akácfa utca 13; ☿ 3pm-dawn; Ⓜ M2 Blaha Lujza tér
Not just jazz and blues, but swing and Latino and even rap, this fab venue has live music nightly from 9pm to 11pm. DJs then take over and dancing continues till dawn. It's a major party place.

TAKE 5 Map pp92-3
☎ 06 30 986 8856; www.take5.hu; VI Paulay Ede utca 2; ☿ 6pm-2am Wed-Sun; Ⓜ M1/2/3 Deák Ferenc tér; 🚊 47 or 49
This newcomer in the basement of Vista travel agency (p216) takes its jazz very seriously indeed, delivering class acts – both local and international – nightly. Move up

to the front; the sound is better in the first half of the hall.

FOLK & TRADITIONAL

Authentic *táncház*, literally 'dance house' but really folk-music workshops, are held at various locations throughout the week, but less frequently in summer. Times and venues often change; consult one of the publications earlier in this chapter (see p154) and expect to pay 500Ft to 1000Ft. Very useful too are the Dance House Guild (www.tanchaz.hu, in Hungarian) and Folkrádió (www.folkradio.hu) websites. The former also lists bands playing other types of traditional music such as klezmer (Jewish folk music). Two of the best are the Budapest Klezmer Band (www.buda pestklezmer.hu) and the Pannónia Klezmer Band (www .pannoniaklezmer.hu) – see p160. Hear the latter at Spinoza Café (p138). For Gypsy music (and we don't mean the three-star hotel ersatz variety), visit the incomparable Giero (p137).

ARANYTÍZ CULTURAL CENTRE Map p85
Aranytíz Művelődési Központ; ☎ 354 3400; www .aranytiz.hu, in Hungarian; V Arany János utca 10; 🚃 15
At this cultural centre in the Northern Inner Town the wonderful Kalamajka Táncház has programs from 8.30pm on Saturday that run till about midnight.

FONÓ BUDA MUSIC HOUSE Map pp70-1
Fonó Budai Zenebáz; ☎ 206 5300; www.fono.hu; XI Sztregova utca 3; 🚃 18 or 41
This place has *táncház* programs several times a week at 8pm as well as concerts by big-name bands throughout each month; it's one of the best venues in town for this sort of thing. Consult the website for more details.

In addition to the above, three cultural houses in Buda have frequent folk programs:

Budavár Cultural Centre (Budavári Művelődési Háza; Map p62; ☎ 201 0234; www.bem6.hu; Bem rakpart 6; 🚃 86) This cultural centre just below Buda Castle has frequent programs for children, including the excellent Fakutya Táncház every third Saturday afternoon.

Marczibányi tér Cultural Centre (Marczibányi téri Művelődési Központ; Map p62; ☎ 212 2820; www .marczi.hu, in Hungarian; II Marczibányi tér 5/a; 🚃 4 or 6) This venue has Hungarian, Moldavian and Slovakian dance and music every Wednesday and *táncház* every second Saturday from 8pm.

Municipal Cultural House (Fővárosi Művelődési Háza; Map pp70-1; ☎ 203 3868; www.fmhnet.hu, in Hungarian; XI Fehérvári út 47; 🚃 18 or 41) There's folk music here every Friday and the first and third Monday of the month at 7pm. A children's dance house hosted by the incomparable Muzsikás (p37) runs every Tuesday from 5pm.

DANCE
CLASSICAL & MODERN

The Hungarian National Ballet (www.opera.hu) company is based at the Hungarian State Opera House (p161) though it occasionally performs at the National Dance Theatre (below) in the Castle District.

CENTRAL EUROPE DANCE THEATRE
Map pp92-3
Közép-Európa Táncszínház; ☎ 342 7163, 06 30 456 3885; www.cedt.hu; VII Bethlen Gábor tér 3; tickets from 1400Ft; trolleybus 74 or 78
This wonderful pan-European dance theatre, Hungary's first when established in 1989, often has cutting-edge contemporary dance performances. Enter from VII István út 4.

MU SZÍNHÁZ Map pp70-1
☎ 209 4014, 466 4627; www.mu.hu, in Hungarian; XI Kőrösy József utca 17; tickets 1500-2000Ft; 🚃 4
Virtually everyone involved in the Hungarian dance scene got their start in the business at this place in south Buda, where excellent modern dance performances can still be enjoyed.

NATIONAL DANCE THEATRE Map p62
Nemzeti Táncszínház; ☎ information 201 4407, tickets 375 8649; www.nemzetitancszinhaz.hu; I Színház utca 1-3; tickets 650-4500Ft; 🚃 16, 16/a or 116
The National Dance Theatre in the Castle District hosts at some point every troupe in the city, including the national ballet company and the Budapest Dance Theatre (www.budapestdancetheatre.hu), one of the most exciting contemporary troupes in the city.

TRAFÓ HOUSE OF CONTEMPORARY ARTS Map pp102-3
Trafó Kortárs Művészetek Háza; ☎ 215 1600; www .trafo.hu; IX Liliom utca 41; tickets 500-3000Ft; Ⓜ M3 Ferenc körút
This stage in Ferencváros presents the cream of the crop of dance, including a good pull of international acts.

PANNÓNIA KLEZMER

Formed in 1997, the Budapest-based Pannónia Klezmer Band (www.pannoniaklezmer.hu) suffered a severe blow 10 years later when their much loved founder and leader Ferenc Gyula Zsákai died unexpectedly. The band, made up of three men and three women ranging in age from 18 to 40, has decided to play on, making their on sound. Their most recent CD is *Best of Pannónia Klezmer Band*.

A rather delicate question but we thought klezmer bands were the last bastion of boys-only clubs. Hey, it's a modern world. Where are you from?

OK, already. Here comes another… Non-Jews playing klezmer? How does that work? Well, that's simple. We're musicians and it's music. Music is music is music. Klezmer is not easy but we like challenges and we get the opportunity to play it at Spinoza (p138). Of course no band can live on just one kind of music.

Then why klezmer? Because it's fun and it's for everyone. And klezmer is a kind of feeling. Everyone says that about all kinds of music but it's true about klezmer.

Is klezmer like anything else? Are there influences? Klezmer and Gypsy music are very close now. Jewish and Gypsy musicians played together for the first time in the same camps and influenced each other greatly. Nowadays people are looking for new sounds so most modern klezmer bands mix in several different types of music — jazz, folk, Gypsy, even techno! It's all improvisation anyway.

And the instruments? What are the must-haves? The violin and clarinet dominate and you can't do much that's modern without piano and drums. We've added tuba and vocals.

Vocals? Klezmer is mainly instrumental music but there are songs in Yiddish too — ballads and pieces for special occasions like *Mazel Tov* at weddings. The 'king of klezmer' Giora Feidman plays the clarinet but he's also one of the greatest male klezmer vocalists in the world. But our singer happens to be female, which restricts our playing at some Jewish events. Orthodox Jews can listen to a male vocalist but not a female one, you see. Male klezmer vocalist are very hard to find in Budapest.

And the fan base? Where's that going? Seems to keep growing. When we played at a *táncház* (folk music workshop) recently we won a new group of fans with klezmer music. Klezmer is very popular right now among non-Jewish people

An interview with Budapest-based Pannónia Klezmer Band.

FOLK

The 30 artistes of the Hungarian State Folk Ensemble (Magyar Állami Népi Együttes) perform at the Buda Concert Hall (Budai Vigadó; Map p62; ☎ 201 3766; I Corvin tér 8; ☐ 86, ☐ 19) in Buda on Tuesday and Thursday from May to early October, with occasional performances the rest of the year. The Rajkó Folk Ensemble (Rajkó Népi Együttes) stages folk-dance performances at the Duna Palota (p156) just off Roosevelt tér in Pest on Friday and Sunday, while the Duna Folk Ensemble (Duna Népi Együttes) dances at the Duna Palota on Monday and Wednesday. The 1½-hour programs begin at 8pm, and tickets cost 3300Ft to5600Ft for adults and 3000Ft to 5100Ft for students. For more information, and bookings contact Hungaria Koncert (☎ 317 1377, 317 2754; www.ticket.info.hu).

Many people attend *táncház* evenings (p159) to learn the folk dances that go with the music. At these events you can actually become part of the program instead of merely watching others perform.

FILM

A couple of dozen cinemas in Budapest screen English-language films with Hungarian subtitles (that is, you can still listen to the film in English). Consult the listings in the *Budapest Sun* newspaper or the freebie *Budapest Funzine* to find out where and when these showings are on. *Pesti Est* and *Pesti Műsor* have more complete listings, but in Hungarian only. Tickets can cost anywhere from 600Ft to 1150Ft.

Be aware though that many foreign films are also dubbed into Hungarian, usually indicated in listings with the words '*magyarul beszélő*' or simply 'mb'. Otherwise, try asking the ticket seller '*Szinkronizált ez a film?*' (Is the film dubbed?) to be sure. Films that have been given Hungarian subtitles *(feliratos)*, rather than being dubbed, will retain their original soundtrack.

KINO Map pp92-3

☎ 349 2773; www.akino.hu; XIII Szent István körút 16; ☐ 4 or 6

Formerly the Szindbád cinema, named after the seminal (and eponymous) 1971 film by director Zoltán Huszárik and based on the novel by Gyula Krúdy (p40), this newly renovated cinema shows good Hungarian and foreign films with subtitles.

MŰVÉSZ Map pp92-3

☎ 332 6726; www.artmozi.hu; VI Teréz körút 30; Ⓜ M1 Oktogon, ⓣ 4 or 6
The 'Artist' shows, appropriately enough, artsy and cult films, but not exclusively so.

ÖRÖKMOZGÓ Map pp92-3

☎ 342 2167; www.orokmozgo.hu, in Hungarian; VII Erzsébet körút 39; ⓣ 4 or 6
Part of the Hungarian Film Institute, this cinema (whose mouthful of a name vaguely translates as 'moving picture') screens an excellent assortment of foreign classic films in their original languages.

PUSHKIN Map p85

☎ 429 6080; V Kossuth Lajos utca 18; ⓣ 7
This long-established cinema shows a healthy mix of art-house and popular releases.

URÁNIA NATIONAL CINEMA
Map pp102-3

Uránia Nemzeti Filmszínház; ☎ 486 3413; www .urania-nf.hu, in Hungarian; VIII Rákóczi út 21; ⓣ 7
This art deco/neo-Moorish extravaganza is a tarted-up film palace. It has an excellent cafe on the 1st floor overlooking Rákóczi út.

OPERA

BUDAPEST OPERETTA Map pp92-3

Budapesti Operettszínház; ☎ 472 2030, bookings 312 4866; www.operettszinhaz.hu; VI Nagymező utca 17; tickets 950-15,000Ft; ☽ ticket office 10am-7pm Mon-Fri, 1-7pm Sat & Sun; Ⓜ M1 Opera
This theatre presents operettas, which are always a riot, especially campy ones such as the *Queen of the Csárdás* by Imre Kálmán, with their over-the-top staging and costumes. There's an interesting bronze statue of Kálmám outside the main entrance.

HUNGARIAN STATE OPERA HOUSE
Map pp92-3

Magyar Állami Operaház; ☎ information 3331 2550, bookings 353 0170; www.opera.hu; VI

Andrássy út 22; tickets 300-16,900Ft; ☽ ticket office 11am-7pm Mon-Sat, 11am-1pm & 4-7pm Sun; Ⓜ M1 Opera
The gorgeous neo-Renaissance opera house should be visited at least once – to admire the incredibly rich decoration inside as much as to view a performance and hear the perfect acoustics. Visits are guided.

THEATRE

BUDAPEST PUPPET THEATRE
Map pp92-3

Budapest Bábszínház; ☎ information 342 2702, 321 5200; www.budapest-babszinhaz.hu; VI Andrássy út 69; tickets 800-2700Ft; ☽ ticket office 9am-6pm; Ⓜ M1 Vörösmarty utca
The city's puppet theatre, which usually doesn't require fluency in Hungarian, presents shows designed for children at 10am or 10.30am and 3pm. Consult the theatre's website for program schedules.

INTERNATIONAL BUDA STAGE Map p82

IBS; ☎ 391 2525; www.ibsszinpad.hu; II Tárogató út 2-4; tickets 1500-2800Ft; ☽ 1 ticket office 0am-6pm Mon-Fri; ⓐ 29, ⓣ 18 or 56
Farther afield on the way to the Buda Hills, the IBS is a more recent arrival than the Merlin, with occasional performances – often comedies – in English.

JÓZSEF KATONA THEATRE Map p85

Katona József Színház; ☎ 318 3725; www.katona jozsefszinhaz.hu; V Petőfi Sándor utca 6; tickets 1000-3500Ft; ☽ ticket office 10am-7pm Mon-Fri, 3-7pm Sat & Sun; Ⓜ M3 Ferenciek tere
The József Katona Theatre is the best known in Hungary and is a public theatre supported mainly by the city of Budapest. Its studio theatre, Kamra, hosts some of the best troupes in the country.

MERLIN THEATRE Map p85

☎ 317 9338, 318 9844; www.merlinszinhaz.hu; V Gerlóczy utca 4; tickets 1500-2500Ft; ☽ ticket office 11am-7pm Mon-Fri; Ⓜ M1/2/3 Deák Ferenc tér, ⓣ 47 or 49
This international theatre stages numerous plays in English, often performed by such local troupes as Scallabouche, Budapest's only alternative British theatre company, and its own Atlantisz troupe. It's usually pretty serious stuff, with little scenery and few props.

NATIONAL THEATRE

Nemzeti Színház; ☎ information 476 6800, bookings 476 6868; www.nemzetiszinhaz.hu; IX Bajor Gizi park 1; tickets 1000-3800Ft; ☯ ticket office 10am-6pm Mon-Fri, 2-6pm Sat & Sun; 🚇 2

This rather eclectic venue is the place to go if you want to brave a play in Hungarian or just check out the bizarre and very controversial architecture built in 2002 according to the designs of Mária Siklós.

SPORTS & ACTIVITIES

top picks

Budapest is chock-a-block with things to keep you occupied outdoors. From cycling and taking the waters to caving and canoeing, it's all in – or within easy access of – the capital. At the same time, like everywhere else, people here enjoy attending sporting matches and watching them on TV as much as they do taking part.

HEALTH & FITNESS

THERMAL BATHS

Budapest lies on the geological fault separating the Buda Hills from the Great Plain; more than 30,000 cu metres of warm to scalding (21°C to 76°C) mineral water gush forth daily from 123 thermal springs. As a result, the city is a major spa centre and 'taking the waters' at a thermal bath (*gyógyfürdő*) is a uniquely Budapest experience. Some baths date from Turkish times, others are art nouveau wonders, and still others are spic-and-span modern establishments.

All baths and pools have cabins or lockers. Find a free one and get changed in (or beside) it. Some new lockers (and cabins in the baths) are 'self-service'; the keys are released when you insert the plastic entry card you've been handed when you paid your admission. Otherwise, after you've got changed, call the attendant who will lock it for you and hand you a numbered tag to tie on your costume. In order to prevent theft should you lose or misplace the tag, the number is not the same as the one on the locker, so commit the locker number to memory.

Though some of the baths look a little rough around the edges, they are clean and the water is changed regularly. You might consider taking along a pair of plastic sandals or flip-flops, however. On single-sex days or in same-sex sections, men usually are handed drawstring loincloths and women apron-like garments to wear. You must wear a bathing suit on mixed-sex days; these are available for hire (1000Ft) if you don't have, or have forgotten to bring, your own.

Almost all the baths now employ a deposit system whereby you are refunded a certain amount from the admission cost (amounts noted in the following reviews) if you stay for less than two hours. Most of the baths offer a full range of serious medical treatments, plus more indulgent services such as massage (15/30 minutes 2800/3800Ft) and pedicure

(1600Ft to 2000Ft). Specify what services you are after when buying your entry ticket.

Please note that some baths become gay venues on male-only days – especially the Király. Not much actually goes on except for some intensive cruising, but those not into it may feel uncomfortable.

An excellent source of information is Budapest Spas and Hot Springs (www.spasbudapest.com).

DANUBIUS HEALTH SPA
MARGITSZIGET Map p74

☎ 889 4700; www.danubiushotels.com; XIII Margit-sziget; admission weekday/weekend 6500/7700Ft; ☙ 6.30am-9.30pm; 🚌 26
The least atmospheric of all the baths, this modern thermal spa is in the Danubius Thermal Hotel Margitsziget on leafy Margaret Island. It is connected via a heated underground corridor with the much nicer Danubius Grand Hotel Margitsziget (p177). The baths are open to men and women in separate sections. A daily ticket includes entry to the swimming pools, sauna and steam room as well as use of the fitness machines.

GELLÉRT Map pp70-1

Gellért Gyógyfürdő; ☎ 466 6166; XI Kelenhegyi út; admission deposit before/after 5pm 3400/3000Ft; ☙ 6am-7pm daily May-Sep, 6am-7pm Mon-Fri, to 5pm Sat & Sun Oct-Apr; 🚊 18, 19, 47 or 49
Soaking in this art nouveau palace, open to men and women in separate sections, has been likened to taking a bath in a cathedral. The eight thermal pools range in temperature from 26°C to 38°C, and the water – high in calcium, magnesium and hydrogen carbonate – is good for pains in the joints, arthritis and blood circulation. You get 400Ft back during the day if you leave within two hours.

KIRÁLY Map p62

Király Gyógyfürdő; ☎ 202 3688; II Fő utca 84; admission deposit 2600Ft; ☙ men 9am-8pm Tue

SPORTS & ACTIVITIES HEALTH & FITNESS

& Thu-Sat, women 7am-6pm Mon & Wed, mixed 9am-8pm Sun; 🚌 86
The four pools here, with water temperatures of between 26°C and 40°C, are genuine Turkish baths erected in 1570 and have a wonderful skylit central dome (though the place is begging for a renovation). Here you get a whopping 1000/500Ft back from your admission deposit if you leave within two/three hours.

LUKÁCS Map p74
Lukács Gyógyfürdő; ☎ 326 1695; II Frankel Leó út 25-29; admission deposit locker/cabin 1790/1900Ft; ⏰ 6am-7pm daily May-Sep, to 7pm Mon-Fri, to 5pm Sat & Sun Oct-Apr; 🚋 17, 🚌 86
Housed in a sprawling, 19th-century complex, these baths are popular with very keen spa aficionados. The thermal baths (temperatures 22°C to 40°C) are mixed and a bathing suit is always required. The renovated mud and weight bath, open from 6am to 6pm weekdays and to 4pm on Saturday, welcomes men on Tuesday, Thursday and Saturday, and women on Monday, Wednesday and Friday. You get 400/200Ft back if you leave within two/three hours.

RUDAS Map pp70-1
Rudas Gyógyfürdő; ☎ 356 1322; I Döbrentei tér 9; admission deposit 2400Ft; ⏰ men 6am-8pm Mon & Wed-Fri, women 6am-8pm Tue, mixed 10pm-4am Fri, 6am-5pm & 10pm-4am Sat, 8am-5pm & 10pm-4am Sun; 🚋 18 or 19, 🚌 7 or 86
These recently renovated baths are the most Turkish of all in Budapest, built in 1566, with an octagonal pool, domed cupola with coloured glass and massive columns. It's a real zoo on mixed weekend nights, when bathing costumes are compulsory. Here you get 400Ft back if you leave within two hours after you arrive.

SZÉCHENYI Map p108
Széchenyi Gyógyfürdő; ☎ 363 3210; XIV Állatkerti körút 11; admission deposit before/after 5pm 2600/2200Ft; ⏰ 6am-10pm; Ⓜ M1 Széchenyi fürdő
At the northern end of City Park, the Széchenyi complex is unusual for its immensity (a dozen thermal baths and five swimming pools), its bright, clean atmosphere and its water temperatures (up to 38°), which really are what the wall plaques say they are. It's open to both

men and women at all times, and you get 400Ft back on your daytime entry fee if you leave within two hours.

SWIMMING
With Hungarians being such keen swimmers, it's not surprising that Budapest boasts dozens of swimming pools. They're always excellent places to get in a few laps (if indoor), cool off on a hot summer's day (if outdoor) or watch all the posers strut their stuff (both).

The system inside is similar to that at the baths, except that rather than a cabin or cubicle you almost always store your gear in lockers. Many pools require the use of a bathing cap, so bring your own or wear the plastic one provided or sold for a nominal fee. Most pools rent bathing suits (1000Ft) and towels.

Following are the best outdoor and indoor pools in the city. Some are attached to thermal baths reviewed previously.

ALFRÉD HAJÓS Map p74
☎ 450 4214; XIII Margit-sziget; adult/child 1320/790Ft; ⏰ outdoor pools 6am-7pm May-Sep, indoor pools 6am-7pm Mon-Fri, to 5pm Sat & Sun Oct-Apr; 🚋 4 or 6, 🚌 26
The two indoor and three outdoor pools at the Alfréd Hajós swimming complex make up the National Sports Pool, where the Olympic swimming and water-polo teams train.

CSÁSZÁR-KOMJÁDI Map p74
☎ 212 2750; II Árpád fejedelem útja 8; adult/child 1320/790Ft; ⏰ 6am-7pm; 🚋 17, 🚌 86
This swimming pool complex, which could use a thorough renovation, is used by very serious swimmers and fitness freaks – so don't come here for fun and games.

CSILLAGHEGY Map pp58-9
☎ 250 1533; III Pusztakúti út 3; adult before/after 4pm 1400/1200Ft, child 1000Ft; ⏰ 7am-7pm May–mid-Sep, 6am-7pm Mon-Fri, 6am-4pm Sat, 6am-noon Sun mid-Sep–Apr; HÉV Csillaghegy
The popular Csillaghegy complex north of Óbuda is the oldest open-air bath in Budapest. There are three pools in a 90-hectare terraced park; in winter they are covered by canvas tenting and heated.

DAGÁLY Map pp58-9

☎ 452 4500; XIII Népfürdő utca 36; admission deposit before/after 4pm 2000/1700Ft; ☼ outdoor pools 6am-7pm May-Sep, indoor pools 6am-7pm Mon-Fri, 6am-5pm Sat & Sun Oct-Apr; Ⓜ M3 Árpád híd, Ⓣ 1

This huge swimming complex has a total of 10 pools, with plenty of grass and shade. If you leave the complex within two hours of entering during the day you get 300Ft back.

DANUBIUS HEALTH SPA HÉLIA
Map pp92-3

☎ 889 5800; www.danubiushotels.com; XIII Kárpát utca 62-64; admission before/after 3pm Mon-Fri 4200/5200Ft, Sat & Sun 5700Ft; ☼ 7am-10pm; Ⓜ M3 Dózsa György út, trolleybus 75

This ultramodern swimming and spa centre in the four-star Danubius Hélia Hotel boasts three pools, a sauna and steam room and an abundance of therapies.

GELLÉRT Map pp70-1

☎ 466 6166; XI Kelenhegyi út; admission deposit to swimming pool & thermal baths with locker/cabin 3000/3400Ft; ☼ 6am-7pm daily May-Sep, to 7pm Mon-Fri, to 5pm Sat & Sun Oct-Apr; Ⓣ 18, 19, 47 or 49

The indoor pools at the Gellért Baths are the most beautiful in Budapest. The outdoor pools (open May to September) have a wave machine and nicely landscaped gardens. The cost of admission with a cabin is reduced to 2700Ft after 5pm from May to September; and from October to April after 5pm Monday to Friday, and after 2pm Saturday and Sunday. You get 400Ft back in you stay less than two hours on your daytime ticket.

LUKÁCS Map p74

☎ 326 1695; II Frankel Leó út 25-29; admission deposit locker/cabin 1790/1900Ft; ☼ 6am-7pm daily May-Sep, to 7pm Mon-Fri, to 5pm Sat & Sun Oct-Apr; Ⓣ 17, Ⓑ 86

In addition to use of the three swimming pools at the Lukács Baths, use of the thermal baths is included in the general admission and the hours are the same.

PALATINUS STRAND Map p74

☎ 340 4505; XIII Margit-sziget; adult/child locker 1500/1300Ft, admission with cabin 1900Ft; ☼ 9am-7pm May-Aug; Ⓑ 26

The largest series of pools in the capital, the 'Palatinus Beach' complex on Margaret Island has a total of 11 pools (three with thermal water), as well as wave machines, water slides, kids' pools etc and is always a good place to watch Hungarians at play.

RÓMAIFÜRDŐ Map pp58-9

☎ 388 9740; III Rozgonyi Piroska utca 2/a; adult/child locker Mon-Fri 1500/1000Ft, Sat & Sun 1700/1200Ft; ☼ 9am-8pm May-Aug; HÉV Rómaifürdő Ⓗ 34 or 134

The outdoor cold-water thermal pools at this 'beach' complex are in a leafy area of Óbuda just north of Aquincum.

RUDAS Map pp70-1

☎ 356 1322; I Döbrentei tér 9; admission with locker/cabin 1400/1700Ft; ☼ 6am-6pm Mon-Fri, to 5pm Sat & Sun; Ⓣ 18 or 19, Ⓑ 7 or 86

You can enter the renovated pool at the Rudas Baths separately without using the thermal bath facilities if you're more interested in swimming than soaking.

SZÉCHENYI Map p108

☎ 363 3210; XIV Állatkerti körút 11; admission deposit before/after 5pm 2600/2200Ft; ☼ 6am-10pm; Ⓜ M1 Széchenyi fürdő

As well as use of the five enormous thermal swimming pools at the Széchenyi Baths, use of the baths is included in the general admission fee and the same 'payback' rules apply.

YOGA & PILATES

A very central place for yoga classes is the Atmas Center (Map p85; ☎ 269 1625, 06-30 914 0839; www.atmacenter.hu; V Vigyázó Ferenc utca 4; Ⓑ 15 or 115) in the same building as the Indian vegetarian restaurant Govinda (p134). Classes begin at 5pm and 7pm Monday, Wednesday and Thursday, at 4pm and 6pm Tuesday, at 2pm and 4pm Friday and at 10am and noon on Saturday. A day ticket is 1700Ft; a season pass with 10 entries is 13,000Ft.

Many of the following gyms and fitness clubs, including Gold's Gym, offer Pilates classes.

GYMS & FITNESS CLUBS

Independent gyms and fitness clubs offering day passes and short-term memberships abound in Budapest. The following are all worth a bend and a stretch.

A&TSA Fitness (Map p62; ☎ 488 7220; www .atsa.hu, in Hungarian; I Pálya utca 9; to 4pm/full day 1400/1900Ft; ☺ 7am-11pm Mon-Fri, 9am-9pm Sat & Sun; ☒ 105)

Arnold Gym (Map p74; ☎ 250 4259; www.arnoldgym .hu, in Hungarian; III Szépvölgyi út 15; 2/10 visits 2000/9000Ft; ☺ 7am-11pm Mon-Thu, 7am-10pm Fri, 9am-10pm Sat & Sun; HÉV Szépvölgyi út, ☒ 86)

Astoria Fitness Center (www.astoriafitness.hu, in Hungarian; adult/student day ticket 1400/1300Ft; ☺ 6.30am-11pm Mon-Fri, 8.30am-6pm Sat & Sun) Erzsébetváros (Map pp92–3; ☎ 343 1140; V Dohány utca 32; Ⓜ M2 Astoria); Belváros (Map p85; ☎ 317 0452; V Károly körút 4; Ⓜ M2 Astoria)

Gold's Gym (Map p62; ☎ 345 8544; www.goldsgym .hu; Mammut II, 4th fl, II Lövőház utca 2-6; monthly from 8000Ft; ☺ 6.45am-10.45pm Mon-Fri, 8am-7.45pm Sat & Sun; Ⓜ M2 Moszkva tér)

OUTDOOR ACTIVITIES
CYCLING

Parts of Budapest, including City and Népliget parks, Margaret Island and the Buda Hills, are excellent places for cycling. There is a total of 180km of dedicated bike lanes around the city, including the path along Andrássy út, though you'll often find yourself fighting for space with pedestrians on them.

There are a couple of places to rent bicycles on Margaret Island (see p77) but these are just for twirling round the island. For places to hire bikes for touring farther afield see p200.

For information and advice on cycling, contact the ever helpful Hungarian Cyclists' Club (MK; Map pp92–3; ☎ 789 5808; http://kerekparosklub .hu/hungarian-cyclists-club; XIII Radnóti Miklós utca 29; ☒ 4 or 6) or the Hungarian Bicycle Touring Association (MKTSZ; Map pp92–3; ☎ 311 2467; www.fsz.bme.hu/mtsz; VI Bajcsy-Zsilinszky út 31, 2nd fl; Ⓜ M3 Arany János utca). You might also check out Hunbike (www.hunbike .hu), an information portal connected to the Hungarian Cyclists' Club (though it's not all in English).

Frigoria (www.frigoriakiado.hu) publishes a number of useful guides and maps, including a 1:60,000 one called *Kerékpárral Budapesten* (By Bike in Budapest) available free from tourist offices. If you want something more detailed, pick up their 1:20,000 *Buda-*

pest Kerékpáratlasz (Budapest Bicycle Atlas; 1700Ft). See p212 for information about joining a city tour by bike.

Bicycles can be transported on the HÉV, the Cog Railway and all Mahart boats, but not on the metro, buses or trams.

BOATING

The best place for canoeing and kayaking in Budapest is on the Danube in Rómaifürdő. To get there, take the HÉV suburban line to Rómaifürdő and walk east towards the river. Reliable places there to rent kayaks and/or canoes include the following:

Béke Boat Club (Map pp58–9; ☎ 388 9303, 06-30 951 5049; www.romaipart.com; III Nánási út 97; per day canoe for 2/4 1900/2600Ft, kayak for 1/2 1300/1900Ft; ☺ 8am-6pm Apr–mid-Oct)

Óbuda Sport Club (ÓSE; Map pp58–9; ☎ 240 3353; www.ose.hu; III Rozgonyi Piroska utca 28; canoes & kayaks per day from 1500Ft; ☺ 8am-6pm May-Sep, 10am-4pm Oct-Apr)

HORSE RIDING

The not-for-profit Hungarian Equestrian Tourism Association (MLTSZ; Map pp102–3; ☎ 456 0444; www .equi.hu; IX Ráday utca 8, 1st fl; Ⓜ M3 Kálvin tér) can provide you with a list of recommended riding schools within easy striking distance of Budapest. Both Equus (Map p82; ☎ 325 6349, 06-20 911 8275; www.lovastura.hu; II Ózgida utca 32; ☒ 11) and Pegazus Tours (Map p85; ☎ 317 1644, 06-30 540 658; www .pegazus.hu, www.ridingtours.hu; V Ferenciek tere 5; Ⓜ M3 Ferenciek tere) organise riding programs around Budapest and farther afield.

One of the closest riding schools to Budapest is the long-established Petneházy Lovascentrum (off Map pp58–9; ☎ 397 5048, 06-20 588 3571; www .petnehazy-lovascentrum.hu; II Feketefej utca 2; ☺ 9am-5pm Fri-Sun; ☒ 63 from Hűvösvölgyi út) at Adyliget near Hűvösvölgy. It offers paddock practice (2500Ft per hour) and open trail riding (4500Ft) as well as pony rides (1500Ft per 15 minutes) for the kiddies and carriage rides (10,000Ft per 30 minutes for eight people).

Other recommended places to ride in and around the city include the following:

Babatvölgyi Lovarda (☎ 06-30 515 2634; www.babat .hu; Babtvölgy; riding per hr 1500-2500Ft) On a 300-hectare property 3km northeast of Gödölő (p191).

Bélapapuszta Equestrian Centre (☎ 22-594 388, 06-20 590 5956; www.belapa.hu; lessons per hr 2600Ft, riding per ½hr 2600/4600Ft) Some 20km northwest of

Martonvásár (p192) and one of the loveliest riding farms in Hungary.

Pasaréti Honvéd Lovarda (Map p82; ☎ 274 5719, 06-70 333 5057; www.honvedlovarda.hu; II Hidász utca 2; lessons per hr 3500-6000Ft; 🚌 5, 🚋 18 or 56) On the way to the Buda Hills; book at least a day in advance.

Sóskúti Lovassport Club (☎ 23-347 579, 06-30 466 1395; www.lovassport.hu; Bajcsy-Zsilinszky út 61; riding per hr 1950-3550 Ft) In Sóskút, 26km southwest of Budapest.

CAVING

Budapest counts something like 200 caves and several can be visited on walk-through guided tours (usually in Hungarian). Most of the hostels also offer adventurous 2½- to three-hour caving excursions (adults/children under 14 for 4500/3500Ft) to Mátyáshegy Cave (Mátyáshegyi-barlang; Map p82; barlangaszat.hu), a cave opposite and linking up with Pálvölgy. Tours usually depart at 4.30pm on Monday, Wednesday and Friday.

PÁLVÖLGY CAVE Map p82

Pálvölgyi-barlang; ☎ 325 9505, 336 0760; www .dinpi.hu; II Szépvölgyi út 162/a; adult/child 1100/900Ft; 🕙 10am-5pm Tue-Sun; 🚌 65 from Kolosy tér in Óbuda
The second largest in Hungary, this 19km-long cave discovered in 1904 is noted for both its stalactites and its bats. Be advised that the 500m route involves climbing some 400 steps and a ladder, so it may not be suitable for the elderly or children under five. The temperature is a constant 8°C so wear a jacket or jumper. Tours lasting 45 minutes depart hourly from 10.15am to 4.15pm.

SZEMLŐHEGY CAVE Map p74

Szemlőhegyi-barlang; ☎ 325 6001; www.dinpi .hu; II Pusztaszeri út 35; adult/child 900/700Ft; 🕙 10am-4pm Wed-Mon; 🚌 29 from III Kolosy tér
A more beautiful cave, with stalactites, stalagmites and weird grapelike formations, Szemlőhegy is about 1km southeast of Pálvölgy Cave. The temperature here is 12°C. The tour lasts 35 minutes.

SKATING

Along with mountain bikes and pedal coaches, Bringóhintó (p77) on Margaret Is-

land rents out inline skates (980/1680Ft per half/full hour).

CITY PARK ICE-SKATING RINK Map p108

Városligeti Műjégpálya; ☎ 364 0013; www.mu jegpalya.hu; XIV Olof Palme sétány 5; admission weekdays/weekends 700/1000Ft; 🕙 9am-1pm & 4-8pm Mon-Fri, 10am-2pm & 4-8pm Sat & Sun
In winter this huge outdoor skating rink operates on the western edge of the lake in City Park. If you want to avoid the crowds, visit on weekday mornings.

GÖRZENÁL ROLLER-SKATING PARK Map p74

Görzenál Görkocsolya Park; ☎ 250 4800; III Árpád fejedelem útja 125; admission weekdays/week-ends 400/600Ft; 🕙 9am-7.30pm daily May-Sep, from 2pm Mon-Fri, from noon Fri-Sun Oct-Apr; HÉV Tímár utca
This outdoor roller-skating rink and karting track on the banks of the Danube in Óbuda rents skates (600Ft) as well as protective equipment such as gloves and shin and elbow guards (150Ft per set).

TENNIS & SQUASH

Budapest counts more than three dozen tennis clubs, which usually charge between 2200Ft and 5600Ft per hour for use of their courts (clay and/or green set). The following includes some of the best in town.

Pasaréti Sport Centre (Pasaréti Sportcentrum; Map p82; ☎ 212 5246; www.pasaretsportcentrum.hu, in Hungarian; II Pasaréti út 11-13; 🕙 7am-10pm Mon-Fri, 9am-9pm Sat & Sun; 🚌 5).

Rozmaring Tennis Club (Rozmaring Teniszklub; Map p74; ☎ 240 4042, 06-30 444 5578; www.teniszpalya.com, in Hungarian; III Árpád fejedelem útja 125; HÉV Tímár utca)

Szépvölgyi Tennis Centre (Szépvölgyi Teniszcentrum; Map p82; ☎ 388 1591; III Virág Benedek utca 39-41; 🕙 7am-10pm; 🚌 65 from Kolosy tér in Óbuda)

Városmajor Tennis Club (Városmajori Tenisz Club; Map p82; ☎ 202 5337; XII Városmajor utca 63-69; 🕙 7am-10pm Mon-Fri, to 8pm Sat & Sun; 🚌 28 or 128)

To play squash, you can book a court at A&TSA Fitness Club or Arnold Gym (p166) for between 1950Ft and 4000Ft per hour; or try Top Squash (Map p62; ☎ 345 8193; www.top-squash .hu, in Hungarian; II Lövőház utca 2-6; court rental 2500-4500Ft; 🕙 10am-11pm Mon, 7am-11pm Tue-Thu, 7am-9pm Fri,

9am-8pm Sat & Sun; Ⓜ M2 Moszkva tér, 🚋 4 or 6) on the 4th floor of the Mammut I shopping mall.

BOWLING

Bowling is enjoying something of a resurgence here and alleys are rolling out across town, especially in shopping malls. One of the best is the Mammut Bowling Club (Map p62; ☎ 345 8300; www.bowlingclub.hu; II Lövőház utca 2-6; games 510-850Ft; 🕙 10am-1am Sun-Thu, to 3am Fri & Sat; Ⓜ M2 Moszkva tér, 🚋 4 or 6) on the 2nd floor of Mammut II.

SPECTATOR SPORT

The most popular spectator sports in Budapest are football and water polo, although motor racing and horse racing – both trotting and flat racing – also have their followers.

For its size and population, Hungary has done very well in the Olympics, though not at the most recent games. It finished 21st overall at the 2008 Olympic Games in Beijing, with 10 medals (three gold, five silver and two bronze). But this compared poorly with its performance at the previous two Olympiads, ending up 13th at both the 2004 Olympic Games in Athens and the ones in Sydney in 2000, each time with exactly the same number of medals (eight gold, six silver and three bronze, making a total of 17). At the 1996 games in Atlanta, Hungary placed 12th with 21 medals, while at Barcelona in 1992 its ranking was eighth with a total of 30 medals.

The best source of information on sport is the mass-circulation daily Nemzeti Sport (National Sport; www.nemzetisport.hu, in Hungarian; 115Ft).

FOOTBALL

Once on top of the heap of European football teams – the national team's defeat of the England team both at Wembley (6-3) in 1953 and at home (7-1) the following year are still talked about as if the winning goals were scored yesterday – Hungary has failed to qualify for any major tournament since 1986. The national team plays at Ferenc Puskás Stadium (Map p108; ☎ 471 4100; XIV Istvánmezei út 1-3; Ⓜ M3 Stadionok), the erstwhile 'People's Stadium' accommodating almost 70,000 fans.

There are five premier league football teams in Budapest out of a total of 16 nationwide,

including the two best: Újpest, which plays at far-flung Ferenc Szusza Stadium (Map pp58–9; ☎ 369 7333; IV Megyeri út 13; 🚌 96 or 196), which accommodates 13,5000 fans; and MTK, based at Nándor Hidegkúti Stadium (Map pp102–3; ☎ 219 0300; VIII Salgótarjáni utca 12-14; 🚋 1), accommodating 12,700 spectators. But no club has dominated Budapest football over the years like Ferencváros Torna Club (FTC), the country's loudest and brashest team. You either love the Fradi boys in green and white or you hate 'em. Watch them play at FTC Albert Stadium (Map pp102–3; ☎ 215 6025; IX Üllői út 129; Ⓜ M3 Népliget), with space for 18,000 raucous spectators. Check Nemzeti Sport for schedules.

WATER POLO

Hungary has dominated the European Championships in water polo a dozen times since 1926 and taken nine gold medals at Olympic Games, so it's worthwhile catching a professional or amateur game of this exciting seven-a-side sport.

The Hungarian Water Polo Association (MVLSZ; ☎ 412 0041; www.waterpolo.hu, in Hungarian) is based at the Alfréd Hajós swimming complex (p165) on Margaret Island. Matches take place here and at two other pools: the Császár-Komjádi swimming complex (p165) in Buda and the BVSC (Map p108; ☎ 251 3888; XIV Szőnyi út 2; trolleybuses 74 or 74/a) in Pest from September to May. If you want to see a match or watch the lads training in summer, call the MVLSZ for times and dates, or get someone to check schedules for you in the daily Nemzeti Sport.

MOTOR RACING

Reintroduced in 1986 following a hiatus of half a century, the Formula 1 Hungarian Grand Prix (☎ 28-444 444; www.hungaroring.hu), Hungary's prime sporting event, is part of the World Championship Series that takes place at the Hungaroring at Mogyoród, 24km northeast of Budapest, in August. Practice is on the Friday, the qualifying warm-up on Saturday and the race begins (after morning practice) at 2pm on Sunday. The only seats with views of the starting grid are the Super Gold ones, which cost €428 for the weekend; cheaper are Gold (€314 to €342), which are near the pit lane, and Silver (€209 to €285) tickets. Standing room costs €114 for the weekend, €105 for Sunday.

HORSE RACING

The descendants of the nomadic Magyars are keen on horse racing. Kincsem Park (Map pp58–9; ☎ 433 0522; www.kincsempark.com; X Albertirsai út 2; Ⓜ M2 Pillangó utca) is the place to go for both trotting (*ügető*) and flat racing (*galopp*). Schedules can change but in general three trotting meetings of 10 or 11 races take place from 2pm to 9pm on Saturday and flat racing from 10.30am to 4pm on Sunday between May and November. The biggest event of the year is Ügetőszilveszter, a vastly popular extraordinary trotting meeting that attracts all ages on the afternoon of New Year's Eve.

SLEEPING

top picks

- **Lánchíd 19** (p174)
- **Papillon Hotel** (pp177)
- **KM Saga Guest Residence** (p185)
- **Gingko Hostel** (p179)
- **Hotel Astra** (pp175)
- **Hotel Parlament** (pp180)
- **Andrássy Hotel** (pp182)
- **Atrium Hotel** (pp184)
- **Radio Inn** (pp182)
- **Home-Made Hostel** (pp181)

SLEEPING

Accommodation in Budapest runs the gamut from hostels in converted flats and private rooms in far-flung housing estates to luxury guesthouses in the Buda Hills and five-star properties charging upwards of €300 a night for a double. The low season for hotels runs roughly from mid-October or November to March (not including the Christmas and New Year holidays); there are often some bargains to be had during the late autumn and winter months. The high season is the rest of the year – a lengthy seven months or so – when prices can increase substantially. The rate quoted for hostel and hotel accommodation almost always includes breakfast. If you're driving, parking at many of the central Pest hotels will be difficult.

The accommodation options in this guide are listed by area and cost from most expensive (top end) to cheapest (budget). For prices at a glance see the box on opposite.

It's difficult to generalise but accommodation in the Buda neighbourhoods is more limited than on the other side of the Danube River, though you will find quite a few luxurious big-name hotels along with some small, atmospheric guesthouses and many rather institutional hostels open in summer time.

Pest has the lion's share of accommodation in Budapest – with everything ranging from the five-star, palatial Four Seasons Gresham Palace Hotel to most of the city's new breed of hostels for the 21st century.

ACCOMMODATION STYLES
Hotels
Hotels, called *szállók* or *szállodák,* can be anything from the rapidly disappearing run-down old socialist-era hovels to luxurious five-star palaces.

A cheap hotel will usually be more expensive than a private room in Budapest, but it may be the answer if you're only staying one night or if you arrive too late to get a private room through an agency. Two-star hotels usually have rooms with a private bathroom; it's almost always in the hall in a one-star place. Three- and four-star hotels can be excellent value compared with those in Western European cities.

Serviced Apartments
Budapest is chock-a-block with serviced apartments and apartment hotels. They all have private bathrooms and usually kitchens – at the very least. Some are positively luxurious (eg Marriott Executive Apartments, p178) while others are bare-bones (eg Peter's Apartments, p181).

Guesthouses
Budapest has scores of *panziók* (guesthouses or pensions), but most of them are in the outskirts of Pest or in the Buda Hills and not very convenient unless you have your own (motorised) transport. Pensions are popular with Germans

and Austrians who like the homey atmosphere and the better breakfasts. Often pensions can cost as much as a moderate hotel, although there are some worthwhile exceptions.

Hostels
Accommodation at Budapest's *ifjúsági szállók* (youth hostels) is available year-round and one of the biggest growth areas in accommodation here is new modern hostels with internet access, laundry facilities, sometimes a bar and an upbeat atmosphere. During the university summer holidays (generally mid-June or July to late August) the number of hostels increases exponentially. During this time, private outfits rent vacant dormitories from the universities and turn them into hostels so you can afford to shop around a bit.

Dormitory accommodation in both year-round and summer hostels costs from a low of 3000Ft to as much as 6000Ft per person, depending on room size. For hostel doubles count on anything between 7500Ft (€25) to 15,500Ft (€50). High season usually means April to October.

A Hostelling International (HI) card or equivalent (p207) is not required at any hostel in Budapest, but it will sometimes get you a discount of up to 10% or an extra night's stay; make sure to ask beforehand.

Hostels usually have laundry facilities (around 1500Ft to 2000Ft for a wash and dry), a fully equipped kitchen, storage lockers, TV lounge with DVDs, no curfew and computers for internet access (almost always free nowadays).

While you can go directly to all the hostels mentioned here, the Express travel agency (p216) and the Mellow Mood Group* (Map pp92–3; ☎ 343 0748; www.mellowmood.hu; VII Baross tér 15, 3rd fl, Ⓜ M2 Keleti pályaudvar) are the best contacts for budget accommodation information. In fact, the latter, which is affiliated with HI, runs two very central year-round hostels as well as five that open in summer only. You can also make bookings through its U Tours travel agency (☎ 343 0748; ☺ 7am-7pm) in Keleti train station (Map p108) near the entrance at the end of platform 6.

Another player in the competitive world of Budapest summer hostels is Universum (☎ 323 2999; www.universumyouthhostels.hu), which has accommodation at one year-round hotel and hostel in Pest, and three hostels (all with fridges in the rooms, safes and washer-dryers) in the vicinity of the University of Technology and Economics (BME; Map pp70–1) in Buda.

Private Rooms

Fizetővendég szolgálat (paying-guest service) here is a great deal and still relatively cheap, but with the advent of stylish and afford-able guesthouses it's not as widespread as it once was.

Private rooms in Budapest generally cost 6000Ft to 7500Ft for a single, 7000Ft to 8500Ft for a double and 9000Ft to 13,000Ft for a small apartment. To get a room in the centre of town, you may have to try several offices. An indexed city map or atlas (p210) might prove useful in finding the block where your room is located.

Individuals on the streets outside the main train stations may offer you a private room, but their prices are usually higher than those asked by the agencies, and there is no quality control. They vary considerably and cases of travellers being promised an idyllic room in the centre of town, only to be taken to a dreary, cramped flat in some distant suburb are not unknown. On the other hand, we've received dozens of letters extolling the virtues of the landlords with whom readers have dealt directly. You really have to use your own judg-ment here.

Tourinform in Budapest does not arrange private accommodation, but will send you to a travel agency, such as To-Ma (Map p85; ☎ 353 0819; www.tomatour.hu; V Október 6 utca 22; ☺ 9am-noon

& 1-8pm Mon-Fri, 9am-5pm Sat & Sun; Ⓜ M1/2/3 Deák Ferenc tér). Among the best places to try for private rooms are Ibusz and Vista (p216) and, in Keleti train station, U Tours (opposite).

ROOM RATES

In this book budget accommodation – hos-tels, private rooms, some pensions and cheap hotels – costs anything under 15,500Ft (€50) for a double. Midrange (usually pensions and hotels) is 15,600Ft (€51) to 33,500Ft (€110) for a double during any season. Top-end hotels start at around 33,600Ft (€111). From there the sky's the limit. Because of the changing value of the forint, many hotels quote their rates in euros. In such cases, we have followed suit.

The price listed will be the price you pay, but it's not as cut-and-dried in Budapest. Travel agencies generally charge a small fee for booking a private room or other accom-modation, and there's usually a surcharge if you stay for less than three nights (at least on the first night). Budapest levies a 3% local tourist tax on those aged 18 to 70. Some top-end hotels in Budapest do not include the whopping 20% VAT in their listed rack rates; make sure you read the fine print.

LONGER-TERM RENTALS

After the fall of communism more than two decades ago, many families in Budapest were given the opportunity to buy – at very low rates – the flats they had been renting from the state since the 1950s. As a result, Budapest is full of fully paid-up flats waiting to be let.

Rental prices vary according to the condi-tion of the property (naturally) and the district it is in; the most expensive areas for renting are districts I, II and XII in Buda and districts V and XIII in Pest. Expect to pay a minimum of 2000Ft per sq metre in the leafy, sought-after neighbourhoods of Buda. In Pest, a flat in central district V will cost from 1500Ft per sq metre and from 1000Ft in districts VI or VII. The diplomatic quarter west of City

PRICE GUIDE

The symbols below indicate the cost per night of a standard double room in high season.

€€€	over 33,500Ft (€111)
€€	15,500- 33,500Ft (€51-110)
€	under 15,500Ft (€50)

SLEEPING ROOM RATES

173

Park will cost as much as districts II and XII in Buda. The cheapest flats are to be found in the housing blocks of some of the more outlying districts (eg districts III and XXII in Buda and almost everything that is situated east of the Big Ring Road in Pest).

Your best source of information is the daily classifieds-only newspaper *Expressz* (198Ft), available from newsstands everywhere. These days, however, many of the advertisements are from agencies, which usually require you to pay a fee just for the address of the property. Monthly property magazines include *Expressz Ingatlan* (398Ft) and *Ingatlan Kavalkád* (298Ft). Since ads are always in Hungarian only – and the landlord is likely to be monolingual – you'll have to get a native speaker to help you.

CASTLE HILL & VÍZIVÁROS

CASTLE HILL

HILTON BUDAPEST Map p62   Hotel €€€
☎ 889 6600; www.budapest.hilton.com; I Hess András tér 1-3; s & d €170-280; 🚌 16, 16/a or 116; ✂ ☒ 🖳 ♿
Perched above the Danube on Castle Hill, the Hilton was built carefully in and around a 14th-century church and baroque college (though it still has its uber-preservationist detractors). It has 322 somewhat sombre rooms, with dark carpeting and low lighting but fantastic views.

BUDA CASTLE HOTEL Map p62   Hotel €€€
☎ 224 7900; www.budacastlehotelbudapest.com; I Úri utca 39; s €95-134, d €110-149; 🚌 16, 16/a or 116; ✂ ☒ 🖳
This very classy new arrival on Castle hill sets a new standard for boutique hotels in Budapest. The building dates from the 15th century, but apart from a bit of vaulted brickwork in the lobby you'd never know that once you've entered. The hotel's 20 rooms and suites, done up in warm shades of brown, tan and beige, look on to a cobbled street or face a relaxing courtyard planted with grass and trees. And that's not a bad choice to have to make.

BURG HOTEL Map p62   Hotel €€€
☎ 212 0269; www.burghotelbudapest.com; I Szentháromság tér 7-8; s €85-105, d €99-115, 2-person ste €109-134; 🚌 16, 16/a or 116; ✂ ☒ 🖳

This small hotel with all the mod cons is in the Castle District, just opposite Matthias Church. The 26 partly refurbished rooms look fresher but are not much more than just ordinary. As they say, though, location is everything and affordable options are as scarce as hen's teeth on Castle Hill.

HOTEL KULTURINNOV Map p62   Hotel €€
☎ 224 8102; www.mka.hu; I Szentháromság tér 6; s/d/tr €60/75/100; 🚌 16, 16/a or 116
A 16-room hotel in the former Finance Ministry, this neo-Gothic structure dating back to 1904 can't be beat for location and price in the Castle District. The guestrooms, though clean and with private bathrooms, are not as nice as the public areas seem to promise.

VÍZIVÁROS

LÁNCHÍD 19 Map p62   Hotel €€€
☎ 419 1900; www.lanchid19hotel.hu; I Lánchíd utca 19; s €120-175, d €140-225, ste €300-400; 🚌 86, 🚋 19; ✂ ☒ 🖳 ♿
We have visited, inspected and stayed in lots of hotels in our time, and we think this new boutique number facing the Danube has the 'wow' factor in spades. The Lánchíd 19 won the European Hotel Design Award for Best Architecture in 2008 and, watching its facade form pictures as light sensors reflect and follow the movement of the Danube, we can't but agree. Each of the 45 rooms and three 'panoramic' suites is different, with distinctive artwork and a unique chair ('can you sit on that?!?') designed by art-college students. And you can't lose with the views: to the front it's the Danube and to the back Buda Castle.

ART'OTEL BUDAPEST Map p62   Hotel€€€
☎ 487 9487; www.artotel.hu; I Bem rakpart 16-19; s/d/ste €198/218/298, with Danube view €218/238/318; 🚌 86, 🚋 19; ✂ ☒ 🖳 ♿
The Art'otel is a minimalist establishment that would not look out of place in London or New York. But what makes this 165-room place unique is that it cobbles together a seven-storey modern building (views of the castle and the Danube) and an 18th-century baroque building and separates them with a leafy courtyard-cum-atrium.

HOTEL VICTORIA Map p62   Hotel €€€

☎ 457 8080; www.victoria.hu; I Bem rakpart 11; s €79-117, d €86-123; 🚌 86, 🚊 19; Ⓟ ✕ 🕸 🖳

This rather elegant hotel has 27 comfortable and spacious rooms with larger-than-life views of Parliament and the Danube. Despite its small size it gets special mention for its friendly service and facilities, including the recently renovated rooms of the 19th-century Jenő Hubay Music Hall attached to and accessible from the hotel. It now serves as a small theatre and series of function rooms.

HOTEL ASTRA Map p62   Hotel €€€

☎ 214 1906; www.hotelastra.hu; I Vám utca 6; s €65-97, d €75-112, ste €129-139; Ⓜ M2 Batthyány tér, 🚌 86; ✕ 🕸 🖳

Tucked away in a small street west of Fő utca and just below the Castle District is this hotel-cum-guesthouse in a centuries-old townhouse. It has nine double rooms and three suites, one of which has a strange niche illustrated with a mosque and is probably a mihrab (Muslim prayer nook) dating back to the Turkish occupation.

CARLTON HOTEL Map p62   Hotel €€

☎ 224 0999; www.carltonhotel.hu; I Apor Péter utca 3; s €75-95, d €85-110, tr €100-130; 🚌 86; Ⓟ 🕸 🖳

This 95-room hotel at the foot of Castle Hill and at the end of a narrow cul-de-sac in Víziváros is a good choice if you plan to divide your time equally between Pest and Buda. Half a dozen rooms lead into a small courtyard garden.

BÜRO PANZIÓ Map p62   Guesthouse €€

☎ 212 2929; www.buropanzio.hu; II Dékán utca 3, 1st fl; s €42-50, d €56-64, tr €72-76, q €82-92; Ⓜ M2 Moszkva tér; 🕸 🖳

A pension just a block off the northern side of Moszkva tér, this place looks basic from the outside, but its 10 rooms are comfortable and have TV and telephone though they are small. Decor is the basic 'just-off-the-assembly-line' look.

GELLÉRT HILL, TABÁN & KELENFÖLD

GELLÉRT HILL

DANUBIUS GELLÉRT HOTEL
Map pp70-1   Hotel €€€

☎ 889 5500; www.danubiusgroup.com/gellert; XI Szent Gellért tér 1; s €67-110, d €135-216, ste €233-268; 🚊 18, 19, 47 or 49; Ⓟ ✕ 🕸 🖳 🚊

Budapest's grande dame is a 234-room, four-star hotel with loads of character. Designed by Ármin Hegedűs in 1909 and completed in 1918, the hotel contains examples of the late art nouveau, notably the thermal spa with its enormous arched glass entrance hall and Zsolnay ceramic fountains in the bathing pools. Use of the thermal baths is free for guests, but overall the Gellért's other facilities are forgettable. Prices depend on which way your room faces and what sort of bathroom it has.

CITADELLA HOTEL
Map pp70-1   Hotel & Hostel €

☎ 466 5794; www.citadella.hu; XI Citadella sétány; dm 3200Ft, s & d with shared shower/shower/bathroom 10,500/11,500/12,500Ft; 🚌 27

This hotel in the fortress atop Gellért-hegy is pretty threadbare, though the dozen guestrooms are extra large, retain some of their original features and have their own shower (toilets are on the circular corridor). The single dorm room has 14 beds and shared facilities. Be warned: this area is something of a tourist trap and you may feel more like a prisoner than a prince or princess here.

HILL HOSTEL Map pp70-1   Hostel €

☎ 787 4321; www.mellowmood.hu; XI Ménesi út 5; r with 1/2/3 beds per person €31/18.50/17.50; 🕙 early Jul-Aug; 🚊 18, 19, 47 or 49, 🚌 7; ✕ 🕸

On the way up to leafy Gellért Hill, this institutional-looking building has 160 beds in 70 rooms, a sports ground and a swimming pool (admission 1200Ft). It's a hostel of the Mellow Mood Group.

top picks

GAY STAYS

- Kapital Inn (p181)
- KM Saga Guest Residence (pp185)
- Connection Guest House (pp181)

HOSTEL LANDLER Map pp70-1   Hostel €

☎ 463 3621; www.universumyouthhostels.hu; XI Bartók Béla út 17; dm €10, r with 1/2/3 beds per person €20/13/12; ☷ Jul-Aug; 🚊 18, 19, 47 or 49, 🚇 7; ✗ 🖳

At the foot of Gellért Hill with 280 beds, Universum's seasonal Hostel Landler has basic rooms for two to four people with washbasins, fridges and shared showers.

TABÁN

HOTEL ORION Map pp70-1   Hotel €€€

☎ 356 8583; www.bestwestern-ce.com/orion; I Döbrentei utca 13; s €75-95, d €95-125, ste €160; 🚊 18 or 19; ✗ 🖳 🖳

Hidden away in the Tabán district, the Orion is a cosy place with a relaxed atmosphere and within easy walking distance of the Castle District. The 30 rooms are bright and of a good size, and there's a small sauna for guests' use.

CHARLES HOTEL & APARTMENTS

Map pp70-1   Serviced Apartment €€

☎ 212 9169; www.charleshotel.hu; I Hegyalja út 23; standard studio s & d €45-65, tr €60-80, deluxe studio s & d €60-80, tr €75-95, apt €75-155; 🚊 8, 112 or 178; 🅿 ✗ 🖳

On the Buda side and somewhat on the beaten track (a train line runs right past it), the Charles has 70 'studios' (larger-than-average rooms) with tiny kitchens and weary-looking furniture as well as two-room apartments. They also have bikes for rent for 2000Ft a day.

BUDA BASE Map pp70-1   Hostel €

☎ 356 2100, 06-20 543 7481; budabase@gmail .com; I Döbrentei utca 16; per person 3500Ft; 🚊 7 or 86, 🚊 18 or 19; ✗ 🖳 🖳

Buda hasn't seen anything like the mushrooming of small independent hostels that

Pest has recently but what exists is all quality. Take the Buda Base, a fantastically located hostel by the Danube with 10 beds in a ground floor dormitory and a loft double with its own bathroom and air conditioning. You won't soon forget the river view, especially when checking your emails via wi-fi from a bench along the riverside walk.

KELENFÖLD

HOTEL VENTURA Map pp70-1   Hotel €€

☎ 208 1232; fax 208 1234; www.gerandhotels.hu; XI Fehérvári út 179; s €49-70, d €62-85, tr €81-122; 🚊 114 or 214, 🚊 47 or 56; ✗ 🖳 🖳

This hotel, done up in various shades of blue, green and purple and with what can only be described as an enormous umbrella cage in the lobby, has 149 rooms spread over two buildings and a modern gym. It's off the beaten track but transport is good.

HOTEL GRIFF JUNIOR

Map pp70-1   Hotel €

☎ 203 2398; www.gerandhotels.hu; XI Bartók Béla út 152; s/d/tr/q with washbasin & toilet €26/30/39/44, with shower €29/39/49/59; 🚊 7E, 🚊 19 or 49; ✗

With 120 rooms – a quarter of them with their own shower – at rock-bottom prices in a low-rise office block, this hotel next to the much larger and pricier Hotel Griff, with which it has no connection, is a great choice for those on a very tight budget. It's easily reached by bus or tram.

BACK PACK GUESTHOUSE

Map pp70-1   Hostel €

☎ 385 8946; www.backpackbudapest.hu; XI Takács Menyhért utca 33; bed in yurt 2500Ft, large/small dm 3000/3500Ft, d 9000Ft; 🚊 7 or 73; ✗ 🖳

We've always loved this laid-back hostel – Budapest's first! – in a colourfully painted suburban 'villa' in south Buda and we're happy to see more and more hostels are copying its style. The Back Pack is relatively small, with just 50 beds, but the fun (and sleeping bodies in high season) spill out into a lovely landscaped garden, with hammocks, a yurt and Thai-style lounging platform. It's the perfect place for one of the low-cost massages available here. The upbeat attitude of the friendly, much travelled owner/manager seems to permeate the place, and the welcome is always warm.

top picks

BOUTIQUE & SMALL HOTELS

- Buda Castle Hotel (p174)
- Lánchíd 19 (pp174)
- Soho Hotel (pp183)
- Hotel Astra (pp175)
- Atrium Hotel (pp184)

MARTOS HOSTEL Map pp70-1   Hostel €

☎ 209 4883, 06-30 911 5755; http://hotel.mar
tos.bme.hu; XI Sztoczek József utca 5-7; s/d/tr/q
4000/6000/9000/12,000Ft, d with shower 8000Ft,
apt 15,000Ft; ⚑ 4 or 6; ✗ ▣
Though primarily a summer hostel with 200
beds, this student dormitory of the Budapest University of Technology and Economics has about two dozen beds available
year-round. It's reasonably well located,
near the Danube, and just a few minutes'
walk from Petőfi Bridge.

ALSO RECOMMENDED

Hostel Universitas (Map pp70–1; ☎ 787 4321; XI Irinyi
József utca 9-11; s/d €27/32; ☺ early Jul-Aug; ⚑ 4 or 6)
With 400 beds, this is Mellow Mood's biggest. liveliest and
most basic hostel, with just washbasins in the twins and
doubles and communal showers in the hallway.

Hostel Vásárhelyi (Map pp70–1; ☎ 463 4326; XI Kruspér
utca 2-4; dm €12, per person s/d & tr €20/13; ☺ Jul-Aug;
⚑ 4 or 6) Universum's Hostel Vásárhelyi has 500 rooms
with two to four beds, all of which have private showers,
and a popular all-night bar in the basement.

Hostel Rózsa (Map pp70–1; ☎ 463 4250; XI Bercsényi
utca 28-30; dm €11, per person s/d/tr €20/13/12; ☺ Jul-
Aug; ⚑ 4 or 6) The quietest of Universum's trio of hostels;
111 double rooms with washbasins and shared showers.

ÓBUDA, RÓZSADOMB & MARGARET ISLAND

ÓBUDA & RÓZASDOM

PAPILLON HOTEL Map p74   Hotel €€

☎ 212 4750; www.hotelpapillon.hu; II Rózsahegy
utca 3/b; s €31-44, d €41-60, tr €56-75, apt for 3/5
people €72/90; ⚑ 4 or 6; ℗ ✗ ▣ ▣ ♿
One of Buda's best-kept accommodation
secrets, this small 20-room hotel in Rózsadomb has a delightful back garden with
a small swimming pool, and some rooms
have balconies. There are also four apartments available in the same building, one
of which boasts a lovely roof terrace.

HOTEL CSÁSZÁR Map p74   Hotel €€

☎ 336 2640; www.csaszarhotel.hu; II Frankel Leó
utca 35; s €33-45, d €43-59, tr €70-91, ste €99-116;
▣ 86, ⚑ 17; ✗ ✂ ▣ ▣
The huge yellow building in which the
'Emperor' is located was built in the 1850s
as a convent, which might explain the size
of the 45 cell-like rooms. Request one of

top picks

GRAND & LUXURY HOTELS

- Four Seasons Gresham Palace Hotel (p179)
- Danubius Gellért Hotel (p175)
- Corinthia Grand Hotel Royal (p183)
- Le Meridien Budapest (p178)
- Danubius Grand Hotel Margitsziget (below)

the superior rooms, which are larger and
look onto the nearby outdoor Olympic-size
pools of the huge Császár-Komjádi swimming complex (p165).

MARGARET ISLAND

DANUBIUS GRAND HOTEL MARGITSZIGET Map p74   Hotel €€€

☎ 889 4700; www.danubiushotels.com; XIII Margit-sziget; s €146-226, d €160-240, ste €206-300;
▣ 26; ✗ ✂ ▣ ▣
Constructed in the late 19th century, this
comfortable – not grand – and tranquil
hotel has 164 rooms that boast all the mod
cons you would want and is connected to
the Danubius Thermal Hotel Margitsziget
via a heated underground corridor, where
the cost of taking the waters is included in
the hotel rate.

HOTEL MARGITSZIGET Map p74   Hotel €€

☎ 450 0105; www.hotelmsz.hu; Hajós Alfréd
sétány 75; XIII Margit-sziget; s €37-53, d €43-55;
▣ 26; ℗ ▣
This 11-room low-priced hotel in the centre
of Margaret Island is surrounded by green-
ery and feels almost like a resort. Choose
this place if you really want to get away
from it all on a budget but remain within
easy striking distance of the action. Rooms
11 to 14 have balconies.

BUDA HILLS & BEYOND

HOTEL NORMAFA Map pp58-9   Guesthouse €€

☎ 395 6505; www.normafahotel.com; XII Eötvös
út 52; s €55-85, d €65-95, ste €80-120; ▣ 90, 90/a
or 190
This recently renovated 62-room hotel sits
atop Sváb-hegy on the edge of the Buda
Hills protected nature area. It has a gorgeous
swimming pool, a fitness room and sauna as

well as a cafe and well-received restaurant. If something should tempt you away from all of this, the Normafa stop of the Cog Railway (p80) is literally across the lawn.

BEATRIX PANZIÓ Map p82   Guesthouse €€

☎ 275 0550; www.beatrixhotel.hu; II Széher út 3; s €50-60, d €60-70, tr €70-80, apt €80-210; 🚌 29, 🚃 18 or 56; 🅿 ✕ 💻

On the way up to the Buda Hills but still easily accessible by frequent public transport, this is an attractive award-winning pension with 18 rooms and four apartments. Surrounding the property is a lovely garden with fishpond, sun terraces and a grill; you might even organise a BBQ during your stay.

BELVÁROS & LIPÓTVÁROS

BELVÁROS

LE MERIDIEN BUDAPEST
Map p85   Hotel €€€

☎ 429 5500; www.budapest.lemeridien.com; V Erzsébet tér 9-10; s €235-385, s & d €399-499, ste from €749; Ⓜ M1/2/3 Deák Ferenc tér; ✕ 📶 💻 🖾 🕭

Le Meridien's public areas and its 218 guestrooms spread over seven floors are dripping in brocade and French polished furniture – think royalty over rock star. And Le Meridien keeps good company, standing shoulder-to-shoulder with the Hotel Kempinski Corvinus.

KEMPINSKI HOTEL CORVINUS
Map p85   Hotel €€€

☎ 429 3777; www.kempinski-budapest.com; V Erzsébet tér 7-8; s & d €299-339, ste from €629; Ⓜ M1/2/3 Deák Ferenc tér; 🅿 ✕ 📶 💻 🖾 🕭

Essentially for business travellers on hefty expense accounts, the Kempinski has European service, American efficiency and Hungarian charm. The hotel's public areas and 366 guestrooms and suites remain among the classiest in town, even with the advent of so many five-star and boutique hotels. There's a lovely spa on the 2nd floor.

MARRIOTT EXECUTIVE APARTMENTS
Map p85   Serviced Apartment €€€

☎ 235 1800; www.execapartments.com; Millennium Court, V Pesti Barnabás utca 4; s €125-195, d €145-215; Ⓜ M3 Ferenciek tere; ✕ 📶 💻 🖾

A rather flash outfit in Pest with 108 serviced studio apartments measuring about 60 sq metres, one-bed apartments of 32 to 64 sq metres and two-bedroom ones of 57 to 87 sq metres. Stays of eight nights and more earn huge discounts. As part of the package, guests staying here get to use the facilities of the Budapest Marriott Hotel, which is just a block to the northwest.

ZARA BOUTIQUE HOTEL Map p85   Hotel €€€

☎ 357 6170; www.zarahotels.com; V Só utca 6; s €95-135, d €105-165, 📶 47 or 49; ✕ 📶 💻 🕭

We normally don't like hotels that tell you what they're all about but we'll make an exception for this well-situated new place with 74 smallish rooms on seven floors. The hotel is cobbled together from two buildings, which are linked by an open-air corridor. Make sure you ask for a room facing Só utca (eg No 37) as half of the total looks down onto an unsightly *udvar* (courtyard).

HOTEL ART Map p85   Hotel €€€

☎ 266 2166; www.hotelart.hu; V Király Pál utca 12; s €70-90, d €90-140; Ⓜ M3 Kálvin tér; ✕ 📶 💻

This Best Western property has art deco touches (including a pink facade) in the public areas, fitness centre and sauna, but the 32 guestrooms are, on the whole, quite ordinary except for the few that have separate sitting and sleeping areas. Rooms on the 5th floor have mansard roofs.

HOTEL ERZSÉBET Map p85   Hotel €€€

☎ 889 3700; www.danubiusgroup.com/erzsebet; V Károlyi Mihály utca 11-15; s €72-102, d €84-114; Ⓜ M2 Ferenciek tere; ✕ 📶 💻

One of Budapest's first independent hotels, the Erzsébet is in a very good location in the centre of the university district and within easy walking distance of the pubs and bars of Ráday utca. The 123 guestrooms – mostly twins – spread across eight floors are small and dark, with generic hotel furniture but comfortable enough.

LEÓ PANZIÓ Map p85   Guesthouse €€

☎ 266 9041; www.leopanzio.hu; V Kossuth Lajos utca 2/a, 2nd fl; s €49-79, d €76-99; Ⓜ M3 Ferenciek tere

This place with a lion ('leo') theme would be a 'find' just on the strength of its central location, but when you factor in the low cost, this attractive pension is the king of the jungle. A dozen of its 14 immaculate rooms look down on busy Kossuth Lajos utca, but they all have double-glazing and are quiet. The other two rooms face a rather dark internal courtyard.

GREEN BRIDGE HOSTEL Map p85   Hostel €€
☎ 266 6922; www.greenbridgehostel.com; V Molnár utca 22-24; dm €12-18, d/tr/q €50/57/72; Ⓜ M3 Kálvin tér; ☒ 🖳
Few hostels truly stand out in terms of comfort, location and reception, but Green Bridge has it all – and in spades. With everything from doubles, triples and quads to an eight-person dormitory available, bunks are nowhere to be seen. It's on a quiet street just one block in from the Danube, and coffee is on offer gratis throughout the day.

DOMINO HOSTEL Map p85   Hostel €
☎ 235 0492; www.dominohostel.com; V Váci utca 77 (enter from Havas utca 6); dm €10-16, d €44-56, q €56-72; 🚋 47 or 49; ☒ 🖳
It's unlikely you'd find more centrally located budget accommodation in central Pest even after searching for a month of Sundays. The Domino, run by the Mellow Mood Group, offers accommodation in dormitories with six or eight beds as well as a total of 10 twins and quads. The bunks in the dorms look a bit rickety but the twins are of a good size. And think of the convenience! There's a hostel-owned Italian restaurant and pub just next door offering Domino guests a 10% discount on food and bev.

11TH HOUR HOSTEL Map p85   Hostel €
☎ 266 2153; www.11thhourcinemahostel.com; V Magyar utca 11; dm €10-15, tr & q from €20 per person; Ⓜ M2 Astoria; ☒ 🖳
This sister property to the Green Bridge Hostel is just as wonderful, with a half dozen dorms with six to 12 beds and two private rooms across three floors in its very own three-storey townhouse. We love the courtyard bar and the low-lit common room with the huge projection screen for watching films.

RED BUS HOSTEL Map p85   Hostel €
☎ 266 0136; www.redbusbudapest.hu; V Semmelweiss utca 14, 1st fl; dm 3900Ft, s & d 9900Ft, tr 13,000Ft; Ⓜ M2 Astoria; ☒ 🖳
One of the very first independent hostels for travellers in Pest, Red Bus is a central

and well-managed place, with four large and airy rooms with four to five beds, as well as five private rooms for up to three people. It's quiet with a lot of rules – a full 16 are listed in reception – so don't expect to party here.

GINGKO HOSTEL Map p85   Hostel €
☎ 266 6107; www.gingko.hu; V Szép utca 5; dm 3500Ft, q/d per person 4500/5500Ft; Ⓜ M3 Ferenciek tere; ☒ 🖳
This very green establishment hostel with between 20 and 30 beds (depending on the season) in seven big rooms is one of the best hostels in town and the font-of-all-knowledge manageress keeps it so clean you could eat off the floor. There are books to share, bikes to rent (2500Ft for 24 hours) and a positively enormous double giving on to quiet Reáltanoda utca.

LIPÓTVÁROS

FOUR SEASONS GRESHAM PALACE HOTEL Map p85   Hotel €€€
☎ 268 6000; www.fourseasons.com/budapest; V Roosevelt tér 5-6; s €305-850, d €340-885, ste from €1090; Ⓜ M1 Vörösmarty tér, 🚋 16; Ⓟ ☒ ⊠ 🖳 🖼 ♿
This magnificent 179-room hotel was created out of the long derelict art nouveau Gresham Palace (1907) and a lot of angst and hard work. No expense was spared to piece back together the palace's Zsolnay tiles, art nouveau mosaics and celebrated wrought-iron Peacock Gates leading north and south from the enormous lobby, and the hotel is truly worthy of its name. You want face and got the dosh? This is simply the best top-end hotel in town.

STARLIGHT SUITEN HOTEL
Map p85   Serviced Apartment €€€
☎ 484 3700; www.starlighthotels.com; V Mérleg utca 6; s/d €159/189; Ⓜ M1 Vörösmarty tér; 🚋 15 or 115; ☒ 🖼 🖳
This very luxurious suite hotel with 54 units is primarily aimed at the German and Austrian business markets. The suites, which are uniform in layout, consist of a bedroom, living room and bathroom and range from 40 to 60 sq metres. There are no kitchens – the suites have microwave ovens only – though breakfast is available in the Starlight Café.

HOTEL PARLAMENT Map p85 Hotel €€€

☎ 374 6000; www.parlament-hotel.hu; V Kálmán
Imre utca 19; s €110-130, d €140-160; Ⓜ M2 Kossuth Lajos tér; ☒ ☒ ▣ ⓓ
This welcome addition to the list of accommodation options in Lipótváros is a minimalist delight with 65 standard (only) rooms
done up in blacks, greys and reds. The anti-
allergenic white pine floors (there's carpet in
the hallways only) are a plus as is the self-
service bar off the lobby, the dedicated iron-
ing room and the adorable wellness centre
with its own private dressing room. Test your
knowledge on the unique 'design wall' in the
lobby with photographs and the names of
famous Magyars etched in the glass.

HOTEL CENTRAL BASILICA
Map p85 Hotel €€€

☎ 328 5010; www.hotelcentral-basilica.hu;
Hercegprímás utca 8; s €98-149, d €109-149, ste
€189-199; Ⓜ M2 Arany János utca; ☒ ☒ ▣ ⓓ
Fancy rolling out of bed and into church?
This new 47-room hostelry house in a
lovely classical building looks the Basilica
of St Stephen square in the face and the
more expensive superior rooms (eg No 105)
offer unparalleled view of same. The black-
and-white photographs of old Budapest
bedecking the guestroom walls and the
hallways are an atmospheric touch and
the signature marble staircase is original.
The entire hotel is nonsmoking which is a
decided benefit in chimney-like Budapest.

CENTRAL BACKPACK KING HOSTEL
Map p85 Hostel €

☎ 06-30 200 7184; www.centralbpk.hu; V Október
6 utca 15, 1st fl; dm €15-19, per person d €27-29,
tr €22-24, q €21-23; Ⓜ M1/2/3/Deák Ferenc tér,
▣ 15 or 115; ☒ ▣
This upbeat place in the heart of the Inner
Town has rooms with between seven and
nine dorm beds on one floor and doubles,
triples and quads on another. There's a small
but scrupulously clean kitchen; a large,
bright common room and views across
Október 6 utca to the lovely 1910 apartment
block at No 16-18 where your humble writer
sometimes stays when in town.

GARIBALDI GUESTHOUSE &
APARTMENTS Map p85 Hostel & Guesthouse €

☎ 302 3457, 06-30 951 8763; garibaldiguest@
hotmail.com; V Garibaldi utca 5, 5th fl; s/d €28/36,
apt per person €25-45; Ⓜ M2 Kossuth Lajos tér

This welcoming hostel-cum-guesthouse
has five rooms with shared bathroom and
kitchen in a flat just around the corner
from Parliament. In the same building, the
gregarious owner has at least a half-dozen
apartments available on several floors, and
a hostel is being built.

NORTHERN RING ROAD AREA
ÚJLIPÓTVÁROS & TERÉZVÁROS

NH BUDAPEST Map pp92-3 Hotel €€€

☎ 814 0000; www.nh-hotels.com; XIII Vígszínház
utca 3; s & d €99-159; ⓡ 4 or 6; ☒ ☒ ▣ ⓓ
There are 160 rooms spread out over this
eight-floor purpose-built hotel and three
rooms on each floor have a balcony. We
especially like the location behind the
Comedy Theatre, the minimalist but welcoming and very bright atrium lobby and
the helpful staff dressed in attractive black
designer togs. The 8th floor fitness centre is
very flashy indeed.

ADINA APARTMENT HOTEL
Map pp92-3 Serviced Apartment €€€

☎ 236 8888; www.adina.hu; XIII Hegedüs Gyula
utca 52-54; studio €160-246, 1-bedroom apt €191-
320, 2-bedroom apt €271-442; Ⓜ M3 Lehel tér,
▣ 15 or 133; ☒ ☒ ▣ ▣
This lovely, recently renovated (and renamed) property hard by Váci út and the
West End City Centre mall has 97 tastefully
furnished units of between 45 and 110 sq
metres in three wings, a gorgeous courtyard garden, marble finishings throughout,
classical music in the lobby and an indoor
swimming pool and fitness centre. Discounted rates are available at the weekend
and after a month's stay.

COTTON HOUSE Map pp92-3 Hotel €€

☎ 354 2600; www.cottonhouse.hu; VI Jókai utca
26; r €70-150; ⓡ 4 or 6; ☒ ▣
This 23-room place has a jazz/speakeasy
theme that gets a bit tired after a while
(though the old radios and vintage telephones do actually work). Prices vary
widely depending on the season and your
room has a shower, tub or Jacuzzi in its
bathroom.

KAPITAL INN Map pp92-3   Hotel €€
☎ 06-30 931 1023; www.kapitalinn.com; VI Aradi utca 30, 4 fl; s & d €79-125; Ⓜ M1 Vörösmarty utca; 🚲 4 or 6; ☒ 🖳 📷
This gay-owned and operated B&B with four rooms offers quite luxurious accommodation up under the stars; the 56 sq metre terrace has to be seen to be believed. Guests get to use a little office with its own laptop, the breakfast room and bar has a fridge stocked with goodies that can be raided at will any time and the entrance to the building (1893) is a stucco masterpiece. Alas, there's no lift here and the cheaper pair of rooms share a bathroom.

CITY HOTEL RING Map pp92-3   Hotel €€
☎ 340 5450; www.cityhotels.hu; XIII Szent István körút 22; s €61-89, d €69-108, tr €89-134; Ⓜ M3 Nyugati pályaudvar; ☒ 🖳
Another feather in the mellow Mood Group's cap, this small, almost motel-like place with 39 rooms is on two floors of a *fin-de-siècle* building (but you'd never know that from the inside looking out). Some of the Ring's rooms gaze down on to the busy, err, ring road, others onto an attractive and very quiet courtyard.

BOAT HOTEL FORTUNA
Map pp92-3   Hotel €€
☎ 288 8100; www.fortunahajo.hu; XIII Szent István Park, Pesti alsó rakpart; with bathroom s €55-80, d €65-100, tr €80-120, with washbasin s €20-25, d €30-35, tr €40-47; trolleybus 76; ☒ 📷 🖳
Sleeping on a one-time river ferry anchored in the Danube may not be everyone's idea of a good time, but it's a unique experience. This 'boatel' has 42 single and double air-conditioned rooms with shower and toilet at water level. An additional 14 rooms with two or three beds and washbasin below deck are not so nice and almost feel like old-fashioned hostel accommodation.

MEDOSZ HOTEL Map pp92-3   Hotel €€
☎ 374 3000; www.medoszhotel.hu; VI Jókai tér 9; s €49-59, d €59-69, tr €69-79, ste €89-100; Ⓜ M1 Oktogon
One of the most central cheap hotels in Pest, the Medosz is just opposite the restaurants and bars of Liszt Ferenc tér. The 68 rooms are well worn but had been slated for a revamp at the time of writing. Each has private bathroom and satellite TV; the

best ones are in the main block, not in the labyrinthine wings.

CONNECTION GUEST HOUSE
Map pp92-3   Hotel €€
☎ 267 7104; www.connectionguesthouse.com; VII Király utca 41; s €45-60, d €50-73; Ⓜ M1 Opera; ☒ 🖳
This very central gay guesthouse above a leafy courtyard attracts a young crowd due to its proximity to queer nightlife venues. Three of the seven rooms share facilities in the corridor and rooms 6 and 7 face partially pedestrianised Király utca.

AVENTURA HOSTEL Map pp92-3   Hostel €
☎ 311 1190; www.aventurahostel.com; XIII Visegrádi utca 12, 1st fl; bed in 5-8-bed dm €14-21, d €50-60, apt €60-70; Ⓜ M2 Nyugati pályaudvar, 🚲 4 or 6; ☒ 🖳
What has got to be the most chilled hostel in Budapest, with four themed rooms (India, Japan, Africa and – our favourite – Space) and run by two affable ladies, is slightly out of the action in Újlipótváros but easily accessible by public transport. We love the colours and fabrics, the in-house massage and the dorms with loft sleeping.

PETER'S APARTMENTS
Map pp92-3   Serviced Apartment €
☎ 06 30 520 0400; www.peters.hu; XIII Victor Hugó utca 25-27; s/d/tr €42-49, d €52-59, tr €62-69; Ⓜ M3 Lehel tér, 🚌 15 or 115, trolleybus 75; 📷 🖳
This budget place in Pest offers 15 studio apartments of approximately 20 sq metres in a basic but clean building at some rock-bottom prices. The more expensive units have air-conditioning and balconies; all have TV. Prices are negotiable, especially during the low season (November to mid-March) and at weekends.

HOME-MADE HOSTEL Map pp92-3   Hostel €
☎ 302 2103; www.homemadehostel.com; VI Teréz körút 22, 1st fl; 8-bed dm €8-15, 6-bed dm €13-17, q per person €14-18, d €40-58; Ⓜ M1 Oktogon; ☒ 🖳
This homey, extremely welcoming hostel with 20 beds in four rooms may not deserve inclusion on Unesco's World Heritage List as its brochure says but it's unique enough, with recycled tables hanging upside down from the ceiling and old valises under the beds serving as lockers. There's a warmth to this place that will make you

want to stay forever, and the old-style kitchen is museum-quality. Maybe it should get that Unesco listing.

BROADWAY HOSTEL Map pp92-3 Hostel €

☎ 688 1662; www.broadwayhostel.hu; VI Ó utca 24-26; dm €12-18, s & d €40; Ⓜ M1 Opera; ⊠ 🖳 🔀
It may be shoehorned into a pretty tight space, but this hostel with three rooms of six, eight and 10 beds and a couple of doubles is among the most modern and upbeat in town. They say orange is the friendliest colour, and this place is positively in the hue. There are no laundry facilities but who's worried? One of Budapest's few laundrettes – the Mosómata (p210) is just across the courtyard. The hostel's name refers, of course, to Nagymező utca – the 'Broadway of Budapest' – within spitting distance to the east.

BÁNKI HOSTEL Map pp92-3 Hostel €

☎ 787 4321; www.mellowmood.hu; VI Podmaniczky utca 8; dm €12, s/d/q per person €28/17/16; ☺ Jul-Aug; Ⓜ M3 Nyugati pályaudvar, 🚋 4 or 6; ⊠ 🖳
This central and relatively small (33 rooms, 104 beds) hostel run by the Mellow Mood Group in a 19th-century building is just minutes away from Nyugati train station. Rooms have fridges but all share a bathroom.

ANDRÁSSY ÚT & SURROUNDS

ANDRÁSSY HOTEL Map pp92-3 Hotel €€€

☎ 462 2100; www.andrassyhotel.com; VI Andrássy út 111; s & d €135-235, ste from €245; Ⓜ M1 Hősök tere; Ⓟ ⊠ 🔀 🖳 ♿
This stunning five-star hotel just off leafy Andrássy út (enter from Munkácsy Mihály utca 5-7) has 70 tastefully decorated rooms (almost half of which have balconies) in a listed building. The lobby and ground-floor restaurant look fresher as do many of the guestrooms since their recent renovation. The use of etched glass and mirrors as well as wrought iron in many is inspired.

RESIDENCE IZABELLA
Map pp92-3 Serviced Apartment €€€

☎ 475 5900; www.residence-izabella.com; VI Izabella utca 61; 1-bedroom apt €180-330, 2-bedroom apt €295-515; Ⓜ M1 Vörösmarty utca; ⊠ 🔀 🖳
This fabulous conversion of a 19th-century Eclectic building has 38 apartments measuring between 45 and 97 sq metres just off

swanky Andrássy út. The units surround a delightful and very tranquil central courtyard garden and the decor mixes materials such as wood, terracotta and basketry to great effect. Service is impeccable.

K+K HOTEL OPERA Map pp92-3 Hotel €€€

☎ 269 0222; www.kkhotels.com; VI Révay utca 24; s €140-168, d €160-209, ste €235-336; Ⓜ M1 Opera; ⊠ 🔀 🖳
This upbeat Austrian-owned place just behind the Hungarian State Opera House has 206 rooms spread over seven floors. They're on the smallish side and decorated in unusually cheerful colours, which raises the tenor of the whole place. Extra touches include the daily distribution of the Good Morning News, world headlines on hard copy.

HOTEL BENCZÚR Map pp92-3 Hotel €€

☎ 479 5662; www.hotelbenczur.hu; VI Benczúr utca 35; s €60-76, d €75-92, tr €90-111; Ⓜ M1 Bajza utca; Ⓟ ⊠ 🔀 🖳 ♿
This rather faded place done up in creams and oranges has 161 serviceable rooms over seven floors, of which about 65 have been renovated in recent years. Some of these look down on a leafy garden. It's got a great location: the hotel is just minutes away from Andrássy út, Heroes' Sq and City Park.

HOTEL DÉLIBÁB Map pp92-3 Hotel €€

☎ 342 9301; www.hoteldelibab.hu; VI Délibáb utca 35; s €57-71, d €68-83, tr €85-100; Ⓜ M1 Hősök tere; Ⓟ ⊠ 🖳
The 34-room 'Mirage' is housed in what was once a Jewish orphanage across from Hősök tere and City Park and is pretty barebones as it still awaits its overdue renovation by the Mellow Mood Group. Ask for one of the nine rooms that face the quiet courtyard to the rear as the rest look onto busy Dózsa György út.

RADIO INN Map pp92-3 Guesthouse €€

☎ 342 8347; www.radioinn.hu; VI Benczúr utca 19; s/d €65/78, apt €80-120; Ⓜ M1 Bajza utca; ⊠ 🖳
Just off leafy Andrássy út, this place is a real find, with 23 large one-bedroom apartments with bathroom and kitchen, 10 with two bedrooms and one with three bedrooms measuring between 44 and 60 sq metres, all spread over five floors. The garden courtyard is a delight; try to get a room with a small balcony. The furnishings could use an upgrade, though.

top picks

HOTELS WITH A GARDEN

- Papillon Hotel (p177)
- Beatrix Panzió (p178)
- Adina Apartment Hotel (p180)
- Hotel Anna (p184)
- Radio Inn (popposite)

ERZSÉBETVÁROS

CORINTHIA GRAND HOTEL ROYAL
Map pp92-3   Hotel €€€

☎ 479 4000; www.corinthia.hu; VII Erszébet körút 43-49; s & d €179-280, ste from €310; ⓡ 4 or 6; ℗ ⊠ ⊠ ▣ ♿

Decades in the remaking, the one-time Royal Hotel on the Big Ring Road is now a very grand 414-room, five-star hotel. Its lobby – a double atrium with massive marble staircase – is among the most impressive in the capital while the restored Royal Spa dating back to 1886 is now as modern as tomorrow. This is truly the 'legend reborn' we've all been waiting for.

HOTEL DOMINA FIESTA
Map pp92-3   Hotel €€€

☎ 328 3000; www.dominahotels.com; VI Király utca 20; s €159-179, d €199-219, tr €259; Ⓜ M1/2/3 Deák Ferenc tér; ⊠ ⊠ ▣ ♿

This attractive boutique hotel, under the management of a small Italian hotel chain, has 112 tastefully furnished rooms and a vaulted wine-cellar restaurant just minutes from Pest's main square.

SOHO HOTEL Map pp92-3   Hotel €€€

☎ 872 8292, 06-20 779 6341; www.sohohotel .hu; VII Dohány utca 64; s €99-125, d €109-135, ste €169-199; Ⓜ M2 Blaha Lujza tér, ⓡ 4 or 6; ⊠ ⊠ ▣ ♿

This delightfully stylish boutique hotel with 68 rooms and six suites has opened just opposite the New York Palace and we know which one feels more like the Big Apple. We lurve the lobby bar in eye-popping reds, blues and lime greens, nonallergenic rooms with bamboo matting on the walls and parquet floors and the music/film theme throughout (check out the portraits of Bono, George Michael and, sigh, Marilyn).

HOTEL BAROSS Map pp92-3   Hotel €€

☎ 461 3010; www.barosshotel.hu; VII Baross tér 15, 4th-6th fl; s €60-82, d €74-98, tr €90-114, q €100-136; Ⓜ M2 Keleti pályaudvar; ⊠ ⊠ ▣

The flagship hotel of the Mellow Mood Group, the Baross is a comfortable, 49-room caravanserai conveniently located directly opposite Keleti train station. The very blue inner courtyard is a delight, and reception, which is on the 5th floor, is clean and bright, with a dramatic central staircase.

STAR HOTEL Map pp92-3   Hotel €€

☎ 479 0420; www.starhotel.hu; VII István utca 14; s €60-85, d €75-95, tr €85-120, q €100-140; trolley-bus 74 or 79; ⊠ ▣

Another addition to the Mellow Mood Group's stable is this brightly coloured midrange hotel just a few minutes' walk north of Keleti train station. The ground floor lobby is quite spacious and a popular meeting place for travellers; most of the guestrooms are doubles spread over four floors.

CARMEN MINI HOTEL
Map pp92-3   Guesthouse €€

☎ 352 0798; carmen@axelero.hu; Károly körút 5/b, 2nd fl; s/d/tr €50/60/75; Ⓜ M1/2/3 Deák Ferenc tér

With nine rooms, the Carmen Mini Hotel is about the nearest you'll find to a rock-bottom B&B in central Pest. It's very close to Deák Ferenc tér and convenient to all forms of transport but expect no frills and lots of spills.

MARCO POLO HOSTEL
Map pp92-3   Hostel €€

☎ 413 2555; www.marcopolohostel.com; VII Nyár utca 6; dm 3000-4500Ft, per person s 10,000-18,250Ft, d 6000-8600Ft, tr 5000-6600Ft, q 4500-6000Ft; Ⓜ M2 Blaha Lujza tér; ⊠ ▣

The Mellow Mood Group's very central flagship hostel is a swish, powder-blue, 47-room place, with telephones and TVs in all the rooms, except the dorms, and a lovely courtyard. Even the five spotless dorms are 'private', with the dozen beds separated by lockers and curtains.

UNITY HOSTEL Map pp92-3   Hostel €

☎ 413 7377; www.unityhostel.com; VI Király utca 60; 3rd fl; dm €12-16, d €36-44; ⓡ 4 or 6; ⊠ ▣

top picks

HOSTELS

- Back Pack Guesthouse (p176)
- Aventura Hostel (p181)
- Unity Hostel (p183)
- Central Backpack King Hostel (pp180)
- 11th Hour Hostel (pp179)

This hostel's location in the heart of party town would be draw enough but add to that a roof terrace with breathtaking views of the Liszt Academy of Music, ceiling fans to cool you down and a resident bearded collie to grab your attention and you've got a winner. There are 24 beds in five rooms over two internal levels – something unique in a Budapest hostel.

SPINOZA APARTMENTS

Map pp92-3   Hotel €

☎ 06-30 491 7069, 413 7488; www.spinoza.hu; VII Dob utca 15; studio €30-40, 2/3-room apt €85/101; 🚊 47 or 49

These four apartments, which rose above a bakery when the building went up in 1903 but now sit contentedly above the Spinoza Café (p137) and its wonderful little theatre, offer some of the best value-for-money in central Pest. There's a three-room unit sleeping up to six on the 1st floor and apartments with one and two rooms on the 2nd but unfortunately no lift. All have modern kitchens but with such a wide range of eateries at your feet it's unlikely you'll be reaching for the frypan.

10 BEDS Map pp92-3   Hostel €

☎ 06-20 933 5965; adrianzador@hotmail.com; VII Erzsébet körút 15, 3rd fl; dm 3000Ft; 🚊 4 or 6

OK, it's misnamed – the place has 14 beds in three rooms – and there's no lift. But that's about the only thing wrong with this laid-back hostel with great kitchen, free use of a washing machine and your own set of keys. The Belváros branch (Map p85; ☎ same; V Molnár utca 53; dm 2500; 🚊 47 or 49) has a dozen beds in just one over-sized room, a big kitchen and common room but million-dollar views of Liberty Bridge and the Danube.

SOUTHERN RING ROAD AREA

HOTEL MERCURE BUDAPEST MUSEUM Map pp102–3   Hotel €€€

☎ 485 1080; www.mercure.com; VIII Trefort utca 2; s €70-180, d €110-210; Ⓜ M2 Astoria, 🚊 7 or 173; ✕ 🐾 🖳 ♿

This hotel, although it is part of an expanding chain, is in a lovely building dating from 1890 that is interesting enough to warrant consideration. The 104 guestrooms, most of which are reserved for nonsmokers and done up in a 'Mediterranean' or 'modern Italian' style, are nothing special, however.

HOTEL SISSI Map pp102-3   Hotel €€€

☎ 215 0082; www.hotelsissi.hu; IX Angyal utca 33; s €90-130, d €100-140, ste €150-180; Ⓜ M3 Ferenc körút; Ⓟ ✕ 🐾 🖳

Named in honour of Elizabeth, the Habsburg empress, Hungarian queen and consort of Franz Joseph much beloved by Hungarians, the Hotel Sissi is decorated in a minimalist-cum-elegant sort of style, and the 44 guestrooms spread over six floors are of a good size. Some rooms look onto a back garden.

ATRIUM HOTEL Map pp102-3   Hotel €€€

☎ 299 0777; www.atriumhotelbudapest.com; VIII Csokonai utca 14; s €88-129, d €98-139, tr €128-179; Ⓜ M2 Blaha Lujza tér, 🚊 4 or 6; ✕ 🐾 🖳

This brightly coloured (think chartreuse and royal blue) venue gets extra points for trying so hard. The enormous pendulum clock swinging in the lobby is an eye-catcher, as are the feline figures striking various poses on each landing of the staircase. Rooms on the top (4th) floor are of an unusual design, with windows that give on to a gallery of grey wrought iron. Depending on the room and the time of year, this could be a very affordable Budapest boutique experience. Location is convenient to public transport.

HOTEL ANNA Map pp102-3   Hotel €€€

☎ 327 2000; www.annahotel.hu; VIII Gyulai Pál utca; s €66-98, d €82-125; ste €88-149; Ⓜ M3 Blaha Lujza tér, 🚊 7 or 78

Run by the same people who own Fülemüle (p140) and just across the street, Anna has 42 fairly basic rooms but feels twice that size – as they are strewn over three floors of two 18th-century buildings surrounding an enormous courtyard and garden. It doesn't tend to offer the greatest value for money in town, but rooms are quieter than the grave and the location is great.

HOTEL PLATÁNUS Map pp102-3 Hotel €€
☎ 333 6505, 210 2592; www.hunguesthotels.hu; VIII Könyves Kálmán körút 44; s/d/tr €99/120/130; Ⓜ M3 Népliget; ✕ ⚙ ⚏
Platánus, with 133 rooms on the noisy outer ring road, is moderately priced in the low season, but room prices jump in summer. It has a fitness centre with a well-equipped gym, sauna and aerobics room, and is a short distance from Népliget Park and the Népliget bus station.

CORVIN HOTEL Map pp102-3 Hotel €€
☎ 218 6566; www.corvinhotelbudapest.hu; IX Angyal utca 31; s €60-85, d €75-99, tr €90-110, apt €105-129; Ⓜ M3 Ferenc körút; Ⓟ ✕ ⚙ ⚏
Hard by the Danube, this purpose-built hotel in up-and-coming Ferencváros has 47 very comfortable rooms with all the mod cons and secure parking in a covered garage. The bright and airy breakfast room is a real plus.

HOTEL THOMAS Map pp102-3 Hotel €€
☎ 218 5505; www.hotels.hu/hotelthomas; IX Liliom utca 44; s €55-65, d €75-95; Ⓜ M3 Ferenc körút; Ⓟ ✕ ⚙ ⚏
A brightly coloured place in an odd location, this hotel has 43 rooms and is a real bargain for its location in still up-and-coming Ferencváros. Some rooms have balconies looking onto an inner courtyard. The goofy-looking kid in the logo is the owner as a young 'un.

ATLAS HOTEL Map pp102-3 Hotel €€
☎ 299 0256; www.atlashotel.hu; VIII Népszínház utca 39-41; s €50-66, d €58-88, tr €75-120, q €92-152; ⚙ 28 or 37; Ⓟ ✕ ⚙ ⚏
This enormous place spread over eight floors in less-than-salubrious district VIII has 102 standard (though comfortable) and renovated singles, doubles, triples and quads as well as another three dozen superior doubles. It is said that you'll always find a room at the Atlas, which may (or may not) be a good recommendation.

KM SAGA GUEST RESIDENCE
Map pp102-3 Guesthouse €€
☎ 217 1934; www.km-saga.hu; IX Lónyay utca 17, 3rd fl; s €42-63, d €55-82; Ⓜ M3 Kálvin tér, 🚌 15 or 115, ⚙ 47 or 49; ⚏ ⚙
This unique place has five themed rooms, an eclectic mix of 19th-century furnishings and a hospitable, multilingual Hungarian-American owner. It's essentially a gay B&B but everyone is welcome. Two rooms share a bathroom. The KM Saga II (Map pp102–3; ☎ same; IX Vámház körút 11, 6th fl; Ⓜ M3 Kálvin tér, ⚙ 47 or 49; ⚏ ⚙) branch is more modern but less atmospheric. It has three rooms with private bathrooms and an 82-sq-metre apartment.

FORTUNA HOTEL
Map pp102-3 Hotel & Hostel €€
☎ 215 0660; www.fortunahotel.hu; IX Gyáli út 3/b; dm €15, s/d/tr 48/66/84; Ⓜ M3 Nagyvárad tér, ⚙ 24; ⚙ ⚏
With 30 rooms (including dorms with four or five beds) this place is not in the best part of Budapest but it's quiet, super clean and the huge Taiwan restaurant (p141) is at your feet. Reception (and all the guestrooms, for that matter) are on the 2nd floor.

HOTEL RILA Map pp102-3 Hotel & Hostel €€
☎ 323 2999; www.hotelrila.com; IX Fehér Holló utca 2; dm 4000-4500Ft, with shared bathroom s 7000-9000Ft, d 10,000-13,000Ft, with bathroom s 9000-12,000Ft, d 12,000-15,000Ft, tr 15,000-18,750Ft; Ⓜ M3 Nagyvárad tér, ⚙ 24; Ⓟ ⚏
A former workers' hostel, the 39-room Rila, the Universum hostel group's flagship property, has been spruced up into quite a nice little property. Open year-round, it has both hostel accommodation and rooms for between one and four people both with and without bathrooms. We like the rustic Hungarian restaurant with old photographs on the walls.

MUSEUM GUEST HOUSE
Map pp102-3 Hostel €
☎ 266 7770, 266 8879; www.budapesthostel.com; VIII Mikszáth Kálmán tér 4, 1st fl; dm 3200-3500Ft; Ⓜ M3 Kálvin tér; ⚏
The Museum is pokey and faded but creatively decorated, with mostly eight beds in three rooms (though there is one room with four beds). Its location on a lovely square and proximity to the nightlife of VIII Krúdy utca and IX Ráday utca are pluses.

More central and upbeat is Museum Guest House II (☎ 266 7774, 266 7775; Károly körút 10, 1st fl; Ⓜ M2 Astoria; 🚋 47 or 49), with 20 beds in six rooms and a lovely modern kitchen for the same price.

KINIZSI HOSTEL Map pp102-3   Hostel €

☎ 787 4321; IX Kinizsi utca 2-6; dm €12.50, s/d/tr per person €25/15/13.50; 🕑 Jul & Aug; Ⓜ M3 Ferenc körút

The only summer hostel in Pest managed by the Mellow Mood hostel group has basic rooms with one to five beds (total 124 beds) in a modern, six-storey student residence close to the Danube and the IX Ráday utca nightlife strip.

CITY PARK & BEYOND

GOLDEN PARK HOTEL

Map pp102-3   Hotel €€€

☎ 477 4777; www.goldenparkhotel.com; VIII Baross tér 10; s/d/tr €140/170/220; Ⓜ M3 Keleti pályaudvar; ✗ 🏋 💻

This old workhorse of a hotel with 180 rooms has been completely de- and recon-structed, and today it is a shimmering four-star caravanserai number within spitting distance of the Keleti train station. We like the bright and airy lobby, the glass doors at either end of the corridors letting in light and some of the old features they managed to retain.

DOMINIK PANZIÓ Map p108   Guesthouse €

☎ 343 7655; www.dominikpanzio.hu; XIV Cházár András utca 3; s €21-36, d €29-45, tr €39-55, apt €69-100; 🚌 7 or 73; Ⓟ

Just off Thököly út and located beside a large church, Dominik Panzió is on a leafy street lined with 19th-century villas and just two stops northeast of Keleti train station by bus. The 36 rooms, which could use an upgrade, come with shared bathroom and there is a five-person apartment available.

HOTEL GÓLIÁT Map p108   Hotel €

☎ 350 1456; www.gerandhotels.hu; XIII Kerekes utca 12-20; s/d/tr/q 6300/7600/8400/9300Ft; 🚌 32, 🚋 14; ✗ 💻

This very basic but spotlessly clean hotel in Angyalföld northeast of the Belváros and Lehel market has 135 basic rooms with between one and four beds. There are washbasins in the rooms, and showers and toilets in the corridor.

HOTEL FLANDRIA Map p108   Hotel €

☎ 350 3181; www.hotelflandria.hu, in Hungarian; XIII Szegedi út 27; s/d/tr/q with washbasin only 6200/7500/10,300/11,600Ft, with shower 10,200/12,400/14,100/16,200Ft; 🚌 4; 🚋 32; Ⓟ ✗ 💻

The Flandria is a classic example of a former workers' hostel that has metamorphosed into a budget hotel. Don't expect anything within a couple of light years of luxury, but the 125 guestrooms, which have from one to four beds, a TV and refrigerator, are clean, serviceable and very cheap.

EXCURSIONS

A lot in Hungary is within easy striking distance of Budapest, and many of the towns and cities in the Danube Bend (to the north of Budapest), Transdanubia (west and south), Northern Uplands (north and northeast) and even the Great Plain (east and southeast) could be visited on a day trip from the capital. You can get to Szentendre to the north in less than an hour by the HÉV commuter train, for example, and Eger, a lovely Mediterranean-like town lying between the Bükk and Mátra Hills to the northeast, is just two hours away by express bus.

This chapter assumes you'll be returning to Budapest after a day of sightseeing, though we've included a few accommodation options in each section in case you miss your train or bus, or simply decide you like the place so much you want to stay a night or two. For fuller treatment of these and other destinations, see Lonely Planet's *Hungary*.

CASTLES & MANOR HOUSES

Some of Hungary's most dramatic castles and opulent manor houses are close to Budapest. First and foremost, is the hilltop fortress at Eger (p194), a castle and a half if there ever was one and the stuff of legend (see the boxed text, p195). The Royal Mansion (p191) at Gödöllő is Hungary's largest baroque – and best preserved – manor house. The Brunswick Mansion (p192) at Martonvásár may not be able to compete in size or opulence, but the guests it has welcomed put it on the A-list.

CHURCHES & CATHEDRALS

If you haven't had your fill of grand churches in Budapest, travel the extra distance south to Pécs, whose Inner Town Parish Church (p196) is housed in a mosque dating from the mid-16th century and the largest building still standing in Hungary from the Turkish occupation. Windy Veszprém, set high up on a plateau, has so many fine churches that the locals exclaim, 'Either the wind is blowing or the bells are ringing in Veszprém'. But first and foremost is the Cathedral of St Michael (p194) with an important Gothic crypt. Eger's neoclassical cathedral (p195), however, is the most important architecturally

and, despite its size and scale, is surprisingly light and airy inside.

WINE

Eger, the birthplace of the famed wine called Bikavér (Bull's Blood; p145), is inextricably linked with wine, and one of the best places in Hungary to sample the fruit of the vine is at the nearby Valley of the Beautiful Women (p196). Pécs is practically next door to Villány, which produces Hungary's biggest and (arguably) best red wines. And from Veszprém the Badacsony region along the northwestern shore of Lake Balaton, famed for its crisp white Olaszrizling and unique Kéknyelű (Blue Stalk), is within easy driving distance.

SZENTENDRE

Szentendre (population 24,000), Hungarian for 'St Andrew', is the gateway to the Danube Bend, the S-shaped curve in Hungary's mightiest river that begins just below Esztergom and twists for 20km before reaching Budapest. As an art colony turned lucrative tourist centre, Szentendre strikes many as a little too 'cutesy', and the town can be crowded and relatively expensive. Still, the many art museums,

---

WAY TO GO

If you're pressed for time or too lazy to do it yourself, a number of travel agencies (p216) and tour operators (p212) organise excursions to destinations away from Budapest. By way of example, a 4½-hour tour by boat and bus to Szentendre with Cityrama costs 11,000Ft (children under 12 free), while one the same length to Gödöllő by bus is 9500/5000Ft per adult/child, and an 8½-hour tour of the Danube Bend by coach and boat with stops at Visegrád and Esztergom costs 14,000/6000Ft. Cityrama also offers day trips to Lake Balaton (Balatonfüred and Tihany) and Herend (18,000/10,000Ft, nine to 10 hours), as well as to Lajosmizse and Kecskemét on the Southern Great Plain (18,000/9000Ft, eight hours). Hungary Program Centrum operates similar tours at almost the same prices, as well as a nine-hour tour of the Eger wine region (19,900/9950Ft).

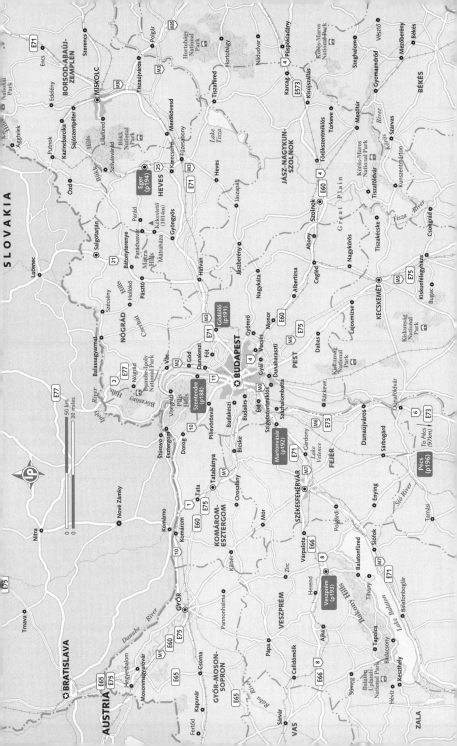

TRANSPORT: SZENTENDRE

Distance from Budapest 19km.

Direction North.

Travel time 40 minutes by HÉV suburban train.

Boat From May to September, one daily Mahart ferry plies the Danube to/from Vigadó tér (Map p85) in Pest and Batthyány tér (Map p62) in Buda, departing at 10.30am and arriving in Szentendre at 11.50am (one-way/return 1490/2235Ft, one hour 20 minutes). The return boat leaves at 5pm. The service dwindles to weekends only in April and October but from June to September there's an extra weekend sailing at 2.30pm (returning 7pm). Additionally, from May to August a daily 9am ferry leaves Budapest, calling in at Szentendre (10.40am) and Visegrád (one-way/ return 1590/2385Ft, 12.30am), before returning from Visegrád at 4.30pm. The service departs weekends only in April, Friday in September, and Friday to Sunday in October.

Bus Buses from Pest's Árpád híd station (Map pp58–9), which is on the M3 blue metro line, run to Szentendre at least once an hour throughout the day (250Ft, 30 minutes).

Car Rte 11 from Buda.

HÉV Trains depart from Batthyány tér (Map p62) in Buda (370Ft, 40 minutes) every 10 to 20 minutes throughout the day. Note that a yellow city bus/metro ticket is good only as far as the Békásmegyer stop on the way; you'll have to pay 100Ft extra to get to Szentendre. Also, many HÉV trains run only as far as Békásmegyer, where you must cross the platform to board the train for Szentendre. The last train leaves Szentendre for Budapest at 11.10pm.

galleries and Serbian Orthodox churches make the trip worthwhile. Just try to avoid it on summer weekends.

Right in the centre of Fő tér, the colourful heart of Szentendre surrounded by 18th- and 19th-century burghers' houses, stands the Memorial Cross, an iron cross decorated with icons on a marble base, erected in 1763 as an ex-votive. Across the square to the northeast is the Serbian Orthodox Blagoveštenska Church (☎ 26-310 554; admission 250Ft; ☽ 10am-5pm Tue-Sun), built in 1754. The church, with fine baroque and rococo elements, hardly looks 'eastern' from the outside, but once you step inside, the ornate iconostasis and elaborate 18th-century furnishings give the game away.

If you descend Görög utca and turn south onto Vastagh György utca, you'll reach the Margit Kovács Ceramic Collection (Kovács Margit Kerámiagyüjtemény; ☎ 26-310 224; Vastagh György utca 1; adult/child 700/350Ft; ☽ 10am-6pm), Szenten- dre's biggest draw. Kovács (1902–77) was a ceramicist who combined Hungarian folk, religious and modern themes to create elon- gated, Gothiclike figures. Some of her works are overly sentimental, but many are very powerful, especially the later ones in which she became obsessed with mortality.

Castle Hill (Vár-domb), which can be reached via Váralja lépcső, the narrow set of steps be- tween Fő tér 8 and 9, was the site of a fortress in the Middle Ages, but all that's left of it is the Parish Church of St John (Szent János Plébániatemplom; Temp-

lom tér; admission free; ☽ 10am-4pm Tue-Sun Apr-Oct), from where you can enjoy views of the town. The red spire of Belgrade Cathedral (Belgrád Székesegyház; Alkot- mány utca; adult/child incl art collection 500/250Ft; ☽ 10am- 6pm Tue-Sun Mar-Sep, 10am-4pm Tue-Sun Oct-Dec, 10am-4pm Fri-Sun Jan & Feb), seat of the Serbian Orthodox bishop in Hungary and built in 1764, rises from within a walled courtyard to the north. One of the church outbuildings contains the Serbian Ecclesiastical Art Collection (Szerb Egyházművészeti Gyűjtemény; ☎ 26-312 399; Pátriárka utca 5; adult/child incl church 500/250Ft), a treasure-trove of icons, vest- ments, and church plate in precious metals (open at the same times as the church).

INFORMATION

Tourinform (☎ 26-317 965; szentendre@tourinform.hu; Dumtsa Jenő utca 22; ☽ 9.30am-4.30pm Mon-Fri year- round, 10am-2pm Sat & Sun mid-Mar–Oct)

www.szentendreprogram.hu Provides loads of online information.

EATING

Promenade (☎ 26-312 626; Futó utca 4; mains 1700-3000Ft) Vaulted ceilings, white-washed walls and a wonderful terrace overlooking the Danube are all highlights here, one of Szentendre's best restaurants serving 'enlightened' Hungarian and international dishes.

Erm's (☎ 26-303 388; Kossuth Lajos utca 22; mains around 2000Ft) Retro-style Erm's, with its walls

DETOUR

The Hungarian Open-Air Ethnographical Museum (Magyar Szabadtéri Néprajzi Múzeum; ☎ 26-502 500; www.skanzen.hu; Sztaravodai út; adult/student 1200/600Ft; ⏱ 9am-5pm Tue-Sun mid-Mar–mid-Nov), 3km northwest of the centre of Szentendre and accessible by bus from bay 7 at the main bus station, is Hungary's most ambitious open-air folk museum, with farmhouses, churches, bell towers, mills and so on set up in five regional units. Craftspeople and artisans do their thing on Sundays and holidays.

festooned with early 20th–century memorabilia and simple wooden tables dressed in lacy cloths, is an unpretentious spot with a wide choice of Hungarian specialities, including some vegetarian choices.

Palapa (☎ 26-302 418; Batthyány utca 4; mains 1500-3000Ft; ⏱ 5pm-midnight Mon-Fri, noon-midnight Sat & Sun) The food at this colourful Mexican restaurant with live music makes it the perfect place for a change from Hungarian fare.

SLEEPING

Centrum (☎ 26-302 500; www.hotelcentrum.hu; Bogdányi utca 15; s/d from 10,000/11,000Ft; Ⓟ 🐾) This quaint guesthouse occupies a well-renovated house a stone's throw from the Danube. Its half-dozen rooms are large and bright and filled with antique furniture.

Ilona (☎ 26-313 599; www.ilonapanzio.hu; Rákóczi Ferenc utca 11; s/d 5500/7700Ft; Ⓟ) Ilona is a perfect little pension with plenty going for it – superb central location, locked parking, inner courtyard for breakfast and six small but tidy rooms.

GÖDÖLLŐ

Easily accessible on the HÉV suburban train, Gödöllő (roughly pronounced 'good-duh-ler') is an easy day trip from Budapest. The main attraction here is the Royal Mansion completed in the 1760s, which is Hungary's largest baroque manor house. The town itself is full of lovely baroque buildings and monuments and hosts a couple of important music festivals each year.

The Royal Mansion (Királyi Kastély; ☎ 28-410 124; www.kiralyikastely.hu; Szabadság tér 1; adult/student & child 1800/900Ft; ⏱ 10am-6pm Apr-Oct, 11am & 2.30pm Mon, 10am-5pm Tue-Sun Nov-Mar) was designed by Antal Mayerhoffer for Count Antal Grassalkovich (1694–1771), confidante of Empress Maria Theresa, in 1741. After the formation of the

Dual Monarchy, the mansion (or palace) was enlarged as a summer retreat for Emperor Franz Joseph and soon became the favoured residence of his consort, the much beloved Habsburg empress and Hungarian queen, Elizabeth (1837–98), affectionately known as Sissi (see boxed text, p96). Between the two world wars, the regent, Admiral Miklós Horthy, also used it as a summer residence, but after the communists came to power, part of the mansion was used as barracks for Soviet and Hungarian troops and as an old people's home. The rest was left to decay.

Partial renovation of the mansion began in the 1990s, and today some 26 rooms are open to the public as the Palace Museum on the ground and 1st floors. They have been restored (some would say too heavily) to the period when the imperial couple were in residence, and Franz Joseph's suites (done up in manly greys and maroons) and Sissi's lavender-coloured private apartments on the 1st floor are impressive. Check out the Ceremonial Hall, all gold tracery, stucco and chandeliers, where chamber-music concerts are held throughout the year but especially in October during the Liszt and International Harp Festivals; the Queen's Reception Room, with a Romantic-style oil painting of Sissi patriotically repairing the coronation robe of King Stephen with needle and thread; and the Grassalkovich Era exhibition, which offers an in-depth look at the palace before the royal couple moved in.

A number of other recently opened rooms and buildings can be visited on guided tour only at extra cost, including the Baroque Theatre

TRANSPORT: GÖDÖLLŐ

Distance from Budapest 26km.

Direction Northeast.

Travel time 45 minutes by HÉV suburban train.

Bus Buses from Stadionok bus station (Map p108) in Pest serve Gödöllő (450Ft, 45 minutes) about once an hour throughout the day. The last bus back is just before 7.30pm weekdays and shortly after 8pm on Saturday and Sunday.

Car Rte 3 from central Pest.

HÉV Trains from Örs vezér tere at the terminus of the M2 metro link Budapest with Gödöllő (570Ft, 45 minutes) every 30 minutes an hour throughout the day. Make sure you get off at the Szabadság tér stop, which is the third to last. The last train for Budapest leaves from this stop just before 10.45pm.

(adult/student & child 1200/600Ft) in the southern wing. A combined ticket offering entry to the Royal Hill Pavilion in the park built in the 1760s, the Royal Baths as well as the museum and the theatre costs 3300/1650Ft for adult/student and child.

INFORMATION

Tourinform (☎ 28-415 402; www.godollotourinform .hu; ⏰ 10am-6pm Tue-Sun Apr-Oct, 10am-5pm Tue-Sun Nov-Mar) Just inside the entrance to the palace.

www.godollotourinform.hu Town website with useful listings in English.

EATING

Szélkakas (☎ 28-423 119; Bajcsy-Zsilinszky utca 27; mains 1300-2250Ft; ⏰ 11.30am-11pm Sun-Thu, 11.30am-midnight Fri & Sat) The 'Weathervane' is a charming, pleasant eatery with covered garden in a neighbourhood of 18th-centuy farmhouses about 500m north of the Szabadság tér HÉV stop.

Pizza Palazzo (☎ 28-420 688; Szabadság tér 2; pizza & pasta 830-1450Ft) This popular pizzeria with more substantial pasta dishes is conveniently attached to the Szabadság tér HÉV station.

SLEEPING

Erzsébet Királyné (☎ 28-816 817; www.erzsebetkiralynehotel .hu; Dózsa György út 2; r €65-85; P ☒ ☒ ☐) Gödöllő's hostelry of choice, the 'Queen Elizabeth' (that would be Sissi) is a new 62-room hotel in a lovely 1912 building. Standard rooms have shower cubicles and look into a courtyard; superior rooms come with bathtub and views of the Royal Mansion.

Galéria (☎ 28-418 691; www.galeriamotel.hu; Szabadság tér 8; s/d with shared bathroom 6900/8900Ft, with shower 10,300/12,900Ft; P) This seven-room pension is 300m northeast of the mansion and in as central a position as you'll find if you want to spend the night in Gödöllő. There's a restaurant attached.

GATE College (☎ 28-522 971; gatekollegium@freemail .hu; Páter Károly utca 1; dm 2500Ft; ☒ ☐) A short distance east of the HÉV terminus, the huge college at St Stephen University has dormitory accommodation from late June to August.

MARTONVÁSÁR

Lying almost exactly halfway between Budapest and the Central Transdanubian 'capital' city of Székesfehérvár and easily accessible by train, Martonvásár (population 5200) is

the site of the former Brunswick Mansion (Brunszvik-kastély; Brunszvik út 2), one of the prettiest summertime concert venues in Hungary. The mansion was built in 1775 for Count Antal Brunswick (Magyarised as 'Brunszvik'), the patriarch of a family of liberal reformers and patrons of the arts; his daughter, Teréz, established Hungary's first nursery school in Pest in 1828.

Beethoven was a frequent visitor to the manse, and it is believed that Jozefin, Teréz' sister, was the inspiration for his *Appassionata* and *Moonlight* sonatas, which the great Ludwig composed here.

Brunswick Mansion was rebuilt in neo-Gothic style in 1870 and restored to its ivory and sky-blue glory a century later. It now houses the Agricultural Research Institute of the Hungarian Academy of Sciences, but you can see at least part of the mansion by visiting the small Beethoven Memorial Museum (Beethoven Emlékmúzeum; ☎ 22-569 500; adult/child incl park 500/250Ft; ⏰ 10am-noon & 2-4pm Tue-Fri, 10am-noon & 2-6pm Sat & Sun) to the left of the main entrance.

A walk around the spacious park (adult/child incl museum 500/250Ft; ⏰ 8am-6pm mid-Mar–Oct, 8am-4.30pm Nov–mid-Mar), which was one of Hungary's first 'English parks' to be laid out when these were all the rage in central Europe in the early 19th century, is a pleasant way to spend a warm summer afternoon. The highlight of the so-called Martonvásár Days (Martonvásár Napok; www.martonvasar.hu, in Hungarian) festival in July are the Beethoven Evenings (Beethoven-estjei) on Saturday at 7pm, when concerts are held on the small island in the middle of the lake reached by a wooden footbridge.

The baroque Catholic church (1776), attached to the mansion but accessible from outside the grounds, has Johannes Cymbal frescoes of saints. There's also the delightful Nursery

DETOUR

Some 20km northwest of Martonvásár in the peaceful Vál Valley, the Bélapapuszta Equestrian Centre (☎ 22-594 388, 06 20 590 5956; www.belapa.hu; lessons per hr 2600Ft, riding per 30min 2600/4600Ft) offers a delightful break from the trials of the outside world. Lessons are available both on the lead and in the paddock; riding is along the delightful trails of this 20-hectare property. Accommodation – four rooms and two apartments – is above the rather grand stables and looks onto open and closed paddocks. The restaurant, with its Italian resident chef, is open for lunch only Tuesday to Sunday though evening meals can be arranged. There's only one direct bus a day from Martonvásár to the closest settlement, Tabajd (375Ft, 30 minutes); otherwise take any of up to seven daily buses to Baracska, Kajászó or Vál and change there. The centre is an easy 1200m walk east of Tabajd, though the Hungarian-American owners will come fetch you if you call in advance.

School Museum (Óvodamúzeum; ☎ 22-569 518; adult/child 340/170Ft; ⏱ 10am-2pm Tue-Fri, 11am-5pm Sat & Sun mid-Mar–Oct, 10am-2pm Tue & Fri, 11am-3pm Sun Nov–mid-Mar) in the park, crammed with school-related materials as well as dolls and other toys.

INFORMATION

www.mgki.hu Website of the Agricultural Research Institute of the Hungarian Academy of Sciences includes some information about the mansion and museums in English.

EATING & SLEEPING

Postakocsi (☎ 22-460 013; Fehérvári utca 1; mains 1200-2350Ft; ⏱ 10am-10pm) In the centre of town, the 'Postal Coach' is a convenient place for lunch and has outside seating in a pleasant courtyard in back. Expect hearty Hungarian fodder, including a killer fish soup (halászlé; 1300Ft).

Macska (☎ /fax 22-460 127, 06 30 904 4897; Budai út 21; s & d 4200-5400Ft) This seven-room pension whose name means 'Cat' is crawling with felines (nine at last count) and is not for hyper-allergenic travellers. The attached restaurant (mains 980Ft to 1980Ft; open noon to 10pm Sunday and Monday, to 11pm Tuesday to Thursday, to midnight Friday and Saturday) serves standard Hungarian csárda (inn) dishes.

VESZPRÉM

Spreading over five hills between the northern and southern ranges of the Bakony Hills, Veszprém (population 60,200) has one of the most dramatic locations in Central Transdanubia. The walled castle district atop a plateau, once the favourite residence of Hungary's queens, is now a living museum of baroque art and architecture, and it's a delight to stroll through the Castle Hill district's single street, admiring the embarrassment of fine churches and civic buildings. What's more, Lake Bala-

ton, the nation's playground, is only 13km to the south and Herend, home of Hungary's finest porcelain (p194) is the same distance to the northwest.

As you walk up Castle Hill (Vár-hegy) and its single street, Vár utca, you'll pass through Heroes' Gate (Hősök-kapuja), an entrance built in 1936 from the stones of a 15th-century castle gate. On the left is the Firewatch Tower (tűztorony; ☎ 88-425 204; Vár utca 9; adult/child 300/200Ft; ⏱ 10am-6pm May-Oct, 10am-5pm mid-Mar–Apr), an architectural hybrid of Gothic, baroque and neoclassical styles. You can climb to the top for excellent views of the rocky hill and the Bakony Hills.

Farther up the hill, the U-shaped Bishop's Palace (Püspöki palota; ☎ 88-426 088; Vár utca 16; adult/child 500/250Ft; ⏱ 10am-5pm Tue-Sun May–mid-Oct), designed by Jakab Fellner in the mid-18th century, is where the queens' residence stood in the Middle Ages. It faces Szentháromság tér, named for the Trinity Column (1751) in the centre.

Next to the Bishop's Palace is the early Gothic Gizella Chapel (Gizella kápolna; ☎ 88-426 088; Vár utca 18; adult/child 200/100Ft; ⏱ 10am-5pm Tue-Sun May–mid-Oct), named after the wife of King Stephen, who was crowned near here early in the 11th century. Inside the chapel are some Byzantine-influenced 13th-century frescoes

TRANSPORT: VESZPRÉM

Distance from Budapest 112km.

Direction Southwest.

Travel time Two hours by train.

Bus Connections with Budapest (1770Ft, 2¼ hours) are excellent, with at least hourly departures.

Car Rte M7 to Székesfehérvár and Rte 8 to Veszprém

Train A half-dozen daily trains link Budapest's Déli and Kelenföld train stations with Veszprém (1770Ft, two hours) via Székesfehérvár.

DETOUR

If you have the time, take a side-trip to Herend (population 3375), 13km west of Veszprém, where a porcelain factory has been producing Hungary's finest hand-painted chinaware for 170 years (see boxed text, p114). The Porcelánium (☎ 88-523 190; www.porcelanium.com; Kossuth Lajos utca 140; adult/child 1700/800Ft; ☽ 9am-5.30pm daily Apr-Oct, 9.30am-4pm Tue-Sat Nov-Mar) is a museum displaying the most prized pieces of the rich Herend collection as well as a minifactory where you can witness first-hand how lumps of clay become exquisite porcelain. Guided tours in four languages, including English, leave every 15 minutes. There's a short film tracing the history of Herend porcelain and a shop selling both antique and new Herend pieces. You can reach Herend from Veszprém by bus at least every 30 minutes (375Ft, 20 minutes, 21km). It's a five-minute walk northeast from the bus station to the museum.

of the Apostles. The Queen Gizella Museum (Gizella Királyné Múzeum; ☎ 88-426 0884; Vár utca 35; adult/child 300/150Ft; ☽ 10am-5pm May–mid-Oct) of religious art is opposite.

The Cathedral of St Michael (Szent Mihály székesegyház; ☎ 88-328 038; Vár utca 18-20; admission free; ☽ 10am-6pm May–mid-Oct), dedicated to St Michael, is on the site of the first bishop's palace. Parts of it date from the beginning of the 11th century, but the cathedral has been rebuilt many times since then. The early Gothic crypt is original, though. Beside the cathedral, the octagonal foundation of the 13th-century Chapel of St George (Szent György kápolna; ☎ 88-426 088; adult/child 200/100Ft; ☽ 10am-5pm Tue-Sun May–mid-Oct) sits under an ugly concrete dome.

From the rampart known as World's End at the end of Vár utca, you can gaze north to craggy Benedict Hill (Benedek-hegy) and the Séd Stream and west to the concrete viaduct (now St Stephen's Valley Bridge) over the Betekints Valley. The statues of King Stephen and Queen Gizella here were erected in 1938 to mark the 900th anniversary of King Stephen's death.

INFORMATION

Tourinform (☎ 88-404 548; www.veszpreminfo.hu; Vár utca 4; ☽ 9am-6pm Mon-Fri, 10am-4pm Sat & Sun Jul & Aug, 9am-5pm Mon-Fri Sep-May) Extremely helpful information office with plenty of brochures on Veszprém and its surrounds.

www.veszprem.hu The city's official website has some useful listings in English.

EATING

Várkert (☎ 88-560 468; Vár utca 13-17; mains 1400-2800Ft) Newly renovated and bubbling with energy, central Várkert is a welcome addition to Veszprém's dining scene. Its menu features unusual dishes, such as wild game ragout and rabbit stew, alongside imaginative Hungarian specialities.

Oliva (☎ 88-403 875; Buhim utca 14-16; mains 1000-3000Ft; ☽ 11.30am-11pm Mon-Thu, 11am-midnight Fri & Sat) Subdued lighting and vaulted ceilings help make Oliva an intimate setting for a romantic evening. The menu changes with the seasons, and in summer there are barbecues on the huge outdoor patio and often live jazz.

Café Piazza (☎ 88-444 445; Óváros tér 4; mains from 1200Ft; ☽ 8.30am-10pm) With seating on pretty Óváros tér and plentiful lunchtime specials, Café Piazza attracts workers and tourists by the droves.

SLEEPING

Oliva (☎ 88-403 875; www.oliva.hu; Buhim utca 14-16; s/d 12,500/14,000Ft; P ☒ ▣) This exquisite little pension is located in a beautifully restored townhouse just below Castle Hill. Its 11 rooms are modern, spacious, and furnished with mock antiques.

Péter Pál (☎ 88-328 091; www.peterpal.hu, in Hungarian; Dózsa György utca 3; s/d 6820/9240Ft; P ☒) Péter Pál is a lovely little guesthouse that borders on being boutique. It has a fine choice of 14 simple yet stylish rooms, a lovely garden, above-average restaurant, and very friendly and helpful staff.

EGER

Everyone loves Eger (population 56,000), and it's immediately apparent why. The beautifully preserved baroque architecture gives the town a relaxed, almost Mediterranean, feel; it is the home of the celebrated Bikavér (Bull's Blood) wine; and it is flanked by two of the Northern Uplands' most beautiful ranges of hills. And it was here that István Dobó and his troops fended off the Turks in 1552 (opposite).

The best overview of the city can be had by climbing up the cobblestone lane from Dózsa György tér to Eger Castle (Egri Vár; ☎ 36-312 744; www.egrivar.hu; Vár köz 1; adult/child castle & grounds

TRANSPORT: EGER

Distance from Budapest 130km.

Direction Northeast.

Travel time Two hours by express bus.

Bus Buses link Eger with Budapest (2040Ft, two hours) hourly via the high-speed M3.

Car Rte 3 from central Pest to Kerecsend and then Rte 25 to Eger

Train There are up to seven direct trains a day to and from Keleti train station (Map pp92–3, F7) in Budapest (2290Ft, 2½ hours).

1200/600Ft, grounds only 600/300Ft; ☺ exhibits 9am-5pm Tue-Sun Mar-Oct, 10am-4pm Tue-Sun Nov-Feb; grounds 8am-8pm daily May-Aug, 8am-7pm Apr & Sep, 8am-6pm Mar & Oct, 8am-5pm Nov-Feb), which was erected in the 13th century after the Mongol invasion. Models and drawings in the István Dobó Museum housed in the former Bishop's Palace (1470) painlessly explain the history of the castle. On the ground floor, a statue of Dobó takes pride of place in Heroes' Hall. The 19th-century building on the northwestern side of the courtyard houses the Eger Art Gallery, with several works by Mihály Munkácsy.

The reconstructed Dobó Bastion (1549) contains a display with the fetching title the World of Weapons (adult/child 500/250Ft). Other exhibits incurring an additional fee include a Waxworks (adult/child 400/300Ft) and a medieval Mint (adult/child 400/300Ft).

A highlight of the town's amazing architecture is Eger Cathedral (Egri Főszékesegyház; Pyrker János tér 1; ☺ 9am-7pm Mon-Sat, 1-5pm Sun), a neoclassical monolith designed in 1836 by József Hild. To the right of the main church steps is the entrance to something called the Town under the Town (☎ 06 20 961 4019; Eszterházy tér; adult/child 800/400Ft; ☺ 10am-9pm Apr-Sep, 10am-5pm Oct-Mar),

which takes you on a history-oriented tour through the casemates that were once the cellars of the Archbishop's Palace (Érseki Palota; Széchenyi István utca 5) to the north.

Directly opposite the cathedral is the sprawling Zopf-style Lyceum (Líceum; ☎ 36-520 400; Eszterházy tér 1; ☺ 9.30am-3.30pm Tue-Sun Apr-Sep, 9.30am-1pm Sat & Sun Oct-Mar) dating from 1765. The 20,000-volume library (library adult/student 700/350Ft) on the 1st floor of the south wing contains hundreds of priceless manuscripts and codices. The trompe l'œil ceiling fresco (1778) depicts the Counter-Reformation's Council of Trent (1545–63) and a lightning bolt setting heretical manuscripts ablaze. The Astronomy Museum (adult/student 800/650Ft) on the 6th floor of the east wing contains 18th-century astronomical equipment and an observatory. Climb three more floors up to the observation deck to try out the camera obscura, the 'eye of Eger', designed in 1776 to spy on the town and to entertain townspeople.

Only nonclaustrophobes will brave the 97 narrow spiral steps to the top of the 40m-high minaret (☎ 36-410 233; Knézich Károly utca; admission 200Ft; ☺ 10am-6pm Apr-Oct) to the north of Dobó István tér. On the southern side of central Dobó István tér stands the Minorite church (Minorita templom; Dobó István tér 6; admission free; ☺ 9am-5pm Tue-Sun), built in 1771 and one of the most beautiful baroque buildings in the world. Statues of István Dobó and his comrades-in-arms routing the Turks fill the square in front of the church.

To the south of the square is Kossuth Lajos utca, a tree-lined street with dozens of architectural gems including the delightful county hall (megyeháza; Kossuth Lajos utca 9), the main door of which is crowned by a wrought-iron representation of Faith, Hope and Charity by Henrik Fazola, a Rhinelander who settled in Eger in the mid-18th century. Walk down the passageway, and you'll see more of his

THE SIEGE OF EGER

The story of the Turkish attempt to take Eger Castle is the stuff of legend. Under the command of István Dobó, a mixed bag of 2000 soldiers held out against more than 100,000 Turks for a month in 1552. As every Hungarian kid can tell you, the women of Eger played a crucial role in the battle, pouring boiling oil and pitch on the invaders from the ramparts.

Also significant was Eger's wine if we are to believe the tale. Apparently Dobó sustained his soldiers with the ruby-red local vintage. When they fought on with increased vigour – and stained beards – rumours began to circulate among the Turks that the defenders were gaining strength by drinking the blood of bulls. Thus was born the name – and brand – Bikavér (Bull's Blood).

Géza Gárdonyi's *Eclipse of the Crescent Moon* (1901), which describes the siege in thrilling detail, can be found in English translation in many Budapest bookshops.

magnificent work – two baroque wrought-iron gates that have superseded the minaret as the symbol of Eger.

Don't miss visiting the wine cellars of the evocatively named Valley of the Beautiful Women (Szépasszony-völgy), which is just over a kilometre southwest of the centre, where local wines are stored. This is the place to sample Bull's Blood – one of very few reds produced in Eger – or any of the whites: Leányka, Olaszrizling and Hárslevelű from nearby Debrő. The choice of wine cellars can be a bit daunting and their characters can change, so walk around and have a look yourself. Be careful, though; those 1dL glasses (around 100Ft) go down easily and quickly. Hours are erratic, but a few cellars are sure to be open till the early evening. The taxi fare back to Eger centre is about 1000Ft.

INFORMATION

Tourinform (☎ 36-517 715; eger@tourinform.hu; Bajcsy-Zsilinszky utca 9; ⏰ 9am-5pm Mon-Fri, 9am-1pm Sat & Sun mid-Jun–mid-Sep, 9am-5pm Mon-Fri, 9am-1pm Sat mid-Sep–mid-Jun)

www.eger.hu The city's official website includes a lot of useful information but in Hungarian only.

EATING

Senator Ház (☎ 36-320 466; Dobó István tér 11; mains 1400-2500Ft) Seats in the antique-filled dining room of this charming hotel are coveted, but the ones outdoors are the hot seat of Eger's main square. The soups and salads are excellent; try the cream of garlic soup.

Szántófer (☎ 36-517 298; Bródy utca 3; mains 1400-1800Ft; ⏰ 8am-10pm) The best choice in town for hearty, homestyle Hungarian, Szántófer oozes a rural-rustic atmosphere. Breakfasts (600Ft to 800Ft) here are particularly good.

Palacsintavár (☎ 36-413 986; Dobó István utca 9; mains 1400-1600Ft) Pop art and postcards line the walls and groovy music fills the rest of the space in this eclectic eatery. Palacsinták (crêpelike 'pancakes') here are served with an abundance of fresh vegetables, and range in flavour from Asian to Italian and back.

SLEEPING

Senator Ház (☎ 36-320 466; www.senatorhaz.hu; Dobó István tér 11; s/d 15,000/19,000Ft; P ✕ 💻) 'Senator House' has 11 warm and cosy rooms on the upper two floors of a delightful 18th-century inn on Eger's main square. Its ground floor is shared between

a quality restaurant and a reception that could easily moonlight as a history museum.

Retur Panzió (☎ 36-416 650; www.returvendeghaz.hu; Knézich Károly utca 18; s/d 4000/6400Ft; P) You couldn't find sweeter hosts than the daughter and mother that own this four-room guesthouse under the eaves. Out back is a huge flower garden with tables and barbecue at your disposal.

Imola Hostel (☎ 36-520 430; www.imolanet.hu/hostel; Leányka utca 2; s 3000-5000Ft, d 6000-8000Ft; ✕ 💻) This former college dormitory has been modernised and comfortable beds and large desks now fill quite smart twin rooms. Each floor shares a kitchen and a computer with internet.

PÉCS

Blessed with a mild climate, an illustrious past and a number of fine museums and monuments, Pécs is one of the most pleasant and interesting cities to visit in provincial Hungary. For those reasons and more – a handful of universities, the nearby Mecsek Hills, a lively nightlife – many travellers put it second only to Budapest on their Hungary 'must-see' list. Be advised that Pécs, which takes on the mantle of European Capital of Culture in 2010, is best visited on overnight excursion from the capital, though.

Dominating Széchenyi tér, a central square of largely baroque buildings, is the 16th-century Pasha Gazi Kassim Mosque. Today it is the Inner Town Parish Church (Belvárosi plébánia templom), more commonly known as the Mosque Church (Dzámi templom; ☎ 72-321 976; admission free; ⏰ 10am-4pm Mon-Sat, 11.30am-4pm Sun mid-Apr–mid-Oct, 10am-noon Mon-Sat, 11.30am-2pm Sun mid-Oct–mid-Apr). It is the largest building from the time of the Turkish occupation still standing in Hungary and the very symbol of the city. The Islamic elements are easy to spot inside: windows with distinctive Turkish ogee arches to the south; a mihrab (prayer niche) carved into the southeast wall; faded verses from the Koran to the southwest.

Kossuth tér to south has two important buildings: an Eclectic town hall (1891) on the north side and Pécs' only remaining synagogue (☎ 72-315 881; adult/child 500/300Ft; ⏰ 10am-noon & 12.45-5pm Sun-Fri May-Oct) to the east. The synagogue was built in the Romantic style in 1869, and a seven-page fact sheet in English explains the history of the building and what's left of the city's once substantial Jewish population.

TRANSPORT: PÉCS

Distance from Budapest 215km.

Direction Southwest.

Travel time Three hours by express train.

Bus Five daily buses link Pécs with Budapest (3010Ft, 4½ hours).

Car High-speed M6 from south Buda towards Mohács and then Rte 57 to Pécs.

Train Up to nine direct trains a day connect Pécs with Budapest (3230Ft to 4550Ft, three to four hours).

Dom tér to the northwest contains the four-towered basilica (székesegyház; ☎ 72-513 030; adult/child 800/500Ft; ☺ 9am-5pm Mon-Sat, 1-5pm Sun Apr-Oct; 10am-4pm Mon-Sat, 1-4pm Sun Nov-Mar) dedicated to St Peter. The foundations date as far back as the 11th century but most of what you see today of the neo-Romanesque structure is the result of renovations carried out in 1881. The most interesting parts of the basilica's very ornate interior are the elevated central altar, the four 14th-century side chapels and the crypt, the oldest part of the structure.

On the southern side of Dom tér is the Cella Septichora Visitors Centre (☎ 72-224 755; www.pecsorokseg .hu; Janus Pannonius utca; adult/child/family 1500/800/3000Ft; ☺ 10am-6pm Tue-Sun Apr-Oct, 10am-4pm Tue-Sun Nov-Mar), which links and explains a series of half-a-dozen early Christian burial sites that have been on Unesco's World Heritage List since 2000. The highlight is the so-called Jug Mausoleum (Korsós sírkamra), a 4th-century Roman tomb whose name comes from a painting of a large drinking vessel with vines found here. Nearby is the Csontváry Museum (☎ 72-310 544; Janus Pannonius utca 11; adult/child 700/350Ft; ☺ 10am-6pm Tue-Sun Apr-Oct, 10am-4pm Tue-Sun Nov-Mar), which shows the major works of master 19th-century painter Tivadar Kosztka Csontváry (p40).

Running east from Dóm tér, Káptalan utca might as well be named 'Museum Street'. If you're time is limited, though, choose between the Vasarely Museum (☎ 72-514 040; Káptalan utca 3; adult/child 700/350Ft; ☺ 10am-6pm Tue-Sun Apr-Oct, 10am-5pm Tue-Sun Nov-Mar) containing the zany works of

ANDREA SZÁSZ

As a trained opera singer and former Magyar Rádió foreign correspondent, Andrea Szász, communications and market-ing director at Pécs2010 (www.pecs2010.hu), is uniquely qualified to prepare the city and the world for Pécs' stint as European Capital of Culture in 2010.

So sing for your supper already. Why Pécs? Apart from Budapest, no other Hungarian city has as many people engaged in artistic activities as this one. But to tell you the truth, another half-dozen cities, including Budapest, Eger and Szeged, tendered for the title and were in the running. The national government nominated Pécs because our bid was the best.

What's the big idea? Well, Pécs has the strong, very solid base of culture necessary for a European Capital of Culture. I mean, we've already got the software. Now we are concentrating on the hardware.

Beg pardon? We've got five major projects on the go, including a new conference centre and conference hall and a regional library and knowledge centre. 'Museum Street' (Káptalan utca) is being fully renovated as are some 70 public squares.

Jó munkát (do a good job), as you say here! Is the fear of missed deadlines keeping you awake at night? The main focus of all this is to put Pécs on the cultural map of Europe. We have to think of the future and the opportunities the project will bring to the city. It's not just about 2010. But sometimes I do think, 'This place looks like another war zone with all the changes.' Maybe I should have stayed in Gaza or Iraq with the radio.

What's the hardest part of the job then? Winning the hearts and minds of local people. There was a lot of euphoria when we went for the bid in 2005; now people are disappointed with the pace of events. They want things now and not tomorrow and they lack a lot of civic pride. I'll consider my work a success when local people find their own way to the project and see how it can effect change in the fibre of their city.

Can a local girl do that? I'm from Kolozsvár (now Cluj-Napoca in Romania). My family came to Budapest when I was 14 after a three-year wait. I feel *pécsi* (a Pécs native) because I'm working and fighting for the city. But local people don't see it that way. Acceptance is not complete even after all these years.

So what keeps you glued to the spot? It's the air, the ambience, the atmosphere – call it what you want – of Pécs. And I can find everything I need here, especially on the cultural front. It's small, it's human and, yes, it does have a Mediterranean feel to it. Sometimes I walk through the streets and think, 'The sea is just around the corner.'

An interview with Andrea Szász, Communications and Marketing Director, Pécs2010

Victor Vasarely, the father of Op Art, and the Zsolnay Porcelain Museum (☎ 72-514 040; Káptalan utca 2; adult/child 700/350Ft; 🕙 10am-6pm Tue-Sun Apr-Oct, 10am-5pm Tue-Sun Nov-Mar). The latter traces the history of the porcelain factory established here in 1853 and which remained at the forefront of European art and design for more than half a century. Many of its maiolica tiles were used to decorate buildings throughout Budapest and contributed to establishing a new pan-Hungarian style of architecture.

INFORMATION

Tourinform (☎ 72-213 315; baranya-m@tourinform.hu; Széchenyi tér 9; 🕙 8am-6pm Mon-Fri, 10am-8pm Sat & Sun Jun-Aug, 8am-5.30pm Mon-Fri, 10am-2pm Sat May, Sep & Oct, 8am-4pm Mon-Fri Nov-Apr) Knowledgeable staff and copious amounts of information on Pécs.

EATING

Az Elefánthoz (☎ 72-216 055; Jókai tér 6; mains 1600-2100Ft) With its enormous terrace and quality Italian cuisine, 'At the Elephant' is a sure bet for first-rate food in the centre of town. It has a wood-burning stove for making pizzas (500Ft to 1800Ft).

Áfium (☎ 72-511 434; Irgalmasok utca 2; mains 1400-1900Ft; 🕙 11am-1am) This welcoming restaurant will fill the needs (and stomachs) of diners in

search of South Slav specialities from just over the border in Croatia and Serbia. Don't miss the 'hatted' (actually a swollen bread crust) bean soup with trotters.

Cellárium (☎ 72-314 453; Hunyadi János út 2; mains 1700-2200Ft) Below the Hotel Főnix but not related to it, this subterranean eatery offers excellent value for money in the city centre.

SLEEPING

Diána Hotel (☎ 72-328 594; www.hoteldiana.hu; Tímár utca 4/a; s 9500-10,500Ft, d 13,000-14,500Ft; ⊠ 🔀 🖳) This very central pension offers 20 spotless rooms, comfortable, 'kick-off-your-shoes' decor and a warm welcome. It overlooks the synagogue.

Hotel Főnix (☎ 72-311 682; www.fonixhotel.hu; Hunyadi János út 2; s/d 7790/12,590Ft; 🔀 🖳) Főnix appears to be a hotel too large for the land it's built upon and some of the 16 rooms and suites are not even big enough to swing a, well, phoenix in. Try to get a room with a balcony; the Mosque Church is just within reach.

Nap Hostel (☎ 72-950 684, 06 30 277 0733; www.naphostel.com; Király utca 23-25; dm 2400-3850Ft, d 9600-10,500Ft; ⊠ 🖳) A new and very welcome addition to Pécs's budget accommodation scene, this place has three dorm rooms with between six and eight beds and a double with washbasin on the 1st floor of a 19th-century bank building. Enter from Szent Mór utca.

TRANSPORT

Budapest is accessible by just about any form of transport you care to name – from plane and train to bus and boat. Flights, tours and train tickets can be booked online at www .lonelyplanet.com/travel_services.

AIR

Budapest can be reached directly from destinations around the world, including the far-flung US and China, but its most important gateways are in continental Europe, especially now that what Hungarians call the *fapados* (wooden bench) airlines – the super discount carriers such as Air Berlin (www.airberlin.com), EasyJet (www.easyjet.com) and Wizzair (www.wizzair.com) – have arrived, bringing the cost of flying between Budapest and dozens of European cities to a level that fits most travellers' budget. Fares vary greatly depending on the destination, availability and the time of the flight.

Please be aware that there are no scheduled flights within Hungary.

Airlines

The national carrier, Malév Hungarian Airlines (MA; www.malev.hu) flies to Budapest from North America, the Middle East and about five dozen cities in continental Europe and the British

THINGS CHANGE...

The information in this chapter is particularly vulnerable to change. Check directly with the airline or a travel agent to make sure you understand how a fare (and ticket you may buy) works and be aware of the security requirements for international travel. Shop carefully. The details given in this chapter should be regarded as pointers and are not a substitute for your own careful, up-to-date research.

Isles. It also flies to/from Beijing in China. Flights may go direct or via the European hubs of Prague, Madrid or Amsterdam.

The main Malév Customer Service Centre (Map pp92–3; ☎ 06-40 212 121 or from abroad +36 235 3888; XIII Váci út 26; 🕒 9am-6pm Mon, 9am-5pm Tue-Fri, 9am-4pm Sat; Ⓜ M3 Nyugati pályaudvar) is 100m north of Nyugati train station. Malév also has ticket-issuing desks at Ferihegy International Airport (p200).

Other major carriers serving Budapest:

Aeroflot (SU; ☎ 318 5955; www.aeroflot.com; hub Moscow)

Air Berlin (AB; ☎ 06-80 017 110; www.airberlin.com; hub Köln)

Air France (AF; ☎ 483 8800; www.airfrance.com; hub Paris)

Alitalia (AZ; ☎ 301 8744; www.alitalia.it; hub Rome)

CLIMATE CHANGE & TRAVEL

Climate change is a serious threat to the ecosystems that humans rely upon, and air travel is the fastest-growing contributor to the problem. Lonely Planet regards travel, overall, as a global benefit, but believes we all have a responsibility to limit our personal impact on global warming.

Flying & Climate Change

Pretty much every form of motor transport generates CO_2 (the main cause of human-induced climate change) but planes are far and away the worst offenders, not just because of the sheer distances they allow us to travel, but because they release greenhouse gases high into the atmosphere. The statistics are frightening: two people taking a return flight between Europe and the US will contribute as much to climate change as an average household's gas and electricity consumption over a whole year.

Carbon Offset Schemes

Climatecare.org and other websites use 'carbon calculators' that allow jetsetters to offset the greenhouse gases they are responsible for with contributions to energy-saving projects and other climate-friendly initiatives in the developing world – including projects in India, Honduras, Kazakhstan and Uganda.

Lonely Planet, together with Rough Guides and other concerned partners in the travel industry, supports the carbon offset scheme run by climatecare.org. Lonely Planet offsets all of its staff and author travel.

For more information check out our website: www.lonelyplanet.com.

Austrian Airlines (OS; ☎ 296 0660; www.aua.com; hub Vienna)

British Airways (BA; ☎ 411 5555; www.ba.com; hub London)

CSA Czech Airlines (OK; ☎ 318 3045; www.czech-air lines.com; hub Prague)

EasyJet (EZY; ☎ 296 5266; www.easyjet.com; hub London)

El Al (LY; ☎ 266 2970; www.elal.com; hub Tel Aviv)

Egyptair (MS; ☎ 266 4300; www.egyptair.com; hub Cairo)

Finnair (AY; ☎ 235 7889; www.finnair.com; hub Helsinki)

German Wings (4U; ☎ 06-80 016 015; www.germanwings .com; hub Köln)

KLM Royal Dutch Airlines (KL; ☎ 373 7737; www.klm .com; hub Amsterdam)

LOT Polish Airlines (LO; ☎ 266 4771; www.lot.com; hub Warsaw)

Lufthansa (LH; ☎ 411 9900; www.lufthansa.com; hub Frankfurt)

Tarom Romanian Airlines (RO; ☎ 235 0809; www.tarom .ro; hub Bucharest)

Turkish Airlines (TK; ☎ 266 4291; www.turkishairlines .com; hub Istanbul)

Wizz Air (W6; ☎ 06-90 181 181; www.wizzair.com; hub Katowice)

Airport

Budapest's Ferihegy International Airport (☎ 296 9696, flight info 296 7000; www.bud.hu), 24km southeast of the city centre, has two modern terminals

side by side and an older one about 5km to the west.

Malév and most of its code-share partners use Terminal 2A. Other international flights arrive at and depart from Terminal 2B, which is next door and within easy walking distance. The super-discount European carriers use the refurbished Terminal 1.

Malév has a service centre in Terminal 2A (☎ 296 7111; ☽ 5am-11pm) and a ticket sales counter at Terminal 2B (☎ 296 5767; ☽ 6am-8.30pm). At the latter you'll also find an exchange desk operated by OTP bank (☽ 5.30am-10pm) with an ATM, six car-rental desks, a hotel booking office and travel agency, and a left-luggage office (☽ 24hr).

BICYCLE

More and more cyclists are seen on the streets and avenues of Budapest these days, taking advantage of the city's growing network of bike paths. The main roads in the city might be a bit too busy and nerve-wracking for enjoyable cycling, but the side streets are fine and there are some areas (City Park, Margaret Island etc) where cycling is positively ideal. For ideas on where to cycle, see p167.

Hire

Long-established and very reliable Yellow Zebra Bikes (Map p85; ☎ 266 8777; www.yellowzebrabikes.com; V Sütő utca 2; per day/24hr 2000/3000Ft; ☽ 10am-6pm Nov-Mar, 8.30am-8pm Apr-Oct; Ⓜ M1/2/3 Deák Ferenc tér) rents

---

GETTING INTO TOWN

Reaching the centre of Budapest is straightforward and inexpensive thanks to a raft of public-transport options.

A company called Zóna Taxi (☎ 365 5555; www.zonataxi.eu) now has the monopoly on picking up taxi passengers at the airport. You might pay a little more than in the past – fares to most locations in Pest are 5100Ft and in Buda 5300Ft to 5700Ft – but at least now you'll know you won't be ripped off. Of course you can take any taxi *to* the airport and several companies have a flat, discounted fare on offer. Buda Taxi (☎ 233 3333; www.budataxi.hu), for example, charges 4600Ft between the airport and Pest, and 5100Ft between Ferihegy and Buda.

The Budapest Airport Minibusz (☎ 296 8555; www.airportshuttle.hu) ferries passengers in nine-seat vans from all three of the airport's terminals directly to their hotel, hostel or residence (one-way/return 2990/4990Ft). Tickets are available at a clearly marked desk in the arrival halls though you may have to wait while the van fills up. You need to book your journey back to the airport at least 12 hours in advance, but remember that, with up to eight pick-ups en route, this can be a nerve-wracking way to go should you be running late.

The cheapest (but most time-consuming) way to get into the city centre from Terminal 2 is to take city bus 200 (270Ft, or 350Ft on the bus) – look for the stop on the footpath between terminals 2A and 2B – which terminates at the Kőbánya-Kispest metro station. From there take the M3 metro into the city centre. The total cost is 540Ft to 620Ft. Bus 93 runs from Terminal 1 to the same metro station.

Trains now link Terminal 1 (only) with Nyugati station. They run between one and six times an hour from 4am to 11pm and cost 300Ft (or 520Ft if you board the hourly IC train). The journey takes just 20 minutes.

out bicycles year-round from just behind the Tourinform office, as well as from behind the Opera House from its Discover Budapest branch (Map pp92–3; ☎ 269 3843; VI Lázár utca 16; ⏰ 9.30am-6.30pm Mon-Fri, 10am-4pm Sat & Sun; Ⓜ M1 Opera).

Budapest Bike (Map pp92–3; ☎ 06-30 944 5533; www.budapestbike.hu; VII Wesselényi utca 13; per 6/24hr 2000/3000Ft; ⏰ 9am-6pm; 🚊 4 or 6 or trolleybus 74) has bikes available year-round. Another outfit is Bike Base (Map pp92–3; ☎ 06-70 625 8501; www.bikebase .hu; VI Podmaniczky utca 19; per 1/2/3 days 2000/3500/5000Ft; ⏰ 9am-7pm; Ⓜ M3 Nyugati pályaudvar).

For places to rent bicycles on Margaret Island, see p77.

BOAT
Local
Between mid-April and mid-October passenger ferries run by BKV (Budapest Transport Company; ☎ 461 6500, 258 4636; www.bkv.hu) depart from IX Boráros tér (Map pp102–3) just north of Petőfi Bridge and head for III Pünkösdfürdő in Óbuda, a 2¼-hour trip with 14 stops along the way. Tickets (adult/child 900/450Ft from end to end or between 250/150Ft and 600/300Ft for intermediate stops) are sold on board. The ferry stop closest to the Castle District is I Batthyány tér (Map p62), and V Petőfi tér is not far from the pier just west of Vörösmarty tér (Map p85). Transporting a bicycle costs 700Ft.

International
A hydrofoil service on the Danube River between Budapest and Vienna (5½ to 6½ hours) operates daily from late April to early October; passengers can disembark at Bratislava with advance notice. Boats leave from both Budapest and Vienna at 9am. Adult one-way/return fares for Vienna are €89/109 and for Bratislava €79/99. Students with ISIC cards receive a €10 discount, and children between two and 14 years of age travel for half price. Taking a bicycle costs €20 one way.

In Budapest, hydrofoils arrive at and depart from the International Ferry Pier (Nemzetközi hajóállomás; Map p85; ☎ 484 4005; V Belgrád rakpart), which is between Elizabeth and Liberty bridges on the Pest side. In Vienna, the boats dock at the Reichsbrücke pier near Mexikoplatz.

For information and tickets contact Mahart PassNave (Map p85; ☎ 484 4013; www.mahartpassnave .hu; V Belgrád rakpart; ⏰ 9.15am-6pm) in Budapest

and Mahart PassNave Wien (☎ 01-72 92 161/2; Handelskai 265) in Vienna.

BUS
Local
An extensive system of buses running on 250 routes day and night serves greater Budapest. On certain bus lines the same bus may have a black or a red number. In such cases, the red-numbered one (also bearing an 'E' after the number) is an express, which makes limited stops and is, of course, faster.

Buses in Budapest run from around 4.15am to between 9pm and 11.30pm, depending on the line. From 11.30pm to just after 4am a network of some 35 night buses (always with three digits and beginning with '9') operate every 10 to 60 minutes, again depending on the line. For information on fares and passes see p204.

Following are bus routes (shown with blue lines on most Budapest maps) that you might find useful:

7 Cuts across a large swathe of central Pest from XIV Bosnyák tér and down VII Rákóczi út before crossing Elizabeth Bridge to southern Buda (7/e to Kelenföld train station).

86 Runs the length of Buda from XI Kosztolányi Dezső tér to Óbuda.

105 Goes from V Deák Ferenc tér to XII Apor Vilmos tér in central Buda.

15 Takes in most of the Inner Town from IX Boráros tér to XIII Lehel tér north of Nyugati train station.

Night bus 906 Follows the tram 6 route along the Big Ring Rd.

Night bus 907 Traces an enormously long route from Örs vezér tere M2 metro stop in Pest to Kelenföld train station in Buda.

Long-Distance & International
All international buses and some (but not all) domestic ones (especially to/from north and north-central Hungary) arrive at and depart from Népliget bus station (Map pp102–3; ☎ 219 8000; IX Üllői út 131; Ⓜ M3 Népliget) in Pest. The international ticket office (☎ 6am-6pm Mon-Fri, 6am-4pm Sat & Sun) is upstairs. Eurolines (☎ 219 8063; www.eurolines.com) is represented here, as is its Hungarian associate, Volánbusz (☎ 382 0888; www.volanbusz.hu). There's a left-luggage office (⏰ 6am-9pm) downstairs that charges 280Ft per piece per day.

Stadionok bus station (Map p108; ☎ 220 6227; XIV Hungária körút 48-52; Ⓜ M3 Stadionok) generally serves cities and towns to the east of Budapest. The ticket office (🕐 6am-6pm Mon-Fri, 6am-4pm Sat & Sun) and the left-luggage office (per piece 280Ft; 🕐 6am-7pm) are on the ground floor. Buses to southwest Hungary use Etele tér bus station (Map pp70–1; ☎ 382 0888; XI Etele tér; 🕐 6am-6pm; 🚌 7/e, 🚊 19 or 49) in Buda.

Árpád Bridge bus station (Map pp58–9; ☎ 412 2597; XIII Árboc utca 1-3; 🕐 ticket office 6am-6pm Mon-Fri, 6am-4pm Sat & Sun; Ⓜ M3 Árpád híd), on the Pest side of Árpád Bridge, is the place to catch buses for the Danube Bend and parts of the Northern Uplands (eg Balassagyarmat, Szécsény, Salgótarján etc). The small Széna tér bus station (Map p62; ☎ 201 3688; I Széna tér 1/a; 🕐 ticket office 6am-6pm Mon-Fri, 6am-4pm Sat & Sun; Ⓜ M3 Moszkva tér) in Buda handles some traffic to and from the Pilis Hills and towns northwest of the capital, with a half-dozen departures to Esztergom as an alternative to the Árpád Bridge bus station.

CAR & MOTORCYCLE

Though it's not so bad at night, driving in Budapest during the day can be a nightmare: ongoing road works reduce traffic to a snail's pace; there are more serious accidents than fender-benders; and parking spots are near impossible to find in some neighbourhoods. The public transport system is good and cheap. Use it.

Foreign driving licences are valid for one year after entering Hungary. If you don't hold a European driving licence, obtain an International Driving Permit (IDP) from your local automobile association before you leave. It is usually inexpensive and valid for one year only. Remember that an IDP is not valid unless accompanied by your original driver's licence.

Third-party liability insurance is compulsory in Hungary. If your car is registered in the EU, it is assumed you have it. Other motorists must show a Green Card or they will have to buy insurance at the border.

Driving

You must drive on the right. Speed limits for cars and motorcycles are consistent across the country and strictly enforced: 50km/h in built-up areas (from the town sign as you enter to the same sign with a red line through it as you leave); 90km/h on secondary and tertiary roads; 110km/h on most highways/dual carriageways; and 130km/h on motorways. Exceeding the limit will earn a fine of between 5000Ft and 30,000Ft, to be paid by postal cheque or at post offices.

The use of seat belts in the front (and in the back – if fitted – outside built-up areas) is compulsory in Hungary, but this rule is often ignored. Motorcyclists must wear helmets, a law strictly enforced. Another law taken very seriously indeed is the one requiring all drivers to use their headlights throughout the day outside built-up areas. Motorcycles must illuminate headlights at all times, everywhere. Using a mobile phone while driving is prohibited in Hungary but this law is universally ignored.

There is a 100% ban on drinking alcohol before driving and this is very strictly enforced (p210). It's not much fun while on holiday, but you'll have to follow the lead of Hungarians and take turns with a companion in abstaining at meals and other times.

Assistance and/or advice for motorists is available from the Hungarian Automobile Club (Magyar Autóklub; Map p74; ☎ 345 1800; II Rómer Flóris utca 4/a; 🚊 4 or 6) off Margit körút near Margaret Bridge. Motorists anywhere in Hungary can call the automobile club on ☎ 188 for assistance.

For information on traffic and public road conditions in the capital, ring Főinform (☎ 317 1173; 🕐 7am-7pm).

Hire

In general, you must be at least 21 years old and have had your licence for at least a year to rent a car. Drivers under 25 sometimes have to pay a surcharge.

All the international car-rental firms have offices in Budapest, but don't expect many bargains. An Opel Corsa or Suzuki Swift from Avis (Map p85; ☎ 318 4158; www.avis.hu; V Szervita tér 8; 🕐 7am-6pm Mon-Sat, 8am-6pm Sun; Ⓜ 1/2/3 Deák Ferenc tér), for example, costs €59/369 per day/week, with unlimited kilometres, collision damage waiver (CDW) and theft protection (TP) insurance. The same car and insurance with 800km costs from €165 for a three-day weekend.

One of the cheapest and most reliable outfits for renting cars is Anselport (Map pp58–9; ☎ 362 6080, 06-20 945 0279; www.anselport.hu; XXII V utca 22; 🕐 9am-6pm; 🚌 213 or 214) in south Buda. Its Suzuki Swifts cost between €19 and €34 per day, including unlimited mileage and insurance, depending on the length of the rental (one day to four weeks). Another possibility is Fox Autorent (Map pp58–9; ☎ 382 9000; www.foxautorent.com; XXII Nagytétényi út 48-50; 🕐 8am-6pm; 🚌 213 or 214), which charges from €38 to €49 per day (€265 per week) for a Smart car and €39 to €50 (€271) for a Fiat Punto (kilometres and insurance included).

Parking

Parking costs between 120Ft and 300Ft per hour on the street (up to 600Ft on Castle Hill), generally between 8am and 6pm Monday to Friday and 8am and noon Saturday. There are 24-hour covered car parks charging from 370Ft to 680Ft per hour below the Millennium Center at V Váci utca 25 (Map p85), V Szervita tér 8 (Map p85), where you'll find Avis, and at V Aranykéz utca 4-6 (Map p85) in the Inner Town as well as at VII Nyár utca 20 (Map pp92–3).

Illegally parked cars are not normally towed in Budapest these days but clamped or booted. If you are trying to trace a vehicle and you believe it has been towed (something that usually only happens during demonstrations) ring ☎ 267 4673. To have a clamp/boot removed, ring ☎ 06-80 220 220 or ☎ 06-80 330 330. It's going to cost you between 7200Ft and 14,400Ft.

METRO & HÉV

Budapest currently has three underground metro lines that converge (only) at Deák Ferenc tér: the little yellow (or Millennium) line designated M1 that runs from Vörösmarty tér to Mexikoi út in Pest; the red M2 line from Déli train station in Buda to Örs vezér tere in Pest; and the blue M3 line from Újpest-Központ to Kőbánya-Kispest in Pest. A possible source of confusion on the M1 is that one station is called Vörösmarty tér and another, five stops later, is Vörösmarty utca. The city's long-awaited M4 metro line (www.metro4.hu) is currently under construction – you can't help but notice the enormous pits being dug in front of Keleti train station and in Kálvin tér – and will run from Kelenföldi train station in southern Buda to XIV Bosnyák tér in northeastern Pest. The first section, between Kelenföldi and Keleti train station, covering 7.5km and 10 stations, is due to open in late 2011.

The metro is the fastest – but obviously the least scenic – way to go. All three lines run from about 4.30am and begin their last journey at around 11.15pm. See the boxed text on page p204 for information about fares and passes.

The HÉV suburban train line, which runs on four lines (north from Batthyány tér in Buda via Óbuda and Aquincum to Szentendre, south to both Csepel and Ráckeve, and east to Gödöllő), is almost like an additional above-ground metro line.

TAXI

Taxis in Budapest remain very cheap by European standards, but with such an excellent public transport network available, you don't really have to use them. We've heard from many readers who were grossly overcharged and even threatened by taxi drivers in Budapest, so taking a taxi in this city should be approached with a certain amount of caution. However, the reputable firms we've listed below have caught on to the concept of customer service and take complaints very seriously indeed nowadays.

Avoid at all costs (operative word) taxis with no name on the door and only a removable taxi light box on the roof; these are just guys with cars and the ones most likely to rip you off. Never get into a taxi that does not have a yellow licence plate and an identification badge displayed on the dashboard (as required by law), the logo of one of the reputable taxi firms on the outside of the side doors and a table of fares clearly visible on the right-side back door.

Not all taxi meters are set at the same rates, and some are much more expensive than others, but there are price ceilings under which taxi companies are free to manoeuvre. From 6am to 10pm the highest flag-fall fee that can be legally charged is 300Ft, the per-kilometre charge 240Ft and the waiting fee 60Ft. From 10pm to 6am the equivalent fees are 420/336/84Ft.

Budapest residents – both Hungarian and foreign – rarely flag down taxis in the street. They almost always ring for them, and fares are actually cheaper if you book over the phone (even if the dispatcher doesn't speak a lot of English, they will generally recognise place names, landmarks and addresses). Make sure you know the number of the landline phone you're calling from, as that's how they establish your address. You can, of course, call from a mobile phone as well but must then establish your location.

Following are the telephone numbers and websites of a half-dozen reputable taxi firms:

Buda (☎ 233 3333; www.budataxi.hu)

City (☎ 211 1111; www.citytaxi.hu)

Fő (☎ 222 2222; www.fotaxi.hu)

Rádió (☎ 377 7777; www.radiotaxi.hu)

Taxi 4 (☎ 444 4444; www.taxi4.hu)

Tele 5 (☎ 355 5555; www.tele5taxi.hu)

ALL ABOARD BUDAPEST'S PUBLIC TRANSPORT SYSTEM

Budapest has a safe, efficient and inexpensive public transport system that is now being upgraded and will never have you waiting more than five or 10 minutes for any conveyance. There are five types of vehicle in general use: metro trains on three (soon to be four) city lines, green HÉV trains on four suburban lines, blue buses, yellow trams and red trolleybuses. All are run by BKV (Budapest Transport Company; ☎ 461 6500, 258 4636; www.bkv.hu). Anyone planning to travel extensively by public transport in Budapest should invest in the invaluable *Budapesti Közlekedési Térképe* (Budapest Public Transport Map), available at most metro ticket booths for 500Ft. You might also try BKV's route planner on http://utvonal.bkv.hu.

To ride the metro, trams, trolleybuses, buses and the HÉV (as far as the city limits, which is the Békásmegyer stop north of Óbuda) you must have a valid ticket, which you can buy at kiosks, newsstands, metro entrances, machines and, in some cases now, on the bus for an extra charge. Children under the age of six and EU seniors over 65 travel free. Bicycles can only be transported on the HÉV.

The basic fare for all forms of transport is 270Ft (2350Ft for a block of 10), allowing you to travel as far as you like on the same metro, bus, trolleybus or tram line without changing/transferring. A ticket allowing unlimited stations with one change within 1½ hours costs 420Ft.

On the metro exclusively, the base fare drops to 220Ft if you are just going three stops within 30 minutes. Tickets bought on the bus and all night buses cost 350Ft.

You must always travel in one continuous direction on any ticket; return trips are forbidden. Tickets have to be validated in machines at metro entrances and aboard other vehicles – inspectors will fine you for not doing this.

Life will most likely be much simpler if you buy a travel pass. Passes are valid on all trams, buses, trolleybuses, HÉV (within the city limits) and metro lines, and you don't have to worry about validating your ticket each time you get on. The most central places to buy them are ticket offices at the Deák Ferenc tér metro station (Map p85), the Nyugati pályaudvar metro station (Map pp92–3) and the Déli pályaudvar metro station (Map p62), all of which are open from 6am to 8pm daily.

A one-day travel card is poor value at 1550Ft, but the three-day pass for 3400Ft and seven-day pass for 4000Ft are worthwhile for most people. You'll need a photo for the fortnightly/monthly passes (5300/8250Ft). All passes are valid from midnight to midnight, so buy them in advance and specify the date(s) you want.

Travelling 'black' (ie without a valid ticket or pass) is risky; with what seems like constant surveillance (especially in the metro), there's an excellent chance you'll get caught. (NB: Tickets are always checked by a conductor on the HÉV.) The on-the-spot fine is 6000Ft, which doubles if you pay it at the BKV office (Map pp92–3; ☎ 461 6800; VII Akácfa utca 22; 🕑 6am-8pm Mon-Fri, 8am-1.45pm Sat; Ⓜ M2 Blaha Lujza tér) up to 30 days later and 24,000Ft after that.

TRAIN

Magyar Államvasutak (☎ 06-40 494 949 or from abroad +36-1 371 9449; www.mav.hu), which translates as Hungarian State Railways and is universally known as MÁV, links up with the European rail network in all directions. Its trains run as far as London (via Munich and Paris), Stockholm (via Hamburg and Copenhagen), Moscow, Rome and Istanbul (via Belgrade). Internally the railway company operates reliable and relatively comfortable train services on just under 8000km of track, a third of which is electrified.

Budapest has three main train stations. Most international and all trains to/from the west go via Keleti pályaudvar (Eastern train station; Map pp92–3; VIII Kerepesi út 2-6; Ⓜ M3 Keleti pályaudvar). Trains to certain destinations in the east (eg Romania) leave from Nyugati pályaudvar (Western train station; Map pp92–3; VI Teréz körút 55-57; Ⓜ M3 Nyugati pályaudvar), while Déli pályaudvar (Southern train station; Map p62; I Krisztina körút 37; Ⓜ M2 Déli pályaudvar) handles trains to some destinations in the

south (eg Osijek in Croatia and Sarajevo in Bosnia). These are not hard-and-fast rules, so always make sure you check which station your train leaves from when you buy a ticket.

The handful of secondary train stations are of little importance to long-distance travellers. Occasionally, though, a through train will stop at Kelenföldi pályaudvar (Kelenföld train station; Map pp70–1; XI Etele tér 5-7; 🚊 19 or 49) in southern Buda.

The train stations are pretty dismal places, with unsavoury-looking characters hanging about day and night, but all have some amenities. The Keleti train station left-luggage office (🕑 24hr) is next to platform six. At Nyugati train station (🕑 6.30am-midnight) it's beside the information and ticketing hall, and at Déli train station (🕑 3.30am-midnight) it's next to platform one. They all charge 150/300Ft for a normal/large piece for six hours and 300/600Ft per 24-hour day. You'll also find post offices and grocery stores that are open late. All three stations are on metro lines and night buses serve them when the metro is closed.

You can buy tickets directly from all the train stations in Budapest, but the queues are often long, passengers are in a hurry and sales staff are not the most patient in the city. It's easier at the centrally located MÁV-Start passenger service centre (Map p85; ☎ 512 7921, 512 7922; www.mav-start.hu; V József Attila utca 16; Ⓜ M1/2/3/Deák Ferenc tér).

TRAMS

BKV currently runs 30 tram lines, some of which now employ spanking-new rolling stock. Buses and trams are much of a muchness, though the latter are often faster and generally more pleasant for sightseeing.

Important tram lines (always marked with a red line on a Budapest map or atlas) include:

2 Scenic tram that travels along the Pest side of the Danube from V Jászai Mari tér to IX Boráros tér and beyond.

4 & 6 Extremely useful trams that start at XI Fehérvári út and XI Móricz Zsigmond körtér in south Buda, respectively, and follow the entire length of the Big Ring Rd in Pest before terminating at II Moszkva tér in Buda.

18 Runs from southern Buda along XI Bartók Béla út through the Tabán to II Moszkva tér before carrying on into the Buda Hills.

19 Covers part of the same route as No 18, but then runs along the Buda side of the Danube to I Batthyány tér.

47 & 49 Link V Deák Ferenc tér in Pest with points in southern Buda via the Little Ring Rd.

61 Connects XI Móricz Zsigmond körtér with Déli train station and II Moszkva tér in Buda.

TROLLEYBUS

Trolleybuses on 15 lines only go along cross streets in central Pest and so, in general, are of little use to most visitors, with the sole exception of the ones to, from and around City Park (70, 72 and 74) and down to Stadionok (75 and 77). A broken red line on a map or atlas indicates a trolleybus route.

BUSINESS HOURS

With few exceptions, the opening hours *(nyitvatartás)* of any concern are posted on the front door. *Nyitva* means 'open', while *zárva* is 'closed'. In this guide, reviews only include business hours if they differ from the standard ones described below.

Generally speaking, grocery stores and supermarkets open from about 6am or 7am to 6pm or 7pm Monday to Friday and 7am to 3pm Saturday; an ever-increasing number also open 7am to noon Sunday. Retail shops and department stores are open from 9am or 10am to 6pm Monday to Friday and 9am or 10am to 1pm Saturday; there's sometimes late-night shopping till 8pm on Thursday. In summer, some private retail shops close early on Friday and shut down altogether for at least part of August.

Most neighbourhoods in Budapest have at least one 'nonstop' – a convenience store open round the clock (or very late/early) that sells basic food items, drinks and cigarettes.

Banking hours change according to institution and location but are usually 7.45am to 5pm or 6pm Monday, 7.45am to 4pm or 5pm Tuesday to Thursday and 7.45am to 4pm Friday. The main post office in most city districts is open from 7am or 8am to 7pm or 8pm weekdays and till noon or even 2pm Saturday. Branch offices close much earlier – usually at 4pm – and are never open at the weekend.

For restaurant opening hours see p125.

CHILDREN

Budapest abounds in places that will delight children (see the boxed texts, p81 and p109, for some suggestions), and there is always a special child's entry rate (and often a family one) to paying attractions. Don't try to overdo things, though; packing too much into the time available can cause problems.

Make sure the activities include the kids as well – balance that morning at the Museum of Fine Arts with an afternoon at the nearby Municipal Great Circus or the Budapest Puppet Theatre. Group visits to many areas of the city can be designed around a rest stop (or picnic) at, say, City Park, or on Margaret Island.

Most car-rental firms in Budapest have children's safety seats for hire at a nominal cost, but it is essential that you book them in advance. The same goes for highchairs and cots (cribs); they're standard in many restaurants and hotels but numbers are limited.

For general information, Lonely Planet's *Travel with Children* is a good resource.

Babysitting

An ever-growing number of midrange and top-end hotels in Budapest offer babysitting services, although purpose-built casual day-care centres are almost nonexistent and babysitters impossible to organise yourself. Reputable hotels hire only local qualified sitters. While most can oblige on short notice, try to give the hotel concierge or front-desk staff at least six hours' advance notice.

CLIMATE

Spring arrives in early April in Budapest and is usually quite wet. Summer can be very hot and humid and Budapest virtually shuts down in August. It rains for most of November and doesn't usually get cold until mid-December. Winter is relatively short, often cloudy and damp but sometimes brilliantly sunny. What little snow the city gets usually disappears after a few days.

January is the coldest month (with the temperature averaging just over 2°C) and July and August the hottest (the average temperature is 26°C during each). The number of hours of sunshine a year averages about 1850 – among the highest in central Europe. From late April to the end of September, you can expect the sun to shine for about 10 hours a day. The mean annual precipitation in the capital is 620mm.

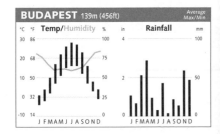

For information on specific weather conditions in Budapest, contact the forecast service of the Hungarian Meteorological Institute (☎ 346 4600, 06-90 304 621; www.met.hu, in Hungarian).

COURSES
Cooking
For a country with such a sophisticated cuisine, cooking courses are thin on the ground in Budapest. The best-known cookery school dealing with foreigners is Chefparade (Map pp102–3; ☎ 210 6042; www.chefparade.hu; IX Ferenc utca 13) just east of Ferenc körút. Course dates vary (consult the website) but usually run from 10am to 1pm, involve visiting a market and preparing a four-course lunch and cost €50 per person. Courses at other times and of a longer duration can be organised in advance.

Language
Schools teaching Hungarian to foreigners have proliferated in Budapest in the past decade, but they vary greatly in quality, approach and success rates. You should establish whether your teacher has a teaching degree in the Hungarian language and whether they have ever taught foreigners. You should be following a text or at least a comprehensive series of photocopies produced by your teacher. Remember also that you'll never get anywhere by simply sitting in class and not studying at home or practising with native speakers. Expect to pay 950Ft to 1100Ft per 45-minute 'hour' in a classroom with six to 12 students, and 3000Ft to 4000Ft for a private lesson.

The most prestigious Hungarian-language school in the land is the Debrecen Summer University (Debreceni Nyári Egyetem; ☎ 52-532 594; www.nyariegyetem.hu; Egyetem tér 1) in eastern Hungary. Its Budapest branch (Map p85; ☎ 320 5751, 06-30 928 6577; www.nyariegyetem.hu/bp; V Báthory utca 4, 2nd fl; M2 Kossuth Lajos tér) offers intensive courses lasting three weeks (60 hours) for 78,000Ft and regular evening classes of 60/84 hours for 58,000/79,000Ft.

In addition, the following schools are recommended for either classroom lessons or one-to-one instruction.

Hungarian Language School (Map pp102–3; ☎ 266 2617; www.magyar-iskola.hu; VIII Bródy Sándor utca 4, 1st fl; M3 Kálvin tér)

InterClub Hungarian Language School (Map pp70–1; ☎ 279 0831; www.interclub.hu; XI Bertalan Lajos utca 17; 47 or 49)

International House Language School (Map p62; ☎ 212 4010; www.ih.hu; I Vérmező út 4; M2 Moszkva tér)

CUSTOMS REGULATIONS
Duty-free shopping within the EU was abolished in 1999 and Hungary, as an EU member, now adheres to the same rules. You cannot, for example, buy tax-free goods in, say, Slovakia or Austria and take them to Hungary. However, you can still enter an EU country with duty-free items from countries outside the EU (eg Croatia).

Allowances on duty-free goods purchased at airports or on ferries originating outside the EU are: 200 cigarettes, 50 cigars or 250g of loose tobacco, 4L of still wine and 1L of spirits. There are no longer any quantitative limits on perfume or eau de toilette. You must declare the import/export of any amount of cash, cheques, securities etc exceeding the sum of 1,000,000Ft.

When leaving the country, you are not supposed to take out valuable antiques without a special permit, which should be available from the place of purchase. For details see p113.

DISCOUNT CARDS
A hostel card is not necessary in Budapest as no hostel here requires you to be a Hostelling International (or associated) member, but it will sometimes get you a 10% discount on quoted rates. Cards valid for a year are issued by the Hungarian Youth Hostel Association (MISZSZ; www.miszsz.hu) and are available to Hungarian citizens and residents for 2300Ft (which includes a 500Ft phonecard) from the Express travel agency (p216).

Useful discount cards:

Budapest Card (☎ 266 0479; www.budapestinfo.hu; per 48/72hr 6500/8000Ft) This card offers free admission to 60 museums and other sights in and around the city, unlimited travel on all forms of public transport, and discounts on organised tours, on car rental, at thermal baths and at selected shops and restaurants. It's available at Tourinform offices, travel agencies, hotels, main metro stations and online.

Hungary Card (☎ 266 3741, 267 0896; www.hungarycard.hu; 13 months 6900Ft) The national equivalent of the Budapest Card, this card gives free admission to many museums nationwide; 50% discounts on a half-dozen return train fares and some bus and boat travel, as well as other museums and attractions; up to 20% off selected accommodation; and 50% off the price of the Budapest Card. It is available at Tourinform branches.

International Student Identity Card (ISIC; www.isic.org; 1 yr 1800Ft) This plastic ID-style card with a photo provides bona fide students with discounts on some forms of transport and cheap admission to museums and other sights. If you're aged under 26 but not a student, you can apply for ISIC's International Youth Travel Card (IYTC; 1 yr 1800Ft) or the Euro<26 card (valid for summer 1600Ft, 1 yr 2200Ft) issued by the European Youth Card Association (EYCA), both of which offer the same discounts as the student card. Teachers can apply for ISIC's International Teacher Identity Card (ITIC; 1 yr 1800Ft).

ELECTRICITY

The electric current in Budapest is 220V, 50Hz AC. Plugs are the European type with two round pins.

EMBASSIES

Selected countries with representation in Budapest are listed here. The opening hours indicate when consular or chancellery services are available, but be sure to confirm these times before you set out as they change frequently.

Australia (Map p82; ☎ 457 9777; www.australia.hu; XII Királyhágó tér 8-9, 4th fl; ☽ 9-11am Mon-Fri)

Austria (Map pp92–3; 479 7010; www.austrian-embassy.hu; VI Benczúr utca 16; ☽ 9-11am Mon-Fri)

Canada (Map p62; 392 3360; www.dfait-maeci.gc.ca; II Ganz utca 12-14; ☽ 8.30-11am & 2-3.30pm Mon-Thu)

Croatia (Map pp92–3; ☎ 354 1315; hrvhu@mail .euroweb.hu; VI Munkácsy Mihály utca 15; ☽ 10am-6pm Mon, Tue, Thu & Fri)

France (Map pp92–3; ☎ 374 1100; www.ambafrance -hu.org; VI Lendvay utca 27; ☽ 9am-12.30pm Mon-Fri)

Germany (Map p62; ☎ 488 3500; www.budapest.diplo .de; I Úri utca 64-66; ☽ 9am-noon Mon-Fri)

Ireland (Map p85; ☎ 301 4960; www.irishembassy .hu; Bank Center, Granite Tower, 5th fl, V Szabadság tér 7; ☽ 9.30am-12.30pm & 2.30-4.30pm Mon-Fri)

Netherlands (Map p74; ☎ 336 6300; www.netherland sembassy.hu; II Füge utca 5-7; ☽ 10am-noon Mon-Fri)

Romania (Map p108; ☎ 384 7689; roembbud@mail .datanet.hu; XIV Thököly út 72, enter from Izsó utca; ☽ 8.30am-12.30pm Mon-Fri)

Serbia (Map pp92–3; ☎ 322 9838; ambjubp@mail.data net.hu; VI Dózsa György út 92/b; ☽ 10am-1pm Mon-Fri)

Slovakia (Map p108; ☎ 460 9010; slovakem@axelero.hu; XIV Stefánia út 22-24; ☽ 8.30am-noon Mon-Fri)

Slovenia (Map p82; ☎ 438 5600; vbp@mzz-dkp.gov.si; II Cseppkő utca 68; ☽ 9am-noon Mon-Fri)

South Africa (Map p82; ☎ 392 0999; www.sa-embassy .hu; II Gárdonyi Géza út 17; ☽ 9am-12.30pm Mon-Fri)

UK (Map p85; ☎ 266 2888; www.britishembassy.hu; V Harmincad utca 6; ☽ 9.30am-12.30pm & 2.30-4.30pm Mon-Fri)

Ukraine (Map p82; ☎ 422 4120; uakovetseg@t-online .hu; XII Istenhegyi út 84/b; ☽ 9am-noon Mon-Wed, by appointment only Fri)

US (Map p85; ☎ 475 4400; www.usembassy.hu; V Szabadság tér 12; ☽ 1-4.30pm Mon-Thu, 9am-noon & 1-4pm Fri)

EMERGENCY

Any crime must be reported at the police station of the district you are in. In the centre of Pest that would be the Belváros-Lipótváros Police Station (Map p85; ☎ 373 1000; V Szalay utca 11-13; Ⓜ M2 Kossuth Lajos tér). If possible, bring along a Hungarian speaker.

Ambulance (☎ 104)

Central emergency number (English spoken; ☎ 112)

English-language crime hotline (☎ 438 8080; ☽ 8am-8pm)

Fire (☎ 105)

Police (☎ 107)

24-hour car assistance (☎ 188)

GAY & LESBIAN TRAVELLERS

For up-to-date information on venues, events, parties and so on, pick up the freebie pamphlet Na Végre! (At Last!; www.navegre.hu) at gay venues throughout Budapest. Useful websites include Budapest Gay Visitor (www.budapestgayvisitor.hu) and the even better Budapest Gay Guide (http://budapest.gayguide .net). The Labrisz Lesbian Association (www.labrisz.hu) has information on Budapest's lesbian scene.

The Háttér Gay & Lesbian Association (☎ 329 3380, 06-80 505 605; www.hatter.hu, in Hungarian; ☽ 6-11pm) has an advice and help line operating daily.

In this book, gay and lesbian bars, clubs and other entertainment venues are listed on p156, and gay-owned and gay-friendly accommodation on p175.

HOLIDAYS
Public Holidays

Hungary celebrates 10 public holidays (ün-nepek) each year:

New Year's Day 1 January

1848 Revolution/National Day 15 March

Easter Monday March/April

International Labour Day 1 May

Whit Monday May/June

St Stephen's/Constitution Day 20 August

1956 Remembrance Day/Republic Day 23 October

All Saints' Day 1 November

Christmas holidays 25-26 December

School Holidays

Hungarian school holidays fall during autumn (first week of November), over the Christmas and New Year period (12 days from around 22 December to 2 January), over Easter (one week in March/April) and in summer (11 weeks from 15 June to 31 August).

INTERNET ACCESS

The internet is very well established in Budapest. Most hostels have at least one terminal available to guests either for free or for a nominal sum; the same cannot be said for hotels, but you may be able to use the reception's computer if you ask nicely. For those travelling with a laptop, many of the latter offer wi-fi, either free or for a small fee.

If you can't log on where you are staying, chances are there's an internet cafe within walking distance; Budapest has an over-abundance of such places. But cafes open and close at a rapid rate, so check with the tourist office whether those mentioned in this book still exist. More and more cafes and bars are now offering wi-fi access, sometimes free of charge as long as you are a paying customer.

Be aware that your modem may not work once you leave your home country. The safest option is to buy a reputable 'global' modem before you leave home, or buy a local PC-card modem if you're spending an extended time in any one country. For more information on travelling with a portable computer, see www.teleadapt.com.

If you are travelling with your own notebook or hand-held computer, remember that the power-supply voltage here may vary from that at home, risking damage to your equipment. The best investment is a universal AC adaptor for your appliance, which will enable you to plug it in anywhere. You'll also need a plug adaptor for European outlets; it's often easiest to buy these before you leave home.

Well-trafficked internet-service providers (ISPs) in Budapest include T-Online Magyarország (www.t-online.hu), GTS-Datanet (www.datanet.hu) and Invitel (www.invitel.hu).

For the best sites to check out before arriving, see p18. The internet icon in this book indicates a computer terminal for guests' use or free wi-fi access.

Internet Cafes

Both Tourinform (p216) and Discover Budapest (p216) offer internet access for 100Ft or 150Ft per 15 minutes.

Among the better equipped internet cafes are the following:

Ami Internet Coffee (Map p85; ☎ 267 1644; V Váci utca 40; per 15/30/60min 200/400/700Ft; 🕙 9am-10pm; M3 Ferenciek tere) This cafe, centrally located in the university area of Pest, has a dozen terminals.

AvoComp (Map pp92–3; ☎ 288 6850; Lehel Csarnok, XIII Lehel tér; per 10/30/60min 150/200/300Ft; 🕙 8am-6pm Mon-Fri, to 2pm Sat; M3 Lehel tér) This very modern facility in eyesore Lehel Market is convenient to Nyugati train station.

Chatman Internet (Map pp92–3; ☎ 266 0856; VII Kazinczy utca 3; per 30/60/120min 100/150/280Ft; 🕙 8am-midnight Mon-Fri, from 10am Sat & Sun; trolleybus 74) This small and very friendly cafe is just north of Rákóczi út in Pest.

Electric Cafe (Map pp92–3; ☎ 413 1803; VII Dohány utca 37; per 30/60min 100/200Ft; 🕙 9am-midnight; M2 Blaha Lujza tér) This huge place is very popular with travellers.

Narancs (Map pp92–3; ☎ 413 6071; VII Akácfa utca 5; per 30/60min 100/200Ft; 🕙 9am-1am; M2 Blaha Lujza tér) *Très* charming French-run neighbourhood internet cafe.

Plastic Net (Map p85; ☎ 317 4638; V Szép utca 5; 🕙 9.30am-11.30pm Mon-Sat, 10am-10pm Sun; M3 Ferenciek tere) Another branch of Plastic Web.

Plastic Web (Map p85; ☎ 337 1374; V Irány utca 1; per 30/60min 200/390Ft; 🕙 9.30am-11.30pm; 📷 2) This friendly place is about as central as you'll find in Pest.

Vist@netcafe (Map pp92–3; ☎ 320 4332; XIII Váci út 6; per 1hr 10am-10pm/10pm-10am 500/400Ft; 🕙 24hr; M3 Nyugati pályaudvar) One of the very few internet cafes open round the clock.

X3 (Map pp102–3; ☎ 313 0893; VIII József körút 52; per 1hr 500Ft; 🕙 24hr; M3 Ferenc körút) Budapest's largest internet cafe with 55 terminals is open round the clock.

LAUNDRY

Most hostels have some sort of laundry facility; expect to pay from 1500Ft to 2000Ft for a wash and dry. Commercial laundries (*patyolat*) are fairly common in Budapest. You can elect to have your laundry done in six hours or one, two or three days – and pay accordingly. About the only self-service laundrettes in town are the following:

Irisz Szalon (Map p85; ☎ 317 2092; V Városház utca 3-5; 7/10kg 1700/2400Ft; ☉ 7am-7pm Mon-Fri, to 1pm Sat; Ⓜ M3 Ferenciek tere)

Liliom Szalon (Map pp102–3; ☎ 215 6782; IX Liliom utca 7-9; 8kg 1740Ft; ☉ 7am-7.30pm Mon-Fri, 8am-noon Sat; Ⓜ M3 Ferenc körút)

Mosoda Laundromat (Map pp70–1; ☎ 06-70 458 0926; XIII Lágymányosi utca 10; 6/10kg 800/1200Ft; ☉ 8am-8pm; 🚊 47 or 49)

Mosómata (Map pp92–3; ☎ 06-20 392 5702; VI Ó utca 24-26; 9kg 1800Ft; ☉ 9am-7pm Mon-Fri, 10am-4pm Sat & Sun; trolleybus 70 or 78)

LEGAL MATTERS

Penalties for possession, use or trafficking in illegal drugs in Hungary are severe, and convicted offenders can expect long jail sentences and heavy fines.

Another law that is taken very seriously here is the 100% ban on alcohol when driving. Do not think you will get away with even a few glasses of wine at lunch; police conduct routine roadside checks with breathalysers. And under new (and even stricter) rules that took effect in 2008, if you are found to have even 0.001% of alcohol in the blood, you could be fined up to 150,000Ft on the spot. If the level is higher than 0.08%, you will be arrested and your licence confiscated. In the event of an accident, the drinking party is automatically regarded as guilty.

The legal age for voting, driving an automobile and drinking alcohol is 18. The age of consent for gays and lesbians was lowered to 14 in 2004 to come into line with that of heterosexuals.

LIBRARIES

Libraries in Budapest with foreign-language books and periodicals include the following:

Ervin Szabó Central Library (Fővárosi Szabó Ervin Könyvtár; Map pp102–3; ☎ 411 5000; www.fszek.hu; VIII Reviczky utca 1; ☉ 10am-8pm Mon-Fri, to 4pm Sat;

Ⓜ M3 Kálvin tér) This stunning place, completed in 1894, is the main repository of Budapest's central library system with access to 800,000 books, 1000 periodicals and 40,000 audiovisual and digital items. You'll need to have an ID with a Hungarian address and to pay a subscription of 2600/3800Ft for six/12 months if you want to take items away.

National Foreign Language Library (Országos Idegennyelvű Könyvtár; Map p85; ☎ 318 3688; www.oik .hu, in Hungarian; V Molnár utca 11; ☉ 10am-8pm Mon, Tue, Thu & Fri, from noon Wed; Ⓜ M3 Ferenciek tere) You can join this library with 270,000 volumes in almost 150 languages for 6000/3000Ft per adult/student for a year. If you just want to borrow CDs and DVDs it's 5000/2500Ft and just books is 2800/1400Ft.

National Széchenyi Library (Országos Széchenyi Könyvtár; Map p62; ☎ 224 3700; www.oszk.hu; Royal Palace, Wing F; ☉ 10am-8pm Tue-Sat) This library allows members (adult/student annual 6000/3000Ft, six months 3000/1500Ft, daily 1000/500Ft) to do research, peruse the general stacks and read the large collection of foreign newspapers and magazines.

MAPS

The best folding maps of the city are Cartographia's 1:22,000 (770Ft) and 1:28,000 (640Ft) ones; a waterproof 1:30,000 map costs 1490Ft. If you plan to explore the city thoroughly, the *Budapest Atlas*, also from Cartographia, is indispensable. It comes in the same scale (1:20,000) but two sizes: a small (2190Ft) and a large (4300Ft) format. There is also a 1:25,000 pocket atlas of just the Inner Town available for 1400Ft.

Many bookshops, including Libri Könyvpalota (p119), stock a wide variety of maps. The national map-making company Cartographia (Map pp92–3; ☎ 312 6001; www.cartographia .hu; VI Bajcsy-Zsilinszky út 37; ☉ 10am-6pm Mon-Fri; Ⓜ M3 Arany János utca) also has its own outlet in Budapest. Even better is Térképkirály (Map pp92–3; ☎ 472 0505; www.mapking.hu; VI Bajcsy-Zsilinszky út 23; ☉ 9am-6pm Mon-Fri, to 1pm Sat; Ⓜ M3 Arany János utca), the 'Map King' nearby, which also has a Buda branch (Map p74; ☎ 315 2729; I Margit körút 1; 🚊 4 or 6).

MEDICAL SERVICES

Medical care in Budapest is generally adequate and good for routine problems but not complicated conditions. Foreigners are entitled to first aid and ambulance services only when they have suffered an accident and require immediate medical attention; follow-up treatment and medicine must be paid for.

Treatment at a public outpatient clinic *(rendelő intézet)* costs little, but doctors working privately will charge much more. Very roughly, a consultation in a Hungarian doctor's surgery *(orvosi rendelő)* costs from around 6000Ft while a home visit is 8000Ft to 10,000Ft.

If you do need health insurance while travelling, consider a policy that covers you for the worst possible scenario, such as an accident requiring an emergency flight home.

Two AIDS lines to contact are the Anonymous AIDS Association (☎ 466 9283; www.anonimaids .hu; ☯ 5-8pm Mon & Wed, 9am-noon Tue & Fri) and the AIDS Help Line (☎ 338 2419; ☯ 8am-4pm Mon-Thu, 8am-1pm Fri).

Clinics

Consultations and treatment are much more expensive in Western-style clinics. Dental work is usually of a high standard and cheap by Western European standards.

FirstMed Centers (Map p62; ☎ 224 9090; www.first medcenters.com; I Hattyú utca 14, 5th fl; ☯ appointments 8am-8pm Mon-Fri, 9am-2pm Sat, urgent care 24hr; Ⓜ M2 Moszkva tér) Modern private medical clinic with round-the-clock emergency treatment that is as expensive as you'll find anywhere in Europe (basic consultation 15,400/30,900Ft for under 10/20 minutes).

SOS Dent (Map pp92–3; ☎ 269 6010, 06-30 383 3333; www.sosdent.hu, in Hungarian; VI Király utca 14; ☯ 24hr; Ⓜ M1/2/3 Deák Ferenc tér) Consultations at this round-the-clock dental surgery are free, with extractions 7000Ft to 9000Ft, fillings 7000Ft to 11,000Ft and crowns from 40,000Ft.

PHARMACIES

Each of Budapest's 23 districts has a rotating all-night pharmacy; a sign on the door of any pharmacy will help you locate the nearest 24-hour place. Conveniently located pharmacies:

Csillag Gyógyszertár (Map pp102–3; ☎ 314 3695; VIII Rákóczi út 39; ☯ 7.30am-9pm Mon-Fri, 7.30am-2pm Sat; Ⓜ M2 Blaha Lujza tér)

Déli Gyógyszertár (Map p62; ☎ 355 4691; XII Alkotás utca 1/b; ☯ 8am-8pm Mon-Fri, 8am-2pm Sat; Ⓜ M2 Déli pályaudvar)

Teréz Patika (Map pp92–3; ☎ 311 4439; VI Teréz körút 41; ☯ 8am-8pm Mon-Fri, to 2pm Sat; Ⓜ M3 Nyugati pályaudvar)

MONEY

Hungary's currency is the forint (Ft). There are coins of 5Ft, 10Ft, 20Ft, 50Ft and 100Ft. Notes come in seven denominations: 200Ft, 500Ft, 1000Ft, 2000Ft, 5000Ft, 10,000Ft and 20,000Ft.

Although Hungary is now part of the EU, it will retain its own currency for the foreseeable future. Prices in shops and restaurants in Budapest are uniformly quoted in forint, but many hotels and guesthouses and even MÁV (the national rail company) quote their prices in euros. In such cases, we have followed suit. You can usually pay in either euros or forint.

ATMs

There are automated teller machines (ATMs) everywhere in Budapest, including in the train and bus stations, and quite a few foreign-currency exchange machines. Be warned that many of the ATMS at branches of Országos Takarékpenztár (OTP), the national savings bank, dispense 20,000Ft notes, which are difficult to break.

Changing Money

If you need to change cash or travellers cheques, avoid moneychangers (especially those on V Váci utca) in favour of banks. The following are among those offering the best rates and service and are very centrally located, but be sure to arrive about an hour before closing time to ensure the *bureau de change* counter is still open.

K&H bank (Map p85; V Váci utca 40; ☯ 8am-5pm Mon, to 4pm Tue-Thu, to 3pm Fri; Ⓜ M3 Ferenciek tere) Conveniently located on the main shopping drag; offers fairly good rates.

OTP bank (Map p85; V Deák Ferenc utca 7-9; ☯ 7.45am-6pm Mon, to 5pm Tue-Thu, to 4pm Fri; Ⓜ M1/2/3 Deák Ferenc tér) The national savings bank offers among the best exchange rates for cash and travellers cheques.

Credit Cards

Credit cards, especially Visa, MasterCard and American Express, are widely accepted here; you'll be able to use them at restaurants, shops, hotels, car-rental firms, travel agencies and petrol stations. They are not usually accepted at museums, supermarkets or train and bus stations.

Many banks, including K&H and Posta Bank (represented at post offices almost everywhere), give cash advances on major credit cards.

Travellers Cheques

You can change travellers cheques – American Express, Visa, MasterCard and Thomas Cook are the most recognisable brands – at most banks and post offices. Banks and *bureaux de change* generally don't take a commission, but exchange rates can vary; private agencies are always the most expensive. OTP has branches throughout the city and offers among the best rates. Ibusz is also a good bet though travel agencies usually take a commission of 2% or so. Shops never accept travellers cheques as payment here.

NEWSPAPERS & MAGAZINES

Three English-language newspapers can be found in Budapest: the long-established weekly tabloid the Budapest Sun (www.budapestsun .com; 399Ft; Thu) has a useful 'Style' arts and entertainment and listings section; the newer Budapest Times (www.budapesttimes.hu; 580Ft; Mon), another weekly with good reviews, opinion pieces and more straightforward news; and the Budapest Business Journal (www.bbjonline .hu; 1250Ft), an almost archival publication of financial news and business, appearing every other Friday.

The erudite Hungarian Quarterly (www.hun garianquarterly.com; €14), which looks at issues in great depth, is a valuable source of current Hungarian thinking in translation. For more information about the Hungarian-language press, see p44. The trilingual Budapest Magic (www .budapestmagic.hu), which appears six times a year, is directed at expatriates living here.

The best place in Budapest for foreign-language newspapers and magazines is Immedio (Map p85; ☎ 317 1311; V Városház utca 3-5; ☼ 7am-7pm Mon-Fri, 7am-2pm Sat, 8am-noon Sun; M M3 Ferenciek tere), which also has a nearby Belváros branch (Map p85; ☎ 318 5604; V Váci utca 10; ☼ 8am-8pm).

ORGANISED TOURS
Boat

From late April to late September, Mahart Pass-Nave (Map p85; ☎ 484 4013; www.mahartpassnave.hu; V Belgrád rakpart; adult/child under 15 2900/1490Ft; ☒ 2) has two-hour cruises along the Danube on the hour from 11am to 7pm and again at 8.30pm and 9.30pm. In the low season, from mid-

March to late April and late September to early November, there are between six and eight departures a day starting at 11am.

Another company running river cruises is Legenda (Map p85; ☎ 266 4190; www.legenda.hu; V Vigadó tér, pier 7; day cruises 1/2hr 2900/3900Ft, night cruises 4900Ft; ☒ 2), which provides taped commentary in up to 35 languages. Check the website for the schedule.

If you don't give a toss about ever getting your land legs back again, set your sights on the Power Hour Booze Cruise (☎ 269 3843; www.power hourboozecruise.com; adult/student 4500/4000Ft; ☼ 8.30pm Wed May-Sep), which is effectively a one-hour piss-up with nonstop beer for an hour while cruising the Danube. Groups assemble on the steps of the Lutheran church (Map p85; M M1/2/3 Deák tér) in V Deák Ferenc tér.

Bus

Many travel agencies, including Cityrama (Map p85; ☎ 302 4382; www.cityrama.hu; V Báthory utca 22; M M3 Arany János utca) and Mr Nilsz (Map p82; ☎ 302 4567; www.budapestcitytourmrnils.hu; XI Törökbálinti út 28; ☒ 8), which departs from V Szent István tér (Map p85), offer three-hour city tours including several photo-op stops. These cost from 6500Ft per adult, while children under 12 or 14 are charged between 3000Ft and 3250Ft.

Increasingly popular are the 'hop-on, hop-off' buses run by Budatours (Map pp92–3; ☎ 374 7070; www.budatours.hu; VI Andrássy út 2; adult/student & child over 6yrs 4000/3000Ft; M M1/2/3 Deák tér), in both open and covered coaches. They depart for 10 different stops every half-hour to an hour between 10am and 5.30pm to 7.30pm from V Andrássy út 3. Though the ticket is valid for 24 hours, it's a two-hour tour if you just stay on and there is taped commentary in 16 different languages. A similar deal is available from Program Centrum (Map p85; ☎ 317 7767, 06-20 944 9091; www.programcentrum.hu; V Erzsébet tér 9-10; M M1/2/3 Deák tér), next to the hotel Le Meridien Budapest, though departures are less frequent.

Cycling

Yellow Zebra Bikes (Map p85; ☎ 266 8777; www.yel lowzebrabikes.com; V Sütő utca 2; ☼ 10am-6pm Nov-Mar, 8.30am-8pm Apr-Oct; M M1/2/3 Deák Ferenc tér), which also has a branch at Discover Budapest (Map pp92–3; ☎ 269 3843; VI Lázár utca 16; ☼ 9.30am-6.30pm Mon-Fri, 10am-4pm Sat & Sun; M M1 Opera), runs cycling tours (adult/student 5000/4500Ft) of the city that take in Heroes' Square, City Park, inner Pest and Castle Hill in around 3½ hours. Tours, which include the bike, depart from in front of the Lutheran church (Map p85; M M1/2/3 Deák tér) in V Deák Ferenc tér at 11am from April to October, with an additional departure at 4pm in July and August.

The same outfit is behind City Segway Tours (www.citysegwaytours.com; tours 14,500Ft), which though not on bicycles involve two-wheeled, electric-powered conveyances. Segway tours, which follow an abbreviated version of the bike tours' Pest route and last 2½ to three hours, depart from the Discover Budapest branch at 10am and 6.30pm daily from April to October. You must book at least a day ahead for these tours.

Walking

Run by the same people behind Yellow Zebra Bikes, Absolute Walking Tours (☎ 266 8777, 269 3843; www.absolutetours.com) has a 3½-hour guided promenade through City Park, central Pest and Castle Hill (adult/student 4000/3500Ft). Tours depart at 9.30am and 1.30pm from April to October and at 10.30am the rest of the year from the steps of the Lutheran church (M M1/2/3 Deák tér) on Deák Ferenc tér. It also has some dynamite specialist tours, including the Hammer & Sickle Tour (adult/child aged 10-18 7000/3500Ft) and the 1956 Revolution Walk (6000/3000Ft).

The walkabouts led by the guides of Free Budapest Tours (☎ 06-20 534 5819; www.freebudapest tours.hu), whose name is as descriptive as it is, err, pedestrian, are unique and highly professional. The tours, which take in the Inner Town, the banks of the Danube and the Castle District in 2½ hours, are free of charge – the guides work for tips only (be generous!) – and departures are at 10.30am and 2pm daily in front of the M1 metro stop in Vörösmarty tér opposite Gerbeaud (p148). An evening thematic tour leaving from Vörösmarty tér at 8pm costs 2500Ft (2000Ft if booked through your hostel) and includes some transport by bus and/or tram.

Focusing on Budapest's Jewish heritage, Hungária Koncert (☎ 317 1377; www.ticket.info.hu) has a 1½- to two-hour tour available at 10am Monday to Friday, again at 2pm Monday to Thursday and at 11am Sunday year-round. The tour includes a visit to the Great Synagogue, the Jewish Museum and the Holocaust Cemetery for 2900Ft. The Grand Tour (about an hour longer) includes the same sights as well as the Orthodox Synagogue, a walking tour of the ghetto and a kosher snack, for 8900/8100Ft per adult/student. Tickets are available from locations throughout the city, including at the entrance to the Great Synagogue (Map pp92–3; VII Dohány utca 2-8) and the Duna Palota (Map p85; V Zrínyi utca 5) entertainment centre.

Paul Street Tours (☎ 06-20 933 5240; www.paulstreet tours.com) offers very personal walking tours covering the Castle District (about two hours), less-explored areas of Pest, such as the Jewish Quarter and Andrássy út (two to three hours), the Little Ring Road, the parks and gardens of Budapest and shopping. Lots of anecdotal information on architecture and social history, especially life in and around the courtyards (*udvar*) of *fin-de-siècle* Pest, is provided. Tours are available in English or Hungarian, by appointment year-round and cost €25 per hour regardless of the number of participants.

POST

The Hungarian Postal Service (Magyar Posta; www.posta .hu), whose logo is a jaunty, stylised version of St Stephen's Crown, has improved greatly in recent years, but the post offices themselves are usually fairly crowded and service can be slow. To beat the crowds, ask at kiosks, newsagents or stationery shops if they sell stamps (*bélyeg*).

If you must deal with the post office, you'll be relieved to learn that most people are there to pay electric, gas and telephone bills or parking fines. To get in and out with a minimum of fuss, look for the window marked with the symbol of an envelope. Make sure the destination of your letter is written clearly, and simply hand it over to the clerk, who will apply the stamps for you, postmark it and send it on its way.

Hungarian addresses start with the name of the recipient, followed on the next line by the postal code and city or town and then the street name and number. The Hungarian postal code consists of four digits. The first indicates the city or town ('1' is Budapest), the second and third the district (*kerület*) and the last the neighbourhood.

Postcards and letters up to 30g sent within Hungary cost 70Ft (100Ft for priority mail) while for the rest of Europe letters up to 20g cost 200Ft (230Ft priority) and postcards 150Ft (170Ft priority). Outside Europe, expect to pay 220Ft (250Ft priority) for letters up to 20g and 170Ft (190Ft priority) for postcards.

To send a parcel, look for the sign '*Csomagfeladás*' or '*Csomagfelvétel*'. Packages sent within Hungary cost around 830Ft for up to 20kg. Packages going abroad must not weigh more than 2kg or you'll face a Kafkaesque parade of forms and queues to fill; try to send small ones. You can send up to 2kg in one box for 4000Ft surface mail to Europe and 4900Ft to the rest of the world. Airmail rates are 5850Ft and 6790Ft respectively.

The main post office (Map p85; V Petőfi Sándor utca 13-15; 8am-8pm Mon-Fri, to 2pm Sat; 1/2/3 Deák Ferenc tér) is a few minutes' walk from Deák Ferenc tér and the main Tourinform office. This is where you buy stamps, mail letters and packages and pick up poste restante. Since the family name always comes first in Hungarian usage, have the sender underline your last name, as letters are often misfiled under foreigners' first names.

Two other convenient post offices with extended hours are the Nyugati train station branch (Map pp92–3; VI Teréz körút 51-53; 7am-8pm Mon-Fri, 8am-6pm Sat; M3 Nyugati pályaudvar) and the Keleti train station branch (Map pp102–3; VIII Kerepesi út 2-6; 7am-9pm Mon-Fri, 8am-2pm Sat; M2 Keleti pályaudvar), which can be most easily reached from platform 6.

RELOCATING

If you are considering moving to Budapest and you are not a citizen of the EU you must have both a residency and a work permit. For details, see p217.

For practical information on moving and getting settled in the Hungarian capital, get a copy of the free *@ Home in Budapest,* a 32-page booklet published annually by the Budapest Sun (www.budapestsun.com), with details on completing paperwork, finding a flat, getting healthcare and so on.

SAFETY

No parts of Budapest are 'off limits' to visitors, although some locals now avoid Margaret Island after dark off-season, and both residents and visitors give the dodgier parts of the 8th and 9th districts (areas of prostitution) a wide berth.

Pickpocketing is most common in markets, the Castle District, Váci utca and Hősök tere, near major hotels and on certain popular buses (eg 7) and trams (2, 4, 6, 47 and 49).

Taking a taxi in Budapest can be an expensive and even unpleasant experience. Never hail a cab on the street; instead, call one from a phone – private, mobile or public – and give the number (almost always posted somewhere in the phone box) to the dispatcher. For more information see p203.

If you've left something on any form of public transport in Budapest, contact the BKV lost & found office (Map pp92–3; 258 4636, 461 6688; VII Akácfa utca 18; 8am-5pm Mon, Tue, Thu & Fri, to 6pm Wed; M2 Blaha Lujza tér).

Scams

Scams involving attractive young women, gullible guys, expensive drinks in nightclubs and a frog-marching to the nearest ATM by gorillas-in-residence, have been all the rage in Budapest for well over a decade now, and we get stacks of letters from male readers complaining they've been ripped off. Guys, please, do us all a favour. If it seems too good to be true, it probably is. These scams have cost some would-be Lotharios hundreds, even thousands, of dollars. Tourinform distributes a brochure called *Well-informed in Budapest* with useful tips on avoiding such problems.

TAXES & REFUNDS

ÁFA, a value-added tax of between 5% and 20%, covers the purchase of all new goods in Hungary. It's usually included in the quoted price but not always, so it pays to check. Visitors are not exempt, but non-EU residents can claim refunds for total purchases of at least 42,000Ft on one receipt as long as they take the goods out of the country (and the EU) within 90 days. The ÁFA receipts (available from where you make the purchases) should be stamped by customs at the border, and the claim has to be made within 183 days of exporting the goods. You can then collect your refund – minus 15% commission – from the Global Refund (www.globalrefund.com) desk at Terminals 1 and 2 at Ferihegy airport in Budapest or at branches of the Ibusz chain of travel agencies at some nine border crossings. You can also have it sent by bank cheque or deposited into your credit-card account.

Like municipalities throughout the land, Budapest levies a tourist tax on most forms of accommodation (see p173).

TELEPHONE

You can make domestic and international calls from public telephones, which are usually in good working order. They work with both coins and phonecards. Telephone boxes with a black and white arrow and red target, and the word *Visszahívható* on the door, display a telephone number so you can be phoned back.

All localities in Hungary have a two-digit telephone area code, except for Budapest, which has just a '1'. To make a local call, pick up the receiver and listen for the neutral and continuous dial tone, then dial the phone number (seven digits in Budapest, six elsewhere). For an intercity landline call within Hungary and whenever you are calling a mobile telephone, dial ☎ 06 and wait for the second, more melodious, tone. Then dial the area code and phone number. Cheaper or toll-free blue and green numbers start with the digits ☎ 06-40 and ☎ 06-80 respectively.

The procedure for making an international call is the same as for a local call except that you dial ☎ 00, wait for the second dial tone, then dial the country code, the area code and then the number. The country code for Hungary is ☎ 36.

The following are useful numbers to know. For emergency numbers, see p208 and the inside front cover of this book under 'Telephone'.

Information Plus (☎ 197) Any inquiry; English spoken.

Domestic operator/inquiries (☎ 198) English spoken.

International inquiries/operator (☎ 199) English spoken.

Time/speaking clock (☎ 180) In Hungarian.

Wake-up service (☎ 193) In Hungarian.

Mobile Phones

In Hungary you must always dial ☎ 06 when ringing mobile telephones, which have specific area codes depending on the telecom company: Pannon GSM (☎ 06-20; www.pannon.hu), T-Mobile (☎ 06-30; www.t-mobile.hu) and Vodafone (☎ 06-70; www.vodafone.hu).

If you're going to spend more than just a few days in Budapest and expect to use your phone quite a bit, consider buying a rechargeable SIM chip, which will reduce the cost of making local calls to a fraction of what you'd pay on your own foreign mobile. For example, Vodafone (Map pp92–3; ☎ 238 7281; West End City Centre, VI Váci út1-3, 1st fl; ⏲ 10am-9pm Mon-Sat, to 6pm Sun; Ⓜ Nyugati pályaudvar) has prepaid vouchers available for 1680Ft with 500Ft worth of credit. Top-up cards cost 3000/7000/12,000Ft and are valid for three/six/12 months.

Pannon (Map p62; ☎ 345 8088; II Mammut I, 2nd fl, Lövőház utca 2-6; ⏲ 9am-8pm Mon-Sat, to 6pm Sun; Ⓜ M2 Moszkva tér) and T-Mobile (Map p85; ☎ 266 5723; V Petőfi

Sándor utca 12; ⏲ 9am-7pm Mon-Fri, 10am-1pm Sat; Ⓜ M3 Ferenciek tere) offer similar deals.

Phonecards

Standard phonecards issued by Magyar Telekom, which are available from post offices, newsagents, hotels and petrol stations, come in values of 500Ft, 800Ft, 1800Ft and 5000Ft, but these are by far the most expensive way to go. As everywhere else these days, there is a plethora of discount phonecards on offer. Among the most widely available are Barangoló (www.telekom.hu), which comes in denominations of 1000Ft, 2000Ft and 5000Ft; NeoPhone (www.neophone.hu), with cards at the same values; and Ezphone (www.ezphone.hu) with cards worth from 500Ft to 5000Ft. It can cost as little as 9Ft per minute to the US, Australia and New Zealand using such cards.

TIME

Budapest lies in the central European time zone. Winter time is GMT plus one hour and in summer it's GMT plus two hours. Clocks are advanced at 2am on the last Sunday in March and set back at the same time on the last Sunday in October.

Without taking daylight-saving times into account, when it's noon in Budapest, it's: 11pm in Auckland, 1pm in Bucharest, 11am in London, 2pm in Moscow, 6am in New York, noon in Paris, 3am in San Francisco, 9pm in Sydney and 8pm in Tokyo.

Like some other European languages, Magyar tells the time by making reference to the next hour – not the one before as we do in English. Thus 7.30 is 'half eight' (*fél nyolc óra*) and the 24-hour system is often used in giving the times of movies, concerts and so on. So a film at 7.30pm could appear on a listing as 'f8', 'f20', '½8' or '½20'. A quarter to the hour has a ¾ in front (thus '¾8' means 7.45) while quarter past is ¼ of the next hour (eg '¼9' means 8.15). Got it?

TIPPING

Hungarians are very tip-conscious and nearly everyone in Budapest will routinely hand gratuities to waiters, hairdressers and taxi drivers. Doctors and dentists accept 'gratitude money', and even petrol station attendants who pump your petrol and thermal spa attendants who walk you to your changing cabin expect a little something. If you aren't impressed with the service at a restaurant, the joyride in a taxi or the way someone cut your hair, leave little or nothing at all. He or she will get the message – loud and clear.

To learn more about the unusual way to tip a waiter see p125.

TOURIST INFORMATION
Tourist Offices

Tourinform (Map p85; ☎ 438 8080; www.tourinform.hu; V Sütő utca 2; ☼ 8am-8pm; M M1/2/3 Deák Ferenc tér) is about the best single source of information about Budapest, but it can get hopelessly crowded in summer, and the staff are not very patient. Less crowded (usually) are the Castle Hill branch (Map p62; ☎ 488 0475; I Szentháromság tér; ☼ 9am-7pm May-Oct, 10am-6pm Nov-Apr; 🚌 16, 16/a or 116) and the Oktogon branch (Map pp92–3; ☎ 322 4098; VI Liszt Ferenc tér 11; ☼ 10am-6pm Mon-Fri; M M1 Oktogon). There are also Tourinform desks in the arrivals sections of Ferihegy International Airport's Terminals 1, 2A and 2B.

Travel Agencies

If your query is about private accommodation, flights or international train travel or you need to change money, you could turn to a commercial travel agency. Ibusz (Map p85; ☎ 501 4910; www.ibusz.hu; V Ferenciek tere 10; ☼ 9am-6pm Mon-Fri, to 1pm Sat; M M3 Ferenciek tere) is arguably the best for private accommodation (p173), and its main office also changes money, books all types of accommodation and sells transport tickets; while youth- and student-orientated Express (Map pp92–3; ☎ 327 7297; www.express-travel.hu; VII Dohány utca 30/a & Kazinczy utca 3/b; ☼ 8.30am-5pm Mon-Fri, 9am-1pm Sat; M M2 Astoria) issues student, youth, teacher and hostel cards (p207) and sells discounted Billet International de Jeunesse (BIJ) train and cheap air tickets. Its main office can also book accommodation in Budapest (particularly hostels and colleges).

Some other options:

Discover Budapest (Map pp92–3; ☎ 269 3843; VI Lázár utca 16; ☼ 9.30am-6.30pm Mon-Fri, 10am-4pm Sat & Sun; M M1 Opera) Visit this one-stop-shop centre for helpful tips and advice, accommodation bookings, internet access and cycling and walking tours with Yellow Zebra Bikes and Absolute Walking Tours (p212).

Vista (Map pp92–3; ☎ 429 9999; www.vista.hu, in Hungarian; VI Andrássy út 1; M M1/2/3 Deák Ferenc tér; ☼ 9.30am-6pm Mon-Fri, 10am-2.30pm Sat) Vista is an excellent destination for all your travel needs, both

outbound (air tickets, package tours etc) and incoming (room bookings, organised tours, study etc).

Wasteels (Map pp102–3; ☎ 210 2802, 343 3492; www .wasteels.hu; VIII Kerepesi út 2-6; ☼ 8am-8pm Mon-Fri, 8am-6pm Sat; M M2 Keleti pályaudvar) This agency next to platform No 9 at Keleti train station sells BIJ-26 discounted train tickets for those 26 years and under, but you must have a student or youth card to get the discounted fares.

TRAVELLERS WITH DISABILITIES

Budapest has made great strides in recent years in making public areas and facilities more accessible to the disabled. Wheelchair ramps, toilets fitted for the disabled and inward opening doors, though not as common as in Western Europe, do exist and audible traffic signals for the blind are becoming commonplace.

For more information, contact the Hungarian Federation of Disabled Persons' Associations (MEOSZ; Map p74; ☎ 388 2387; www.meoszinfo.hu; III San Marco utca 76).

VISAS

Citizens of virtually all European countries as well as Australia, Canada, Israel, Japan, New Zealand and the US do not require visas to visit Hungary for stays of up to 90 days. Nationals of South Africa (among others) still require visas. Check current visa requirements at a Hungarian consulate, any Hungarian National Tourism Office (HNTO) or Malév Hungarian Airlines office or on the website of the Hungarian Foreign Ministry (www.mfa.gov.hu) as requirements often change without notice.

Visas are issued at Hungarian consulates or missions, most international highway border crossings, Ferihegy International Airport and the International Ferry Pier in Budapest. They are rarely issued on international buses and never on trains. Be sure to retain the separate entry and exit forms issued with the visa that is stamped in your passport.

Short-stay visas (€60), which are the best for tourists as they allow stays of up to 90 days, are issued at Hungarian consulates or missions in the applicants' country of residence. Be sure to get a short-stay rather than a transit visa; the latter – also available for €60 – is only good for a stay of five days.

Short-stay visas are only extended in emergencies (eg medical ones; 5000Ft) and this must be done at the central police station (*rendőrkapitányság*) of any city or town 15 days before the original one expires.

WOMEN TRAVELLERS

Hungarian men can be sexist in their thinking, but women in Budapest do not suffer any particular form of harassment (though domestic violence and rape get relatively little media coverage here). Most men – even drunks – are effusively polite with women. Women may not be made to feel especially welcome when eating or drinking alone, but it's really no different from most other countries in Europe.

If you do need assistance and/or information ring the Women's Line (Nővonal; ☎ 06-80 505 101; 6-10pm) or Women for Women against Violence (NANE; ☎ 267 4900; www.nane.hu).

WORK

Travellers on tourist visas in Budapest are not supposed to accept employment, but many end up teaching, doing a little writing for the English-language press or even working for foreign firms without permits. Check the English-language telephone book or advertisements for English-language schools in the *Budapest Sun*, which also has job listings, though pay is generally pretty low. You can do much better teaching privately (up to 4000Ft per 45-minute 'hour' depending on your experience).

For the most part (and this varies with some states), EU nationals can come and work freely in Hungary, though they do require a residency permit, which can only be obtained in Budapest. For non-EU nationals, however, obtaining a work permit *(munkavállalási engedély)* involves a considerable paper chase lasting up to a month. You'll need a letter of support from your prospective employer, proof that the job has been advertised publicly for a fixed period of 15 days, copies of your birth certificate, your academic record and results of a recent medical examination. The employer then submits these to the local labour centre *(munkaügyi központ)*, and you must return to your current country of residence and apply for the work permit at the Hungarian embassy or consulate there.

When you return to Hungary, you have 15 days to gather all the documents required to apply for a one-year renewable residence permit *(tartózkodási engedély)* through the Residency Department of the Ministry of Internal Affairs' Immigration office at XI Budafoki út 60 in Budapest or through the main police station *(főkapitányság)* in your district or city.

Doing Business

The main source of information in English for businesspeople in Budapest is the Budapest Business Journal (BBJ; www.bbj.hu; 1250Ft), which has been around since 1992 and appears every other Friday. Another useful publication for businesspeople is the feature-oriented *Business Hungary*, compiled monthly by the American Chamber of Commerce and available free around town. *Diplomacy & Trade*, which appears 10 times a year, is more of a vanity publication. A good business website is www.portfolio.hu/en.

Following are some important addresses and/or useful sources of information:

American Chamber of Commerce in Hungary (Map p85; ☎ 266 9880; www.amcham.hu; V Deák Ferenc utca 10, 5th fl; M1 Vörösmarty tér)

British Chamber of Commerce in Hungary (Map pp92–3; ☎ 302 5200, www.bcch.com; XIII Szent István körút 24, 3rd fl; 4 or 6)

Budapest Chamber of Commerce & Industry (Budapesti Kereskedelmi és Iparkamra; Map p62; ☎ 214 1826; www.bkik.hu; I Krisztina körút 99; 18)

National Development & Economy Ministry (Nemzeti Fejlesztési és Gazdasági Minisztárium; Map p85; ☎ 374 2700; http://nfgm.gov.hu; V Honvéd utca 13-15; M2 Kossuth Lajos tér)

Finance Ministry (Pénzügy Minisztérium; Map p85; ☎ 318 2066; www.meh.hu, in Hungarian; V József nádor tér 2-4; M1 Vörösmarty tér)

Hungarian Chamber of Commerce & Industry (Magyar Kereskedelmi és Iparkamra; Map p85; ☎ 474 5100; www.mkik.hu; V Kossuth Lajos tér 6-8, 5th fl; M2 Kossuth Lajos tér)

For photocopying, digital printing and computer services like scanning, visit any of the eight outlets of Copy General (www.copygeneral.hu, in Hungarian), including its district V branch (Map p85; ☎ 302 3206; V Kálmán Imre utca 22; 24hr; M3 Nyugati pályaudvar). A similar – and aptly named – place nearby is CopyCat (Map p85; ☎ 312 7636; www.copycat.hu; V Alkotmány utca 18; 7am-10pm Mon-Fri, 10am-8pm Sat & Sun; M3 Nyugati pályaudvar).

All the major courier companies are represented here, including DHL (☎ 382 3499; www.dhl.hu), FedEx Hungary (☎ 29-551 900; www.fedex.com/hu), TNT Express (☎ 431 3131; www.tnt.hu) and UPS (☎ 06-40 262 000; www.ups.com).

The Hungarians like to boast that their language ranks with Japanese and Arabic as among the world's most difficult tongues to learn. All languages are hard for non-native speakers to master, but it is true: Hungarian is a bitch to learn to speak well. This should not put you off attempting a few words and phrases, however.

For assorted reasons – the compulsory study of Russian in all schools until the late 1980s being one of them – Hungarians are not polyglots and even when they do have a smattering of a foreign language, they lack experience and are generally hesitant to speak it. Attempt a few words *magyarul* (in Hungarian) and they will be impressed, take it as a compliment and be encouraging.

The best foreign language for getting around with here was always German; historical ties, geographical proximity and the fact that it was the preferred language of the literati until almost the 20th century have given it almost semi-official status. But with the advent of the internet

and the frequency of travel, most young people now have at least a smattering of English – so, if you are desperate to make yourself understood in English, look for someone under the age of 25.

For obvious reasons, Russian is best avoided; there seems to be almost a national paranoia about speaking it, and many people revel in how little they know 'despite all those years in class'. Italian is understood more and more in Hungary because of tourism. French and Spanish are virtually useless.

If you want to learn more Hungarian than we've included here, pick up a copy of Lonely Planet's user-friendly *Hungarian* phrasebook.

PRONUNCIATION

The letters ö and ő, and ü and ű, are listed as separate pairs of letters in dictionaries (following o, ó and u, ú respectively). The consonant combinations cs, dz, dzs, gy, ly, ny, sz, ty and zs also have separate entries.

Vowels

a	as in 'hot'
á	as in 'father'
e	as in 'bet'
é	as in 'air"
i	as in 'hit'
í	as in 'meet'
o	as in 'law' but short
ó	as in 'awl'
ö	as in 'curt' but short (with no 'r' sound)
ő	as in 'her' (with no 'r' sound)
u	as in 'pull'
ú	as in 'rule'
ü	like i but with rounded lips (like 'u' in French *tu*)
ű	as in 'strewn'

Consonants

c	as the 'ts' in 'rats'
cs	as the 'ch' in 'cheese'
dz	as in 'adze'
dzs	as the 'j' in 'joke'
gy	as the 'du' in 'dune' (British)
j/ly	as in 'yes'
ny	as the 'ny' in 'canyon'
r	as in 'run' (but rolled)
s	as the 'sh' in 'ship'
sz	as the 's' in 'sit'
ty	as the 'tu' in 'tube' (British)
zs	as the 's' in 'pleasure'

SOCIAL
Meeting People

In the following phrases, the polite form of 'you' (*Ön* and *Önök*) is given except for situations where you might wish to establish a more personal relationship.

Note that when you want to say 'Hello', 'Hi', or 'Bye', the word will change depending on whether you are speaking to one person or more than one. Look for the symbols 'sg' (singular) or 'pl' (plural) to determine which word to use.

Hello.	Szervusz. (sg)
	Szervusztok. (pl)
Hi.	Szia/Sziasztok. (sg/pl)
Good ...	Jó ... kívánok.
morning	reggelt
afternoon/day	napot
evening	estét

Goodbye.	Viszlát. (pol)
	Szia. (inf sg)
	Sziasztok. (inf sg/pl)
Good night.	Jó éjszakát.
Yes.	Igen.
No.	Nem.
Please.	Kérem. (pol)
	Kérlek (inf)
Thank you (very much).	(Nagyon) Köszönöm.
You're welcome.	Szívesen.
Excuse me. (to get attention)	Elnézést kérek.
Excuse me. (to get past)	Bocsánat.
Sorry.	Sajnálom.
How are you?	Hogy van? (pol)
	Hogy vagy? (inf)
Fine. And you?	Jól. És Ön/te?
What's your name?	Mi a neve? (pol)
	Mi a neved? (inf)
My name is …	A nevem …
I'm pleased to meet you.	Örvendek.
Where are you from?	Ön honnan jön?
I'm from …	Én … jövök.
Do you speak English?	Beszél angolul?
I (don't) understand.	(Nem) Értem.
What does … mean?	Mit jelent az, hogy …?
Could you please write it down?	Leírná, kérem.

Going Out

What's on …?
Mi a program …?

locally	helyben
this weekend	ezen a hétvégén
today	ma
tonight	ma este

Where can I find …?
Hol találok …?

clubs	klubokat
gay venues	meleg szórakozó-helyeket
places to eat	egy helyet, ahol enni lehet
pubs	pubokat

Is there a local entertainment guide?
Van itt helyi programkalauz?

PRACTICAL

Directions

Where's (the market)?	
Hol van (a piac)?	
What's the address?	
Mi a cím?	
How do I get there?	
Hogyan jutok oda?	
How far is it?	
Milyen messze van?	
Can you show me (on the map)?	
Meg tudja mutatni nekem (a térképen)?	
It's straight ahead.	
Egyenesen előttünk van.	

Turn …
Forduljon …

at the corner	a saroknál
at the traffic lights	a közlekedési lámpánál
left/right	balra/jobbra

Signs

Bejárat	Entrance
Kijárat	Exit
Nyitva	Open
Zárva	Closed
Foglalt	Reserved/Occupied
Belépni Tilos	No Entry
Tilos	Prohibited
Tilos a Dohányzás	No Smoking
Toalett/WC	Toilets
Férfiak	Men
Nők	Women

Question Words

How many?	Hány?
How much?	Mennyi?
What?	Mi?
What kind?	Milyen?
Where?	Hol?
When?	Mikor?
Which?	Melyik?
Who?	Ki?
Why?	Miért?

Numbers & Amounts

The word kettő is used when expressing the number two on its own, while két is used when it is followed by the counted noun.

0	nulla
1	egy
2	kettő/két

3	három
4	négy
5	öt
6	hat
7	hét
8	nyolc
9	kilenc
10	tíz
11	tizenegy
12	tizenkettő
13	tizenhárom
14	tizennégy
15	tizenöt
16	tizenhat
17	tizenhét
18	tizennyolc
19	tizenkilenc
20	húsz
21	huszonegy
22	huszonkettő
30	harminc
31	harmincegy
32	harminckettő
40	negyven
41	negyvenegy
42	negyvenkettő
50	ötven
60	hatvan
70	hetven
80	nyolcvan
90	kilencven
100	száz
200	kétszáz
1000	ezer

Days

Monday	hétfő
Tuesday	kedd
Wednesday	szerda
Thursday	csütörtök
Friday	péntek
Saturday	szombat
Sunday	vasárnap

Banking

I'd like to …
Szeretnék …

change a travellers cheque	beváltani egy utazási csekket
change money	pénzt váltani

Do you accept …?
Elfogadnak …?

credit cards	hitelkártyát
travellers cheques	utazási csekket

Where is …?
Hol van …?

an ATM	egy bankautomata
a foreign exchange office	egy valutaváltó ügynökség

Post

Where's the post office?
Hol van a postahivatal?

I want to send a …
… szeretnék küldeni.

letter	Levelet
parcel	Csomagot
postcard	Képeslapot

I want to buy a/an…
… szeretnék venni.

airmail envelope	Légipostai borítékot
ordinary envelope	Sima borítékot
stamp	Bélyeget

Phones & Mobiles

Where's the nearest public phone?
Hol a legközelebbi nyilvános telefon?
I want to make a collect/reverse-charge call.
'R' beszélgetést szeretnék kérni.

I want to …
Szeretnék …
 buy a phonecard
 telefonkártyát venni
 call (Singapore)
 (Szingapúr)ba telefonálni
 make a (local) call
 (helyi) telefonbeszélgetést folytatni

I'd like a …
Szeretnék egy …
 charger for my phone
 töltőt a telefonomhoz
 mobile phone/cellphone for hire
 mobiltelefont bérelni
 (prepaid) SIM card
 (előre kifizetett) SIM-kártyát

Internet

Where's the local internet cafe?
Hol van a legközelebbi internet kávézó?

I'd like to …
Szeretném …
 check my email
 megnézni az e-mailjeimet
 get internet access
 rámenni az internetre

Transport

Which ... goes to (the Parliament)?
Melyik ... megy (a Parlamenthez)?

bus	busz
train	vonat
tram	villamos
trolleybus	trolibusz
metro line	metró

When's the ...?
Mikor megy ...?

first	az első
last	az utolsó
next	a következő

Is this taxi available?
Szabad ez a taxi?
Please put the meter on.
Kérem, kapcsolja be az órát.
How much is it to ...?
Mennyibe kerül ... ba?
Please take me to (this address).
Kérem, vigyen el (erre a címre).
What time does it leave?
Mikor indul?

EMERGENCIES

Help!	Segítség!
Could you please help?	Tudna segíteni?
Call the police!	Hívja a rendőrséget!
Call a doctor!	Hívjon orvost!
Where's the police station?	Hol a rendőrség?
Go away!	Menjen el!

HEALTH

Where's the nearest ...?
Hol a legközelebbi ...?

dentist	fogorvos
doctor	orvos
hospital	kórház
medical centre	orvosi rendelő
(night) pharmacist	(éjszaka nyitvatartó) gyógyszertár

I'm allergic to ...
Allergiás vagyok ...

antibiotics	az antibiotikumokra
penicillin	a penicillinre

Symptoms

I have a headache.	Fáj a fejem.
I have a sore throat.	Fáj a torkom.

I have (a) ...
... van.

asthma	Asztmám
diarrhoea	Hasmenésem
fever	Lázam
nausea	Hányingerem

FOOD
Useful Phrases

breakfast	reggeli
lunch	ebéd
dinner	vacsora
snack	snack

Can you recommend a ... ?
Tud/Tudsz ajánlani egy ...? (pol/inf)

bar/pub	bárt/pubot
beer bar	sörözőt
restaurant	éttermet
self-service restaurant	önkiszolgálót

Is service included in the bill?
A kiszolgálás díja benne van a számlában?
I'm hungry/thirsty.
Éhes/szomjas vagyok.
The menu, please.
Az étlapot, kérem.
Is there an English-language menu?
Van angol nyelvű étlap?
What would you recommend?
Mit ajánlana?
I'd like a local speciality.
Valamilyen helyi specialitást szeretnék.
I'm (a) vegetarian.
Vegetáriánus vagyok.
Do you have vegetarian food?
Vannak önöknél vegetáriánus ételek?
I'm allergic to (nuts/peanuts).
Allergiás vagyok a (diófélékre/mogyoróra).
I'd like..., please.
Legyen szíves, hozzon egy...
Another..., please.
Még (egy)... kérek szépen.
Please bring the bill.
Kérem, hozza a számlát.

Food Glossary
BASICS

bors	pepper
cukor	sugar
cukorral/cukor nélkül	with/without sugar
étel	food
étlap	menu
gyümölcs	fruit

MENU READER

Restaurant menus are often translated into German and English, with mixed degrees of success. The following is a sample menu as it would appear in many restaurants in Budapest. It's far from complete, but it gives a good idea of what to expect. The main categories on a menu include those listed here; *készételek* are ready-made dishes that are kept warm or just heated up, while *frissensültek* are made to order. Other words you might encounter are *halételek* or *halak* (fish dishes), *szárnyasok* (poultry dishes) and *sajtok* (cheeses).

Előételek (Appetisers)
Hortobágyi palacsinta Meat-filled pancakes with paprika sauce
libamájpástétom Goose-liver pâté
rántott gombafejek Breaded, fried mushroom caps

Levesek (Soups)
csontleves Consommé
Jókai bableves Bean soup with meat
meggyleves Cold sour-cherry soup (in summer)
tyúkhúsleves Chicken soup with carrot, kohlrabi, parsley and celery roots

Saláták (Salads)
cékla saláta Pickled beetroot salad
ecetes almapaprika Pickled (apple) peppers
paradicsom saláta Tomato salad
uborka saláta Sliced pickled-cucumber salad
vegyes saláta Mixed salad of pickles

Köretek (Side Dishes)
rizi-bizi Rice with peas
sült hasábburgonya Chips (French fries)

Készételek (Ready-Made Dishes)
csirke paprikás Chicken paprika
(marha)pörkölt (Beef) stew (many types)
töltött paprika/káposzta Stuffed peppers/cabbage

Frissensültek (Dishes Made to Order)
Bécsiszelet Wiener schnitzel
Brassói aprópecsenye Braised pork Braşov-style
cigánypecsenye Roast pork Gypsy-style
csülök Smoked pork knuckle
hagymás rostélyos Beef sirloin fried with onions
rántott hátszínszelet Breaded, fried rump steak
rántott pulykamell Breaded, fried turkey breast
sertésborda Pork chop
sült csirkecomb Roast chicken thigh
sült libacomb Roast goose leg

Édességek (Desserts)
Dobos torta Multilayered 'Dobos' chocolate and cream cake with caramelised brown sugar top
Gundel palacsinta 'Gundel' flambéed pancake with chocolate and nuts
rétes Strudel
Somlói galuska Somló-style sponge cake with chocolate and whipped cream

hús	meat
jéggel/jég nélkül	with/without ice
meleg/forró/hideg	warm/hot/cold
sajt	cheese
só	salt
tojás	egg
vaj	butter
zöldség	vegetables

MEAT & FISH
borjúhús	veal
csirke	chicken
disznóhús	pork
hal	fish
hús	meat
marhahús	beef
pulyka	turkey

VEGETABLES
gomba	mushroom
káposzta	cabbage
karfiol	cauliflower
sárgarépa	carrot
spenót	spinach
zöldbab	string (green) bean
zöldborsó	pea

FRUIT
alma	apple
banán	banana
cseresznye	(sweet) cherry
eper	strawberry
körte	pear
meggy	sour (Morello) cherry
narancs	orange
őszibarack	peach
sárgabarack	apricot
szőlő	grape

COOKING METHODS
füstölt	smoked
főtt or főve	boiled

főzelék	frying or boiling vegetables, then mixing into a roux
párolt	steamed
pirított	braised
rántva or rántott	breaded and fried
roston	grilled
sült or sütve	fried or roast

NONALCOHOLIC DRINKS

almalé	apple juice
ásvány víz	mineral water
gyümölcslé	fruit juice
kávé	coffee
narancslé	orange juice
üdítőital	soft drink
tej	milk
víz	water

ALCOHOLIC DRINKS

barackpálinka	apricot brandy
barna sör	dark beer/stout
bor	wine
csapolt sör	draught beer
édes bor	sweet wine
fehér bor	white wine
fél barna sör	dark lager
fröccs	spritzer (wine soda)
korsó sör	mug (½L) of beer
körtepálinka	pear brandy
pezsgő	champagne/sparkling wine
pohár sör	glass (one-third litre) of beer
sör	beer
szilvapálinka	plum brandy
világos sör	lager
vörös bor	red wine

GLOSSARY

ÁFA – value-added tax (VAT)

alagút – tunnel

ÁVO – Rákosi's hated secret police in the early years of communism; later renamed ÁVH

bélyeg – stamps

BKV – Budapest Közlekedési Vallálat (Budapest Transport Company)

bolhapiac – flea market

borozó – wine bar; any place serving wine

Bp – commonly used abbreviation for Budapest

búcsú – farewell; also a church patronal festival

büfé – snack bar

centrum – town or city centre

cukrászda – cake shop or patisserie

Eclectic – an art and architectural style that was popular in Hungary in the Romantic period, drawing from sources both indigenous and foreign

eszpresszó – coffee shop, often also selling alcoholic drinks and snacks; strong, black coffee; same as *presszó*

étkezde – canteen that serves simple dishes

étterem – restaurant

fapados – wooden bench; budget (in reference to airlines)

fasor – boulevard, avenue

forint (Ft) – Hungary's monetary unit

főkapitányság – main police station

gyógyfürdő – thermal bath or spa

gyógyszertár – pharmacy

gyűjtemény – collection

hajóallomás – ferry pier or landing

ház – house

hegy – hill, mountain

HÉV – Helyiérdekű Vasút (suburban commuter train in Budapest)

híd – bridge

HNTO – Hungarian National Tourism Office

ifjúsági szálló – youth hostel

kastély – manor house or mansion (see *vár*)

kávéház – coffee house

képtár – picture gallery

kertek – literally 'gardens', but in Budapest any outdoor spot that has been converted into an entertainment zone

kerület – city district

kincstár – treasury

Kiskörút – 'Little Ring Road' in Budapest

kökény – sloe

könyvtár – library

korsó – 0.4L glass

körút – ring road

korzó – embankment or promenade

köz – alley, mews, lane

központ – centre

krt – abbreviation for *körút* (ring road)

labdarúgás – football

lángos – deep-fried dough with various toppings, usually cheese and sour cream

lépcső – stairs, steps

Mahart – Hungarian passenger ferry company

Malév – Hungary's national airline

málna – blackberry

MÁV – Magyar Államvasutak (Hungarian State Railways)
megyék – counties

Nagykörút – 'Big Ring Road' in Budapest
nyitva – open
nyitvartás – opening hours

önkiszolgáló – self-service
OTP – Országos Takarékpenztár (National Savings Bank)

pálinka – fruit brandy
palota – palace
pályaudvar – train or railway station
panzió – pension, guest house
patyolat – laundry
pénztár – cashier
piac – market
pince – wine cellar
pohár – 0.3L glass
presszó – same as *eszpresszó* (coffee shop; strong, black coffee)
pu – abbreviation for *pályaudvar* (train station)
puttony – the number of 'butts' of sweet *aszú* essence added to other base wines in making Tokaj wine

rakpart – quay, embankment
rendőrkapitányság – police station
rendörség – police
romkocsmák – ruin bars

Secessionism – art and architectural style similar to art nouveau

sedile (pl sedilia) – medieval stone niche with seats
sétány – walkway, promenade
söröző – beer bar or pub
szálló or szálloda – hotel
székesegyház – cathedral
sziget – island
színház – theatre

táncház – folk music and dance workshop
templom – church
tér – town or market square
tere – genitive form of *tér* as in Hősök tere (Square of the Heroes)
tó – lake
turul – eagle-like totem of the ancient Magyars and now a national symbol

u – abbreviation for *utca* (street)
udvar – court
út – road
utca – street
utcája – genitive form of *utca* as in Ferencesek utcája (Street of the Franciscans)
útja – genitive form of *út* as in Mártíroká útja (Street of the Martyrs)

vár – castle
város – city
városház or városháza – town hall
vásárcsarnok – market hall
vendéglő – a type of restaurant

zárva – closed

BEHIND THE SCENES

THIS BOOK

This 4th edition of *Budapest* was written and updated by Steve Fallon, as were the previous three editions. This city guide was commissioned in Lonely Planet's London office and produced by the following:

Commissioning Editors Fiona Buchan, Jo Potts

Coordinating Editor Angela Tinson

Coordinating Cartographer Barbara Benson

Coordinating Layout Designer Jacqui Saunders

Managing Editor Sasha Baskett

Managing Cartographers Shahara Ahmed, Herman So

Managing Layout Designer Sally Darmody

Assisting Editors Piers Kelly, Janet Austin, Kate Evans, Diana Saad

Assisting Cartographers Ross Butler, Alex Leung

Cover Designer Jennifer Mullins

Project Manager Craig Kilburn

Language Content Coordinator Quentin Frayne

Thanks to Charlotte Amelines, Imogen Bannister, Andras Bogdanovits, Xavier Di Toro, Owen Eszeki, Bruce Evans, Kyla Gillzan, Mark Griffiths, Corey Hutchison, Indra Kilfoyle, Chris Lee Ack, Robyn Loughnane, Trent Paton, Tom Webster

Cover photographs Parliament building, Simeone Huber/ Getty Images (top); swimmers in Gellért Baths, Martin Moo/LPI (bottom).

Internal photographs p5 (#3) by Laszlo Beliczay/epa/Corbis. All other photographs by Lonely Planet Images, and by Richard Nebesky except Bruce Bi p7 (#2), p9 (#4), p52 (bottom); Gavin Gough p2, p7 (#3), p9 (#5), p48 (right); David Greedy p4 (#2), p11 (#5), p12 (#2), p47 (left), p51 (top and bottom); Holger Leue p5 (#4), p6 (#2); Martin Moos p4 (#1), p12 (#3), p49 (bottom); Stephen Saks p3, p12 (#1); Jonathan Smith p6 (#1), p45, p48 (left), p50, p52 (top).

All images are copyright of the photographer unless otherwise indicated. Many of the images in this guide are available for licensing from Lonely Planet Images: www .lonelyplanetimages.com.

THANKS
STEVE FALLON

First and foremost, I'd like to thank my excellent friend Bea Szirti for her helpful suggestions and more pedestrian assistance on the ground. Thanks also to Ildikó Nagy Moran for steering me in the right direction on several occasions. Péter Lengyel and Balázs Váradi showed me the correct wine roads to follow, and Brandon Krueger, Adrian Zador and Erik D'Amato again provided useful insights into what's on in Budapest after dark. Special friends and Budapest 'virgins' Kini McDonald and Maria Tassé were fine and helpful travel companions. It was great 'rekindling' with old mate Judy Finn and meeting the angelic trio.

I'd like to dedicate this book to my civil partner, Michael Rothschild, with love and gratitude, as well as to the memory of two people whose life travels came to an end as I wrote: Erzsébet 'Zsóka' Tiszai, my one-time Hungarian teacher, and my father-in-law, William Baer Rothschild. One was my friend and the other friend and family. *Nyugodjatok békében* (Rest in peace).

THE LONELY PLANET STORY

Fresh from an epic journey across Europe, Asia and Australia in 1972, Tony and Maureen Wheeler sat at their kitchen table stapling together notes. The first Lonely Planet guidebook, *Across Asia on the Cheap*, was born.

Travellers snapped up the guides. Inspired by their success, the Wheelers began publishing books to Southeast Asia, India and beyond. Demand was prodigious, and the Wheelers expanded the business rapidly to keep up. Over the years, Lonely Planet extended its coverage to every country and into the virtual world via lonelyplanet.com and the Thorn Tree message board.

As Lonely Planet became a globally loved brand, Tony and Maureen received several offers for the company. But it wasn't until 2007 that they found a partner whom they trusted to remain true to the company's principles of travelling widely, treading lightly and giving sustainably. In October of that year, BBC Worldwide acquired a 75% share in the company, pledging to uphold Lonely Planet's commitment to independent travel, trustworthy advice and editorial independence.

Today, Lonely Planet has offices in Melbourne, London and Oakland, with over 500 staff members and 300 authors. Tony and Maureen are still actively involved with Lonely Planet. They're travelling more often than ever, and they're devoting their spare time to charitable projects. And the company is still driven by the philosophy of *Across Asia on the Cheap*: 'All you've got to do is decide to go and the hardest part is over. So go!'

OUR READERS

Many thanks to the travellers who used the last edition and wrote to us with helpful hints, useful advice and interesting anecdotes:

Bárbara Albuquerque, Sara Asadullah, Ralph Bengtsson, Erik Bomberen, Daniel Boutet, Myles Brandt, Elizabeth Carbone, Melani Clark, Glenn Craig, Emma-Jane Crozier, Graeme Currie, Martin Elofsson, Ridi Faruque, Gergo Foti, Peter Gillett, Clover Hatcher, Paul Hatton, Barbara Helm, John Hemingway, Jaima Holland, Garrett Holmes, Vivian Hsieh, Tom Humphrey, Robin Hunt, Livia Jakab, David Johnston, Peter Jones, Andre Jordan, Tim Julian, Marjan Knossenburg, Aili Kytökivi, Marcus Lloyd, Mercedes Malloy, Hannah Mcmurray, Heather Monell, Kelley Moore, Zsolt Orban, Andrew Page, Antony Peries, Summer Prejean, Sally Russell, Valerie Schnee, Neil Stevenson, Charlotte Stockley, Can Togay, Yoav Valin, Olorin Vancoillie, Wim Vanden-bussche, Alice Wood, Manuele Zunelli

SEND US YOUR FEEDBACK

We love to hear from travellers — your comments keep us on our toes and help make our books better. Our well-travelled team reads every word on what you loved or loathed about this book. Although we cannot reply individually to postal submissions, we always guarantee that your feedback goes straight to the appropriate authors, in time for the next edition. Each person who sends us information is thanked in the next edition — and the most useful submissions are rewarded with a free book.

To send us your updates — and find out about Lonely Planet events, newsletters and travel news — visit our award-winning website: lonelyplanet.com/contact.

Note: We may edit, reproduce and incorporate your comments in Lonely Planet products such as guidebooks, websites and digital products, so let us know if you don't want your comments reproduced or your name acknowledged. For a copy of our privacy policy visit lonelyplanet.com/privacy.

Notes

Notes

Notes

Notes

INDEX

498

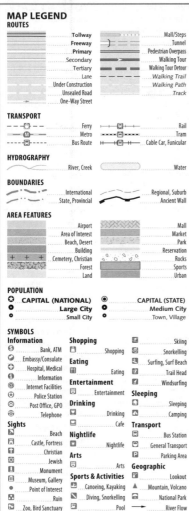

MAP LEGEND

ROUTES

Tollway	Mall/Steps
Freeway	Tunnel
Primary	Pedestrian Overpass
Secondary	Walking Tour
Tertiary	Walking Tour Detour
Lane	Walking Trail
Under Construction	Walking Path
Unsealed Road	Track
One-Way Street	

TRANSPORT

Ferry	Rail
Metro	Tram
Bus Route	Cable Car, Funicular

HYDROGRAPHY

River, Creek	Water

BOUNDARIES

International	Regional, Suburb
State, Provincial	Ancient Wall

AREA FEATURES

Airport	Mall
Area of Interest	Market
Beach, Desert	Park
Building	Reservation
Cemetery, Christian	Rocks
Forest	Sports
Land	Urban

POPULATION

✪ CAPITAL (NATIONAL)	◉ CAPITAL (STATE)
● Large City	● Medium City
○ Small City	○ Town, Village

SYMBOLS

Information
Ⓢ	Bank, ATM
Ⓔ	Embassy/Consulate
Ⓗ	Hospital, Medical
Ⓘ	Information
@	Internet Facilities
Ⓟ	Police Station
⊗	Post Office, GPO
☎	Telephone

Shopping
	Shopping

Eating
	Eating

Entertainment
	Entertainment

Drinking
	Drinking
	Cafe

Nightlife
	Nightlife

Arts
	Arts

Sports & Activities
	Canoeing, Kayaking
	Diving, Snorkelling
	Pool

	Skiing
	Snorkelling
	Surfing, Surf Beach
	Trail Head
	Windsurfing

Sleeping
	Sleeping
	Camping

Transport
	Bus Station
	General Transport
	Parking Area

Geographic
	Lookout
▲	Mountain, Volcano
	National Park
→	River Flow

Sights
	Beach
	Castle, Fortress
	Christian
	Jewish
	Monument
	Museum, Gallery
●	Point of Interest
	Ruin
	Zoo, Bird Sanctuary

Published by Lonely Planet Publications Pty Ltd
ABN 36 005 607 983

Australia Head Office, Locked Bag 1, Footscray, Victoria 3011,
☎03 8379 8000, fax 03 8379 8111,
talk2us@lonelyplanet.com.au

USA 150 Linden St, Oakland, CA 94607,
☎510 250 6400, toll free 800 275 8555,
fax 510 893 8572, info@lonelyplanet.com

UK 2nd fl, 186 City Rd, London, EC1V 2NT,
☎020 7106 2100, fax 020 7106 2101, go@
lonelyplanet.co.uk

© Lonely Planet 2009
Photographs © Richard Nebesky and as listed (p225) 2009

Printed by SNP Security Printing Pte Ltd, Singapore.

Mixed Sources
Product group from well-managed forests and other controlled sources
www.fsc.org Cert no. SGS-COC-005002
© 1996 Forest Stewardship Council